CORVETTE
SPORTS CAR SUPERSTAR

BY THE AUTO EDITORS OF CONSUMER GUIDE®

Publications International, Ltd.

Louis Weber, CEO
Publications International, Ltd.
7373 North Cicero Avenue
Lincolnwood, Illinois 60712

Permission is never granted for commercial purposes.

Manufactured in China.

8 7 6 5 4 3 2 1

ISBN: 1-4127-1222-X

Library of Congress Card Catalog Number: 2005924025

CREDITS

Photography:
The editors gratefully acknowledge the cooperation of the following people who have supplied photography to help make this book possible:

John Biel; Mark Bilek; Mitch Frumkin; Thomas Glatch; David Gooley; Sam Griffith; Bud Juneau; Dan Lyons; Vince Manocchi; Doug Mitchel; Mike Mueller; David Newhardt; Neil Nissing; Nina Padgett-Russin; Jeff Rose; Phil Toy; W.C. Waymack; Nicky Wright.

Owners:
Special thanks to the owners of the cars featured in this book for their enthusiastic cooperation:

John Adams; John Angwert and Les Bieri; Stanton P. Belland; Lon and Barbara Berger; Blackhawk Auto Collection; Peter Bose; Classic Showcase; Gordon and Dorothy Clemmer; Collier Auto Museum; Patrick and Kay Collins; Robert C. Corley, Jr.; Corvette Mike; Brad Damico; Gary Dargai; Dobby Dobbins; Jack Dunning; John M. Endres; Marc Erwin; Joe and Cathy Fazio; John Finley; Gateway Classic Cars; Steve George; Jack Gersh; Jack Gillette; Joe Giordano; Jim Glass Corvette; Fred Grasseschi; Glenn Hutchinson; Mark Hyman; Joe D. James; John E. and Barbara E. James; James Keller; Edward S. Kuziel; Al and Carol Lawrence; Robert Luebbe; Dan Lyons; Michael MacDonald; Gene Marburger; Rich Mason; Gordon McGregor; Werner Meier; Bob Meyer; Ed Milas; Wesley Muddle; Edward Mueller; Marcel Nadeau; Edward E. Ortiz; Dr. Dennis Pagliano; Glenn and Barbara Patch; Robert Paterson; Gerald Potter; Prestige Motor Cars; Dennis Reed; Frank and Mary Lou Riccardo; Larry K. Riesen; Jack Rikert; Don and Denise Sanzera; Ed and Judy Schoenthaler; Richard Stanley; Martin Swig; Jim Valerio; Bill and Val Wade; Steven Weissman; Rosalie and Jim Wente; Ray and Debbie West; Tim and Carol Whitford; Ken Whitney.

Special thanks to Dan Lyons.

Thanks also to Chevrolet Public Relations; GM Photographic; Lockheed Martin; Wieck Media Services.

CONTENTS

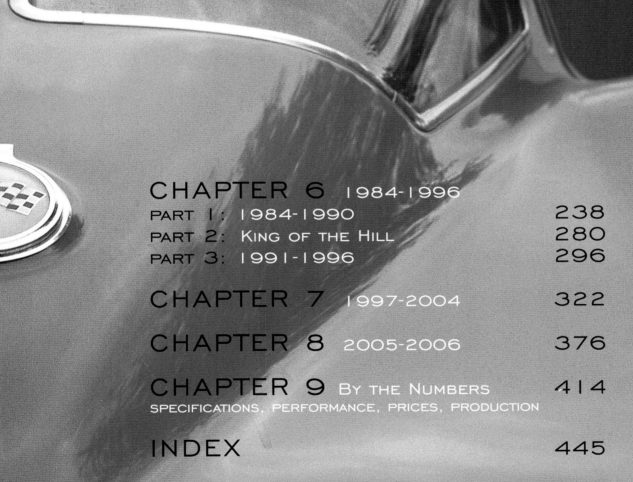

Foreword

Corvette was born of the post-war sports-car boom, an optimistic time when nearly anything seemed possible, including the world's largest automaker building a two-seat "image" car. But despite the Corvette's initial impact as a sensational show car, the first production model was dismissed as more poseur than performer, and the so-called "plastic bathtub" was nearly axed from the Chevrolet lineup. Fortunately, the venerable 'Vette developed a raw sporting nature during the formative years of rock-and-roll, and got its kicks on Route 66.

Corvette came into its own, both on the road and at the racetrack, during the go-go space-age Sixties. It flexed its muscle during the subsequently turbulent years of civil unrest, antiwar protests, and political scandals. It survived an onslaught of adversity throughout the Seventies. And while it welcomed the button-down Eighties with its portfolio secure, the car's fortunes plummeted over the course of the ensuing decade.

Again turning the tide, Chevy's legendary sports car was reborn in the late Nineties as a technologically advanced performance machine for the new millennium, and it enjoyed a well-earned resurgence in popularity. Then, when we didn't think it could get any better, Corvette engineers unleashed the C6, the most precise and refined Corvette yet. They soon topped themselves with the next-generation Z06, a 500-horsepower track-bred beast that upped per-

FORMANCE TO NEW HEIGHTS.

Plenty of sports cars would come and go since 1953, but through it all, the Corvette survived. In fact, the Corvette thrived, outlasting and outpacing the competition.

This is the detailed account of the Corvette's journey from its roots as a brash young show car to the sophisticated gran turismo it is today. It is also the story of the people behind the legend, the visionary designers and engineers who created and nurtured it, the race-car drivers whose victories helped gain the respect of its most steadfast critics, and the boardroom boosters and corporate detractors who debated its very existence.

Corvette's biography is one of drama, intrigue, and passion. Back-room battles and locked-door secrets lurk within. It's a tale of the underdog overcoming great hurdles, living up to prior successes, and suffering through the inevitable failures.

It's a story straight out of Hollywood, populated with strong leading men and crafty bit players, heroes, villains, plot twists, and red herrings. Packed into a six-act script played out against the backdrop of America's ever-changing landscape, this is the tale of a cultural icon like no other.

CHAPTER 1

Before Corvette

Though the Corvette is claimed to be "America's first production sports car," it was, of course, far from being the first bona fide sporting model to put rubber to the road. And it most certainly wasn't the first auto built solely to accommodate the sheer pleasure of motoring.

While Henry Ford was rolling millions of cookie-cutter basic-transportation Model Ts off his assembly lines, a number of automakers were building more expressive models in limited numbers for the lucky few who could afford them. Legendary coachbuilders such as Locomobile, Packard, Peerless, and Pierce-Arrow all built large, luxurious touring sedans for the wealthy to enjoy in a flamboyant, cost-be-damned manner. Soon, lighter, open-top two-seat varieties were introduced that promised a more sporting approach to driving. Though they were more manageable than their larger closed-cabin counterparts, they would hardly be considered sporty today. Still, they excelled in the speed runs, durability trials, and cross-country marathons that were the primary modes of competition throughout the horseless-carriage era.

Perhaps the first recognized example of what we might now consider to be a true sports car was

the Mercer Type 35 Raceabout, which was introduced for the 1911 model year. A bare-bones open-top auto with only spartan bodywork, the Raceabout could hardly be considered stylish. And at $2150, it cost more than twice as much as an average motor car of the day, yet offered far less in the way of comfort. Not surprisingly, only about 150 were sold in any given model year.

The Raceabout carried what was known as a "T-head" engine, similar to a flathead except that the valves were situated on opposite sides of the cylinder to produce a "cross-flow" effect. While it generated a mere 58 horsepower at 1700 rpm, that was enough to propel the relatively lightweight (2400 pounds) and nimble car to over 75 mph, with race-ready versions topping out at a then-staggering 100 mph. Its three-speed transmission used an oil-immersed multiple-disc clutch that offered what were, at least for the times, relatively smooth and quick gear changes; it was upgraded with a four-speed version for 1913. The Raceabout won five of the six races in which it was entered during 1911 and finished 12th and 15th in the inaugural Indianapolis 500, averaging 63 mph. (According to some reports the cars were so trouble-free during the first Indy race that their

hoods didn't have to be opened once for the entire 500-mile run.) The car would continue to be a formidable presence on America's tracks through 1916 and would count among its premier drivers the legendary Barney Oldfield.

Mercer's prime racetrack competitor was Stutz, a company that had recorded many wins with its own T-head racers. In 1912, the company won 25 out of the 30 contests in which it was entered with a modified version of one of the most famous models of its time, the Stutz Bearcat. Conceived as a "sportsman's car" and eschewing personal comfort in favor of performance, the muscular Bearcat would come to be symbolic—along with flappers, raccoon coats, and the Charleston—of the Roaring Twenties. Indicative of the vehicle's adventurous attitude, Cannon Ball Baker would set a transcontinental land-speed record in 1915 by piloting a Stutz Bearcat from San Diego to New York City in 11 days, 7 hours, and 15 minutes.

Derived from Stutz's more passive passenger-car line, but with a shorter wheelbase and lower ride-height, the Bearcat offered a choice of four- or six-cylinder engines and delivered superior roadholding. Styling on the open-top roadster was about as sparsely utilitarian as

The Corvette's sporting predecessors were many and varied, but all shared a common theme: to wring every ounce of pleasure and driving enthusiasm out of an engine, chassis, and four wheels. Their goal was to make a driver feel like the pilot of a race car, taking the checkered flag at the finish line of a long and satisfying run.

its rival, the Raceabout, though the Bearcat would receive a makeover for 1917 that included more-attractive bodywork. Also new that year was a lustier 80-bhp 360-cubic-inch four-cylinder engine. It was among the first powerplants to include a four-valves-per-cylinder head, an automotive engineering innovation that wouldn't come into widespread use for several decades. The new engine enabled the Bearcat to reach a then-amazing 85 mph; a later revision in 1920 increased that to nearly 90 mph. A push to recast the company's image as a builder of stylish and sophisticated motorcars—rather than raucous racers—brought about the original Bearcat's demise at the end of the 1925 model year. Though the company would later revive the name, it was carried by a sporty roadster with somewhat more luxurious trimmings.

Meanwhile, throughout the post-World War I era, the American auto industry hit its stride, developing a broad range of elegantly attractive and mechanically interesting vehicles that continued to push the envelope on performance. Romantic roadsters like the elegant two-seat Auburn boattail Speedster and the then-futuristic-looking Cord 810 Sportsman won the hearts of the elite and were competitive on the

track. Today they are considered among the top models in this country's "Golden Age" of autos. But while they lived up to their reputations for delivering a pleasurable driving experience, they were not by and large true sports cars. Some were merely fun-to-drive and stylish luxury cars, while the friskiest of the bunch would be considered gran touring (GT) or "sports tourer" cars that emphasized passenger comfort over sheer performance. A few models, like the early Duesenbergs, leaned even more toward the sporting end of things, but they were more competition cars than road machines, being too powerful and unwieldy for everyday use. Besides, they were built in miniscule numbers and cost a fortune.

Meanwhile, the sports-car idea was being pursued in pre-WWII Europe along several different lines. Bugatti in France put the emphasis on small, almost delicate, open-wheel racers and two-place road cars. From Germany's Mercedes-Benz came the super-expensive supercharged S/SS/SSK roadsters of the late Twenties/early Thirties and the more civilized 500/540K touring cars of 1935–39. Italy's Maserati and Alfa Romeo, along with England's Squire, Morgan, and Morris Garages (MG), were building amazingly

agile road cars that combined race-bred performance with curvaceous, two-seat styling.

Sports-car development would, unfortunately, come grinding to a halt along with the rest of the world's automotive production for the duration of World War II. However, the welcome return of peace in 1945 enabled a new generation of automakers to indulge car-hungry enthusiasts with sporting automobiles. In Europe, Enzo Ferrari was beginning to work his magic with both race and road cars, while Dr. Ferdinand Porsche was transforming the essential underpinnings of the Volkswagen Type 1 (Beetle) into a line of what would become legendary sports cars. In England, venerable marques like Aston Martin, Jaguar, MG, and Triumph were developing what would become their trademark vehicles.

MG is widely credited as the automaker that introduced sports cars to America (as the company itself once boasted). However arguable the claim, the MG TC, first imported in 1945, undeniably helped kindle the sports-car fever that swept the nation during the early postwar years. With its appealing vintage-Thirties open-top styling and cozy two-seat cockpit—and despite a lack of conveniences

1

2

3

1. One of the earliest examples of what might be considered a "sports car" was the Mercer Type 35 Raceabout introduced for 1911. It traded creature comforts for light weight that resulted in vivid performance, but since it cost far more than the average car of the day, sales were meager. **2.** Though it wears solid wheels instead of wires, this 1919 Paige 6-66 Daytona Speedster prototype otherwise closely reflects the production model offered in the early Twenties. As sports cars go, it was nicely trimmed and equipped for the era, but a large engine in a relatively lightweight chassis gave it performance worthy of the name. **3.** Auburn's boattail Speedster exemplified the large sporting machines popular in America during the 1920s and early '30s. **4.** The beautiful and expensive Mercedes-Benz 500K of 1935–39 was a classic in its own time. **5.** At the opposite end of the price scale was the spartan MG TC. Introduced to America after World War II, it became the iconic sports car that started a revolution.

4

5

and a notoriously stiff ride—the TC's svelte agility was a revelation to Yanks raised on lumbering Detroit iron. With a particularly tiny 1250-cc four-cylinder engine that generated a mere 54 bhp, the TC was hardly a quick ride, topping out at well under 80 mph. Still, it familiarized domestic drivers with the then-foreign (literally) concept that a car needn't have a huge engine under the hood in order to be fun to drive. The fact that it was a relatively uncomplicated vehicle only added to the car's charm. That it had a folding top (and a difficult one to operate at that) and only two seats seemed almost superfluous.

But perhaps the TC's greatest contribution was that it combined all the basic elements that had evolved over the previous 50 years and actually defined the modern sports car for a growing legion of aficionados in the U.S. Traditionally, a "true" sports car is an open-top two-seat roadster that, by its nature, sacrifices a certain level of comfort for performance. (Though in later years the definition would be extended to include hardtops, and recent developments in engineering would minimize the trade-offs between performance and punishment.)

Detroit nevertheless decided to sit out the sports-car craze during

the early post-war era, and for good reason: The end of World War II brought the promise of prosperity unknown since before the Depression. Since Detroit factories had been devoted to building tanks, aircraft, and military vehicles during the war, there was four years' worth of pent-up demand for new cars. As a result, consumers began snapping up most anything and everything Detroit turned out for the 1945 model year, even though most were only warmed-over 1942 models.

Besides, the idea of a taut-and-tiny two-seater just didn't make sense for most returning GIs starting to raise families. When most

1

1. Jaguar's XK-120 was both a styling and performance benchmark in the early Fifties. But its 1949 introductory price of about $3500 could be justified by few buyers. **2.** Even more costly was the Nash-Healey, which mated a rather mundane Nash six-cylinder engine to an aluminum body by Pinin Farina of Italy. Few were sold.

U.S. automakers issued their first completely new postwar models for 1949, they mirrored the mindset of the nation perfectly, with increasingly larger engines and brazenly longer, lower, and wider designs. While a great many people may have been intrigued by sports cars in the late Forties, few were actually willing to buy one. Even by 1952, registrations of what could be considered "sports cars" came to a grand total of 11,000—a mere 0.26 percent of the 4.2 million cars registered in the U.S. that year.

Regardless, the post-war sports-car phenomenon had begun to gain momentum. The Sports Car Club of America (SCCA) had already been formed, organizing road races as well as something called a "rally," a motorsports event that was then new to the United States. On highways, sports-car drivers began waving and honking at one another to signal their kindred interest, and many enjoyed playing tag with larger, more powerful American cars.

And a steady stream of new models from overseas only fueled their enthusiasm. England exported the exquisite Jaguar XK-120 to the U.S. in 1949: curvy, envelope-bodied roadsters and coupes with twin-cam sixes that were capable of speeds up to 120 mph. They were quite costly—selling for around $3500—but the XK-120 was the car every MG owner aspired to own. In 1950, MG itself issued an improved model, the TD. Three years later, the MG/Jaguar price-and-performance gap was bridged by the low-slung Triumph TR2, which delivered 90 mph for around $2300, and the handsome Austin-Healey 100-4, a genuine 100-mph roadster that was still priced under $3000.

The booming postwar market had encouraged a number of enterprising individuals back in the States to try their luck in the auto business, and many did so with a sports car. Soon the idea began to

2

germinate among auto dealers that, even if average Americans couldn't afford a sports car, having a seductive sportster on the showroom floor might boost sales of the more sedate, higher-volume models.

Automotive entrepreneurs were behind most of America's early-postwar sports cars. Many of these were little more than a sleeker-than-average two-seat body fitted onto an existing production-car chassis carrying the largest engine that could be crammed under the hood. Limited knowledge and shoe-string budgets precluded most of these dreams from going beyond the prototype stage. Others, like the 1948–49 two-seat Kurtis convertible and its later higher-performance derivative, the 1950–54 Muntz Jet (under the aegis of legendary promoter and radio king Earl "Madman" Muntz), saw only a few models leave the factory before their companies' demise.

However, one such fledgling car builder that managed a highly respectable effort was Cunningham. The man behind it was wealthy California sportsman Briggs Swift Cunningham, who not coincidentally also engineered the most successful American efforts in international sports-car competition

up to the early Fifties. The 1952 C-4R, for example, finished fourth in the grueling 24-hour marathon at LeMans in France. Its 1953 successor, the C-5R, finished third behind two D-Type Jaguars, which had the main advantage of disc brakes. (Cunningham, on the other hand, was thwarted in his efforts to buy disc brakes from their British manufacturer.)

For power, Cunningham relied on what many considered to be the finest American powerplant of his day: the 331-cid Chrysler hemi-head V-8, which produced 180 bhp in its production version and up to 300 bhp for competition. His one road-going "production" model, the 107-inch-wheelbase C-3, introduced for 1953, carried handsome but expensive Italian bodywork by Vignale and was painstakingly crafted; it was cited as being among the world's ten best designs by the New York Museum of Modern Art. However, even with the car selling for $10,000 or more (then several times the annual salary of most Americans), Cunningham lost money with every car he sold, which amounted to only 19 coupes and 9 convertibles. As a result, production was halted in 1955.

13

1

Another notable post-war American sportster emerged in 1951 in a joint venture between the Nash-Kelvinator company and England's Donald Healey, a one-time racing driver. The Nash-Healey, as it was called, was powered by the Nash Ambassador's ohv six-cylinder engine. Fitted to Healey's 102-inch-wheelbase chassis, it was wrapped in a stylish, though slab-sided, British-built aluminum body. Nash's 234.8-cid straight-six was already dated, and generated only 125-bhp, even in heated-up Healey tune. Nevertheless, the N-H was a strong track competitor: A prototype finished fourth at LeMans in 1950. The following year, a stock '51 model ran sixth overall and fourth in class. It came in third the following year, beating out the fourth-place Cunningham and just trailing two more-powerful Mercedes-Benz racers. Unfortunately, the car was

priced high in the $4000-to-$6000 range and sales were limited to a relative handful. Even the addition of a curvaceous steel body with styling by Pininfarina for 1952, and a long-wheelbase closed coupe the following year, didn't help boost interest in the car. When Nash merged with Hudson to form the American Motors Corporation in 1954, the N-H was left by the wayside, and AMC concentrated on building more utilitarian cars, most notably the Rambler.

Elsewhere in early-Fifties America, the 100-inch-wheelbase chassis from Kaiser-Frazer's compact Henry J became the basis for two very different machines: the Kaiser-Darrin and the Excalibur J. Designated DKF-161, for its 161-cid F-head Willys six-cylinder engine, the 1954 Kaiser-Darrin was a sleek two-seater that combined a European-roadster profile with unique front-end styling. It was

designed by Dutch Darrin, who created the outstanding 1951 Kaiser DeLuxe. The car offered three novel features: a fiberglass body, a three-way folding top that could be left half-up for a landau or town-car effect, and unique sliding doors. Its performance was more than respectable; the car could hit 0–60 mph in around 13 seconds and approached 100 mph. Darrin's sports car wasn't in production for long, however, as just 435 production examples were completed, all for model year 1954. Its high price—around $3700—limited sales, and the fast-failing fortunes of Kaiser-Frazer, or Kaiser-Willys as it had become by then, rendered the car expendable.

The trim little Excalibur J embodied even more of the true sports car spirit than the Darrin. Though the Excalibur employed the same chassis and an overhead-valve version of the Willys six, it was far more

14

2

3

4

5

1. Race-car designer Frank Kurtis introduced a roadgoing model in 1948 as the Kurtis Sport. Most were powered by Ford flathead V-8s. After a short run, Kurtis sold the tooling to Earl Muntz, who offered a modified version as the Muntz Jet. **2.** Though a price tag of around $3700 limited sales to just 435, the 1954 Kaiser-Darrin was a commendable American effort with novel features and respectable performance. **3.** Cunningham built race cars before bringing out a street car in 1953. The beautiful C-3 was powered by a 331-cid Chrysler Hemi, but its $10,000 price attracted few buyers. **4.** Where Cunningham made its name was on the race track, and the highly successful 1952 C4-R was one of the reasons. **5.** Triumph's TR2, introduced for 1953, was faster than the contempory MG and, at $2300, far less expensive than a Jaguar.

sparsely equipped, in line with designer Brooks Stevens' desire to hold the car's price to around $2000. Several prototypes were built for SCCA racing purposes and held their own with some prestigious competitors. But once again, Kaiser-Frazer's dire financial straits deep-sixed the project before the car could reach volume production.

Another well-respected but short-lived series of limited-production sports models from the post-war era came from economy-car (and radio) manufacturer Crosley. The 1949 Crosley Hotshot was a bantam bare-bones roadster that weighed in at only about 1200 pounds. It was built on an 85-inch-wheelbase chassis with Crosley's primitive solid-axle suspension at each end. The down-right diminutive 44-cid four-cylinder engine produced only 26.5 bhp, but it was enough to propel this light-weight two-seater to a top speed of around 85 mph. The car was joined

in the line a year later by the Super Sports, which was a more deluxe version of the Hotshot that featured opening doors instead of bodyside cut-outs. Even in stock form these cars offered tenacious cornering, and one modified model showed its ruggedness by winning the Index of Performance at the 1950 Sebring 12 Hours of Endurance in Florida. The company's fortunes were sagging, however, and founder Powel Crosley, Jr. abandoned carmaking in 1952.

Still, these ill-fated early domestic efforts all proved that otherwise-ordinary passenger-car components could work in a production-volume sports car. This, plus a reborn interest in genuine sports cars (at least among a small but growing legion of enthusiasts), stirred the imaginations of those who would become true automotive visionaries at General Motors, and the creation of the Corvette was at hand.

CHAPTER 2

Corvette Dreams

As post-war America began to satiate its pent-up hunger for new automobiles and other goods that were in short supply for the duration of World War II, a welcome level of prosperity and optimism returned to the nation. As such, many would-be enthusiasts were giving more than just passing glances to the growing number of sports cars that were entering the market from abroad, most notably the MG TC roadster from England. With all-new models finally rolling off the assembly lines and into buyers' driveways by the late 1940s, automakers were eager to return to the business of "selling the sizzle instead of the steak" to help maintain their lofty sales pace.

The term "dream car" had reentered the lexicon, with automakers once again drafting concepts created not only to flex the imaginations of their own engineers and designers, but to gauge the public's interest in and acceptance of leading-edge styling and newly introduced features. Harley J. Earl, founder and head of General Motor's Art

The booming postwar economy had brought vigor and vitality back to the automobile business, and in light of their growing popularity, Detroit finally began to take sports cars seriously. In the early 1950s, a handful of foresighted individuals at Chevrolet pioneered a new concept car that would bring an enthusiast's dream to reality, and a bona fide automotive legend was born.

and Colour Section, the American auto industry's first in-house styling department, virtually invented the dream car with his renowned Buick Y-Job concept, first displayed in 1938. This long, low, two-seat convertible not only set the tone for company styling themes in the

years immediately preceding and following the war, it proved the value of giving the public a "sneak preview" of things to come. To that end, GM had great success with its Motorama expositions, held between 1949 and 1961. These were true extravaganzas of chrome and

choreography that toured America to showcase the company's current offerings along with enticing concepts for the future.

Earl was eager to tackle new experimental projects soon after completing his work on the corporation's 1949 and '50 models, which

The Corvette was strikingly lower than Chevy's standard 1953 passenger cars and represented a dramatic departure for General Motors. It remains among the few "dream cars" to reach production virtually unaltered.

included the stylish Buick Roadmaster Riviera and Cadillac Coupe deVille. Significantly, his first postwar dream cars were two-seaters: the aircraft-inspired Buick LeSabre of 1951 and the Buick XP-300, shown a year later. Both boasted advanced ideas, including a wraparound windshield, a folding top hidden beneath a metal cover just aft of the cockpit, a sculptured rear deck with prominent tail fins, and a low, ground-hugging stance.

He then turned to creating a concept for a low-priced sporty car during the late fall of 1951. Earl figured he could outsell the foreign sports cars that were attracting enthusiasts' attention by offering more vehicle for the money with the added benefit of ubiquitous dealer sales and service. He had access to a small enclosure adjacent to the company's main Body Development Studio where he could work privately with a personal crew on projects that he wanted to shield from premature exposure. It was here he would create what would eventually become the Corvette.

With a target price of around $2000—then about 15 percent less than an MG TD—Earl went about creating a few initial design studies and scale models. These were reportedly along the lines of the bare-bones British roadsters of the day and based on a stock GM chassis. Along the way, Earl found inspiration in a concept car that had been displayed for a time in the GM Styling auditorium. Called "Alembic 1," it was a fiberglass-bodied vehicle derived from an original design by Bill Tritt for the U.S. Rubber Company. Tritt was founder of a company called Glasspar, which in the early Fifties was the most successful and influential supplier of kit-car bodies made from GRP (for "glass-reinforced plastic," as fiberglass was originally known).

Earl now stepped up the pace, and work proceeded under the guise of "Project Opel" (this was

1

likely chosen to confuse outsiders, as Chevy frequently did advanced studies for GM's German subsidiary at the time). Access was limited to a chosen few for security purposes, and employees who were not directly involved would probably have never even heard of the "Opel" project.

It was at about this time that Edward N. Cole was transferred from GM's Cadillac Division to Chevrolet, where he took over as chief engineer and would become another key figure in Corvette history. Once in his new position, he tripled the engineering staff—from 850 to 2900—then turned to designing a new engine, the landmark 265-cubic-inch small-block V-8 that would debut for 1955. Meanwhile, Earl tapped Robert F. McLean, a young sports-car enthusiast with degrees from Cal Tech in both engineering and industrial design, to come up with a basic layout for Project Opel.

McLean started visualizing the vehicle from the back forward, and not from the front rearward, as was the usual practice. With the rear axle as a reference point, he placed the engine and passengers as close to it as possible, the goal being the balanced 50/50 weight distribution desirable for optimum sports-car

handling. The final figure was a still-creditable 53/47 percent. The concept's wheelbase was set at 102 inches, the same as that of the Jaguar XK-120, one of Earl's favorite sports cars. At 57 inches front, 59 inches rear, the concept's track was wider than the Jaguar's but not as wide proportionally as that of the rear-engine Porsches of the early 1950s.

A technical paper delivered to the Society of Automotive Engineers in October 1953 by veteran Chevy engineer Maurice Olley outlined the design criteria that dictated the Corvette's engineering goals. These included the assumptions that a sports car must have a cruising speed of over 70 mph, a weight-to-power ratio of better than 25 to 1, and "ample brakes and good handling qualities." The last were said to mean quick steering with light handling, a low center of gravity, a minimum overhang with a low moment of inertia relative to wheelbase, a smooth yet firm suspension, and a quick steering response without oversteer.

Earl's Art and Colour Section soon coordinated its efforts with those of GM's engineers, leaning rather heavily on styling cues borrowed from the Buick LeSabre and XP-300 show vehicles. These included a panoramic windshield, toothy oval grille, "definition" at the rear fenders, and a shadow-box rear license-plate frame.

Earl shelved earlier plans for a conventional steel body and turned to fiberglass as the basis for the car's exterior. GRP would make it possible to mold very complex shapes that would have been prohibitively expensive to stamp in steel. This would afford designers greater flexibility to create nicely rounded shapes and graceful curves in a limited amount of time and on budget.

But there were still two big, unanswered questions regarding the car's proposed fiberglass body:

Namely, would it provide the requisite structural strength, and would it work in mass production? The second couldn't be resolved without a production go-ahead, of course, but the first was answered dramatically in "accidental" fashion. Chevy had built a full-size convertible with a GRP body strictly for investigative research and development purposes in early 1952. During high-speed testing at the proving grounds, the driver unexpectedly rolled the car but escaped uninjured. The car's body suffered no major damage, with doors, hood, and decklid all intact. Earl was now more convinced than ever that fiberglass would form the shell of his dream car.

With Earl aiming for completion in time for the first 1953 Motorama, to be held in January at New York's Waldorf-Astoria Hotel, McLean and the Chevrolet engineers redoubled their efforts to find production chassis and drivetrain components compatible with the developing plastic body. Time was short, so the ability to utilize off-the-shelf hardware was crucial. Needless to say, Chevrolet had quite a bit of componentry available for the team to appropriate.

Ultimately, though, the chassis had to be designed from scratch, both for rigidity's sake and because McLean wanted to position the engine behind the front axle instead of directly over it. Weighing just 213 pounds, the new chassis was a special X-member design with sturdy box-section siderails. What's more, the vehicle's rear-end arrangement was also unique. For the first time in Chevrolet history, an open or Hotchkiss drive was used instead of the traditional torque-tube drive. Conventional leaf springs were located on the rear axle, but again breaking with Chevy tradition, they were positioned outboard of the main frame rails for added stability, a feature picked up for the division's all-new

1955 passenger cars. While the Corvette's front suspension was borrowed from then-current Chevy passenger cars, its shock rates were recalibrated and a larger-diameter anti-roll bar was fitted.

Steering was basically an off-the-shelf Saginaw recirculating-ball system but with its ratio quickened to 16:1. The steering idler arm was redesigned to accommodate the lower engine mounting. Also, the concept car's steering wheel was an inch smaller in diameter than that of production Chevys.

As for the engine, there was only one available: the tried-and-true 235.5-cid ohv six, which produced 105 horsepower in standard tune. Modifications made to boost power included a high-lift, long-duration camshaft (similar to that found in Chevy's 261-cid truck engine), solid valve lifters (instead of the hydraulic variety), and dual valve springs (to cope with the higher engine speeds). While other 1953 Chevrolet engines mated to the company's Powerglide automatic transmission specified aluminum pistons, the show car would have cast-iron pistons for durability's sake. The head casting was modified to produce an 8.0:1 compression ratio, versus the 7.5:1 squeeze of top-line Chevy passenger cars. Water pump flow capacity was increased, and the pump itself was lowered at the front of the block so that the large, four-blade fan could clear the anticipated low hoodline.

The engine's stock induction system was exchanged for triple Carter "YH" sidedraft carburetors mounted on a special aluminum intake manifold. The carbs worked together instead of via a progressive linkage, each feeding a pair of cylinders through a separate choke. Automatic chokes were initially used, but tests showed that all three couldn't be synchronized because they didn't warm at the same rate. Thus, only the Motorama Corvette carried auto-

2

3

1. Harley Earl, head of GM styling, pushed the Corvette through as his secret "pet" project. **2-3.** Prior to the Corvette, Earl worked on a pair of postwar two-seat concept cars, the LeSabre (*top*) and XP-300 (*bottom*). Both were too large to be considered sports cars, however.

matic chokes; production models used a manual setup. A redesigned rocker-arm cover became necessary to clear the low hoodline, and the oil filler was repositioned to the rear, eliminating the final obstruction. Equally effective was the special dual exhaust system that reduced back pressure for more power and better sound.

In all, the various changes yielded a freer-breathing "Blue Flame Special" engine that produced 150 bhp at 4500 rpm, with maximum revs considerably higher than that.

Chevy's Powerglide two-speed automatic transmission was selected for the original Motorama show car and would prove one of the most controversial features of the eventual production Corvette (to purists, the terms "sports car" and "automatic transmission" are mutu-

19

1

1-2. The Corvette built for the 1953 Motorama differed only in detail from the production version. A couple of the changes are noticeable in these photos: On the production model, "Corvette" was removed from below the hood badge, the side trim was extended and its "wing" turned up, the fender air scoops in front of the windshield and external door buttons were removed, and the interior armrests and knobs differed. Smiling is the '50s TV personality Art Baker.

ally exclusive). Unfortunately, the engineering staff didn't believe it had a manual gearbox at hand that was strong enough for the fortified engine, and it had no time to design one, so it was forced to use Power-glide by default.

The transmission was essentially unchanged from its conventional specifications except for shiftpoint rpms, which were raised to match the new engine's 11-percent increase in torque. Tests showed that the stock transmission oil cooler wasn't necessary in this lighter

car, so all oil lines normally running forward to the cooler were plugged. Shift control was floor-mounted for both practical and aesthetic reasons.

The fiberglass bodywork for the Motorama show car was $\frac{2}{10}$-inch thick, and was hand-laid into a mold that was cast directly from Earl's pre-production full-scale plaster styling model. The result, as shown in a widely circulated GM press photo, was a body composed of only nine major subassemblies: floorpan, trunklid, top cover, the two doors, hood, front fenders/nose, front gravel pan, and rear fenders/gravel pan.

As the '53 show car neared completion, Ed Cole, by virtue of his new position, was one of the first within Chevrolet Division to see the fiberglass-bodied concept. Enraptured by its sight, he enthusiastically promised to support Earl in his efforts to win production approval for the vehicle. This support went all the way to the GM Building's 14th Floor executive suite and company president Harlow Curtice. Earl took Curtice and Chevrolet Division general manager Thomas H. Keating on a walk-around tour of a full-scale plaster model, explaining enthusiastically that here was not only a profitable new product but also one that would add much-needed sparkle to Chevrolet's sedate family car image.

His persuasiveness worked, and the car was approved as part of the 1953 Motorama show. At the same time, it was decided that the engineering staff should work on the car with a view to eventual production and would proceed as Project EX-122, with the final go/no-go decision to be based largely on showgoers' reactions.

But what to name this pioneering concept? In late 1952, Chevrolet's top executives met to attach a moniker to their latest dream car. After the group rejected nearly 300 proposed names as being unsuitable, Chevy's assistant advertising manager Myron Scott found one that seemed to strike the right chord. While perusing a dictionary, he found the word "corvette" was defined as "a type of small, agile 19th century warship," and implied speed, strength, and maneuverability. It was perfectly suited to the powerful and nimble compact sports car the company was developing. (Interestingly, one early press release introduced the car with the British spelling "Courvette.")

2

Finished in gleaming Polo White with a bright Sportsman Red interior, the Corvette was a hands-down sensation in its Motorama debut, and the inevitable inquiries soon started pouring in: When will it be at my dealer's, and how much will it cost? Based on the wealth of positive public reaction, Chevy decided to start building Corvettes as soon as possible. Amazingly, they would be in production by June of that year—and sold as 1953 models, no less.

Except for its cowl-mounted fresh air scoops (which reappeared in non-functional form for 1956–57), the Motorama Corvette was one of the few show cars to reach production with its styling virtually intact. The fact that Earl's pure original was retained unsullied by committee modifications—something that was as virtually unheard of then as it is today—enhances the appeal of early Corvettes among collectors and enthusiasts. The car's original styling has aged well, and it remains a classic a half-century later.

But as Harley Earl, Ed Cole, and company would soon discover, it was one thing to design and engineer a prototype sports car that would turn heads at an auto show; it was quite another to actually bring it to production and sell it for a profit.

PART 1 1953-1955

Buoyed by a wildly enthusiastic introduction as a concept car at GM's New York 1953 Motorama debut in January, company executives put production of the Corvette on a fast track to capitalize on the favorable public and media opinion. In reality, the decision to proceed with the project was actually made well before then, when GM president Harlow Curtice and Chevy Division chief Tom Keating gave their blessing to Harley Earl's mock-up. But the positive public reaction only bolstered the company's resolve to bring the car to market as soon as possible.

Chevrolet scrambled to tool up for production, having to set up shop in a temporary facility adjacent to Chevrolet's main plant in Flint, Michigan. To keep the process moving, any manufacturing problems would have to be addressed along the way, leaving engineers to effectively master the art of building Corvettes as they went along. Fiberglass molding techniques, for example, were still far from perfected and more experimentation was needed before actual production could begin.

Ultimately, improvements in process chemistry allowed the production body to be only $\frac{1}{10}$-inch thick, with no loss in surface quality or structural strength. Still, Chevy had to build several interim bodies as trials before it was convinced that fiberglass was really feasible.

After months of frantic activity, Corvette production got underway, with the initial target set at just 50 cars a month—a maximum of 300 units for the balance of the calendar year. Actually, much of the first model-year's run of 300 cars would be hand-built, as more-efficient production processes for assembling the vehicle's fiberglass body were still being perfected. All cars would be built the same way so workers could concentrate on putting the bodies together properly without being rushed and without the distraction of trim and equipment variations. As a result, all '53 Corvettes were painted Polo White and had Sportsman Red interiors, black tops, 6.70 × 15 four-ply whitewall tires, Delco signal-seeking radios, and recirculating hot-water heaters. Also standard was a complete set of

This promotional scene notwithstanding, Americans hadn't widely embraced the idea of sports cars when Chevrolet unveiled the Corvette in 1953. The two-car family was still rare, and the 'Vette proved too primitive for everyday use, too pedestrian for driving enthusiasts—and too expensive for almost everyone. At $3513, a Corvette cost twice as much as a Chevrolet Deluxe sedan and $1300 more than Chevy's top-line Bel Air convertible. All '53 Corvettes wore the same color combination: Polo White paint over Sportsman Red vinyl with a black top.

Rushed into production, the Corvette stumbled coming out of the gate. Expectations were largely unfulfilled, reviews were mixed, and sales fell far short of expectations throughout the car's early years. The project was nearly canceled, but Chevrolet would ultimately stay the course and Harley Earl and company would transform the 'Vette into a true world-class sports car.

1

1. Corvette's fiberglass body comprised 46 separate pieces glued together to form the nine major subassemblies. **2.** Large jigs were used to position the individual pieces to assure proper fit. **3.** Fiberglass made for a much lighter car than traditional steel construction and could be more easily molded into complex shapes like this floorpan.

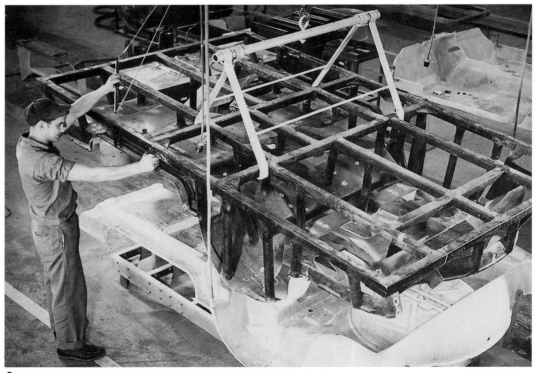

2

3

analog instruments, including a 5000-rpm tachometer and a counter for total engine revolutions (a feature that would continue through 1959).

The first Corvette to come off the assembly line was driven by Tony Kleiber, a Chevrolet body assembler, on June 30, 1953—just six months after its public unveiling as a Motorama dream car. Amazingly, the first production Corvette was changed little from its concept display model. Some chrome-plated engine parts were now painted, manual doors and hood replaced the hydraulically operated versions, a manual choke was used instead of an automatic one, exterior door pushbuttons were left off, and there

were some minor trim variations. Yet at a suggested retail price of $3513, the car had evolved into a considerably costlier vehicle than the austere roadster Harley Earl had originally conceived as selling for around $2000 as "Project Opel."

Though reaction to the Corvette as a show car was strongly positive, early reviews of the production version were mixed. For starters, sports-car enthusiasts took extreme umbrage to the vehicle's only available transmission, the Powerglide automatic. What's more, Harley Earl's body design, though clean and appealing, was still considered to be too gimmicky for some tastes. Coming under particular scrutiny in some quarters were the rocket-

like rear fenders with their tiny fins, the dazzling vertical grille teeth, and the sunken headlights covered by mesh stone guards. The shadow-box license-plate housing was covered by plastic that tended to turn cloudy. The car's convertible top was not power operated, but it folded neatly beneath a flush-fitting cover and could be managed with some ease by one person. The clip-in side curtains, perhaps favored over roll-down windows as a cost-cutting measure, were every bit as inconvenient and annoying as they were on the less-expensive British roadsters of the period. Even worse, not having exterior door buttons meant that the only way to open a door from the out-

25

side was to reach inside the car for the release.

Performance-wise, however, the Corvette was quite a good sports car. Even with Powerglide and the six-cylinder engine, a well-tuned example could do 0–60 mph in 11 seconds and reach 105 mph flat out, which was commendable at the time. Furthermore, road testers from contemporary enthusiast magazines judged the ride/handling balance to be excellent.

Unfortunately, for all the demand the Motorama car had generated, neither consumers nor dealers could as yet obtain one. Early production models went to project engineers for testing and engineering purposes (production cars 001001 and 001002 are believed to have been destroyed), and the balance went to GM managers and other visible people. Word was

released that the year's entire contemplated production had already been spoken for. That was a nice way of saying that Chevy didn't really intend to sell Corvettes to the general public, at least not just yet. Indeed, a dealer notice issued by the division's Central Office on July 10, cautioned that, "No dealer is in a position to accept firm orders for delivery of a Corvette in 1953." In fact, Chevrolet couldn't begin addressing customers' orders until a new plant would subsequently be geared up for '54 production.

In effect, Chevrolet was employing what we'd now call a "controlled production start-up," which made sense, all things considered. Given the company's lack of experience with fiberglass manufacturing techniques, the quality of the finished product was very much in doubt. And GM definitely did not

want to risk embarrassment should something go wrong with new cars in the dealer pipeline, especially with a brand new "image" car that had already attracted so much attention.

It was just as well, because quality problems surfaced early. Predictably enough, they involved the fiberglass body. Each body began as 46 separate pieces that were supplied by the Molded Fiber Glass Company of Ashtabula, Ohio. Workers had to fit all these into wooden jigs, then glue them together into the larger subassemblies, all of which took time and left vast room for error. Worse, some pieces didn't fit together well as delivered because of molding flaws that required still more hand labor to correct.

As a result, the fit-and-finish of early Corvette bodies was variable

Each '53 Corvette required considerable hand labor on the makeshift Flint, Michigan, assembly line, which was housed in the same factory that turned out Chevy passenger cars. Due to variances in the supplied fiberglass components, body fit-and-finish were inconsistent, especially during the first model year.

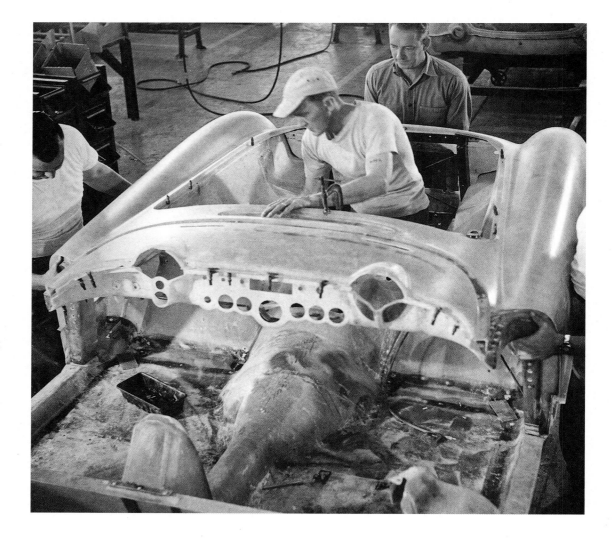

1.

2.

1. For model-year '54, production was moved to a plant in St. Louis that was capable of much higher volume than the temporary Corvette line in Flint—up to 10,000 units a year versus only 600. Still, it would be quite some time before sales reached so high. **2.** Job 1 came off the Flint line on June 30, 1953, just months after the car's public debut.

1

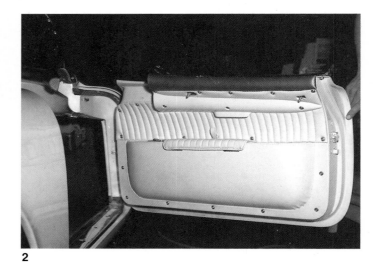

2

3

to say the least, with judgments on the fiberglass ranging from fair to excellent compared to steel construction. What's more, creaks and groans as well as drumming from the fiberglass body structure plagued the new vehicles—as they would on most every Corvette built through 1962.

In the fall of 1953 as a promotional endeavor, Chevrolet began to use the first available production cars as dealer-display attractions. Each of the eight Chevrolet wholesale regions was assigned a car to send from dealer to dealer for one- to three-day showings during the last three months of the year. In an effort to enhance the Corvette's image as a prestige car, dealers restricted sales to VIPs in each community: mayors, celebrities, industrial leaders, and favorite customers. The 'Vette was glamorous and exciting, especially compared to the rest of the company's more-mundane passenger-car line, and

Chevrolet's publicists played it up for all it was worth.

Coming on the heels of the big pre-launch buildup, this public-relations maneuver had an unintended effect. With ads and stories about the car appearing everywhere but no vehicles being genuinely available, some began to wonder whether Chevy was pulling a fast one. While it's common today for limited-production models to sell out before their release, with potential buyers paying a premium to get on the waiting list, this type of product launch was unheard of in the early 1950s. Some wondered whether this "dream car" was still just a dream after all.

As it turned out, Chevy's marketing plan backfired in a big way. While the company's judgment was fundamentally sound in turning to VIPs as opinion leaders, unfortunately these folks didn't end up liking the car as much as the marketers had hoped. Many com-

plained of the "jet-age" styling, clumsy side curtains, off-the-rack mechanicals, and the vehicle's high price. British sports-car partisans condemned the Corvette as being nonfunctional and faddish. Potential buyers went looking at MGs, Jaguars, and Triumphs, instead.

Production for the 1954 models was shifted to a renovated St. Louis assembly plant in December 1953, which was designed to build more than 10,000 Corvettes a year (the first 14 or 15 '54 models were actually built in Flint, however, as were all engines). Finally, anyone who wanted and could afford a Corvette could readily find one in stock at their local Chevy store.

Not surprisingly, the 1954 model differed little from the '53, though running refinements occurred throughout the model year. For instance, the 1953 Corvette had two short stainless-steel exhaust outlets protruding inboard of the rear fenders. When it was found that air turbulence tended to suck exhaust gases back against the car, soiling the paint, the outlets were lengthened and routed below the body. But even this alteration didn't entirely solve the problem, which would persist until the 1956 redesign, when the tips were shifted to the rear fender extremities. In addition, gas and brake lines were better protected by being moved inboard of the right-hand main frame rail, and tops and top irons changed from black to tan. The storage bag for carrying the side curtains in the trunk was mildly reshaped and newly color-keyed to the interior.

Some initial inconveniences were also remedied on the '54s. For example, the original two-handle exterior hood latch was replaced by a more manageable single-handle mechanism after the first 300 or so units were built. The choke control was moved from the right to the left of the steering column,

4

1. Corvette's dash design previewed that of 1955 passenger Chevys.
2. Contoured, padded-vinyl door trim was quite dressy for the era.
3. Bucket seats were deemed a sports car must—even for one with only automatic transmission. Note the short floor-mounted shift lever.
4. Name script was contemplated but not used. Only a small hood badge proclaimed "Corvette."

swapping places with the wiper switch. This eliminated having to reach across or through the steering wheel to operate the choke with the left hand while turning the ignition key with the right. Moisture in the rear license plate recess tended to cause its plastic cover to fog up, so Chevy included two little bags of a desiccant material to keep the area dry.

Under the hood, a new camshaft gave the Blue Flame six an extra five horsepower, boosting the total to 155 bhp, though the increase wasn't announced until the following year. Other alterations included a new-style rocker-arm cover

(about 20 percent of which were finished in chrome—serial numbers 1363 through 4381), a tidier wiring harness, and more plastic-insulated wire (replacing fabric). Also, the three bullet-shaped air cleaners were replaced by a two-pot configuration after the first 1900 cars rolled off the line.

Another niggling problem the '54

1. Chevy's workaday Blue Flame six was fitted with triple carburetors to become the Corvette Special Six. The extra carbs plus some internal changes boosted horsepower from 115 to 150. **2.** This early ad quoted no mechanical specifications but promised that Corvette "smooths a turn" and "levels out a hill."

model addressed concerned the convertible top mechanism. On early cars, the main irons had to poke through slots in the chrome moldings behind the seats and were capped with spring-loaded flippers. Beginning with serial number 3600, the irons were redesigned with a dogleg shape that allowed them to slip between the body and the seatback. Unhappily, this led to another annoyance—the top irons rubbed against the upholstery. Since the preferred top-folding procedure was not particularly obvious, the factory began sticking explanatory decals on the underside of the top cover.

1

bushing. Then it was fine—very neutral."

Those slight, but significant, changes were typical of Duntov, whose seat-of-the-pants feel for what was right—and wrong—with Corvettes would make him a legend among GM insiders and Corvette enthusiasts alike. So respected was he that when it came to management showdowns over suggested changes, the white-haired wizard usually won. "Fiddling" with Corvettes would become Duntov's life's work for the next 20 years.

Throughout the discussion of whether or not the Corvette should be put to pasture, Harley Earl remained the car's biggest booster. For 1955 he proposed a mild facelift, with a wide eggcrate grille similar to that of Chevy's forthcoming new passenger cars, plus a functional hood scoop, dummy front-fender vents, and a redesigned rear deck with the aforementioned outboard exhaust tips. But with sales in the cellar and the high cost of tooling the standard '55 models, there was simply no money left to sink into such a slow-selling product.

Lack of funds also precluded further development of two follow-up concept cars Earl designed for the 1954 Motorama tour. One was a lift-off hardtop that turned the Corvette into a handsome, thin-pillar coupe. It was a natural, but it would have to wait until 1956 to join the model line. The other concept, a closed fastback coupe, wouldn't make production until much later still, with the advent of the Bill Mitchell-designed 1963 Sting Ray. Interestingly, the Motorama fastback was dubbed "Corvair," a name that had actually once been favored over Corvette. (It would, of course, resurface for Chevy's notorious rear-engine compact of 1960.) A third '54 Motorama

Corvette's renaissance: the brilliant new 265-cid small-block V-8 he'd been working on for Chevy's totally redesigned 1955 passenger cars.

At about this time, a new member joined the Corvette team, who, as it turned out, would help ensure the vehicle's long-term viability. Zora Arkus-Duntov was a 45-year-old German-trained enthusiast, race driver, designer, and engineer who had been "fiddling" with Corvettes

in his spare time since joining the GM Research and Development Staff in 1953. As a racer, he not only knew what serious drivers demanded of sports cars but how to achieve it, and he was appalled by what the Corvette had to offer. "The front end oversteered [and] the rear end understeered," he explained. "I put two degrees of positive caster in the front suspension and relocated the rear spring

1

2

concept was the handsome Corvette-based Nomad sports wagon. A running exercise built on a standard 1953 Chevy wagon chassis, it led to the production 1955 model of the same name that would be built on that year's new passenger-car chassis. There's no evidence that GM ever seriously considered a Corvette-based wagon for volume production, however.

As for the car that was in production (however meager), the '55 looked to be just a repeat of the 1953-54 Corvette, but it was much improved in many respects. The biggest improvement was Ed Cole's superb small-block V-8, which, for an extra $135, was fitted to all but six of the '55 models sold that year; it was identified externally only by

exaggerated gold "V's" overlaid on the existing "Chevrolet" name on the lower front fenders. Chevy's ads heralded it as "The V-8 that goes like a V-2," comparing the eight-cylinder Corvette to a "guided missile."

One of the many interesting innovations that made the 265 such a pivotal development was the lack of a common rocker shaft. Each rocker arm was entirely independent of the others, so that the deflection of one had no effect on the rest. Each was assembled over a valve stem and pushrod, retained by a fulcrum ball and lock nut. Regardless of whether mechanical or hydraulic lifters were used, the valves were lashed by turning the lock nut. In addition, the arrangement reduced

reciprocating weight, which allowed higher rpm and cut down on raw materials.

Other features included an intake manifold that provided a common water outlet to both heads, which were die cast with integral valve guides and were completely interchangeable. A short stroke meant short connecting rods were used, which was another way to achieve higher rpm. Pressed-in piston pins eliminated the need for split rods and the required locking bolts. Five main bearings of equal diameter carried maximum loads in their lower halves. Engine weight was saved by circulating the oil through hollow pushrods, providing splash lubrication to the rocker arms and valve stems, thus eliminating the

3

need for separate and costly oil feeder lines. Pistons were modern slipper-type "autothermic" aluminum units with three rings; a circumferential expander for the single oil ring provided axial and radial force to control oil burning. Instead of iron, the crankshaft was forged of pressed steel because of its higher specific gravity and modulus of elasticity.

The V-8 certainly did wonders for the Corvette's performance in 1955. Though it was essentially the same engine that became newly optional in that year's passenger Chevys, the Corvette version ran a special camshaft that raised horsepower 33 above standard tune—to a total 195 bhp at 5000 rpm. Replacing the finicky multiple carbs was a single Rochester four-barrel version. Final-drive gearing remained at 3.55:1, but the V-8's higher rev limit prompted a revised tachometer redline of 6500 rpm. Because the engine was lighter, fore/aft weight distribution improved, though the benefit was slight (now set at 52/48 percent).

There was no doubting the V-8's performance improvement—it was nothing short of stunning. The benchmark 0–60-mph sprint now took just 8.5 seconds; the standing quarter-mile only 16.5 seconds. Top

"Loaded for bear"

There's mighty potent ammunition under the hood of the new Corvette—for now the "Blue-Flame" 6 is joined by a very special 195-h.p. version of the astonishing Chevrolet V8 engine!

This is the engine sports car drivers have been waiting for—compact, low in weight, ultra-rigid, with all the inherent virtues of Chevrolet's three-inch stroke, massive crankshaft, and short manifolds. And when you add an almost pressure-free dual exhaust system, a high-lift camshaft and four-barrel carburetor, you get GO in great big capital letters!

How does it go? Like "The Ride of the Valkyries," the takeoff of a V-2 rocket, the plunge down the Cresta bobsled run—all wrapped up in one! You never felt anything like this sheer triumphant surge of power . . . or the way the V8 Corvette cruises, as effortlessly as a flame burns.

Even if you have known the Corvette before . . . if you have tested its rock-solid stability on curves, its polo-pony compactness, its fantastic grip on the road, and its hairline 16 to 1 steering . . . the V8 version will stun you. But if you have never driven any Corvette, then you are to be envied. You have an experience coming—a singing jubilation that will tingle in your memory all the rest of your life!

True, you risk spoiling yourself for every other kind of car. But why not phone your Chevrolet dealer, now, and set up a date with the new V8? . . . Chevrolet Division of General Motors, Detroit 2, Michigan.

CHEVROLET CORVETTE

4

1-2. Only detail changes occurred for '54. Paint colors expanded to include black, Pennant Blue, and Sportsman Red. **3,5.** Mild styling changes were proposed for '55, then quickly shelved due to slow sales. **4.** Corvette did get a V-8 option for '55 that was a boon to performance but had little sales impact. Most all the '55s were so equipped.

speed was up to nearly 120 mph. Despite this, gas mileage was actually better too. *Road & Track*, for example, recorded 18–22.5 mpg with Powerglide, some 2–3 mpg better than the standard six-cylinder engine.

Other changes made to accommodate the V-8 included an automatic choke for the first time since the Motorama show Corvette and a

modern 12-volt electrical system, though the older six-volt setup was retained for the few six-cylinder Corvettes built that year. The previous vacuum-operated wiper motor gave way to an electric unit, and a foot-operated windshield washer returned. Tires changed from tube-type to the tubeless variety in both white- and blackwall versions.

For a time, Powerglide remained

5

A '55 V-8 'Vette struts its stuff at the Pure Oil Trials on the sands at Daytona Beach, Florida. These and other tests confirmed the 'Vette's newfound vigor. Where the six-cylinder car did 0–60 mph in 11 seconds and topped out at 105 mph, the V-8 dropped the 0–60 time to 8.5 seconds and raised top speed to nearly 120 mph.

the only transmission, though its vacuum modulator was eliminated (as on other '55 Chevys) so that kickdown was governed solely by speed and throttle position. But later in the model run, about 75 cars were built with Corvette's first manual gearbox. This was a new close-ratio three-speed manual, which shifted via a stubby chrome stalk rising from the side of the transmission tunnel, capped by a small white ball and surrounded by a boot that was clamped to the floor by a bright metal ring showing the shift pattern. Final drive was shortened to 3.7:1, which combined with the lighter

gearbox and that potent V-8 to make this the fastest 'Vette yet.

As in 1953–54, the Corvette received several running changes during 1955 production. Soon after start-up, the Pennant Blue color option was replaced by Harvest Gold, with contrasting green trim and a dark green top, which became a popular combination. Metallic Copper also became available, and Sportsman Red was replaced by Gypsy Red. The latter came with white vinyl interior, red saddle stitching, and tan carpeting and top. What's more, the '55s had smoother bodies constructed of

slightly thinner sections than the 1953–54 models. Fit-and-finish was tidier and tighter. Early '55s retained holes in the frame rails for mounting the six-cylinder engine, but these were soon plugged once it was realized they'd probably never be used again. In addition, the X-brace on the underside of the hood was replaced by a lateral brace to clear the V-8's air cleaner.

On balance, 1955 marked a great leap forward for Corvette engineering, but not even genuine high performance, improved workmanship, and fine-tuned details could turn around the car's failing fortunes, at least not immediately. Sales actually declined to only 700 units for the model year. Chevy was still wrestling with problems that kept production from being either efficient or significant, and the market was still dubious and elusive. Despite 1955's vast improvements, the overall package still wasn't completely "right."

That the Corvette wasn't dropped from the line right then and there likely has more to do with Chevrolet's corporate hubris than its own bottom line. Ford's own two-seat sporty car, the Thunderbird, was a rousing success, selling 16,155 for the model year—a 23 to 1 margin over the plastic-bodied Chevy. Not wanting to eat the dust of its closest competitor without a fight, management allowed Harley Earl, Ed Cole, and Zora Arkus-Duntov to make the car "right" once and for all. They would soon transform the awkward two-seater of 1953–55 into the genuine article—"America's only true sports car," as Chevy would proudly proclaim. Like those of Lazarus and Mark Twain, the reports of the Corvette's demise would prove to be greatly exaggerated.

All 1953 Corvettes were finished in Polo White with Sportsman Red interiors, red wheels, and black tops. Early cars, like this restored example, left the factory wearing '53 Chevy passenger-car wheel covers, reflecting the somewhat makeshift nature of initial Corvette production. Triple-carburetor "Blue Flame Special" six mated to a Chevy Powerglide automatic transmission controlled by a stubby lever between the seats. "Twin cowl" instrument panel would be a 'Vette hallmark for many years, as would the "toothy" grille, but critics chided the overall styling for mixing Detroit flash with traditional sports-car elements like mesh headlamp stone shields. Exactly 300 of the '53 Corvettes were built, but only 183 were sold in that first calendar year.

Corvette production shifted during '54 from Flint, Michigan, to a larger plant in St. Louis. Colors expanded to include red, blue, and black paint as well as white, plus a beige interior and top. The early 'Vette's clip-in plastic side curtains included a small vent window to augment the regular cowl ventilator (open at right). A revised camshaft boosted the 235.5-cubic-inch six by five bhp to 155, but acceleration remained relatively tepid at about 11 sec 0–60 mph. Chevy hoped to move 10,000 of the '54s but ended up building just 3640, many of which were unsold at year's end.

Looking very Ferrari-like, this one-of-a-kind *gran turismo* coupe combines a 1954 Corvette chassis and power-train with aluminum bodywork constructed by Ghia Aigle of Switzerland, an affilate of Italy's famed Ghia coach-works. Built for the 1957 Geneva Auto Show, it was designed by Giovanni Michellotti, who later penned several sports cars for Triumph in England. The custom interior is stitched in black leather and features a Ferrari-style wood-faced dashboard and matching wood-rim steering wheel. Road wheels are period Borrani wires. The car was recently discovered in Portugal, where it had been stored with only 3800 km (about 2350 miles) on its odometer.

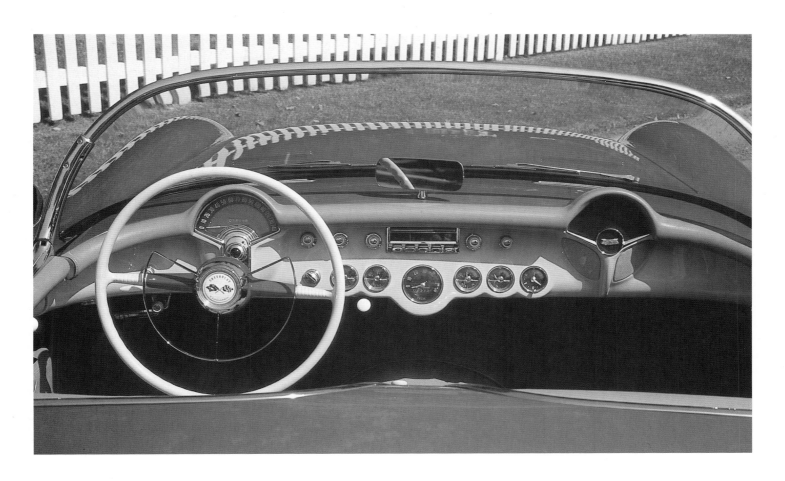

Only 700 Corvettes were built for '55, but nearly all packed Chevy's brilliant new small-block V-8, signalled by an exaggerated "V" in the bodyside namescript. With 265 cubic inches and 195 bhp, the V-8 trimmed the 0–60 sprint to well under nine seconds. A newly optional three-speed manual transmission also helped make that year's 'Vette a much more exciting performer.

Profile: Harley Earl

Enthusiasts generally agree that the impetus for the first Corvette came from Harley Earl, pioneering automotive stylist and founder of GM's Art and Colour Section. Some observers consider him to be more the Corvette's "father" than even Zora Arkus-Duntov.

To be sure, the fiberglass-bodied two-seater could not have progressed from Motorama dream car to production reality without Earl's backing. He fought for the Corvette from the very first, against some fairly stiff odds, and for a reason: It was just his sort of car. Of course, Earl carried considerable clout with GM management, the kind that comes from a swift, sure rise to fame—and a winning track record.

Harley Earl was born to be a stylist. His father had designed horse-drawn carriages in Los Angeles, and by the time young Harley had graduated from Stanford, he was a genuine car buff. In the early Twenties he secured a job designing dashing custom bodywork for Don Lee, a Cadillac dealer who catered to the Hollywood elite. While at the Lee shops, Earl was discovered by Lawrence P. Fisher, then general manager of Cadillac, who hired the 32-year-old as a consultant.

One of Earl's first assignments upon arriving in Detroit was the body design for the 1927 LaSalle, the first edition of Cadillac's lower-cost companion make. It would be the first mass-produced car to be styled in the modern sense. Its lines were gracefully handsome, reminiscent of the contemporary Hispano-Suiza—not much of a surprise, since Earl was quite familiar with European design trends of the day.

That first LaSalle was an instant hit, and many attributed its success to styling. GM president Alfred P. Sloan, Jr., soon invited Earl to establish an in-house styling department. Earl organized it as the Art and Colour Section; the English spelling for "color" was his way of denoting prestige. Earl surrounded himself with talented designers, many of whom would owe him their careers. Virgil Exner, destined to win fame with Chrysler Corporation's "Forward Look" in the mid-Fifties, trained under Earl and headed the Pontiac studio in the Thirties. Other luminaries like Frank Hershey, Art Ross, Ned Nickels, and William L. Mitchell learned their craft from Earl, making their marks at Cadillac and Buick. (Mitchell would succeed his mentor following Earl's retirement in 1958.) Clare MacKichan, who helped create the classic 1955 Chevy, was yet another pupil.

Earl's impact on the shape of GM cars was enormous. To evolve the form of various body components, he pio-neered the use of modeling clay, then considered a highly unusual material for the purpose. As chief designer for the world's largest automaker, Earl put his personal stamp on more different cars during his 31 years with the company than any other individual up to that time. His way of seeing things explains the distinctive ribbed or fluted roof of the 1955–57 Chevrolet Nomad, as well as the use of brushed aluminum—one of his favorite materials—on the roof of the 1957–58 Cadillac Eldorado Brougham and, before that, a variety of show cars.

Show cars were Earl's favorite projects. Nothing pleased him more than personally designing many of the Motorama concepts, including the original Corvette. His very first "dream car" may well have been his most influential. The Buick Y-Job of 1938 literally defined the shape of Detroit cars for the next two decades with its dramatically low body, absence of traditional running boards, strong horizontal lines, and long boattail deck.

Aircraft design influenced much of Earl's work. For example, the trend-setting tailfins that first appeared in production on the 1948 Cadillac were inspired by the twin-tail Lockheed P-38 Lightning, a World War II pursuit plane powered by GM-built Allison engines. The pontoon fenders, fastback roofs, and heavy chrome accents that came to characterize GM's early postwar look were likewise inspired by Earl's fascination with the fighter plane. Even the first Corvette sported rocket-like fins. History has already recorded the first Corvettes as some of his best efforts.

The following quotes from Harley Earl include excerpts from a 1954 interview conducted by Arthur W. Baum:

On GM Art and Colour: "When I refer to 'myself,' I am merely using a short cut to talk about my team. There are 650 of us, and collectively we are known as the Styling Section. I happen to be the founder of the section and the responsible head, but we all contribute to the future appearance of GM automobiles.

"We work informally and, of course, secretly. Since our job is to generate and present design ideas, we have methods of keeping new ideas popping and stirring. To help keep us young, we introduce a freshman squad every year, mostly from two design schools on the East and West coasts. We have contests and idea races."

Inspiring Designers: "I often act merely as prompter. If a particular group appears to be bogging down over a new fender or grille or interior trim, I sometimes wander into their quarters, make some irrelevant or even zany observation, and then leave. It is surprising what effect a bit of peculiar behavior will have. First-class minds will seize on anything out of the ordinary."

His Office: "It is a hidden room with no telephone. The windows are blacked out and a misleading name is

on the door. In it is a scale model of the first sedan I ever designed for the company, a 1927 LaSalle. I have a great affection for the old crock, but I must admit it is slab-sided, top-heavy, and stiff-shouldered. [Still] there is something on it that explains what I have been trying to do. On the line we now call the beltline, running around the body, there is a decorative strip like half a figure eight fastened to the body. This strip was placed there to eat up the over-powering vertical expanse of that tall car. It was an effort to make the car look longer and lower."

The Motorama Expositions: "A Motorama is more than a good show with good promotion. Frankly, it makes my styling job easier, as visitors express themselves vividly, and by the time hundreds of thousands of these critics have examined your show and commented on your exhibits, you have a firm idea of their likes and dislikes. And it is hardly necessary for me to say that it is vital for us to keep in tune with American thinking about automobiles."

A Few Thoughts on Automotive Design: "My primary purpose [with 'longer-lower-wider' styling] has been to lengthen and lower the American automobile, at times in reality and always at least in appearance. Why? Because my sense of proportion tells me that oblongs are more attractive than squares, just as a ranch house is more attractive than a square, three-story flat-roofed house, or a greyhound is more graceful than a bulldog.

"American cars have always had a comfortably blunt, leonine front look. This is good as long as the car as a whole is poised right. There was a time when automobiles tilted down in front as if they intended to dig for woodchucks. Subsequently, they went tail-heavy and appeared to be sitting up and begging. Now I think we have them in exactly the right attitude of level alertness, like an airplane at take-off.

"I am not particularly committed to chrome. But when chrome arrived as a decorative trim for the industry, it was imperative that I find out how people felt about it. I dispatched my staff to key cities to pose as reporters. They asked hundreds of questions about customer response to or rejection of chrome trim. The conclusions were in favor of chrome, more so on used-car lots.

"Highway regulatory bodies keep us fenced in [in terms of design limitations]. If we wanted a single headlight on a car, the states would prohibit it, since many of them control the number, brightness, position, and height of headlights. They exercise similar control over tail and stop lights. [Similarly], the engineers quite properly will not let us interfere with the efficiency and soundness of their powerplants. If we wanted to try our hands on a three-wheeled car, I am sure the engineers wouldn't encourage us. They think three-wheeled cars are inherently dangerous. They won't give us a rear engine either, until problems like weight distribution are solved, and only then if there is a compelling advantage to the owner.

"Most of our thousands of hours of work every year are small refinements and revisions to improve the comfort, utility, and appearance of our automobiles. But we also need explosive bursts of spanking-new themes, and somehow we get them. I have enjoyed every minute of both kinds of this labor for 28 years. I hope designing is always like that."

Left: Harley Earl (standing) virtually invented the idea of "styling" at GM, and influenced the corporation's designs from the late '20s to the late '50s. He's shown here discussing future concepts with (from left) Albert Bradley, chairman of the board of GM; C.E. Wilson, Secretary of Defense; and Harlow H. Curtice, President of GM. Above: Earl took particular interest in designing show cars; here he sits at the wheel of the LeSabre concept vehicle of 1952, which lent some of its styling features to the Corvette. Had the Corvette not been one of his pet projects, it likely would have been killed after the '54 or '55 model year—if it would ever have been built at all. Earl retired in 1958, passing the baton to one of his chosen protégés, William Mitchell—who would go on to leave an indelible mark of his own.

PART 2 1956-1957

Fitting Chevrolet's landmark 265-cid small block V-8 under the 1955 Corvette's hood added a welcome measure of performance to the struggling sports car, and it was greeted with great enthusiasm. Still, boosters and critics alike agreed the vehicle was badly in need of a makeover, both cosmetic and functional, to make it a world-class contender.

Truth was, the 1953–55 Corvette had lost sight of its original objective. It was neither a serious performance sports car nor a small, fun-to-drive roadster that anyone could afford. It had instead become a well-equipped and flamboyant image car, though it wasn't exactly clear what that image was supposed to project. Plus it was expensive—at around $3500, the Corvette cost about twice as much as a typical family sedan.

That Ford's 1955 Thunderbird outsold the Corvette by such a wide margin (23–1) was more than a mere slap in Chevy's face—it was a direct challenge to the company's market supremacy. Electing to not only continue building the Corvette but also to make it superior to the T-Bird in every respect wasn't just a matter of pride.

Ironically, just as Chevrolet would commit to turning the Corvette into a genuine sports car, Ford was taking the other route by transforming the Thunderbird into

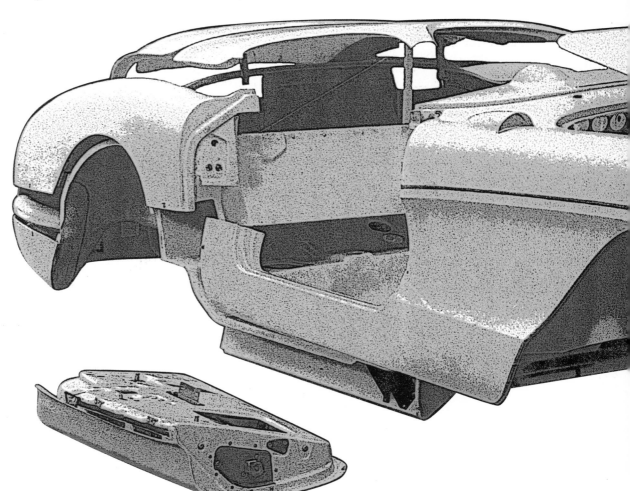

Corvette came of age with the fully redesigned
1956 model and got a solid new lease on life.
GM design chief Harley Earl made it stunning to
behold. Engineering whiz Zora Arkus-Duntov
gave it handling to match newfound V-8 sizzle.
The '57 offered more of the same—*much* more.
No doubt about it: Chevrolet's sports car was
now "America's only *true* sports car."

a more passive four-seater, which would debut for the 1958 model year. Though the T-Bird's 1955 sales tally of 16,000 units certainly outpaced the Corvette's puny 700 cars on the year, Ford wanted to further boost sales by broadening the vehicle's appeal. Making the Thunderbird more practical and civilized seemed the way to achieve this goal.

Harley Earl, who'd been taking the many Corvette criticisms of the past few years to heart, was busily at work addressing them. On February 1, 1955, just as Thunderbirds were beginning to be seen on the street in serious numbers, Earl had all but finalized a full-scale clay model of a new Corvette body. With minor trim changes, Earl showed the mockup to GM management in mid-April and the new design was approved on the spot. The result was a '56 Corvette and a nearly identical '57 model

Corvette's styling transformation for 1956 is apparent even on this "naked body" shot. The new look was more coherent and purposeful, without the "dream car" gimmicks of 1953–55. The original's slab-sidedness was gone too, replaced by sweeping concave indentations long called "coves" by Corvette lovers. Adding interest to the hood were twin slim longitudinal bulges, a likely crib from the contemporary Mercedes 300SL Gullwing.

1

2

that are still regarded by many as the epitome of Corvette styling (at least until the famed Sting Ray hit the market for 1963).

This second-generation styling was rooted in three Motorama concept cars shown during 1955: the Chevrolet Biscayne and a pair of showstoppers dubbed "LaSalle II" (a nostalgic bow to GM's departed luxury-car division). The Biscayne was a compact four-door hardtop painted light green with a color-keyed interior. Appearance features included so-called "bugeye" headlamps that were set high and inboard of fender-mounted parking lights, flanking a grille that was made up of a series of vertical bars. Shallow air-intake slots were positioned in the cowl just ahead of and

below a huge compound-curve windshield, and the flat cabin floor was level with the bottom of the frame. The LaSalle II was a similarly styled hardtop sedan and sporty roadster combo; both versions likewise had prominent vertical-bar grilles but sported a styling touch the '56 Corvette would inherit: an elliptical concave section at the rear of the lower bodysides that was swept back from the front wheel wells.

One of the last GM production cars to be designed before the styling staff moved from Detroit to the new corporate Technical Center in Warren, Michigan, the '56 Corvette was not only fresh looking but was a vast improvement over the first generation in virtually

every respect. While its changes were more evolutionary than revolutionary, all the former version's inferior elements were removed and the superior ones were now emphasized. At $3120, the price had jumped by only a nominal amount—around $200—over the previous year's (V-8-equipped) model.

A definite "face" was regarded as the most appealing element of the first-generation design, and the next generation's visage looked even more attractive. Wire screens had made the "eyes" seem veiled on the 1953–55 models—hardly appropriate, it was thought, for a "man's" car—so the headlamps were uncovered and moved forward out of their recesses.

8

3

4

5

6

7

1-2. Corvette's '56 styling was finalized just months before production. This February 1955 workout wears stubby front "coves" and matching rear indents above a side-exit exhaust. **3-4.** What is likely the other side of the same model was closer to final form, including a two-toning scheme. **5-7.** The design was all but locked up by May 1955. **8.** February 1955 sketches suggest the '56 'Vette could have been much like the one-off LaSalle II roadster shown at that year's GM Motorama.

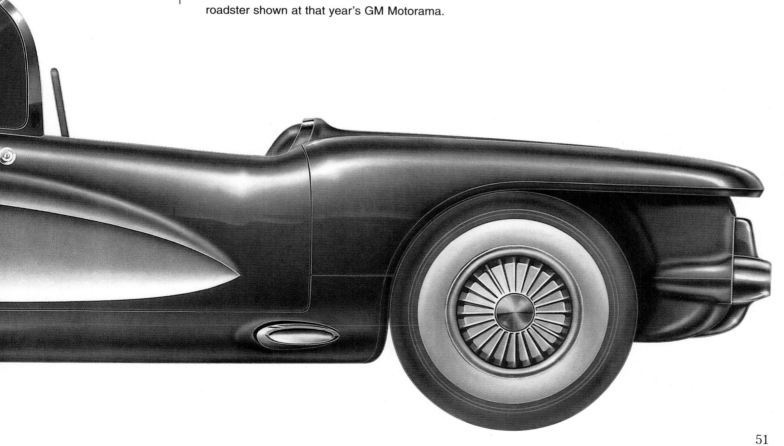

Complementing this was a larger version of the round Corvette nose emblem, with the racy crossed-flags motif that survives to this day. The original front grille, which formed the "mouth" and its magnificent chrome "teeth," were unchanged from the 1955 model.

Rear-end styling revisions to the '56 were just as tastefully executed. The '53–'55's finny fenders and jet-pod taillamps were trimmed down to artful French curves contoured to match rear deck curvature, and new taillights were neatly "frenched" above a vertical bumperette on each fender. The trunklid "shadow box" was discarded and the license plate moved to below the trunk opening, where it was flanked by horizontal bumperettes with little inboard bullets. The result was a smooth, gently curved tail, with the fenders protruding just slightly.

The bodyside "coves," as they came to be called, gave the '56

'Vette a truly unique styling personality. They also helped correct the slab-sided look that had led some to mock the first-generation's design as a "plastic bathtub." Even with the coves' narrow chrome outlines—one of the few last-minute trim changes made to the production prototype—the flanks were clean and attractive.

To be sure, the car was now largely devoid of styling gimmicks, though two obvious ones remained: faux vent scoops atop the front fenders near the windshield (originally designed to be functional—for cowl ventilation—but cost considerations rendered them merely decorative) and the often-lambasted fake wheel-knockoff hubs (the car's wheel covers were all-new and more ornate than before). Those wheel covers, however, remained standard issue until 1963 and have since become some of the best-known wheel covers in automotive history.

What's more, the '56 Corvette didn't just look better than its predecessor; it worked better, too, and was an all-around more "livable" car. The fussy side curtains were gone forever, replaced by proper roll-up door glass. Even power window lifts were available at extra cost. The welcome addition of outside handles ended the annoyance of having to reach into the cabin to open a door.

The Corvette's standard convertible top was now tighter fitting and offered in beige and white in addition to the standard-issue black cloth; design-wise it was more integrated and was rounded at the rear to echo the aft-quarter design. A power-operated top was offered for the first time as a $170.60 option, though it was technically only semi-automatic—it had to be unlatched and partially collapsed manually before pressing the fold button. Capping the new design was a detachable hardtop taken directly

1

from the production-based prototype seen at the 1954 Motorama show. The hardtop cost an extra $215.20, though it could be swapped for the soft top at no charge. The new factory hardtop was also obviously curved and, with its rear side windows, afforded much better over-the-shoulder vision than the soft top.

Except for new waffle-pattern upholstery and revised door panels to go with the wind-up windows, the cockpit was changed little from 1955, retaining the existing "twin cowl" dashboard with its awkward, near full-width instrument spread. A new spring-spoke steering wheel was added, and the heater was changed from the old recirculating type to a new "fresh air" version after the first 145 production cars were built. Seats remained separate, flat-bottomed affairs that were buckets in name only. The passenger's seat could be adjusted fore and aft for the first time, and seat belts were newly available as a dealer-installed accessory kit. A then-leading-edge transistorized signal-seeking radio was another new option, available for $198.90.

1. The '56 dashboard was similar to the 1953–55 design, but the old awkward side curtains gave way at last to proper roll-up windows. Power windows were optional. Outside door handles were another innovation. **2.** A three-speed manual transmission returned from late '55 but was standard for '56, not optional, and used an improved linkage providing more positive shift action. Two-speed Powerglide automatic shifted to option status. Contemporary road tests indicated the manual gearbox cut the 0–60 time to about 7.3 seconds versus 8.9.

There was more good news under the hood for '56, where the small-block V-8 was now standard. And it had been given even more muscle to boot, now up to a rated 210 bhp at 5200 rpm with a single four-barrel carburetor and higher 9.25:1 compression. That was 15 bhp more than the '55 version and a significant improvement over the 155-bhp six of just two years earlier. A special "high lift" camshaft was available as an extra-cost item at $188.30, but was only available in tandem with the optional 225-bhp dual-four-barrel-carburetor-equipped engine for another $172.20. The latter also included a cast aluminum intake manifold. Chevy recommended this combination "for racing purposes only," however, and while a horsepower figure was never officially given for this configuration, it's said to be around 240 bhp on premium fuel. The special cam, developed by Zora Arkus-Duntov, helped raise torque on the 225-bhp powerplant to an impressive 270 pound-feet at 3600 rpm. The original Blue Flame Six was gone for good, and few were sorry to see it go.

The car's running gear was beefed up to handle the extra power, and the day's enthusiast magazines were quick to catch the racing implications. Like the V-8, the three-speed manual gearbox was now standard—Powerglide at last became a true option, at an honest $189 extra. The manual was tweaked with much closer gear ratios than in the '55 version (for the record, the spread was 2.2:1 in 1st, 1.31:1 in 2nd, and 1:1 in 3rd). In addition, the shifter was now attached directly to the transmission housing, which afforded more positive shifts. A stronger 10-inch-diameter clutch with 12 heat-treated coil springs was added, replacing

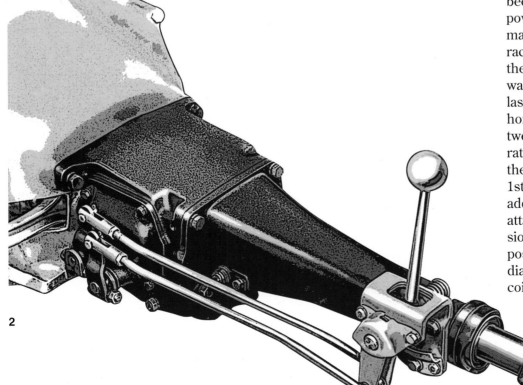

2

1. The rakish '56 Corvette was a big draw at auto shows and Chevy showrooms. This one beautified the lobby of the GM Building in downtown Detroit. **2.** We don't know the man, but we do know the narrowband whitewalls on this 'Vette weren't publicly available until 1959. **3.** One '56 ad poked fun at sports-car purists. **4.** Optional fuel injection made big news for '57.

1

2

"REALLY, OLD BOY, YOU AREN'T SUPPOSED TO BUILD THAT SORT OF THING IN AMERICA, Y'KNOW."

The unforgivable thing, of course, is this: The new Corvette not only looks delightful and rides like the Blue Train—but it also is quite capable of macerating the competition out on the road circuits.

This dual nature is the classic requirement before you can call a pretty two-seater a *sports car.* And properly so, for this is an honorable name, and only a vehicle with race-bred precision of handling, cornering and control can make a mortal driver feel quite so akin to the gods.

Unlike the gentleman above, who has been a little slow in catching up with current events, most sports car people are becoming aware that the Corvette is truly one of the world's most remarkable cars. Because it does two disparate things outstandingly well: It provides superbly practical motoring, with every luxury and convenience your heart might covet, and accompanies this with a soul-satisfying ferocity of performance.

We could recite the full specifications. But if you are the kind of driver who is meant for a Corvette, you'll want to find out firsthand—and that, sir, would be our pleasure! . . . *Chevrolet Division of General Motors, Detroit 2, Michigan.*

SPECIFICATIONS: 283-cubic-inch V8 engine with single four-barrel carburetor, 220 h.p. (four other engines* range to 283 h.p. with fuel injection). Close-ratio three-speed manual transmission standard, with special Powerglide automatic drive* available on all but maximum-performance engines. Choice of removable hard top or power-operated fabric top, Power-Lift windows.* Instruments include 6000 r.p.m. tachometer, oil pressure gauge and ammeter.   *Optional at extra cost.

CORVETTE

by Chevrolet

3

the previous diaphragm-spring unit. Final drive was still 3.55:1, but a 3.27:1 cog was newly available. The differential itself was new as well and was shared with other 1956 passenger Chevys. The car's front suspension array with its integral front cross-member was unchanged from the 1955 version, as were the car's brakes—11-inch Bendix drums.

With all this, the Corvette now shed its image as a half-finished plastic toy car. The '56 offered genuine sports car performance with smart new styling and a full complement of amenities. And despite employing a few design clichés of

the era, the '56 Corvette still turns heads and draws admiring glances over four-and-a-half decades later.

Enthusiast magazines generally praised the new Corvette: Its manual shifter was lauded as being raceworthy, while the car's handling was judged "good to excellent" in its class, though it was noted to suffer somewhat from understeer. The steering gear was hailed as being amply quick—just 3.5 turns lock-to-lock—and weight distribution was cited as nearly perfect at 52/48 percent front/rear. Brakes remained a weak point, however. With just 158 square inches of total lining area, they "faded into oblivion," as one

tester said after a hard application. In all, the critics agreed that the car's road behavior had been greatly improved, though it continued to offer a fairly harsh, albeit controlled, ride.

Other criticisms were minor, and were addressed mainly at the car's confusing instrument array, flat-bottomed seats, and lack of storage space. Still, the consensus was that Chevrolet was now building a true sporting machine that could be considered a worthy dual-purpose competitor with any of the day's formidable British or European marques.

There was no doubt about it—

TOWARD AN AMERICAN CLASSIC . . . THE 1957 CORVETTE WITH FUEL INJECTION! It is with considerable pride that Chevrolet invites you to examine an engineering advance of great significance, available on the 1957 Corvette. It is fuel injection, and in the Corvette V8 it permits a level of efficiency hitherto unrealized in any American production car: *one horsepower for every cubic inch of displacement* . . . 283 h.p.! In addition, there is unprecedented responsiveness, even during warm-up; virtually instantaneous acceleration and significant gains in overall gas economy.

This is another major step in the creation of a proud new kind of car for America: a *genuine* sports car, as certified by its record in competition. But a *unique* sports car in its combination of moderate price, luxurious equipment and low-cost maintenance with fiery performance, polo-pony responsiveness and granite stability on curves.

It is our intention to make of the Corvette a classic car, one of those rare and happy milestones in the history of automotive design. We take pleasure in inviting you to drive the 1957 version—and see just how close we have come to the target. . . . *Chevrolet Division of General Motors, Detroit 2, Michigan.*

SPECIFICATIONS: 283-cubic-inch V8 engine with single four-barrel carburetor, 220 h.p. (four other engines* range to 283 h.p. with fuel injection). Close-ratio three-speed manual transmission standard, with special Powerglide automatic drive* available on all but maximum-performance engines. Choice of removable hard top or power-operated fabric top, Power-Lift windows.* Instruments include 6000 r.p.m. tachometer, oil pressure gauge and ammeter. **Optional at extra cost.*

CORVETTE

by Chevrolet

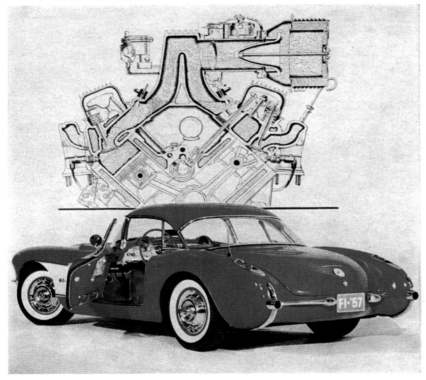

4

America's sports car had finally come of age. No one knew that better than Zora Arkus-Duntov, who believed that a race-winning image was vital to Corvette sales. He would be proven correct. Duntov had developed his high-lift camshaft specifically with an eye to competition. If the 'Vette could set a few speed records and win some races, Chevy advertising would be able to capitalize on those feats.

Accordingly, the Duntov camshaft was slipped into a modified '56 Corvette specially prepared at GM's Arizona proving grounds. The car was then shipped to Florida, where Betty Skelton and John Fitch would drive it at the Daytona Speed Weeks trials in January. The goal was 150 mph. Though beach conditions weren't favorable, the car managed an impressive two-way run of 150.583 mph, with Duntov himself behind the wheel.

Development work continued and yielded a new high-compression head that raised the engine's output to a claimed 255 bhp—nearly one horsepower per cubic inch. At the Speed Weeks trials, a Thunderbird prepped by ex-racer Pete DePaolo and driven by Chuck Daigh bested the 'Vette in the production standing-mile contest, but the plastic-bodied Chevy proved fastest in the modified class, as Fitch won with a two-pass average of 145.543 mph.

By September, ads were exclaiming that "The 1956 Corvette is proving—in open competition—that it is America's only genuine production sports car," an obvious swipe at the Thunderbird, which Chevy had already started calling a "scaled-down convertible." Another ad proclaimed, "Bring on the hay bales! The new Corvette, piloted by Betty Skelton, has established a new record for American sports cars at Daytona Beach. But that's only the start. Corvette owners may enter other big racing tests in the months ahead—tests that may carry America's blue-and-white colors into several of the most important European competitions."

And so they did. A modified car made a decent showing at Sebring in 1956, finishing ninth in the grueling 12-hour run. Out at Pebble Beach, California, a Corvette, piloted by "Dr." Dick Thompson (a Washington, D.C., dentist who had previously been known for racing a Porsche 356) finished a strong second behind a Mercedes-Benz 300SL. Thompson would end up winning that year's national championship in the SCCA's C-Production class—with a little help from Duntov and other friends. Here was yet another boost to the "competition-proved" image Chevrolet wanted to attain.

The Corvette also began performing better in the race that mattered most to GM—the production race—with sales volume at 3467 units now accounting for about a fifth of the Thunderbird's level for 1956. That may have disappointed the accountants, but it heartened those at Chevrolet who had been fighting to keep the 'Vette alive. Even more importantly, the Corvette was again boosting dealer floor traffic while enhancing Chevrolet's newly won perform-

55

1

ance reputation. Chevrolet managers seemed quite happy to sustain the car despite modest sales. In fact, there'd been no talk about dropping the Corvette since 1955. And now that Corvette was beginning to be taken seriously, its supporters argued, it should sell even better for 1957, which it did by a wide margin.

Major improvements for 1957 included a larger V-8 and, as a midyear addition to the options list, a four-speed manual gearbox that had long been demanded by enthusiasts. The Corvette's appearance didn't change—not that it needed to—except that the bodyside "coves" could now be finished in a contrasting color as a $19.40 option.

The 283-cid V-8 has since become one of Chevy's most revered engines—the definitive small-block enshrined by a generation of car enthusiasts and all the collectors who followed. It was essentially the existing 265 engine that had been bored out ⅛-inch (to 3.875 in.; stroke remained a short 3.00 in.). In Chevrolet passenger

56

2

3

1. A GM engineer checks out a 283 Chevy V-8 with Ramjet fuel injection, two power-boosting improvements for 1957. 2. A tall, central two-piece aluminum manifold gave "fuelie" 283s a distinctive underhood appearance. 3. Straight-talking auto writer "Uncle" Tom McCahill (*right*) gets the lowdown on Ramjet from Corvettemeister Zora Arkus-Duntov.

ers in the 1950s. Chevrolet turned to the technology as a way of gleaning added performance out of its two-year-old V-8 while its competitors were preparing all-new eight-cylinder powerplants of their own. GM initially considered using supercharging, which Kaiser had employed for 1954–55 and one Studebaker would use for 1958, but nixed the idea because of potential reliability problems. So the engineers borrowed a page from the European automakers' performance books and settled on obtaining more horsepower via a more precise fuel metering system than a carburetor allowed, namely fuel injection. Model year '57 was closing fast, so a development team was formed—and hustled. The key figures were Ed Cole, who'd been promoted to Chevrolet's chief in 1955; Harry Barr, Cole's one-time collaborator on the 1949 Cadillac V-8 and now his successor as Chevy chief engineer; John Dolza, head of fuel injection development for the GM Engineering Staff; and Zora Arkus-Duntov.

Duntov had been working on a fuel injection system since early 1956 and under unusual circumstances. An accident while driving a prototype Corvette hardtop equipped with experimental disc brakes at the GM Proving Grounds in April left him with a broken vertebra in his back. For the next six months, he would work on the fuel-injection program while standing up, confined by a body cast.

In a relatively short period of time, the engineers put together a fuel injection system that appeared to be relatively inexpensive to manufacture and promised significant power gains. Yet initial dyno-testing showed the "fuelie" to be no more powerful than a standard dual-carburetor V-8. Cole, however, was a believer who wanted nothing less than to offer fuel injection across

cars, the 283 delivered 185 bhp in base form, but the standard Corvette version with a four-barrel carburetor developed 220 bhp at 4800 rpm. Dual four-barrels took it to 245 and 270 bhp, and GM's newly developed "Ramjet" fuel injection system yielded 250 or 283 bhp. The last was the magic "one-horsepower-per-cubic-inch" threshold, and Chevy ads blared the news. (It wasn't a first, though; Chrysler had actually exceeded that goal the previous year— and by more conventional means—with its 355-bhp 354-cid hemi V-8 in the 300B.)

Though almost universal today, fuel injection was a foreign concept—literally—to Detroit automak-

continued on page 60

Profile: Zora Arkus-Duntov

Known among industry insiders and enthusiasts alike as "Mr. Corvette," Zora Arkus-Duntov was a true original. While he did not participate in the car's birth, he helped nurse it back to life when its days were seemingly numbered and nurtured the vehicle throughout its Golden Age. More than anyone else behind the scenes, Duntov was responsible for making the Corvette a respected sports car both at home and abroad.

An engineer by trade, the Belgium-born Duntov had worked for the renowned British automaker Sydney Allard. Duntov collaborated in the development of the appropriately named "Ardun" cylinder-head conversion used to wring more power out of Ford's V-8 flathead engine. He came to Chevrolet's attention shortly after Ed Cole became the division's chief engineer when Duntov submitted a paper on high-performance engines for Cole's review. Chevrolet had not been known for employing high-salary European high-performance engineers. But Cole had *carte blanche* from GM executives Tom Keating and Harlow Curtice for a massive upgrade and enlargement of Chevrolet's engineering department, and Duntov came aboard.

Duntov was one of the original 1953 Corvette's most outspoken critics, and time would prove his judgment to be right on target. He found the first Corvette's handling to be abominable for what might otherwise be a world-class sports car, and Duntov immediately set about correcting it—unofficially at first. He was initially hired to work on the full Chevrolet line, where the Corvette was but a peripheral product.

Duntov was not only a superb engineer but a capable racing driver. In 1956, for example, he and Betty Skelton drove modified Corvettes at better than 150 miles per hour at the Daytona Speed Weeks. The feat marked the birth of the famous "Duntov cam," which enhanced the performance of Chevy's new small-block V-8—and its reputation among enthusiasts. In 1957 he was involved with track testing of the futuristic Corvette-based SS racer at Sebring, although the car retired after only 23 laps.

When the Automobile Manufacturers Association (AMA) agreed that its members should cease all racing activities and performance advertising in the spring of 1957, Duntov advocated violating the edict in secrecy. He was soon involved with GM's "closet" NASCAR program and other under-the-table competition efforts, which helped end the impractical and ill-conceived AMA ban by the mid-Sixties.

Duntov retired in 1974 after almost 20 years as chief Corvette engineer, and he remained close to the company and to the car until the end of his life. His product accomplishments are too numerous to recount in full, so we'll confine ourselves to highlights. Duntov created the prototype mid-engine Corvette Q-model of 1960, which was never produced. He designed the 1963 Sting Ray chassis, which remained in production essentially unchanged for 20 years. He also lent his name to the "Duntov Corvette," a conversion that turned a stock, post-1975 coupe into a rip-snorting powerhouse with full roadster bodywork. He was inducted in the Corvette Hall of Fame in 1988.

Zora Arkus-Duntov passed away in April 1996, only months before the fifth-generation Corvette's introduction. Upon his death, columnist George Will wrote, "If you do not mourn his passing, you are not a good American."

What follows is the result of several interviews with Zora Arkus-Duntov over the years. The editors and Mr. Duntov covered all aspects of the Corvette—a vivid experience that reflected his remarkable drive and personality.

Q: Why did you leave Allard and join General Motors?

Zora Arkus-Duntov: I wished to return to America. I had talked to an American general who was stationed in England, and he told me to write to Ed Cole at Chevrolet. I did, but it was not promising. I found a position with Fairchild Aviation, and after I had been in the States for some time, I sent to Ed Cole a copy of a research report on high-performance engines that I had written. We discussed salary and benefits for some time before I accepted. I came to GM in May 1953.

Q: What did you think of the new Corvette at that time?

Duntov: That it was the most beautiful car I had ever seen. The engine was a let-down, but the proportions and aesthetics were right. I borrowed one in May, when I first joined GM. The handling was not good. I took it upon myself to give this car better handling. This was not part of my normal assignment—just fiddling on the side.

Q: When, then, did you formalize the Corvette relationship?

Duntov: On the '55, when I was assigned to investigate exhaust staining on the rear of the fenders, which was connected with fumes in the passenger compartment. I attached streamers to a test car and took motion pictures of the air flow. If you opened the vent pane, the exhaust was carried from the rear to the front and into the passenger compartment. Moving the exhaust tips to the very rear of the fenders on the 1956 model corrected both problems.

Q: Tell us about the Duntov cam.

Duntov: I wished to start building a racing image and to exceed 150 mph at the Daytona Speed Weeks. I calculated that I needed an additional 30 horsepower from the 265 V-8 in high-performance trim. I changed the camshaft design to hold the valves open longer but not to lift them higher. This provided a fuller valve-opening curve. Engine speed rose to 6500 rpm, and I had the horsepower I needed. But the Corvette was still too heavy for racing, and we were not ready yet.

Q: So you kept testing and had that terrible accident?

Duntov: Yes, in April 1956. It was my own fault. I arrived at the proving grounds to make carburetor tests and found that this car had no seat belts. It had experimental disc brakes. There were many things wrong with this car. Still, I drove it. Sure, like hell. I got sideways and went off the track. I was in a cast for six months. I couldn't bend. I had strings to lift my dress in the rest room. I was quite a sight.

Q: But you kept working, especially on fuel injection.

Duntov: The fuel-injection project had top priority, because we needed it on both the 1957 Corvette and Chevrolet passenger cars.

Q: Why didn't the fuel injection work out?

Duntov: It was too expensive. In 1965, when it was dropped, the option cost almost $500 extra. For only $150, we could offer the big-block with more power and torque at lower speeds. The fuel-injection engine had to be wound up first. The big engine was superior. It was not the bugs that killed fuel injection. They could have been worked out.

Q: How did the Sebring Corvette SS come about?

Duntov: Harley Earl had a D-Type Jaguar and wanted us to fit it with a Corvette V-8. This was absurd, and I said that if Chevrolet wanted to go racing, we should build an entire car. The SS was the result—a combined project between Styling and Engineering.

Q: Did its styling influence aerodynamics?

Duntov: No. I had them build a full-size model for aerodynamic testing, so that I could have some input on this body. I had them use considerable tuck-under to achieve maximum air velocity under the car. They did not want to do this at first. I could see that they would not have the car ready in time for testing, so I put the test body on a spare chassis.

Q: And that was the famous "mule"?

Duntov: Yes. It was not a beautiful car, but Juan Fangio and Stirling Moss beat the Sebring track record with it.

Q: But Fangio did not drive it in the actual race?

Duntov: As the race got closer and Styling failed to complete the car, Fangio feared that it would not be ready and asked to be released from his contract. Carroll Shelby was also signed and released. Finally, the drivers were John Fitch and Piero Taruffi, but that overtight bushing failed after 23 laps.

Q: Were there long-range plans for the SS?

Duntov: Yes, I was preparing four SS cars to compete at Le Mans, under a fictitious name. But it really was a terrible "lifter" [aerodynamically]. Right away I lost interest in this car. It's beautiful all right, but [it has] the profile of a wing. I drove the Corvette SS racer at the proving grounds at 183 mph, and I ran about 155 mph at the opening of the Daytona track in 1959. But the AMA ruling in 1957 was a tremendous shock. Until 1961, I promoted racing in secrecy.

Q: Why did the AMA ban finally come apart at GM?

Duntov: Bunkie Knudsen replaced Ed Cole as general manager of Chevrolet in 1961. Both wanted to see Corvettes winning races. Knudsen approved a plan for another pure-racing Corvette. I wanted to build at least 100 specials that would weigh only 2000 pounds and which would have powerful new engines. That was the start of the Corvette Grand Sport.

Q: What happened to the Grand Sport program? Why was it cut?

Duntov: Higher management.

Q: Didn't Carroll Shelby approach Chevrolet with the Cobra idea before he went to Ford?

Duntov: Yes. He got two chassis from us and had them bodied in Italy, but nothing ever came of that project. He settled with Ford instead.

Q: When did work begin on the first Sting Ray?

Duntov: Both chassis and engine work began in 1959. I had by then been named director of high-performance vehicles. I took pride in the small-block Chevrolet engine.

Q: What do you recall about designing the Sting Ray chassis?

Duntov: Mainly that everything worked as designed—it lasted up to the 1982 model. In 1962 we produced the Grand Sport with the disc brakes, vented

in front, solid at the rear. In '64 we had the Girling Brake Company throw their hands in the air and say they couldn't make discs because Corvettes have too much weight for their performance. I worked with Kelsey-Hayes, and they succeeded in providing excellent brakes for the Corvette.

Q: But the brakes were by Delco, weren't they?

Duntov: Kelsey-Hayes didn't get the contract because Delco Division [of GM] used their leverage. Delco produced a brake identical to Kelsey-Hayes'. For '65 we produced four-wheel disc brakes, and they were so good they stayed until 1982. With the mid-engine Corvette we used a Bendix brake identical to the Delco brake—four pads per caliper.

Q: Overall, how did you view the '63 Sting Ray?

Duntov: The ergonomics were very good. It was quite adequate as an envelope, with such things as a shift lever location that would fall into the hand readily, good legibility of the gauges, and performance that was nonpareil overall.

Q: Did you like Bill Mitchell's styling?

Duntov: Overall, we were on the same wavelength. I only remember one disagreement—the split window on the '63 Sting Ray [coupe]. We took it out [of the '64 model].

Q: What was your opinion of the 1968 Corvette styling?

Duntov: As a whole, design-wise, it was a very good car. Something got lost in the ergonomics, though. You had to move to operate the gearshift. At that time, Bill Mitchell was impressed by supersonic jets. The first thing I did was to provide more shoulder room. It was so pinched you couldn't drive it without leaning. To gain a half-inch per side, I spent $120,000 retooling door inners. This half an inch was very significant. Another consideration: The '63–'67 car was a terrible lifter. The subsequent design was also a lifter, but not to that extent.

Q: How important was racing?

Duntov: At that time, very important. I considered that it was necessary. To establish the sports car, you have to race it. After a car gets established, like in the mid-Seventies, the racing is second place. We had all the optional items to enable people to race. CERV 1 [an experimental open-wheel single-seat racer] was the progenitor of the Sting Ray suspension-wise.

Q: Did you like GM's experimental rotary engine?

Duntov: Not at all. But as things began to shape up in '71, I had either a

mid-engine car and a rotary engine or not at all. Therefore, I had to accept the rotary engine. Ed Cole [by then, GM's president] was enamored with the rotary engine. Therefore, I showed him the two- and four-rotor Corvettes. The four-rotor engine was interchangeable with a reciprocating engine; it could easily be replaced with the small-block V-8. When GM got off the Wankel kick, they went back to a reciprocating engine. The Aerovette [the four-rotor design] got a 400-cid small-block engine. It also had the space to accept four-wheel drive. I told them....four-wheel drive [would be important in the future]. First with rear-wheel drive and, two years later, four-wheel drive. If you look at the Aerovette, you see a big tunnel to fit four-wheel drive. But it was just a styling exercise. The mid-engine Corvette minus energy-absorbent bumpers was under 3000 pounds with the 400 or 350 small-block. Torsional stiffness was in the area of 6000 pounds-feet per degree. It was a very good car. It had good luggage space. When I think about it, it's a pity it did not come about.

Q: Who killed the mid-engine design?

Duntov: In 1974, I had a conversation with the chairman of the board [Thomas A. Murphy]. He said, "Let's wait. Right now we cannot build enough cars to satisfy the demand. When we see the demand will slacken, we'll bring the mid-engine car out." I disagreed with him. I thought Chevrolet should be at the forefront, but he had the last word.

Q: What do you think of the fourth-generation Corvette [introduced around the time this interview was conducted], and what would you have done differently with it?

Duntov: [I think it's] very good. I tried to promulgate the mid-engine car. If I was not forced to retire, [the 1984 model] would probably be a mid-engine car. The mid-engine design in '69 and '73–'74 was in the picture on and off. I think I would have won the fight given time, but, unfortunately, I was forced to retire. Styling-wise, aerodynamic-wise, [the '84 generation] is excellent. It is ergonomically well thought out. The chassis is not as good as I wish it were. But second guessing is unfair. Digital gauges I don't care for at all. They're good for slow-moving processes, like fuel gauge, clock, or oil level. But the speedometer and tach should have round faces to show where you have been and where you are going. Instantaneous readouts have no place in a sports car.

1

"UND SO HELFE MIR, HERMANN, I WAS HOLDING 5900 R.P.M. AND HE CAME PAST ME LIKE A STUKA . . . AND PLAYING THE RADIO, TOO!"

CORVETTE
by Chevrolet

2

1. GM designers and engineers loved playing with Corvettes from the very first. This September 1956 photo shows some of their more signficant experiments to that point. **2.** Many 1956–57 Corvette ads made the point that accomplished sports cars were no longer the sole province of Italy, Britain, and Germany.

the entire '57 Chevrolet line. "Win on Sunday, sell on Monday" was still a cherished marketing maxim, and with merely facelifted '57 passenger cars to sell, Chevy as a whole needed the extra boost that stock-car racing victories—aided by the fuel-injected horsepower bump—would provide. The image enhancement of using an exotic "high tech" feature in the division's car line would be secondary. So it was back to the lab for more research.

Ultimately Chevrolet and GM's Rochester carburetor division came up with a workable system that not only increased top-end output but spread power over a wider rpm range. Alas, reliability problems surfaced quickly, which together with the option's high price tag—$500—rendered fuel injection a scarce commodity, even among Corvettes. Installations ran to only 240 in a total '57 production run of 6339 'Vettes. Ramjet fuel injection was subsequently dropped from Chevy's other passenger car lines after 1958, though it remained as a Corvette option through the 1965 model year.

Despite its problems, fuel injection provided the necessary per-

formance ability. "Fantastico!" began one ad that pictured a Corvette being unloaded from a freighter, a half-covered Ferrari just visible in the background. "Even in Turin, no one has fuel injection!" Ironically in view of all the hubbub about "1 h.p. per cu. in.," the top fuelie actually delivered closer to 290 bhp—more than the advertised 283. This was attained on 10.5:1 compression, shared with the dual-carb 270-bhp engine. The milder 250-bhp fuelie ran a lighter 9.5:1 squeeze, same as that of the 245-bhp twin-carb unit. Some historians think that in its zeal to promote Ramjet, Chevrolet deliberately underrated power on the dual-carb engines—certainly unusual for the day—so they may have actually had more power than advertised.

The 283-cid/283-bhp motor was sold as a $484.20 option; it carried the EL order code and should not be confused with the EN racing version, which, at $726.30, was sold as a package complete with column-mounted tachometer and a cold-air induction system. Chevy warned potential buyers that the EN option was not for the street and actually

continued on page 65

Show With Go: Super Sport and SR-2

With Corvettes starting to win races, GM built the all-out SR-2 in 1956 with an eye to long-distance events in '57. First tested in June, as shown here, it was later owned by Harley Earl's son Jerry. A similar street car was built for GM president Harlowe Curtice. Taking the wheel up top is Ed Cole, then Chevy chief engineer.

Show cars have always loomed large in Corvette history. Perhaps it's because the Corvette was born as one (the original Motorama prototype was officially GM experimental EX-122), but more likely because designers and engineers find conjuring up sports cars a lot more fun than creating sedans and station wagons. In any case, production Corvettes over the years have inspired many of GM's most memorable one-of-a-kind dream cars—including a few conceived mainly to gauge the public's

reactions to styling and features intended for a new production Corvette.

That was certainly true of the three Corvette-based experiments shown at the 1954 Motorama, one of which, as mentioned elsewhere, provided a sneak preview of the optional hardtop being planned for 1956. The next Corvette show cars were a bit wilder: a pair of race-inspired designs reflecting the competition prowess of the redesigned 1956–57 production models and presented concurrently with them.

The lesser of these was the Super Sport or SS of 1957. Essentially a mildly customized version of the standard model, it carried that year's new fuel-injected 283 V-8, four-speed manual gearbox, and heavy-duty racing suspension package. Exterior differences were confined to a low "double-bubble" windscreen, broad dorsal racing stripes, and forward-facing scoops built into the aft

continued on page 62

The "racing" or "Jerry Earl" SR-2 went through several incarnations, but survives today looking much like the first fall 1956 version (*black-and-white photos*). The high fin/headrest, covered headlamps, and white paint striping were added by GM designer Bill Mitchell for the 1957 Sebring 12 Hour race, where the car finished 16th overall.

portions of the bodyside "coves," which were finished to contrast with the otherwise all-white body. Overall, the SS looked a lot like the competition-prepped Corvette that had appeared at Sebring and elsewhere beginning in early 1956.

Road & Track spotlighted the Super Sport in an April 1957 feature with Jaguar's then-new SS competition car, the implication being that the two might

soon meet on some race track. They wouldn't, mainly because Chevy had something even better in the works: the slinky but ultimately unsuccessful Sebring SS and an open-top model designated SR-2.

One of the first projects completed at GM's new Warren, Michigan, Technical Center, the SR-2 was originally built for Harley Earl's son Jerry in March 1956.

Though recognizably related to the production Corvette, it was far more aggressive, with a longer snout, a wider and "toothier" grille, and a huge "Shark" fin capping a racing style driver's headrest, faired in the bodywork just aft of the cockpit on the left. "Cove" scoops and double-bubble windscreen were also featured (and would be picked up for the aforementioned '57 show car). Chassis

design and drivetrain components borrowed heavily from the Sebring SS.

The SR-2 looked ready to race, and it did. Bill Mitchell, who'd soon succeed Jerry's father as head of GM Styling, put white paint scallops on the front, making the racy red roadster look something like a racing airplane. He also fitted headlight domes and flat wheel discs for better aerodynamics and added small,

quadruple side-exit exhausts just aft of the front wheels. For cold-weather events, there was a special canopy running forward from the headrest to mate with a higher, single-bubble windscreen. The canopy arrangement was unnecessary at the 1957 Daytona Speed Weeks, where the SR-2 turned in a creditable performance despite inadequate preparation time. Buck Baker averaged

93.047 mph to win the modified-class standing mile and placed second in the flying mile at 152.866 mph, bested only by a D-Type Jaguar. The car was better prepared for Sebring on March 23, where Pete Lovely brought it home 16th after 12 hours of time-consuming pit stops.

There was also a second SR-2, constructed at about the same time for GM

Though strictly for show, the 1957 Super Sport looked almost as a racy as the all-out SR-2. It even had similar design elements like a "double-bubble" windshield and cove air scoops, but not the SR-2's extended snout and wider grille. Essentially, this was a modestly customized stock '57 'Vette.

president Harlow Curtice. It carried similar side and nose treatments, plus a more modest shark fin mounted centrally, but was otherwise a standard '57 Corvette hardtop. Wheels were chrome Dayton wires with genuine knock-off hubs; the Earl car rolled on Halibrand magnesium rims.

Thought the fate of the Curtice car is unclear, the original SR-2 passed briefly into Bill Mitchell's hands. With his personal sponsorship, it raced for several more years at places like Daytona, Sebring, and Road America, though with no notable success. It was ultimately acquired by race-driver Jim

Jeffords (who'd driven the 15th-place Corvette at Sebring '57, along with Dale Duncan and John Kilbourn).

Mitchell, meantime, got hold of the "mule" chassis left over from the abortive Sebring SS effort, on which he built the racing Stingray that inspired the production 1963 Corvette.

refused to include heaters on cars equipped with the racing package.

In the long run, the four-speed manual gearbox option was probably more significant than fuel injection for the Corvette's overall performance aura. Priced at only $188.30, Regular Production Option (RPO) 685 was essentially the existing three-speed Borg-Warner transmission with the reverse gear moved into the tailshaft housing to make room for a fourth forward speed. Ratios were again closely spaced: 2.20:1 (1st), 1.66 (2nd), 1.31 (3rd), and 1.00 (4th). "Positraction," Chevy's new limited-slip differential, was a separate option available with four different final-drive ratios to help get the most out of the new engines and gearbox in each particular driving or competition situation.

Answering the previous generations' complaints about handling and braking deficiencies, Chevrolet also issued RPO 684. This was a $780.10 "heavy-duty racing suspension" package comprising heavy-duty springs, a thicker front anti-sway bar, the aforementioned Positraction, larger-piston shock absorbers with firmer valveing, a faster steering ratio that reduced turns lock-to-lock from 3.7 to 2.9, and ceramic-metallic brake linings with finned ventilated drums. Add the 283-bhp fuelie V-8, and you had a car that was ready to go racing right off the showroom floor.

And race it did. At Sebring, two production examples finished 12th and 15th overall and 1-2 in the GT class. Just as impressive, the lead car, driven by Dick Thompson and Gaston Andrey, crossed the line some 20 laps ahead of the nearest Mercedes-Benz 300SL. Back at SCCA, the larger V-8 had bumped the 'Vette into the B-Production category, but it didn't matter. Dr. Thompson had taken the national championship.

But that wasn't all. The Corvette took an early-season contest down in New Smyrna Beach, Florida, besting the likes of Jaguar XK-140, Thunderbird, and the Mercedes 300SL. Chevy's sports car also swept the first four places at that year's Nassau Speed Weeks and dominated C-Production at Daytona, finishing 1-2-3 in both standing-start acceleration and the flying mile.

In almost any form, the '57 Corvette delivered certifiably staggering performance. *Motor Trend* clocked a 250-bhp fuelie at just 7.2 seconds in the 0–60-mph sprint. The 283-bhp version was even more formidable, with *Road & Track* running the same test in a four-speed with the short 4.11:1 final drive in just 5.7 seconds; it breezed through the quarter-mile in 14.3 seconds at better than 90 mph and sailed on to a maximum of 132 mph. *Motor Trend* took a version with the 283-bhp engine, dual exhausts, special cam, and solid lifters all the way up to 134 mph.

Corvette's great progress, both mechanical and social, was reflected in model-year 1957 production: 6339—a new record and almost double the 1956 total. Thunderbird's withdrawal from the two-seater market, which Chevrolet saw well in advance, promised at least 10,000 units for 1958, which was almost achieved despite one of the most dismal sales years in postwar Detroit history.

But there was a cloud on the horizon, and it involved racing—just at the time when the Corvette was beginning to show its mettle on the track. In June 1957, the Automobile Manufacturers Association, responding to critics of the Detroit "horsepower race," adopted a two-point resolution that required members to cease performance-oriented advertising as well as competition sponsorship, including technical assistance. GM president Harlow Curtice was among those voting solemnly in favor of the measure, which effec-

tively banned all factory-sponsored racing activities, including the Corvette's blossoming competition efforts. Duntov called it "a tremendous shock," though he'd never paid much mind to such executive decisions at General Motors.

The last major Fifties event at which an American production car ran as an official factory entry was the Grand Prix of Endurance at Sebring on March 23, 1957. Two Corvette Super Sport models (a flashy prototype racer Ed Cole and Harley Earl had created especially to run at Sebring) were in the race—which was won by a 4.5-liter Maserati—but they did not finish.

The self-imposed ban on racing would be loosely enforced, however. By the time the ink had dried on the resolution, industry insiders had already figured out how to circumvent it. Engineers surreptitiously continued to further automakers' racing development, supplying owners and drivers with under-the-counter contraband components. Duntov himself saw to it that anyone who wanted a racing Corvette could have one by choosing the right options, and he began working on even higher-performance gear. He also continued to appear—"casually," of course—at several races, where other GM executives could also be spotted—just as "casually"—in or near the pit areas.

Back on the street, the Corvette was finally establishing itself with the media and buyers alike. Chevrolet's sports car experiment was an experiment no longer, now being firmly entrenched as part of the automaker's lineup. With success at their doors, the development team had to find a way to improve upon what was, for them, the fruit of seven years of hard labor and unbridled enthusiasm. As they would find, however, it's not always easy to top yourself when you're already on top.

Corvette sales recovered to 3467 with a slick, all-new 1956 model boasting a much-improved chassis, standard roll-up windows, and an optional lift-off hardtop (shown). The old six was dropped, while the V-8 was upped to 210 or 225 bhp, and manual transmission was now standard. Performance improved dramatically, with 0–60 mph in as little as 7.5 seconds, a 120-mph top speed, and genuine sports-car handling. Amazingly, the $3149 base price was nearly $400 less than 1953–54 and just $215 over '55.

The big news for '57 was a V-8 enlarged to 283 cubic inches and offered in five versions. Two featured Chevy's new "Ramjet" fuel injection, a pricey $500 option signalled by discreet lettering in the concave bodyside "coves." Only 240 cars got the 250-bhp "fuelie" or the landmark 283-bhp edition. Ads touted the latter for making an impressive "1 h.p. per cu. in." Relatively few '57s wore the small hubcaps and monotone paint shown here.

Carbureted '57s offered 220, 245, or 270 bhp depending on the setup. This year also introduced many other new performance-oriented options, including Borg-Warner four-speed manual transmission ($188), a variety of rear axle ratios, and a "heavy-duty racing suspension" ($725) that made the 'Vette virtually track-ready right off the showroom floor. Among accessories reprised from '56 were whitewall tires, full wheel covers with simulated knock-off hubs, a contrast color in the bodyside "coves," and power soft top. The beauty shown here has them all but is missing the ever-popular factory radio. Despite a base price hiked $316 to $3465, model-year sales jumped over 80 percent to 6339 units.

Even everyday '57s, like this midrange 245-bhp example, were strong performers. But the new 283 "fuelie" was blazing, especially with four-speed and a stump-pulling axle ratio (as tight as 4.11:1). A published test of one such car showed 0–60 mph in just 5.7 seconds, 0–100 in 16.8, a standing quarter-mile of 14.3 seconds at 96 mph, and 132 mph all out. Most gauges, including the all-important standard tachometer, still spread across the lower dashboard. Racy three-spoke steering wheel continued from '56.

Dreams of Glory: The Super Sport Racer

Chevrolet was riding high in 1956. Though barely a year old, Ed Cole's brilliant 265-cubic-inch small-block V-8 had already won performance laurels for the division in NASCAR stock-car racing and in events like the annual Pikes Peak Hill Climb. Now the newly V-8-powered Corvette sports car began adding to this growing performance reputation with slick new styling, courtesy of General Motors design chief Harley Earl and a more competent chassis engineered by Zora Arkus-Duntov.

The payoffs were dramatic. Dick Thompson, in the first of what would be many Corvette drives for him, took a near-stock '56 to a surprising first-in-class and second overall at Pebble Beach against the best racing hardware Europe could muster. Perhaps even more impressive was the ninth-place finish by Walt Hansgen and John Fitch at the 1956 Sebring 12 Hours of Endurance.

But Cole, recently promoted from chief engineer to Chevy general manager, knew that there was no way a stock Corvette could ever win Sebring outright. The competition was just too strong. Chevy's sports car might do well in the production classes or even the Modified category, but sophisticated, purpose-designed racers like the birdcage Maserati, 3.0-liter Ferrari, and Jaguar D-Type would inevitably cross the finish line first.

Both Cole and Earl, however, were great believers in the old Detroit maxim, "Race on Sunday, sell on Monday" and the Corvette needed whatever help it could get to garner additional sales in 1956. Encouraged by the stock car's strong showing at Sebring, Earl set in motion a series of events that would lead to an all-out assault on the Florida enduro with one of the most singular cars GM would ever build: the Corvette Super Sport.

In retrospect, the SS was one of

those expensive indulgences for which GM was so often criticized in the mid-Fifties. Though the company possessed some of the best design and engineering talent anywhere, GM was relatively new to the production sports-car business, let alone experienced with purpose-built long-distance racers. But for Cole and Earl, the lure of Sebring was irresistible.

Other than the fabled 24 Hours of Le Mans, Sebring was the most important international sports-car race in those days. Run on a bumpy old airport course near the central Florida town, it attracted competitors from around the world. The most prestigious marques were usually well represented, all vying for the acclaim and notoriety associated with a Sebring win. Duntov also knew that a good showing at this one event would be a tremendous boost to the Corvette's image, and more than anything, he wanted his car to be respected—not regarded as a mere plastic toy

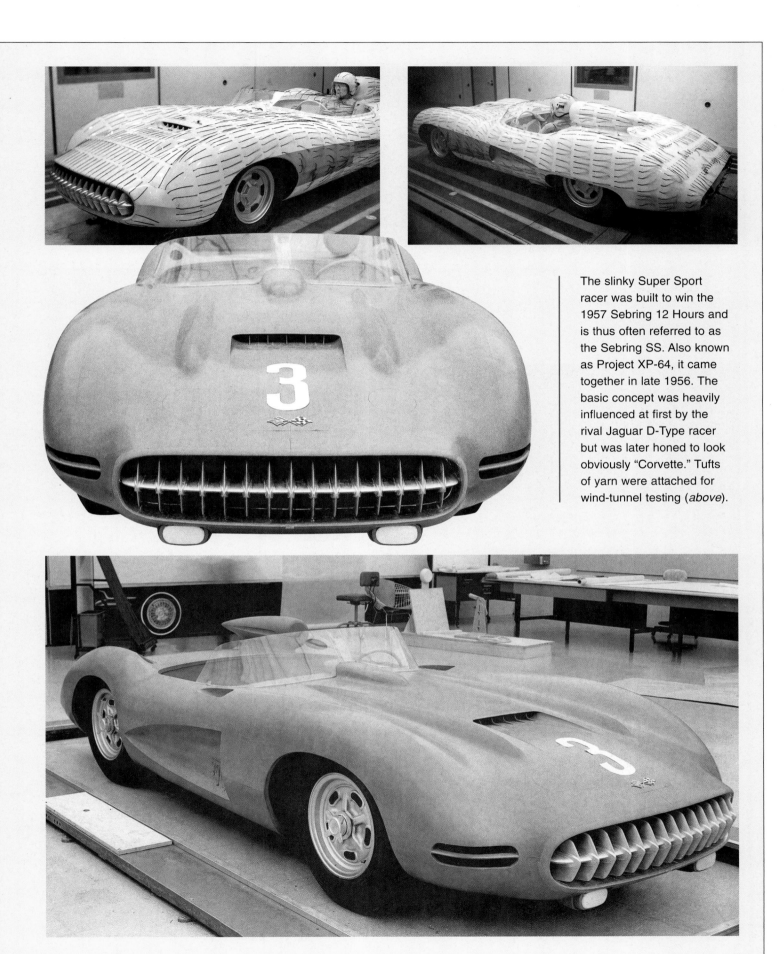

The slinky Super Sport racer was built to win the 1957 Sebring 12 Hours and is thus often referred to as the Sebring SS. Also known as Project XP-64, it came together in late 1956. The basic concept was heavily influenced at first by the rival Jaguar D-Type racer but was later honed to look obviously "Corvette." Tufts of yarn were attached for wind-tunnel testing (*above*).

the way some had viewed the 1953–55 models.

Dreams of glory must have occupied Harley Earl in the spring of 1956, for he managed to borrow the Jaguar D-Type that had placed third at Sebring just weeks before. Owned by Jack Ensley of Indianapolis, who'd driven it in Florida with 1955 Indy winner Bob Sweikert, the bright-yellow machine was brought to Earl's styling-staff area without its engine, which had been the victim of over-revving. Earl's idea was to install a new Chevy V-8, modify the British bodywork, and race the Jag at Sebring in 1957 as an "experimental Corvette."

To that end, the D-Type was first sent to Bob McLean's Research Studio for evaluation. Then, in June '56, it went to

"Studio Z," which was assigned the actual conversion. This would involve fitting the Corvette powerplant onto the Jaguar chassis, converting the steering to left-hand drive, and masking the body so no one could tell it was originally a Jaguar, while retaining the original vehicle's aerodynamics.

But Earl's "Jag-Vette" racer would not come to be. When Harry Barr, Cole's replacement as Chevy chief engineer, got wind of the project, he hurriedly called Duntov, then vacationing in New York City. "Harley Earl wants to put one of our engines in a Jaguar and run it at Sebring," he told Duntov. "What do you think about it?" Evidently not much, for Duntov rushed back to Detroit and drew up his own proposal for a special

all-Chevy sports/racing Corvette. Management approved Duntov's persuasive proposal, and the yellow D-Type Jag was returned to its owner.

By July, Chevy designers and engineers were hard at work on what had been designated project XP-64. Styling, evolved under Clare MacKichan, was initially much like the racing Jaguar's in sketches, with the same swoopy cigarlike profile and a prominent driver's headrest capped by a large trailing fin. The first full-scale clay model looked more like the production '56 Corvette, but sported a long bullet-style headrest, twin exhaust pipes exiting each bodyside cove, hidden headlamps, and a wider rendition of the toothy Corvette grille in an elongated snout. This basic

design would persist through XP-64's completion, though the original fully open rear wheel arches were eventually made semi-enclosed, and the external exhausts were moved down a bit and the coves given detachable covers to hide them.

Dimensionally, XP-64 was quite compact. Its wheelbase was initially pegged at 90 inches, but this was eventually trimmed to just 72 inches—a full 30 inches shorter than the production Corvette. For long-distance events, MacKichan designed a clear bubble canopy of the sort then common on GM show cars, with a rear cutout for the headrest. With this in place, the SS stood just 48.7 inches tall; without the bubble, its overall height was a mere 36 inches.

There was no time, however, to work out the intricacies of the Jaguar-style full monocoque structure that Duntov wanted for its strength and minimum weight. A separate frame was desirable anyway since body changes to fine-tune aerodynamics might require major under-skin alterations. Accordingly, a Mercedes-Benz 300SL tubular frame was selected as the starting point for the SS chassis. In final form, however, the revised platform resembled its German counterpart only in having a pyramidal cowl structure and a truss-type latticework beneath each (conventional) door. Square instead of tubular sections were used to facilitate the mounting of brake servos, suspension, and other components, and the use of chrome-moly steel held total frame weight to a reasonable 180 pounds.

Weight-saving measures figured extensively throughout the development of the SS. For example, the body was made of sheet magnesium rather than the 'Vette's highly touted fiberglass. Magnesium also appeared in the engine's special oil pan, whose finned bottom cover contained a maze of cooling passages. The sump itself was cast with two one-way lateral baffles, or doors, to prevent oil starvation in hard cornering, a feature later to be incorporated on production Corvettes. Aluminum was used for the specially designed cylinder heads, stock water pump, the clutch housing, transmission case, and radiator. The last included a separate oil-cooling section and, because of its steeply raked-forward mounting (necessary to clear the low nose), a cylindrical coolant header tank.

The racer's suspension was fairly straightforward, with the usual upper and lower A-arms in front, a semi-independent de Dion rear axle, coil springs at all four corners, and an anti-roll bar at each end. All components, including bushings and mounting hardware, were specially crafted, however, and the springs were wound so that the coils "collapsed" over each other on upward wheel deflection; an early example of what we would now call variable-rate springing. Duntov would have ordinarily preferred all-independent suspension for the bumpy Sebring course, but settled for the de Dion axle since it was

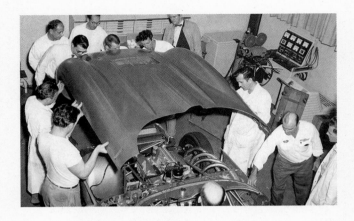

sturdier over long hauls. This characteristic was favored mainly for the 24-hour race at Le Mans in June 1957, where Duntov hoped the SS might compete after a successful Sebring debut. GM's Saginaw Division supplied a special recirculating-ball steering gear with a fast overall ratio of 12.0:1. This was linked to a height-adjustable steering column with a quick-release steering wheel mechanism to speed entry/exit—and thus driver changes—during the course of the race.

Duntov wanted disc brakes like the racing Jaguars had. But though GM's Delco-Moraine Division had been experimenting with discs, there was no time to develop a sufficiently reliable system for Sebring. This left conventional drum brakes the only choice. Trouble was, the usual American duo-servo type

was deemed less desirable than a twin-leading-shoe mechanism, and Chevy had no such parts on its shelf. But Chrysler did, so Highland Park's beefy 1956 "Center-Plane" front brakes—a foot in diameter and 2.5 inches wide— were

used at all four wheels of the XP-64. Rear binders were mounted inboard to minimize unsprung weight. Brake cooling was provided via a heat-dissipating aluminum "muff" around each drum, plus transverse fins on the outer surfaces of the front brakes and strategically placed body air ducts fore and aft. All braking surfaces were cast iron, carried on sheet-steel faceplates.

The SS braking system also incorporated two rather predictive features. One was separate front and rear servos and hydraulic lines, anticipating a federal requirement for production cars in the late Sixties. The other was a kind of primitive mechanical antilock braking system (as compared to the electronically-controlled systems used today). A special air link was employed to keep rear braking effort proportional

Period "record" photos show the racing Super Sport nearing completion at the GM Tech Center before being sent on its way to Sebring. No expense was spared to make it a winner. The body, for instance, was made of light, costly magnesium, while the chassis boasted a unique racing-style suspension and even an embryonic form of antilock brakes.

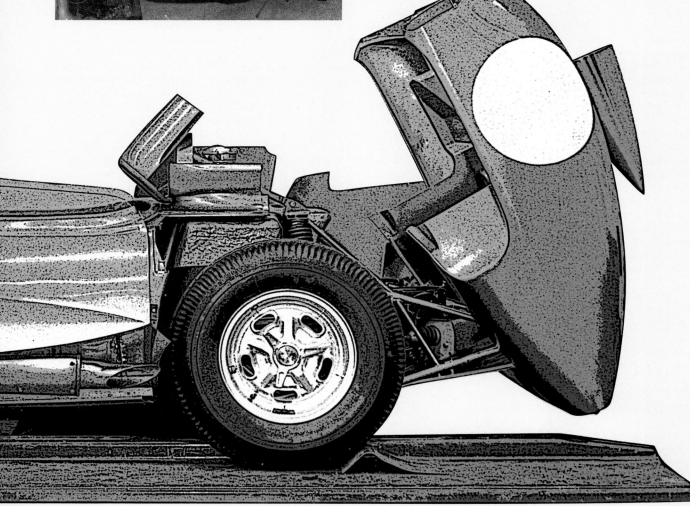

to front braking force in a fixed ratio of 30 to 70.

Mechanically, there was no question that the XP-64 would carry the enlarged 283-cid small-block V-8 slated for production 1957 Corvettes, along with its new Rochester Ramjet fuel injection system. However, Duntov envisioned more complex intake manifolds, with straighter ram pipes that crossed each other to feed separate plenum chambers, each with its own air-metering venturi; the manifolds, in turn, would connect to a special hood air intake. But wind-tunnel tests showed that the hood intake was ineffective due to unfavorable aerodynamic flow at the proposed location, so Duntov had to settle for production-stock manifolds. However, these were fed from special ducts in the grille, which provided enough "ram effect" to add 10 horsepower at 150 mph. Valve sizes were stock 283, as was the rest of the SS engine except for the special aluminum cylinder heads, whose ports were given a mild "tulip" shape that further improved output. Exhaust valves received heat-dissipating aluminum inserts. For long-distance reliability, compression was kept to a modest 9.0:1.

All this resulted in a rated 307 horsepower at 6400 rpm, versus 283 bhp for the production '57 fuel-injected V-8, which ran on 10.5:1 compression.

Because final curb weight came in at a satisfactory 1850 pounds, about 100 pounds lighter than the Jaguar D-Type, the SS promised to be competitively fast.

The rest of the drivetrain was fairly orthodox by late-Fifties standards. Power flowed to a four-speed manual gearbox, then back to a conventional differential with racing-type Halibrand quick-change case. A limited-slip differential was planned but, again, there was no time to have it fully ready for Sebring. The de Dion axle's differential was frame-mounted, which reduced unsprung weight, and the final drive chosen for Sebring was 3.55:1.

Duntov had planned to use the March 1957 Florida race as a shakedown for the SS before contesting Le Mans in June. Chevy's futuristic racer was thus entered in the prototype class, along with a brace of production models again running in the GT category. John Fitch was selected as team manager, but Duntov was on hand to supervise the entire operation, which got underway with preliminary track testing in mid-February.

Because development had been so frenzied, Duntov deemed this pre-race testing vital. Without it, the SS would surely make a poor showing. GM officials had approved construction of only one

car, but Duntov, ever the corporate conniver, managed to get approval for enough spare parts to construct a second, if incomplete, SS "mule" for testing purposes. And it turned out to be a good thing, too, because the mule revealed a number of problems— including faults in the cooling and braking systems—that might not have otherwise surfaced and been rectified in enough time to run at Sebring. Duntov himself reportedly clocked about 2000 test miles on the mule.

Continuing delays in completing the actual racing SS forced a change in drivers. Understandably seeking to give its new showcase sports/racer the best possible chance for outright victory, Chevy had signed the incredibly talented Juan Manuel Fangio to drive the SS at Sebring. It seemed a smart move, especially when the Formula 1 ace made a practice run—in the overweight, underpowered mule—and nipped his own lap record, set the previous year in a Ferrari. The great Stirling Moss, Fangio's choice as co-driver, turned in similarly promising practice laps. Despite the mule's incomplete nature, both drivers commented favorably on its dynamic behavio, but still ended up piloting Maseratis on race day. It seemed that Fangio's contract with Chevrolet was conditional on his approving the

car. With no race-ready SS in sight, Fangio begged off and Chevy released him (and Moss) to the Italian automaker. Fitch agreed to take over as lead driver and suggested Piero Taruffi as his relief. The Italian veteran dutifully answered the call, despite having to travel some 6000 miles on short notice.

And soon the race car was likewise on the road, being trucked to Florida. There was still work to be done on the SS after it reached Sebring, however. Despite overtime efforts by Duntov and the pit crew, Fitch was still trying to sort out inconsistent braking behavior almost up to the moment of the running Le Mans-type start. Sizzling heat within the magnesium-clad cockpit had already prompted some awkward last-minute body alterations.

During the first few laps of the race, the SS proved even faster than the mule and was more than up to the D-Type Jags and 3.5-liter Ferraris, but it lagged behind the big 4.5-liter V-8 Maseratis. Then a host of problems began to surface. The last-minute brake testing had flat-spotted the tires, causing bad vibrations, so Fitch pulled in on lap three for two new tires. After a few more laps, the engine began making unnatural sounds. Fitch pulled in again, and the crew spent 15 minutes tracking down a faulty coil connection, only to watch him replace the coil out on the track soon afterward. Then the rear suspension began to act up. Undrivable and overheated, the Corvette SS retired after its twenty-third lap.

The gremlin in the works, as was later explained, was relatively minor—a rubber bushing at the chassis end of one of the lower rods that provided the de Dion tube with lateral location. It had been inadvertently split during assembly of the joint and was a figura-

tive ticking time-bomb waiting to explode.

Despite this discouraging debut, Cole had ambitious plans for the future, including a three-car SS team for Le Mans, an improved SS for the 1958 season, and special racing (SR) versions of the production Corvette. But it all came to an abrupt end with the racing "ban" enacted by the Automobile Manufacturers Association in June 1957. (Actually, GM had issued its own cease-and-desist order about a month earlier.) As a result, Chevy was told to scrap every aspect of the SS project except the actual car itself. What's more, the test mule would likewise survive, thanks to designer Bill Mitchell, who would soon give it a glorious new lease on life. But the SS would never race again.

The production Corvettes didn't win Sebring '57 either, but both finished respectably. Dick Thompson and co-driver Gaston Andrey managed 12th overall and first in the GT class. A second entry, piloted by Bill Kilborn and Jim Jeffords, took the checkered flag 15th overall and second in class. These finishes were actually more significant for the Corvette's reputation than an outright SS win would have been, because they came in production cars that Sunday's racegoers—Monday's prospective buyers—would more readily identify with. Even fussy European auto writers had to agree that the Corvette was no longer to be regarded as a "plastic toy," but rather as a world-class sports car that was as capable on the raceway as it was on the highway.

Nevertheless, the Corvette SS (sometimes called the Sebring SS) remains one of the most memorable and consistently intriguing cars in General Motors history. That's largely because it came from GM, a giant out-

Delays in finishing the Sebring SS forced Chevy to use a cobbled-up "mule" (*above*) for pre-race testing. Things looked promising, but the actual race car was forced to retire after just 23 laps, never to compete again. It would, however, have a brief second life as a GM show car (*below*), often displayed with the clear canopy roof that was required for Sebring but not used on race day.

fit which once admitted that its main concern was "making money, not cars," and certainly not sleek, specially designed long-distance racers. Thus, it's remarkable that the SS displayed such potential, especially considering its hasty preparation. That the SS would likely have been a winner with further development only enhances its "what if" fascination among automotive and racing historians.

But the story doesn't quite end with Sebring. The SS was the first car to officially circle the new Daytona International Speedway, driven by none other than Duntov himself at the track's formal opening in February 1959. And two months earlier, the car had recorded an amazing 183 mph on the five-mile high-speed track at GM's Mesa, Arizona, proving grounds.

Looking almost as fresh as the day it arrived at Sebring, the SS would later appear at the 1988 Monterey Historic Races in a weekend saluting Chevrolet performance. The Corvette SS remains a vivid symbol of that tradition, which is why it will always be revered despite its shattered dreams of glory.

John Fitch, a veteran Corvette pilot even in '57, drove the Sebring SS in pre-race tests and for most of the few laps it completed. But the day wasn't a total loss for Chevy, thanks to strong finishes by stock-based 'Vettes (*right*).

The SS was a crowd favorite at Sebring—and a strong contender while it lasted. A broken rear suspension put it back on the trailer way too soon, but the main problem was lack of development.

With Corvette starting to make its mark in competition by 1957, Chevrolet devised the Sebring SS for that year's fabled 12-hour Florida race. A trim 70-inch wheelbase supported an advanced tubular "space frame" chassis topped by a sleek body made of lightweight magesium. Also on hand were racing-style suspension, special metal-lined drum brakes, four-speed gearbox, and a unique aluminum V-8 with over 300 bhp. Though faster than the race-day competition, the SS had to retire after just 23 laps and would never race again. But Chevy also entered stock Corvettes, and they finished 1-2 in the GT class and a creditable 12th and 15th overall.

PART 3 1958-1962

As the auto industry approached model year 1958, America as a whole seemed to be in transition. The unabashed exuberance and rampant prosperity of the post-World War II era had faded, the economy had slowed considerably, and unemployment was on the rise. The festering cynicism and social turbulence that would dominate the nation in the mid-to-late 1960s would soon be at hand.

The Soviet Union had sent its first satellites into space and was successfully testing intercontinental ballistic missiles, putting America's military and technological superiority into question, and both the space race and the Cold War would switch into high gear as a result. Soviet premier Nikita Khrushchev warned bourgeois Americans, "We will bury you." Back home, federal troops were sent to Little Rock, Arkansas, to quell unrest over public-school integration and the budding civil rights movement. The quiz-show scandals would ultimately rock the integrity of America's new trusted household companion, the television, and give rise to moral self-doubt.

The late 1950s and early '60s would also be recorded as a period of vast and fairly rapid change for the automotive industry in general, and for General Motors in particular. These were the years that ushered in Bill Mitchell to replace Harley Earl at GM Styling and gave us the last Corvettes in the original mold. They also witnessed the breakdown of what was a largely monolithic automotive business in favor of the much more highly segmented and competitive marketplace that persists to this day. Meanwhile, the poorly received Edsel was fast becoming both a financial and public-relations embarrassment to Ford, and a funny little foreign car called the Volkswagen Beetle was confounding the cognoscenti in Detroit by selling 200,000 or more units a year. An anonymous GM executive was quoted at the time saying, "If the public wants to lower its standard of living by driving a cheap crowded car, we'll make it."

Still, American autos in the late

The 1956–57 Corvette was a tough act to follow. For 1958, GM considered an all-new aluminum-body design with out-of-this-world styling, but finally had to settle for a thorough makeover of the existing car. Many thought the result a step backward, yet the '58 represented genuine progress in many ways. More importantly, it ushered in a period of record sales that would assure Corvette a permanent place in the Chevy lineup.

1950s were anything but cheap and crowded. This was a time of big cars that sported increasingly excessive styling. Clean, classic lines from the first generations of post-war hardware would give way to bloated, heavier, and more ornately adorned vehicles, before lower, leaner, and more sharply edged designs would eventually manifest themselves in the early '60s.

The Corvette would see many changes throughout this time, marking the vehicle's transition from a Spartan take-no-prisoners sports car to a more civilized—albeit high-performance—and well-appointed gran turismo. But the era would start with what its staunchest boosters would consider to be a stumble, finding the

Corvette, fresh from its highly regarded 1957 model, falling prey to the unfortunate styling largesse of the day.

Despite the fact that the Corvette had yet to earn a profit, GM management was sufficiently impressed by what Harley Earl had wrought for his 1956 treatment to allow preliminary work toward a 1958 model. At the time, GM engineers were entertaining thoughts of unit-body construction, while the styling staff was still enamored of the famed Mercedes-Benz 300SL gullwing coupe that had burst onto the scene in 1954. Both influences joined to inspire a futuristic show

car for the '56 Motorama that nearly became the basis for an all-new Corvette.

The Oldsmobile Golden Rocket was a unit-body two-seat coupe that came wrapped in then-futuristic styling. It sported a slim vertical grille on a protruding snout that flanked quad headlamps—then the rage that was sweeping Detroit styling. Matching front fenders swept back to a torpedo-like rear end that was topped by small fins running about halfway back from the rear roof pillars. Gullwing-like "flipper" sections were cut into the roof to assist entry/exit in this low-riding show car. The roofline tapered back in a boattail fashion, with a large rear window that wrapped down and around the roof. Intriguingly, the backlight was split

1

2

on its vertical centerline by a body-color bar—a remarkable forecast of the treatment Bill Mitchell would use on the Corvette Sting Ray coupe seven years later.

Work reportedly began on clay—and later fiberglass—models of a new Corvette to be based on the Golden Rocket's styling. It had unitized construction and a body made of sheet metal, not fiberglass. Unit construction was nothing new by the late '50s; Nash had introduced the concept in its 1941 Ambassador. GM had long experience with it at its Opel and Vauxhall subsidiaries in Europe, and Chevrolet had envisioned it for a never-produced compact, the Cadet, back in 1946. GM thought unit construction would permit lower unit cost and higher volume, two things the Corvette

desperately needed to begin paying its own way. But this "Son of Golden Rocket" 'Vette was not meant to be—the project would have to be shelved as the development team was needed elsewhere in the division to better compete in the overall sales race with Ford. For 1958, Corvette would just have to get along with a facelift.

It emerged as a fairly heavy-handed one at that. The front end seemed to take some cues from last year's SR-2 prototype racer, but the overall package was far more excessive than any previous Corvette. The basically clean, rounded lines of 1956–57 were still evident, only ostentatiously dressed up with simulated hood louvers, nonfunctional air scoops on either side of the grille and in the body-

side "cove" areas, and twin chrome-bar "suspenders" running down the trunklid. Quad headlamps were now featured, with thick chrome bezels meeting bright strips that continued back atop the fenders. Stylists considered replacing the distinctive grille teeth but later thought better of it, though they did reduce the number of teeth to nine instead of the previous 13.

Inevitably, the '58 Corvette not only looked heavier than its predecessor, but it was. The car's curb weight now exceeded 3000 pounds for the first time, which was up about 200 pounds from the '57 model. Much of this was due to 9.2 inches in added length and 2.3 inches in added width, bringing its overall dimensions to 177.2 and 72.8 inches, respectively.

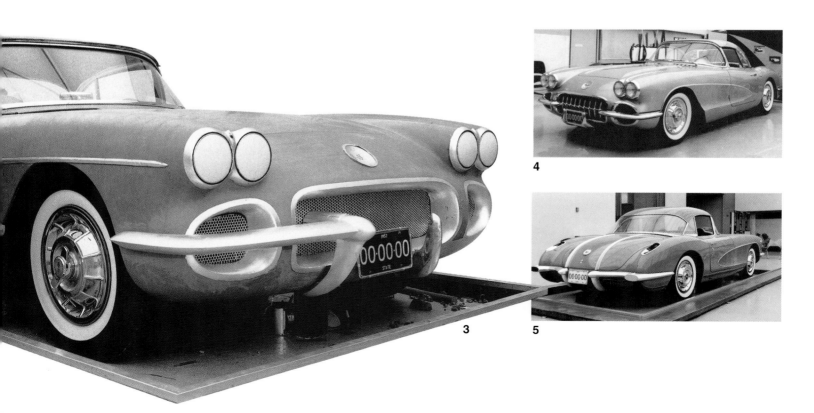

3   5

4

1-2. Initial '58 design work started with the 1956 Olds Golden Rocket show car. This modified version is also pictured on pages 86–87 with a Mercedes 300SL Gullwing coupe, then a favorite of Corvette designers. **3-5.** Out of this work came a "four-lamp" nose that became the heart of a major facelift once GM ditched plans for an all-new '58.

On the other hand, the new design afforded a couple of minor improvements: Bumpers, for example, were no longer attached to the body but to the frame, secured by long brackets that providing significantly greater protection. Paint was switched from enamel to acrylic-lacquer.

Key revisions made to the '58 Corvette's interior were just as substantial but were ultimately more successful. Stung by criticism of the former model's awkward instrument panel layout, interior designers made sure every dial (except the clock) was right in front of the driver. Dominating the new arrangement was a large, semicircular, 160-mph speedometer; perched ahead of it on the steering column was a round, 6000-rpm tachometer. The customary four engine gauges were arrayed in pairs on either side of the tach. A vertical console dropped down from the center of the dashboard where the heater controls, clock, and the optional "Wonder Bar" signal-seeking radio were located, essentially the arrangement found in most cars and trucks today. A grab bar in front of a semicircular cutout made up the passenger's side of the dash. A locking glove compartment was fitted between the seats just below the release button for the integral convertible-top tonneau cover. The car's door panels were again restyled, with reflectors added at armrest level for nighttime safety. Upholstery was

6

6. Interior designers penned a new '58 dashboard grouping all gauges ahead of the driver. **7.** Exterior styling was largely locked up by February '56. **8.** Chrome strips adorned the '58's decklid. **9.** Styling work was frozen in August '56, but this front end with a strong SR-2 flavor was briefly contemplated.

7

8

9

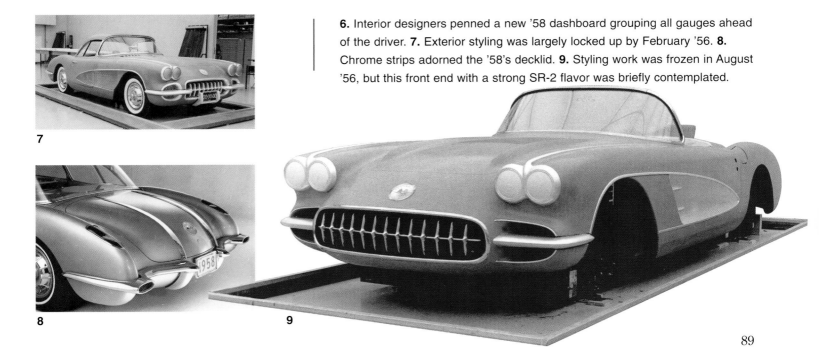

1

changed to a new "pebble-grain" fabric. Seat belts were factory installed for the first time.

While the '58 Vette may have been flashier than some purists would have liked, there were few complaints with its overall perform- ance, as the '57 engine lineup returned with few changes. The top powerplant remained the high-com- pression, fuel-injected, Duntov-cam 283 with a now-official 290 horse- power at 6200 rpm. A similar arrangement with twin carburetors continued at 270 bhp, but few buy- ers opted for this version. In fact, the base 230-bhp V-8 accounted for nearly half of '58 engine installa- tions, and only 1500 cars were fitted with fuel injection—1000 with the 290-bhp setup, 500 with the 250-bhp version.

Nevertheless, determined speed freaks could still order a near race- ready Corvette from their local Chevrolet dealers, and at a reason- able price. Even the hottest engine, ($484.20), Positraction ($48.45), heavy-duty metallic brakes and sus- pension ($780.10), and four-speed manual transmission ($188.30) added only about $1500 to the '58's reasonable $3591 base price. That was a remarkable value considering that the 'Vette was more than a match for the likes of Jaguar,

Porsche, and other higher-priced European performers. Even off-the- chart exotics like Ferrari weren't far beyond it in performance.

Car magazines were mostly pos- itive about the '58's mechanical changes, continuing to laud the car's performance and handling characteristics. Sprints from 0–60 mph well under 8 seconds and top speeds of around 125 mph with the 250-bhp fuelie/four-speed con- figuration were reported. How- ever, the performance-minded "Cerametallic" brakes in the afore- mentioned heavy-duty package were cited as not being for the faint of heart, as they tended to pull strongly to one side or the other until sufficiently warmed up. Corvettes delivered with this pack- age reportedly carried a sticker on the windshield that warned, "This car is not for street use."

Back on the track, thanks to the efforts of Jim Jeffords and his "Purple People Eater," Corvette again won the SCCA's B-Production crown in 1958. Jim Rathmann and Dick Doane took the GT class at Sebring that year, and veteran Ak Miller won the sports-car class at the Pikes Peak Hill Climb with a time of 15 minutes, 23.7 seconds. None of these triumphs were men- tioned in Corvette advertising,

however, as Chevrolet was officially shying away from hawking per- formance in the wake of the Automobile Manufacturers Association "anti-racing" edict of the previous year. The Corvette's ad copy now emphasized things like a "silken cyclone of a V-8" and a "beautifully compact body" with "a chassis that clings to the road like a stalking panther."

Despite the somewhat extreme styling updates, which critics deride even today, the '58 Corvette turned a profit for the first time in its brief existence. Model-year pro- duction was well above 1957's record level, totaling 9168 units. As a result, the 'Vette was one of the few domestic models to score increased sales in that recession- wracked season, the others being limited to Rambler, Lincoln, and Ford's new-for-'58 four-seat Thunderbird.

Bill Mitchell once admitted that he and his associates at GM Styling in the Fifties were too willing to "ladle on chrome with a trowel." Fortunately they were more spar- ing with the Corvette than any other car in the corporate fleet, and it's to Chevrolet's credit that the busied '58 styling was cleaned up considerably for the otherwise lit- tle-unchanged 1959 model. The oft-

2

3

1. Despite a sharp recession and gripes about the styling, Corvette sales set another new sales record for model-year '58, jumping almost 45 percent from the '57 tally.

2-3. The '59 looked cleaner and more purposeful, thanks to removal of the decklid chrome and a hood shorn of the '58's gimmicky "washboard" ribbing.

derided faux hood louvers and decklid chrome bars were now nowhere to be found.

Interior alterations were just as minor and just as effective. There were repositioned armrests and door handles, a shelf added beneath the passenger grab bar for extra small-item stowage space, and reshaped seats that at least now offered token lateral support. Sunvisors were a newly added option, and concave instead of flat instrument lenses (to cut down on reflections) were added to the instrument panel; a T-handle lockout for the manual transmission was included to prevent a driver from accidentally engaging reverse gear.

Powertrain choices were again unchanged, but the '59 featured a minor mechanical alteration of major benefit: the addition of rear-trailing radius rods that helped contribute to a slightly softer ride and noticeably less rear-end steering on irregular surfaces. The rods also helped counteract rear-axle windup, which was an unfortunate byproduct of the a problem with the explosive torque produced by the most powerful engines, and the RPO 684 heavy-duty brakes/suspension option was given even stiffer springs—all of which made for bet-

ter handling. Most Corvettes could shoot through the quarter-mile in under 15 seconds, and 0–60 mph times of less than eight seconds were typical. *Road & Track* clocked a 290-bhp fuelie engine from 0 to 60 mph in 6.6 seconds and on to the quarter-mile mark in 14.5 seconds at 96 mph. Top speed was listed at 128 mph with the short 4.11:1 final drive.

Brakes also received some attention, with newly optional sintered-metallic linings (RPO 686) developed by GM's Delco-Moraine Division. Priced at a mere $26.90, the option comprised three pairs of lining segments that were riveted to the primary brake shoes and five pairs of slightly thicker segments for the secondary shoes. Drums were finless with this option but were flared at their open ends to enhance cooling. The sintered linings made braking less harsh than the Cerametallic material and needed far less warming up to provide maximum braking effectiveness.

At about this time Chevrolet was working on a new and far more radical concept for America's sports car—the so-called Q-Corvette. This was a much smaller and lighter two-seat coupe with very streamlined styling, an independent rear suspension, and a rear transaxle

derived from the one being developed for Chevy's new rear-engine compact, the 1960 Corvair. Unfortunately, the Q-model would be another false start on the road to a truly new second-generation Corvette.

Production totaled 9670 units for the 1959 model year, a slight increase over the year before. Chevy still wasn't making much money on Corvettes, but it wasn't losing any either. Sales continued their steady if modest climb for 1960, exceeding the psychologically important 10,000-unit level by exactly 261 cars.

The 1960 Corvette was virtually indistinguishable from the '59, but there were some power increases made to the top two engines. Solid lifters and higher 11.0:1 compression boosted the most potent 283 fuelie to 315 bhp at 6200; a second version with hydraulic lifters for easier maintenance pumped out 275 bhp at 5200 rpm. Because of these gains, the Powerglide automatic transmission was no longer available with the fuel injected engines—it simply couldn't handle the torque. Carbureted engines remained much the same as before. The tamest was still the 230-bhp unit with single four-barrel carburetor, followed by a dual-quad 245-

91

bhp hydraulic-lifter version and the solid-lifter 270-bhp engine with twin four-barrel carbs.

Mechanical refinements for 1960 included new aluminum clutch housings for manual transmissions, which allowed the car to shed 18 pounds, and aluminum radiators for cars running the Duntov cam. A power-saving thermostatically controlled cooling fan was a new option, as was a long-range, 24-gallon fuel tank. A larger-diameter front anti-roll bar, matched by a new rear bar were made standard. These changes, plus an extra inch of rear-wheel travel in rebound, yielded a smoother ride and more neutral handling.

Despite the shift away from racing in favor of promoting the Corvette as a smooth, no-fuss touring car, there were still plenty of reasonably priced performance options available for 1960. Aside from the 315-bhp engine at $484.20, you could still order Positraction ($43.05) and the four-speed gearbox ($188.30). The metallic brake linings (RPO 687) returned as a $26.90 option. A set of blackwall 6.70 × 15 nylon tires cost only $15.75 (5.50 × 15 whitewalls remained standard).

By now, most everyone acknowledged the Corvette's on-road abilities. And Chevy hadn't abandoned sports car competition despite the AMA decision. In fact, the Corvette had one of its finest hours—or rather, 24 of them—that year. Renowned yachtsman and one-time car-builder Briggs Cunningham entered three Corvettes in the 1960 running of the fabled 24 Hours of Le Mans, where Bob Grossman and John Fitch finished a respectable eighth overall in a field of formidable contenders.

Chevrolet offered Cunningham cylinder heads cast from a high silicon aluminum alloy. Based on a design that was first tried with the Corvette SS prototype racer from Sebring in 1957, they maintained the stock 11.0:1 compression ratio but featured improved intake and exhaust flow. The high silicon content prefigured the block construction of the four-cylinder Vega engine of a decade later, which proved to be just as troublesome. The aluminum heads were fine in theory, but they tended to warp if the engine overheated, and Chevy had quality-control hassles with the castings. It is not believed that any of these heads were made available to retail customers.

Lending credence to the rumors of an all-new Corvette in the offing was the track debut of a dramatic special called Stingray that was being "privately" campaigned by GM design chief Bill Mitchell. The fact that Mitchell had succeeded to that position upon Harley Earl's retirement in 1958 convinced many 'Vette watchers that the Stingray was the shape of things to come for America's sports car. In some ways, it was.

Also noteworthy for 1960 was the premiere that fall of a dramatic television show that would help boost the Corvette's cache beyond that of sports-car devotees—an hour-long CBS series called *Route 66*. The premise of *Route 66* was

Styling was untouched for 1960, but that year's 'Vette was the quickest and most nimble yet. It was also the most popular Corvette to date, as model-year sales broke the psychologically important 10,000 barrier (by 261 units). Corvette had proved itself to GM bean-counters, and its long-term future was assured.

1

simple and appealingly visceral: Two guys in a sports car traversed the highways and backroads of America looking for adventure wherever they could find it. Chevrolet sponsored the program, of course, as part of the division's prime-time network "saturation" advertising strategy that also encompassed NBC's *Bonanza* and ABC's *My Three Sons*. (It was common at the time for an automaker to sponsor a show and, in the process, ensure that all the characters drove that particular brand of car—though this was obviously impossible with *Bonanza*, which was set in the Old West.)

Actors Martin Milner and George Maharis (later replaced by Glenn Corbett) co-starred each week with a shiny new Corvette. This was initially a 1960 model, but with each new season the boys got a new model just like the ones at local Chevy dealerships. The car was revealed to be a bequest from Milner's character's late father, but how the duo managed to trade it in with each successive season for what would have been one of the first new models out of the factory (or paid for gas and insurance, for that matter) was anyone's guess. Sure the boys worked—at least occasionally—as oil riggers, farm hands, stevedores, or similar occupations that could further that week's plot, but in the end they'd jump back into their 'Vette and drive off into the following week's episode.

Though well received, the series lasted only through the 1963–64 season before running out of gas. Still, four years of weekly exposure in a successful prime-time TV series helped enhance the Corvette's image as a freewheeling vehicle for those with an innate sense of freedom and adventure. Truly, the Corvette got its kicks on *Route 66.*

Meanwhile, Bill Mitchell had been working diligently to breathe new life into the existing Corvette styling, which had been around in its basic form since 1956. But though his studios had no shortage of ideas, the Corvette would see relatively few changes through 1962. Chevrolet had other priorities, among them the Corvair. Ed

Bridging the "Generation Gap"

The experimental XP-700 bowed in 1958 as a trial balloon for future Corvette styling elements. It returned to the show circuit two years later with a "facelift" that included a clear "bubble" top. This car reflected the thinking of GM's new design chief, Bill Mitchell.

1

2

1-2. With Corvette sales rising, GM brass okayed a restyle that materialized for 1961. The louvered front-fender coves and large circular grille emblem here were among many discarded ideas. **3.** Shapely new "ducktail," however, persisted to production and mated nicely with the existing four-lamp front.

3

Cole's technically advanced compact was the most interesting of the Big Three's new 1960 small cars, but it was beset with service problems—oil leaks, thrown fan belts, and tuning difficulties, among others. When it failed to outsell the conventional Ford Falcon, money was set aside for the development of a more conventional compact, which emerged for '62 as the Chevy II (later called the Nova). Once more, the Corvette would have to soldier on with relatively minor changes.

Even so, the 1961–62 models are regarded as the best Corvettes since the "classic" '57. Mitchell executed a tasteful exterior makeover that took a welcome step back from the chrome-laden 1958–60 models. Accompanying this body redesign were assorted mechanical modifications aimed at improved efficiency and higher performance. The result was two years worth of vintage 'Vettes that stand as the ultimate expression of the original 1953 concept.

A freshened rear design was the most pronounced external change for 1961, a kind of "ducktail" design that had been lifted virtually intact from Mitchell's Stingray racer and also used on his XP-700 show car. Besides improved aesthetics, the new posterior brought a practical bonus: luggage space (such as it was) increased by around 20 percent. The new tail also sported a pair of small round taillamps on each side of the central license-plate recess, plus a modest longitudinal trunklid creaseline running through the traditional, big, round Corvette medallion. Simple chrome bumperettes bracketed the license plate, which itself gained a small "arch" bumper. And for the first time, the dual exhausts exited below the body rather than through it or the bumper guards.

On the leading end of the car, Mitchell crafted a cleaner version of the existing four-lamp nose. Headlight bezels were now painted body color, and the trademark vertical teeth were jettisoned in favor of a fine, horizontal-mesh insert finished in argent silver. The round medallion gave way to separate block letters spelling out the car's name, topped by a larger version of the Corvette's crossed-flags insignia. The '61 would be the last Corvette available with bodyside coves in a contrasting hue, a mere $16.15 option that most buyers ordered. Even the fiberglass exterior's build quality was improved, as the car's fit-and-finish for 1961 was the best yet.

Carrying a base price of $3934, standard features now included windshield washers, sunvisors, a thermostatically controlled radiator fan, and a parking-brake warning light. A heater was still optional for '61, however, priced at $102.25. While air conditioning, power steering, and power brakes still weren't offered, the "Wonder Bar" signal-seeking AM radio remained available, as did the Positraction limited-slip differential, "wide" whitewall tires, electric windows, and the power-operated top. Nearly three-quarters of all Corvette customers that year gladly paid $188.30 for the four-speed manual transmission, which was now clad in aluminum, trimming 15 pounds from the car's heft.

Within the two-seat cockpit, the only change for '61 was a narrower transmission tunnel that afforded a bit more interior room. Four interior color schemes were available: black, red, fawn, and blue.

Mechanically, the 1961 Corvette was much like the 1960 model. However, an aluminum radiator took the place of the previous copper-core unit, which not only

1

2

3

1-2. A new front end was proposed in early '59 to complete the styling makeover begun with the "ducktail," but went no further than this work-out. **3.** Instead, the '62 ended up a cleaner-looking '61. **4-5.** The 1961 Shark show car built on XP-700 ideas. **6.** Racing 'Vettes won the SCCA's national A- and B-Production championships in 1962.

improved cooling capacity some 10 percent, but weighed half as much as before—which was another weight-saving improvement. Side-mount coolant-expansion tanks were added as a running change. Engine choices were basically car-ryovers. There were still five ver-sions of Chevy's renowned 283-cubic-inch small-block V-8: 230, 245, 270, 275, and 315 bhp, the last two being fuel injected. The three-speed manual remained the stan-dard gearbox but was now offered with a wider choice of axle ratios. Powerglide automatic continued as optional, but was now unavailable with the three hottest engines.

Even with the mildest 283 and Powerglide, the '61 Corvette was quick by any standard: Magazine testers recorded 0–60-mph acceler-ation between 6.7 and 7.7 seconds. Top speed with the automatic was listed at 109 mph and was limited mainly by gearing. The four speed lacked the long-legged overdrive ratio of most modern five-speed manuals, yet many of the fuel-inject-ed and twin four-barrel models could reach in excess of 130 mph.

Although Corvette didn't yet have an independent rear suspension like some costlier European models, this didn't seem to hurt the vehicle on either the street or the track. Testers sang the praises of the '61's handling virtues, and almost none of them discerned any particular deficiencies. By the standards of that day, the Corvette was now one of the most roadworthy cars in the world, and it turned in another fine performance at that year's running of the Sebring 12 Hours of Endurance, with a near-stock model finishing 11th overall.

If the '61 'Vette was good, the '62 was even better. With still more power and even cleaner looks, it ranks as perhaps the most desir-able Corvette between 1957 and 1963. The car's base price broke the $4000 barrier for the first time, at $4038. A heater was finally made standard for 1962, more than negat-ing the price increase over the pre-vious year's model, but it could be deleted if so desired, which was intended for racing purposes.

Though the basic styling of the C1 generation was beginning to

look a bit dated, the last of its worst excesses disappeared on this final variation. The most obvi-ous deletion was the chrome out-line around the bodyside coves, which also shed their triple chrome accent spears in favor of more conservative ribbed alu-minum appliqués, which were fin-ished in black for subtlety. Omitting the coves' optional two-tone treatment only enhanced this more cohesive look. Other ele-ments were similarly refined. The previous silver mesh grille and its flanking cutouts were now finished in black, as was the background of the trunklid medallion. Narrow-band whitewalls were in vogue that year and looked great on the 'Vette. The only place where any form of decoration was added was to the rocker panels, which were newly adorned with ribbed anodized-aluminum moldings.

Under the hood, the 283 engine was bored and stroked to bring its cylinder dimensions to 4.00 × 3.25 inches and displacement up to 327 cid. The small-block V-8 would con-tinue in this form as the Corvette's

4

5

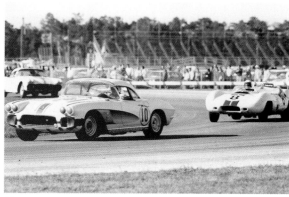

6

main muscle through 1965. And muscular it was. Even the base 327 pumped out 250 bhp, and in top form could generate an explosive 360 bhp. The deeper-breathing 327 block necessitated a small but important change in the Rochester fuel-injection system, and heavier-duty bearings, larger ports, and a longer duration camshaft were fitted to all but the base 250-bhp engine. The solid-lifter Duntov cam was now specified for the most potent of the three carbureted engines, now up to 340 bhp (as well as continuing in the top fuelie). Both of these ran tight 11.25:1 compression, versus 10.5:1 for the base and step-up 300-bhp engines. The latter two were perhaps the best choices for all-around use, offering more than enough power plus the simplicity and easy maintenance of hydraulic tappets and a single four-barrel carburetor.

To that end, the troublesome twin four-barrel carbs were now gone altogether, replaced by big, single four-barrel Carters. Peak power in the top two versions came at a screaming 6000 rpm—quite

high for a pushrod powerplant—while the 250- and 300-bhp versions ran out of steam at 4400 and 5000 rpm, respectively. The latter two were the only engines available with optional Powerglide, which was treated to a weight-saving aluminum case like the one given the four-speed manual the previous year.

The extra power and torque of the larger 327 V-8 translated into truly ferocious 0–60-mph and quarter-mile acceleration: The four-speed/fuelie routinely hit the quarter-mile mark in 15 seconds or less at speeds of 100 mph or more in magazine tests. And with the appropriate options, the 'Vette was still a winning production-class racer. Again in 1962, The Sports Car Club of America's A-Production champion was Dr. Dick Thompson. The Corvette was a serious competitor even with only minor modifications. Don Yenko, for example, took the SCCA's B-Production title that season.

The '62 Corvette marked the end of an era for America's sports car, with the first completely new model

in its history now a mere model year away. Still, the '62 was a transitional model in that it introduced the venerable 327 V-8, which would be carried over to the new design. While the car harkened back to its roots as a 1953 introduction, thanks to Bill Mitchell, Zora Arkus-Duntov, and company, the '62 was faster, handled better, looked handsomer, and was more civilized than any previous Corvette, but retained much of the charm of the original roadster concept. Sales on the year jumped by nearly 40 percent to 14,531 units, and the Corvette was firmly in the black as far as GM's bottom line was concerned. This was a sizable relief to the likes of Duntov, Cole, and Mitchell, who'd kept faith with the 'Vette in its darkest days by using all their influence to keep it alive.

And they weren't resting on their laurels, either. The first completely redesigned model in its history would soon come to be realized as the epitome of Chevy's plastic-bodied sports car, and the appellations "Corvette" and "Stingray" would become synonymous.

The 1958 Corvette kept the usual 102-inch wheelbase, but stood 10 inches longer, more than two inches wider, and some 200 pounds heavier than the '57. Extra chrome, a "washboard" hood, and four-headlamp front were typical period Detroit glitz, but there was also a new, more driver-friendly dashboard, and all the '57 engines returned to keep performance exciting; the top "fuelie" V-8 even gained seven bhp for 290 total. Helped by a still-reasonable $3631 base price, sales rose smartly to 9168.

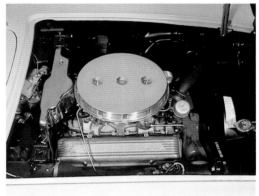

Corvette cleaned up its act somewhat for 1959, losing the washboard hood and chrome decklid strips, but was otherwise little changed. Though larger and plusher than earlier models, late-Fifties 'Vettes were no less fast or agile when equipped with options like Positraction limited-slip rear differential, race-ready suspension and brakes, and four-speed manual shift. Buyers could still choose from five 283 V-8s in '59, ranging from 245 bhp to 290 with fuel injection and high compression. Base price rose again, this time by $244, but sales rose again too, reaching 9670 for the model year, thus vindicating Chevy's decision to continue Corvette after 1955.

The 1960 Corvette was unchanged outside but further improved inside. The top "fuelie" V-8 went to a thumping 315 bhp, and a revised suspension gave all models the same handling prowess as the heavy-duty chassis option, which was dropped. Some drivetrain components switched from steel to aluminum to save weight. Meantime, Corvette was adding competition trophies, winning its class at Pikes Peak and Sebring in 1958, SCCA national championships in 1958–59, and 8th overall at the 1960 LeMans 24 Hours. The 'Vette also claimed an important showroom victory as 1960 sales broke the magic 10,000 barrier.

A "toothless" grille and a handsome new "ducktail" gave the '61 Corvette a cleaner look—and more luggage space. Performance remained sizzling, as powertrains were little altered. Sunvisors were newly standard and much appreciated. Base price rose a modest $62 to $3934. Sales climbed once more to nearly 11,000 for the model year.

The Corvette was a genuine TV star by 1961, thanks to the weekly *Route 66* series, in which two young adventure-seekers roamed the country in a brand-new 'Vette. The '61's styling updates were the work of Bill Mitchell, recently installed as GM design chief, replacing the legendary Harley Earl. The distinctive new rear end was inspired by that of Mitchell's late-Fifties Stingray racer, which was salvaged from the short-lived Sebring SS project and was later used as a show car.

The '62 'Vette looked even cleaner via a blacked-out grille, simple vents instead of chrome windsplits in the "coves," ribbed rocker-panel trim—and no optional two-toning. But the big news was a small-block V-8 enlarged to 327 cubic inches in four versions offering 250 bhp to a thundering 360. Sales leaped past 14,000 in this final year for "solid axle" 'Vettes.

PART 1 A Racing Lineage

While the Automobile Manufacturers' Association ban against automakers taking part in racing activities had been in effect since 1957, several prominent players in the car business—GM in particular—were still participating in high-performance race-track projects. Zora Arkus-Duntov, of course, continued to ensure that anyone with the need for speed could order a race-ready Corvette by simply checking off the right boxes on the options sheet. Bill Mitchell couldn't stay away from the track, either, especially after working on the handsome and capable Corvette Super Sport project in 1957.

The SS cut a striking profile, with its lightweight magnesium alloy body highlighted by what insiders called a "flying football" headrest that tapered back to the rear of the vehicle. A wide toothy grille up front and gracefully sculptured lines leading back to a boattail rear end would hint at styling cues from both current and what would become future production Corvettes. (Animation aficionados would see the same basic look a few years later in the early-'60's classic Japanese cartoon series *Speed Racer,* embodied in the title character's Mach 5 race car.)

Power for the Super Sport came from a 283-cid small-block fuel-injected V-8 from the 1957 produc-

For Corvette's second generation, Bill Mitchell revisited the Super Sport racer and would subsequently reinvent the Corvette with radical new styling, heart-pounding performance, and an assortment of added accoutrements—including a first-ever coupe. The resulting Corvette Sting Ray would become an instant classic, setting sales records year after year, and it remains one of the most coveted of collectors' cars. With a winning attitude on the track that would benefit from each successive engineering innovation, the car's competitive spirit would culminate with one of the best Corvette racers ever, the Grand Sport.

Built on the 1957 Sebring SS "mule" chassis, Bill Mitchell's Stingray competed in the SCCA's C Sports Racing class as a private entry. It had little success in 1959, but then won the 1960 national class championship. Here, Dr. Richard Thompson tackles the "corkscrew" at Laguna Seca in the 1960 season closer, the car's final outing.

1-3. Mitchell quickly devised a slick new competition body for the rescued Sebring SS "mule" chassis, assisted by staff at his special "Studio X" near the GM Tech Center. The Stingay's basic shape was set by December 1957, when the car posed in the GM Design courtyard. GM brass didn't like Mitchell violating their "no racing" edict but looked the other way once he promised to keep the Stingray off GM property—and to race it strictly on his own. **4.** Exposed side-exit exhausts were added by February 1958, when the design was all but complete. **5.** After a two-year racing career, the Stingray got "Corvette" and "Fuel Injection" badges, plus other modifications, to become an offical GM show car. It looked like this when unveiled at the Chicago Auto Show in February 1961. **6-7.** The Stingray raced in red paint during 1959, then got a new replica body finished in silver for the 1960 campaign. Here it is again at Laguna Seca before and during the season closer.

tion 'Vette that generated 307 hp. Duntov had created an all-new lightweight tubular space-frame platform for the racer that was loosely based on the Mercedes-Benz 300SL. The car's suspension was fairly straightforward, with the usual upper and lower A-arms in front, a semi-independent de Dion rear axle, coil springs at all four wheels, and an anti-roll bar at each end. Steering was a special recirculating-ball type with a fast overall ratio of 12.0:1. Extreme weight-saving measures kept the car's bulk down to a svelte 1850 pounds.

The Super Sport development "mule" was successfully track-tested at Sebring in 1957 by Juan Manuel Fangio and Stirling Moss. The actual racecar would prove to be problematic, however, and before Duntov would have a chance to work out the bugs, the industry's voluntary racing ban would take effect. Fortunately, as it would turn out, the car would escape the clutches of GM's corporate crusher thanks to the efforts of Bill Mitchell, who would soon give it a new lease on life, though the SS would never formally race again.

Not long afterward, Bill Mitchell would revisit the original Sebring SS development mule that had

been consigned to a GM storage facility. Using his own money and without GM's blessing, Mitchell decided to transform the mule into the thoroughbred racer he felt it was destined to become and to campaign it under his own banner. In recrafting the Super Sport's exterior, Mitchell adapted lines from the ill-fated Q-Corvette concept to create a dazzling new open body. Stylist Larry Shinoda further contributed to the car's sleek appearance, and the Stingray Special was born.

As one of Mitchell's infamous "bootleg" projects, the Stingray Special took shape at his "Studio X" special projects area at the GM Tech Center in Warren, Michigan. While the racer retained a version of the SS's football-shaped headrest, the Stingray came wrapped in more-linear styling, highlighted by a pronounced crease line running around the car, with exaggerated humped wheel flares on all four fenders and exhaust pipes that poked out and ran along the outside of the lower body.

Duntov, of course, would devote his energies to improving the chassis and mechanical components to make the car eminently race-worthy. The Stingray featured a 92-inch

5

wheelbase and was nearly 1000 lbs lighter than a typical production car from 1960. Its fuel-injected 283-cubic-inch V-8 engine produced 315 horsepower at 6200 rpm, thanks to a Duntov camshaft and a compression ratio of 10:1. It was said the car could hit 60 mph from a standing start in a blazing four seconds.

As the story goes, Dr. Dick Thompson, one of SCCA's top Corvette competitors, dropped by the studio, took one look at the radical new racer, and promptly promised to drive it in C-Modified events. His subsequent showing in that hotly contested class, which was then dominated by the aristocratic European brands, stunned everyone including Mitchell, for Thompson took the championship in 1960.

Unfortunately, the car would have a short racing career, as the cost of sponsoring his own team proved to be prohibitively high for Mitchell to finance. After its championship season, Mitchell modified the Stingray and exhibited it as an experimental show car, touted as a concept that was "built to test handling ease and performance."

6

Ironically, the Stingray Special racer would carry neither the Corvette nor Chevrolet designations in light of the manufacturers' racing prohibition, though it would later be called a Corvette on its subsequent tour as a show car. The vehicle made quite an impression on the viewing public, and many believed it to be a preview of the next-generation Corvette. Time—and Bill Mitchell—would prove this to be closer to the truth than most observers outside of GM realized.

7

Profile: William L. Mitchell

As vice president of design at General Motors in the Sixties and Seventies, William L. "Bill" Mitchell influenced the shape of American production cars more than any other single person. He had a great deal to do with contemporary Ford, Chrysler, and American Motors products—more, perhaps, than those companies were willing to admit. To be sure, with the sole exception of Chrysler's 1955-58 "Forward Look" cars, GM led Detroit styling for a full half-century—from Harley Earl's very first LaSalle in 1927 to Mitchell's Cadillac Seville of 1980.

When Harley Earl retired as head of GM Styling in 1958, he picked Bill Mitchell to succeed him. Mitchell found himself with legendary shoes to fill—shoes that some said were too big for anyone. But fill them he did—so well that he might be said to have invented a new shoe style. Admittedly, he got the job at a good time. Earl, who hadn't been on the cutting edge of car design for several years, had surrendered the styling initiative to resurgent Chrysler and Virgil M. Exner. Mitchell reclaimed it in a hurry, bringing GM back to the styling pinnacle for a generation. How? Simply by giving upper management—and usually the customers themselves—exactly what they wanted, and sometimes a lot more.

Candor was one of Mitchell's most admirable characteristics, which is unusual in a field that's built largely on ego. In interviews he rarely failed to mention the numerous people at GM Design who'd made his accomplishments possible. He was equally frank—and often colorful—about his likes and dislikes. For example, he once compared designing a small economy car to "tailoring a dwarf," which has since become one of his most quoted phrases. What he liked working on most, he said, were luxury and sports models—preferably a combination of both.

Mitchell's first great design was the 1938 Cadillac Sixty Special sedan, which is now recognized as one of the most significant styling achievements of the prewar era. Later, Mitchell would be the creative force behind such memorable production cars as the 1963 Buick Riviera and stunning show models like the Corvair Monza GT and SS. But his greatest achievement—certainly his greatest love—was the Corvette, which owed its glamour and allure to Mitchell from 1960 through the mid-

Seventies. He devoted a good deal of his time to Corvette, which was by far his favorite work of the many projects he supervised at GM. His penchant for the 'Vette is hardly surprising given the personality of the man, who has been described by many of the same adjectives applied to the car itself: brash, flamboyant, even beefy. For Mitchell, like Harley Earl before him, the Corvette was an opportunity not only to have fun as a designer but also to make a personal statement about what a high-performance American automobile should be.

Like most pioneers in a burgeoning field, Mitchell came to his career quite by accident. He grew up in Pennsylvania, where he fell in love with cars on regular visits to his father's Buick dealership. In the Thirties, he secured a job as an illustrator for the Barron Collier advertising agency in New York City. He spent his spare time drawing cars and, in the evenings, attending classes at the Art Students' League. The Collier family also liked cars, especially the racing variety, and spent many weekends in upstate New York at the Sleepy Hollow racetrack, which they owned. Mitchell went with them, and one weekend his sketches came to the attention of one of Harley Earl's friends.

Earl then contacted Mitchell, asking for more sketches and wanting to know what the young man thought cars "ought to look like in the future." Six months later, Mitchell was at work at the GM Art and Colour Studio under Earl's watchful eye. Six months after

that, he was chief designer at Cadillac. Twenty years later, Mitchell replaced his boss and mentor as head of what was by then known as GM Styling Staff. He soon changed the name again, to GM Design Staff, while establishing what's been called the "Mitchell Style."

Controversial, highly visible, and never given to halfway measures, Mitchell pulled few punches in his work. The same can be said for his arguments over policy with GM managers, and, as can be seen in the following excerpts from various interviews, in his public pronouncements. Sadly, that voice was silenced forever with his passing in late 1988.

Q: It must have been something, going from virtually nowhere to styling head of Cadillac in just 12 months.

William L. Mitchell: It sounds great now, but there were only a hundred of us then at the whole place [Art and Colour]. When I left General Motors [in 1977], I had 1600 people.

Q: How long were you with Cadillac?

Mitchell: Until I went into the Navy in the war. I came back in '49. After that, I was taken out of General Motors. Earl wanted me to run a business for his sons; he wanted to put them in design. So I took over Harley Earl Design. I did that for four years and got big accounts like Clark Equipment, General Electric, Westinghouse, Parker Pen. Oh, I really went. I didn't like the products, but the newness of it was good for me.

Q: How did you return to GM?

Mitchell: Earl brought me back as director. I didn't love [Harley Earl Design], but it was good background for me, because when I came back . . . I didn't have to take any lip from any general manager. [Earl] told me four years ahead I was going to take his job. He talked to [then GM board chairman Alfred] Sloan and [then president Harlow] Curtice. I guess you can't do that any more; committees have to put you in.

Q: How did you first get involved with the Corvette?

Mitchell: Harley Earl—this was his idea. After the war, he was a good friend of [General Curtis] LeMay. They had these activities at the bases to keep the uniformed men happy. They started sports-car racing. They got GM and a lot of different companies to put a lot of money into it to give them some fun. We built a Jeep with a Cadillac engine in it for LeMay, I remember. He said, "Harley, why don't you build an

Mitchell's styling career was launched with the milestone 1938 Cadillac Sixty Special (*above*). Other significant designs included Buick's sleek 1963 Riviera (*right*).

American sports car?"

We showed the first Corvette to a group at the proving grounds, and Earl told Sloan he'd like to put it in the [Motorama] show at the Waldorf. This was a prototype—no engine, nothing. It went over so good, Chevrolet said they'd build it.

Q: What were some of the problems with the early Corvettes?

Mitchell: It didn't have a good engine. There wasn't a good V-8 then.

Q: How did the decision to use the V-8 come about?

Mitchell: [Former chief engineer Edward N.] Cole became the head of Chevrolet, and he was a young fireball. He liked to race. Prior to that, people started to try to race [Corvettes] and they weren't any good. But when you got the V-8 in it—boy, she started to go. When we beat the Jaguars—that was something. And then we beat the Mercedes. From then on it was all hell to pay. It was like a Ferrari: It looks good, but it's got to go. Performance is part of the act.

Q: What was the closest that the Corvette project came to being halted?

Mitchell: There were times when [James M.] Roche [distribution vice president 1960-62, later GM president and chairman] wanted to discontinue the Corvette. I raised hell. I knew Roche well, but he was a Cadillac man. I said, "The Corvette's got far greater owner loyalty than any damn Cadillac made." And the sales manager backed me up. That was before the Sting Ray got going.

Q: What was your involvement with racing?

Mitchell: I did a lot of bootlegging at GM. I had a studio right down underneath my office. I called it Studio X. [It was] where I'd bootleg all kinds of cars I wanted to do. Chevrolet was racing on a [significant] scale, and then that stopped. I knew they had three chassis they didn't use [after the 1957 Sebring race]. So I went to Cole, and he gave [one] to me for 500 bucks. I did [the racing Stingray] down in Studio X; nobody knew about it. I always liked its looks. It's my favorite Corvette. That strong shadow underneath makes it very photogenic. The early Corvettes were too rounded, too soft. The Sting Ray has that sharp body edge, and that makes it work.

Q: When did you have to take the Corvette SS chassis out of GM?

Mitchell: I raced it first in Washington with Dick Thompson [in early 1959]. At the engineering policy committee, [then president John F.] Gordon made a statement: "I thought everybody realized we're not going to do any racing." After the meeting I said, "Were you talking to me?" and he said, "I sure as hell was." He was tough. Instead of taking it lying down, I got a couple good friends of mine who could write better than I could, and we wrote a letter to him saying, "I got my job racing with the Collier boys; racing is in my blood."

In those days, they'd come out in those big limousines. He came out one day and I said, "Jack, did you get my letter?" And he said, "You're a pretty damn good salesman. Go ahead." But he said, "Keep it off [GM Tech Center] property and spend your own money." So I did,

and I raced for two years until he said, "Stop it, they're getting back after me for racing." So I had a little bit of my own way, and on my income tax I got away pretty good.

Q: Where did you keep the race car outside of the Tech Center?

Mitchell: [I had] a shop on Twelve Mile Road that's just five minutes from my office, and I did the work out there. But I got GM engineers and I had a lot of talent at GM helping me. I got good mechanics to go to the races with me. I got a lot of things I wanted.

Q: Did it cost you?

Mitchell: Plenty. I financed it all out of my own pocket. I couldn't afford to build and race the Stingray today. But back then, it pleased me no end to go up against Cunningham and those boys with the faster cars, and take any of them.

Q: Did the body design help its performance?

Mitchell: Oh, yes. It was very slippery. It would take a D-Jag, which had a very smooth body and about the same horsepower. The Stingray would do 0-to-60 in four seconds. It had a beautiful engine—first fuel injection, then we tried four Webers with different cams. Tear your head off! The only weakness that car had was the brakes. They never did work right.

Q: How did the shape translate to production cars?

Mitchell: It was the same, wasn't it? I just took all those lines and turned the Stingray racer into the production 1963 Sting Ray. That made the Corvette. And overnight, the sales just boomed. So I knew I had something.

I went to the races in Europe and saw the cars there. I didn't want a car that looked like everything out of Europe. All their cars looked like Ferraris or Maseratis. They didn't have any sharp identifying features. I wanted a car that—by God, you'd know it a mile away. That was my whole theme. And it did have identity.

Q: How did the Stingray (Sting Ray) get its name?

Mitchell: I just did it. Jack Gordon never liked those names of mine, the fish names. They wanted everything to start with a "C." But we'd get them anyway. I don't know how the Stingray got to be two words, though.

Q: The Mako Shark was another of your names, then?

Mitchell: Yes. I love sharks because, in the water, they're exciting. They twist and turn. I caught a mako off Bimini, and it's in my studio in Palm Beach. I've got pictures of my Corvettes below it. That's where I got the impetus to do the experimental Manta Ray. I'd do a lead car on my own. Then we built things off of it.

Q: Why did you remove the split window on the '64 coupe?

Mitchell: I had to admit it was a hazard. Duntov won that one. By the way, I stole that back line from Porsche. I wasn't above stealing things from European cars. Not American cars—there was nothing over here to steal! There isn't anything today, unless you want a cake of soap. Then you get a Ford. You need identity on a car. If you took the antlers off a deer, you'd have a big rabbit!

Q: What was your relationship like with Zora Duntov?

Mitchell: Anyone with a foreign accent can get away with arguments because they're hard to understand. He'd mumble around. But he was a good guy.

Q: Did the Corvette have much influence on other cars?

Mitchell: Remember the early Pontiac Grand Prix and the 1963 Buick Riviera? When they were built, the sales people still thought that the more chrome, the better. The Corvette didn't have much chrome, and it sold! So I did those two like the Corvette and eliminated the chrome. They sold fantastically. That changed a lot of old-fashioned thinking. The European designers recognized it. They had never liked our cars before, but they liked the Corvette—and the Riviera, too. It was the same idea—trim, stylish, classic.

Q: How close did the Corvair Monza GT come to being a 'Vette?

Mitchell: The Corvair was a great car—very unusual. The Monza GT and SS were the cars that might have replaced the Corvette. The GT was first. It was a rush job, done over several times in less than 10 weeks. Engineering did a box-section chassis for it and tested it at different tracks. It outperformed the fuel-injection Corvette and was very aerodynamic. It only weighed 1500 pounds.

Q: Why wasn't it mid-engine?

Mitchell: I wanted that, but Chevrolet said they could make the car handle the same way with the engine hanging out the back. I got Roger Penske, who was then a great Porsche racer, to drive the Monza GT. He liked it better than the Porsche. Right at that time the whole Corvair program started to wane, and I couldn't interest management in doing anything with that car. It was just no go.

Q: The Monza seems like the cleanest design of that era.

Mitchell: Well, you can see where it relates to the Sting Ray shape in many ways. It could have been sold as a small Corvette and done wonderfully. It's one of the classic designs. If you've got a good design, it's timeless. If you drive a Monza GT down the street today, you'll draw a crowd.

Q: The Monza GT reminds us of the early-'70's Opel GT.

Mitchell: Oh, yes, of course. The Opel GT was derived from this. It relates to the [1968] Sting Ray and could have been a small Corvette. It was a pretty car, with that same classic Sting Ray look. It could have sold alongside the big Corvette as a cheaper model with no problem at all. But nobody was interested.

Q: It seems like a big car such as the Corvette would be easier to style than a small car like the Monza GT or Opel GT, even though the body is similar.

Mitchell: That's why today, with all the small cars on the road, it would be hard for me. I'm glad I retired when I did [in 1977]. After all my years of designing cars, I was being asked to make them shorter, narrower, and higher instead of longer, lower, and wider. And you know what I used to say: "Designing a small car is like tailoring a dwarf." That's true. It's really tough to do a good small car.

Q: How did the Mako Shark fit into all this?

Mitchell: That car's a real favorite of mine. We used a dark top and light underbody, and nobody had ever done that. It works very well. It's even got nice lines from the top. On so many cars, the tops just fall away. But the Mako Shark looks good from the top. The Mako has the old chassis, and it's heavy. But it's got a 650 horsepower CanAm engine. It goes like hell. And it holds the road.

Q: Rumor has it that at one time there was some thought of discontinuing the Corvette and treating the Camaro as the General Motors' sports car.

Mitchell: That's very true. The first-series Camaro was done too fast. We didn't get a chance to do much. But the second-series cars [were] in production for a decade, and selling. That [was] really a hell of a package. Stirling Moss saw the first Camaro, and he said to me, "Bill, you've really got a classic. The detail . . . it's not all carved up. It's got a nice swoop to it." He was right. That car's been very popular in Europe, too. Much more than the [1968-82] Corvettes, which they consider over-styled. No matter what we do to it, [the second-series Camaro] body always works. The Camaro Berlinetta was a show car, you remember, with brass trim. I drove it here for a few months, and everybody liked it. So I said to myself, maybe I've got something here.

Q: There must be a pretty fine line between a classic design and a dull design.

Mitchell: Well, like they say, a designer's got to know when to lift his brush.

Q: Let's talk about the famed Aerovette concept. Originally, it was thought to be the 1980 Corvette design, but that never came about.

Mitchell: What's to tell? They took the most beautiful car ever styled and let it hang around. It's a shame, but that car had problems from the beginning. Originally, they were going to hire that Italian—Giorgetto Giugiaro—to do it. The Aerovette [was] my answer to Giugiaro. Giugiaro's cars are all full of angles. He can't draw a simple perspective, you know. He makes a side view and a top view. All his cars look like they've been cut out of cardboard.

Q: Isn't that deliberate?

Mitchell: I hope not. It's horrible. Now take my Aerovette by comparison. The Aerovette has nice contours, soft curves, and still a certain sharpness. It has really good balance. It's a design you can look at from any angle. A car is like a girl, you know. You wouldn't want

to see a girl from only one angle. You want to get more views.

Q: You must have spent most of your time with the Corvette.

Mitchell: Well, it was my pet. Nobody bothered me. No high power in Chevrolet was interested—the volume and profit wasn't there. You could do what you wanted without anybody monkeying around. In the other divisions, when you'd have a showing, you'd have the chief engineer and six assistants plus an audience in the studio that would drive you nuts. Committees, committees, committees. The first Camaro and Firebird were so "committeed" that I don't remember what they look like. They were just nothing. The other ones we got done so damn fast that they never saw 'em! But with the Corvette, they would always leave you alone.

Q: They never tried to make you build it out of steel?

Mitchell: With fiberglass, you can only make, say, 70,000 [units] at most [from a mold]. But you can change it. You can't do that so easily with metal. Every Corvette was different because you can do that. That's where [John] DeLorean screwed up [with the ill-fated sports car of the same name]. That thing he had—half metal, half plastic—you couldn't do anything with it.

Q: How important were show cars to production plans?

Mitchell: That's how you'd find out what people wanted. That's how the Eldorados were born and the Toronados and all that—at the Motorama. Now they don't make those anymore. Show cars were more fun to work on [because] you didn't have a bunch of committeemen telling us, "You can't do this, you can't do that." We did it, and if people liked it they'd say, "Go make it." It would do more for us in the studio to see one come out of the shop. People want to see something new.

Q: What do you think of the 1984-generation Corvette?

Mitchell: I think [it] looks like a grouper—a blunt look. I think the Camaro and Firebird are sharper. Although—I'll eat my own words—on the highway it looks pretty damn good from the front. But I don't like this lack of whip in the side view—it isn't exciting. And the big taillights look like it was done for A.J. Foyt. I think it should have been done for women as well as men. I like more interest in the car. You look at watches—there's millions of them and they look different all the time. You don't want cars all looking alike. I'd have put more accents on it. The new Corvette is engineering perfect, but design? No. The engineers ran the whole damn show. They wouldn't have done that with me.

You need two things in a car: You need road value and showroom value. You need a little sparkle in a car. On a little misty day they all look dull. You don't want to put chrome on with a trowel like we did in '58, but you need some. There isn't showroom value in these cars today. If I had one, I'd touch it up. You have to have enough interest to keep looking at it. That goes for all the cars.

Q: What are some specific changes you'd make?

Mitchell: I'd put more flow in the line. I wouldn't have the sideline straight through. I know it wouldn't be as aerodynamic, but I'd put some curve in that. Like a shark is so much more interesting than a grouper because there's so many little things happening to it. This ['84 Corvette] is a big potato. On the road, yes; but you walk up to it—blah. Black rubber around everything. I like to have a car that when I pull up, somebody says, "Whose car is that?" I want a car that, when it's stopped, people walk around it for an hour. Exciting automobiles.

1

2

3

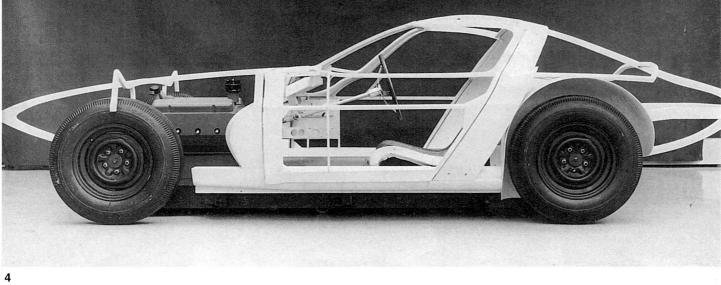

4

5

6

7

While Mitchell was building his race car, the Corvette team contemplated a smaller, all-new 1960 production model with Stingray-like lines, rear-mounted transmission, and fully independent suspension. Work on this so-called "Q-Corvette" was underway by fall 1957. **1-2.** First thoughts involved replacing the convertible with a radical fastback coupe. **3, 5-6.** Wild early shapes were soon refined into a more practical, producible form that accurately prefigured the eventual 1963 Sting Ray coupe. **4, 7.** A "space buck" was built to check interior dimensions and mechanical packaging. **8-9.** The project went as far as a full-scale clay model, which was compared to a '58 Corvette in the GM Design courtyard circa spring 1958. The planned rear transmission and other components would have come from a new line of passenger Chevys, also eyed for 1960. But when those higher-volume cars were nixed as uneconomical, so was the Q-Corvette...though it would not be forgotten.

8

9

PART 2 Birth of the Sting Ray

The original 1953 Corvette was born of Harley Earl's Motorama dream car that had become, much to the delight of a growing legion of aficionados, a vivid reality. Nurtured over the ensuing decade by the enthusiasm, energy, and talents of Ed Cole, Zora Arkus-Duntov, and Bill Mitchell, among others, the 'Vette had grown to fulfill its promise as "America's only true sports car." The 1961-62 model had been lauded as among the finest performance machines in the world. Sales were on a continued upswing and the car was finally and firmly profitable. The 'Vette was tearing up the nation's racing circuit, even though General Motors had "officially" signed on to the industry's self-imposed racing ban that was then in effect. The car had come to be known as a symbol of freedom and fun for a generation

Continuing a long tradition at Chevy Public Relations, photographers were on hand as the first Sting Rays came off the line at St. Louis in late 1962. A version of this photo was apparently circulated with the hood's simulated air vents touched out, forecasting a change that would actually be made for 1964. Note the convertible directly behind.

Virtually all-new from road to roof, the Sting Ray stunned the automotive world in 1963. Like the very first Corvette, it was a "dream car" come true but more sophisticated than any previous 'Vette, blending world-class handling with unmistakable all-American style and performance. It would have a great five-year run that many still regard as the high point of Corvette history.

that was dying to break free of the constrictive conformity of post-war America.

But the Corvette's designers and engineers—and GM's own top brass—knew that after 10 years in its basic form, albeit much improved, it was time to move on. By decade's end, the machinery would be put into motion to fashion a fitting successor to debut for the 1963 model year. After years of tinkering with the basic package, Bill Mitchell and his crew would finally break the mold of Earl's original design once and for all. Like his successor, Mitchell always considered the car to be his "pet" project. The car's second generation, which he would dub "Sting Ray" after the earlier race car of the same name (but now spelled out in separate words), would be the first Corvette to bear Mitchell's signature.

The production Sting Ray's lineage can be traced to two separate GM projects: the Q-Corvette, and perhaps more directly, Mitchell's racing Stingray.

The Q-Corvette, initiated in 1957, envisioned a smaller, more advanced Corvette as a coupe-only model, boasting a rear transaxle, independent rear suspension, and four-wheel disc brakes, with the rear brakes mounted inboard. Exterior styling, articulated by the same Bob McLean who was responsible for the original Motorama Corvette's layout, was purposeful, with peaked fenders, a

121

1

2

3

long nose, and a short, bobbed tail. The car was originally envisioned as one of a full line of large rear-transmission cars with which the Q-'Vette would share major components. But the passenger-car line was scrapped as being too radical, and the Corvette variant suffered the same fate by default—with no high-volume models from which to borrow components, the Q-coupe would have been prohibitively expensive to build.

Meanwhile, Zora Arkus-Duntov and other GM engineers had become fascinated with mid- and rear-engine designs, likely inspired by Porsche's success. It was also likely encouraged by Chevrolet general manager Ed Cole, who had championed a rear engine configuration for the division's first compact, the Corvair. It was during the Corvair's development that Duntov took the mid/rear-engine layout to its limits in the CERV I concept.

The Chevrolet Experimental Research Vehicle was a lightweight, open-wheel single-seat racer in the image of the British Coopers and Lotuses that were then starting to make their mark in international racing competition. A rear-engined Corvette was briefly considered during 1958-60, progressing as far as a full-scale mock-up designed around the Corvair's entire rear-mounted power package, including its complicated air-cooled flat-six as an alternative to the Corvette's usual water-cooled V-8.

By the fall of 1959, elements of the Q-Corvette and the Stingray Special racer would be incorporated into experimental project XP-720, which was the design program that led directly to the production 1963 Corvette Sting Ray. The XP-720 sought to deliver improved passenger accommodation, more luggage space, and superior ride and handling over previous Corvettes.

Duntov would personally ensure that the latter two goals got the greatest emphasis.

The starting point was a ground-up chassis design that would reflect lessons learned from the Sebring SS, the Q-coupe, CERV I, and the Stingray Special. It was, however, decided early in the project that the new Corvette would continue to offer a conventional drivetrain lay-out. Passengers were placed relatively far to the rear so that the engine/transmission package could sit somewhat behind the front-wheel centerline (in a so-called "front mid-engine" position) for optimum weight distribution—the same reasoning that had guided McLean on the plans for the original 1953 Corvette. The car's center of gravity was purposely kept low in the interest of both handling and ride quality, ending up at 16.5 inches above the road, versus the previous 19 inches. Ground clearance

7

4

6

was now down to a mere five inches.

Also in the name of improved handling characteristics, passengers were placed within the frame, rather than on top of it, and the car's wheelbase was trimmed four inches to 98. For greater torsional rigidity, and also to allow the driveline to ride low and fairly close to the car's longitudinal center, the old Fifties-fashion X-brace frame was abandoned for a new ladder-type design with five cross members. The extra rigidity was deemed necessary not only because of the more potent engines being planned

for the future, but because Duntov insisted that the new model would come with a fully independent rear suspension, which would generate higher lateral stresses than previous 'Vettes had ever known.

The independent rear suspension Duntov created for Sting Ray was simple yet effective. It was essentially a frame-mounted differential with U-jointed half-shafts tied together by a transverse leaf spring—a design derived from the CERV I concept. Rubber-cushioned struts carried the differential, which reduced ride harshness while improving tire adhesion,

The Sting Ray originated in Project XP-720, begun in summer 1959. **4, 7.** Designers initially focused on the planned new fastback coupe, with the aborted Q-Corvette and Bill Mitchell's racing Stingray as templates. Styling went together very quickly. These early workouts date from October. **1-2.** This full-size mockup from early April 1960 differs from the final design mainly in its grille treatment and various details. **3.** Closer still is this revised version of the same clay from late April, which was painted and given chrome-like foil trim for management review. Wheel covers, rear bumper, and fender-mount gas cap here would not survive. **5-6.** These undated photos suggest that designers briefly tried for a very literal rendition of the Stingray racer.

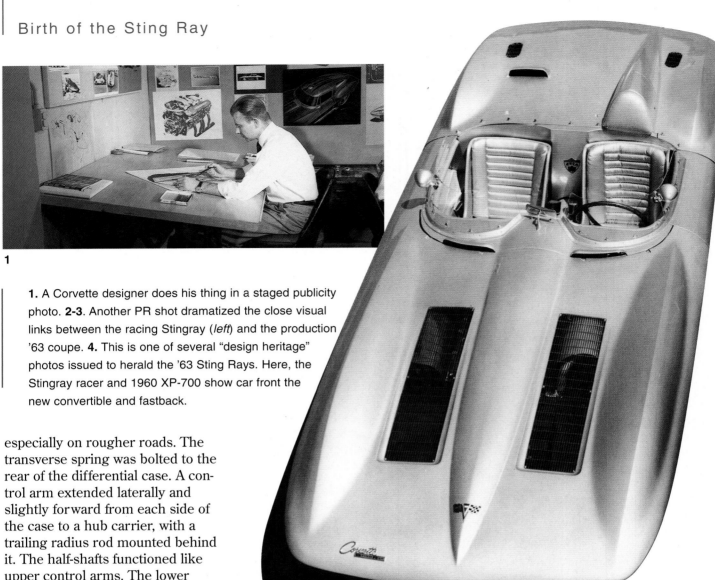

1. A Corvette designer does his thing in a staged publicity photo. **2-3.** Another PR shot dramatized the close visual links between the racing Stingray (*left*) and the production '63 coupe. **4.** This is one of several "design heritage" photos issued to herald the '63 Sting Rays. Here, the Stingray racer and 1960 XP-700 show car front the new convertible and fastback.

especially on rougher roads. The transverse spring was bolted to the rear of the differential case. A control arm extended laterally and slightly forward from each side of the case to a hub carrier, with a trailing radius rod mounted behind it. The half-shafts functioned like upper control arms. The lower arms controlled vertical wheel motion, while the trailing rods took care of fore/aft wheel motion and transferred braking torque to the frame. Shock absorbers were conventional twin-tube units.

Considerably lighter than the old solid axle, the new rear suspension array delivered a significant reduction in unsprung weight, which was important since the '63 model would retain the previous generation's outboard rear brakes.

The new model's front suspension would be much as before, with unequal-length upper and lower A-arms on coil springs concentric with the shocks, plus a standard anti-roll bar. Steering remained the conventional recirculating-ball design, but it was geared at a higher 19.6:1 overall ratio (previously 21.0:1). Bolted to the frame rail at one end and to the relay rod at the

other was a new hydraulic steering damper (essentially a shock absorber), which helped soak up bumps before they reached the steering wheel. What's more, hydraulically assisted steering would be offered as optional equipment for the first time on a Corvette—except on cars with the two most powerful engines—and offer a faster 17.1:1 ratio, which reduced lock-to-lock turns from 3.4 to just 2.9.

While Duntov was developing an innovative new chassis, designers were adapting and refining the basic look of the racing Stingray for the production model. The styling staff had been thinking mainly of

coupes ever since the Q-Corvette, and early XP-720 mock-ups looked a lot like Mitchell's Stingray racer fitted with a fastback roof.

A fully functional space buck (a wooden mock-up created to work out interior dimensions) was completed by early 1960, production coupe styling was locked up for the most part by April, and the interior—instrument panel included—was in place by November. Only in the fall of 1960 did the designers turn their creative attention to a new version of the traditional Corvette convertible and, still later, its detachable hardtop. A four-place coupe would be briefly considered, getting as far as a full-size mockup,

3

4

but would never see production.

For one of the few times in automotive history and for the first time in the Corvette's, wind tunnel testing helped refine the final shape, as did practical matters like interior space, windshield curvatures, and tooling limitations. Both body styles were extensively evaluated as production-ready ¾-scale models at the Cal Tech wind tunnel.

The vehicle's inner structure received as much attention as its exterior aerodynamics—again for reasons of refinement, though also for greater longevity. Fiberglass outer panels were retained, but the Sting Ray emerged with nearly twice as much steel support in its

central structure as the 1958-62 Corvette. The resulting extra weight was balanced by a reduction in fiberglass thickness, so the finished product actually weighed a bit less than the old roadster. Passenger room was as good as before despite the tighter wheelbase, and the reinforcing steel girder made the cockpit both stronger and safer.

Symbolic of the car's transformation was the first-ever production Corvette coupe—a futuristic fastback that sported one of the most unique styling elements in automotive history—a divided rear window. This feature, which dated from the Olds Golden Rocket show

car of 1956, had once been considered for an all-new '58 Corvette, and Mitchell thought enough of the backlight backbone to resurrect it for the '63 redesign. The rear window's basic shape, which was a compound-curve "saddleback," had been originally conceived by Bob McLean for the Q-model.

The split window proved quite controversial. Duntov, for one, was opposed because it hampered rearward visibility. But Mitchell insisted upon it, and most Corvette fans agree he was right. It certainly met one of Mitchell's prime criteria: It wouldn't be mistaken for anything else.

The rest of the Sting Ray design was equally stunning. Quad headlamps were retained but newly hidden—the first American car so equipped since the 1942 DeSoto. The lamps were mounted in rotating sections that matched the pointy front end with the "eyes" closed. An attractive beltline dip was added at the door's trailing upper edge, a result of cinching up the racing Stingray at the midriff. Coupe doors were cut into the roof, a common design element today, which made entry/exit easier in such a low-slung closed car. Faux vents were located in the hood and on the coupe's rear pillars; functional ones had been intended but were nixed by cost considerations. Furthermore, in the case of the hood vents, a problem cropped up caused by aerodynamics. It was

1

2

1-3. Chevy briefly considered a four-seat Sting Ray coupe at the urging of division chief Ed Cole, who thought it would sell better than the two-seat version. Designers obliged in 1962 with this full-size mockup, which was photographed alone and with a current Ford Thunderbird. But Bill Mitchell and Zora Duntov were strenuously opposed, believing the "2+2" would dilute Corvette's image as a red-blooded sports car. Cole finally relented, and the idea was abandoned.

found that warm engine air exiting from the top of the hood would flow right back into the cowl intake for the new windows-up interior ventilation system.

The Sting Ray's interior carried a new interpretation of the twin-cowl Corvette dash motif used since '58, with the scooped-out semicircles now standing upright instead of lying down. It was also more practical, now incorporating a roomy glovebox, an improved heater, and the aforementioned cowl-ventilation system. Also on hand was a full set of easy-to-read round gauges that included a huge speedometer and tachometer set dead ahead of the driver. The control tower center console returned, somewhat slimmer but now containing the clock and—another unusual touch—a vertically situated radio with a dial oriented to suit.

Luggage space was improved as well, though due to a lack of an external trunklid, cargo had to be stuffed behind the seats. If you wanted to carry anything other than passengers in the convertible, you also had to disconnect the folded top from its flip-up tonneau panel. The spare tire was located at

the rear in a drop-down fiberglass housing beneath the gas tank (which now held 20 gallons instead of 16). The big, round deck emblem was newly hinged to double as a fuel-filler flap, replacing the previous left-flank door.

The 1963 Corvette Sting Ray was an instant sensation and a certifiable blockbuster. Bill Mitchell's styling vision and Zora Arkus-Duntov's engineering wizardry proved to be just what the marketing department had been looking for, and Chevrolet's second-generation sports car hit the ground running at full throttle. "Only a man with a heart of stone could withstand temptation like this," the inaugural Sting Ray ad copy read. It would prove to be prophetic. Corvette sales would skyrocket to heights never imagined, even by the car's noted corporate boosters who nursed the vehicle along when few buyers paid attention. The St. Louis factory where the 'Vette was assembled would add a second shift, yet still couldn't keep up with demand. Customers were forced to wait up to two months for delivery—and to pay full retail price for the privilege. Even so, the Sting

Ray maintained tradition by offering remarkable sports-car value for the money. Base price was $4037 for the convertible and $4257 for the split-window coupe.

What's more, used-car values for previous years' models began heading upward, making this one of the first postwar cars to surpass its original list price on the collectors' market. Today the Sting Ray generation stands as perhaps the most desirable Corvette of all—the 1963 split-window coupe in particular.

Though not as obvious as the car's radical styling, the new chassis was just as important to the Sting Ray's success. Maneuverability was improved thanks to the faster "Ball-Race" steering (as the ad copywriters called it) and shorter wheelbase. The latter might ordinarily imply a choppier ride, but the altered weight distribution partly compensated for it. Less weight on the front wheels also meant easier steering at a time when power steering wasn't commonly ordered on Corvettes. And with some 80 additional pounds on the rear wheels, the Sting Ray offered improved traction over its predecessors.

3

Stopping power improved, too. Four-wheel cast-iron 11-inch drum brakes remained standard but were now wider, for an increase in effective braking area. Sintered-metallic linings, segmented for cooling, were again optional. So were finned aluminum ("Al-Fin") drums, which not only provided faster heat dissipation (and thus better fade resistance) but less unsprung weight. Power assist was available with both brake packages. Evolutionary engineering changes included positive crankcase ventilation, a smaller flywheel, and an aluminum clutch housing. As elsewhere in Detroit, a more efficient alternator replaced the old-fashioned generator.

Drivetrains were carried over from the previous model, comprising four 327 V-8s, a trio of transmissions, and six axle ratios. Carbureted engines came in 250-, 300-, and 340-horsepower versions. As before, the base and step-up units employed hydraulic lifters, a mild cam, forged-steel crankshaft, 10.5:1 compression, single-point distributor, and dual exhausts. The 300-bhp engine produced its extra power via a larger four-barrel carburetor (Carter AFB instead of the 250's Carter WCFB), plus larger intake valves and exhaust manifold. Again topping the performance chart was a 360-bhp fuel-injected powerhouse, available for an extra $430.40.

The car's standard transmission remained the familiar three-speed manual, though neither it nor the optional Powerglide automatic wound up finding their way into many units. The preferred gearbox continued to be the $188.30 Borg-Warner manual four-speed, delivered with wide-ratio gears when teamed with the base and 300-bhp engines, and close-ratio gearing with the top two powerplants. Standard axle ratio for the three-speed manual or Powerglide was 3.36:1. The four-speed gearbox came with a 3.70:1 final drive, but 3.08:1, 3.55:1, 4.11:1, and 4.56:1 gearsets were available. The last was quite rare in production, however.

Although GM was still nominally adhering to the Automotive Manufacturers' Association's 1957 racing ban, Duntov was determined that anyone who wanted to race his sophisticated new Sting Ray—which was, after all, the best-handling Corvette yet—should have the best possible chance for victory. This was the rationale behind RPO Z06, a new competition-oriented package. To get it, you had to specify a fuelie coupe equipped with four-speed and Positraction limited-slip differential—then pay a formidable $1818.45 for the Z06 option. In exchange you received the top-line Al-Fin power brakes with sintered metallic linings, plus a heavy-duty front stabilizer bar, stronger shocks, much stiffer springs, a dual master cylinder, and a long-distance 36.5-gallon fuel tank. The package was also listed for the convertible, but production records show that no such cars were ever built.

Chevy had intended to offer beautiful cast-aluminum wheels with tri-spinner knock-off hubs as part of the Z06 package and as a separate option. But though often shown in ads and press photos, these weren't "factory equipment" for '63. Chevy withdrew them before the car went into production due to casting problems that made the wheels so porous that they wouldn't hold air in the tires. The problem was solved for 1964 and later models, and some dealers installed the "working" wheels on '63s post-purchase, but all Z06-equipped 1963 models left St. Louis on conventional steel rims.

The Sting Ray was lauded in the automotive press almost unanimously for its handling, road adhesion, and sheer explosive power. *Car Life* bestowed its annual Award for Engineering Excellence on the 1963 Sting Ray. Chevy's small-block V-8—the most consistent component of past Corvette performance—was rated by the buff books to be even better in the Sting Ray. The '63 was noted to have an edge over past models in both traction and handling because the new independent rear suspension reduced wheelspin compared to the live-axle cars. Testing a four-speed fuelie with 3.70:1 axle, *Motor Trend* reported 0-30/45/60 mph in 2.9/4.2/5.8 seconds and a 14.5-second standing quarter-mile at 102 mph. The magazine also recorded better than 18 miles per gallon at

GM Photographic had been documenting "body drops" for decades when this Sting Ray coupe went together on the St. Louis assembly line. Readily apparent here is the Sting Ray's new independent rear suspension, a relatively simple but very effective setup created by Corvette chief engineer Zora Arkus-Duntov.

legal highway speeds and 14.1 mpg overall.

Ironically, the split backlight for which the first Sting Ray would become so well known took a beating in the automotive press from both a design standpoint and because of the hampered rearward view. Mitchell would be listening—perhaps too closely—and eliminate it after one year of production, which only served to boost the '63's value among future collectors. (Further, many split-window coupes were lost to customizers, some of whom replaced the small panes with one-piece windows made of Plexiglas. Chevy itself didn't help

matters by subsequently offering replacement one-piece windows through its dealers. As a result, a good many 1963 coupes lost considerable collector value.)

Other criticisms were limited mainly to the inconvenient access to the luggage compartment. On the other hand, creature comfort, not typically associated with previous models, was noted as one of the Corvette's high points, performance notwithstanding. The days of Plexiglas side curtains, doors without handles, and wheezing heaters were gone for good—after all, even British two-seaters were now getting roll-up windows

and two-minute tops.

But the Sting Ray was a notch above even the best European sports cars with its contoured bucket seats, telescopic steering wheel adjustment, functional instrumentation, and a heating/ventilation system fully able to cope with the greater extremes of the North American climate. True, the steering column adjustment demanded a little wrench work. And yes, the seats were a little low for some, though that was because Duntov wanted them that way for a low center of gravity. But overall, the Sting Ray was the most civilized Corvette ever and one of the most refined sporting cars built anywhere on the planet. Buyers now even had the option of ordering the car with leather upholstery and air conditioning.

Chevrolet's advertising for 1963 made the most of the Corvette's improved accommodations with a pair of ads. One headline offered, "Power brakes, power windows, power steering, air conditioning, automatic transmission...why do they call this a sports car?" The second reversed the same basic theme with, "Looks like a sports car, feels like a sports car, performs like a sports car, how come it's a luxury car?"

Racers, of course, cared less for accoutrements and instead went for the aforementioned Z06 package, a reflection of Duntov's determination that the Sting Ray coupe at least should be a GT-class and SCCA contender. Appropriately enough, a quartet of Z06-equipped fastbacks was dispatched to the Los Angeles Times Three-Hour Invitational Race at Riverside on October 13, 1962, for the Sting Ray's competition coming-out party. Dave MacDonald, Bob Bondurant, Jerry Grant, and Doug Hooper did the driving honors. As fate would have it, that was also the debut for Carroll Shelby's awesome Ford-powered Cobra, but the Sting Ray

was well up to the challenge of that Anglo-American hybrid. Though three of the four Chevys failed to finish, Hooper took the checkered flag in a car owned by Mickey Thompson.

The Sting Ray would go on to other victories, but it was the Cobra that would come to dominate production-class racing in the Sixties. But by now, the Corvette's street manners were so good the car didn't really need a racing image to support sales anymore. Duntov still hoped for a full-blown competition version, and his dream would be realized, if briefly, in the spectacular Corvette Grand Sport (see Chapter Four, Part Three).

An astounding 21,513 units would be built for the 1963 model year, which was up 50 percent from the record-setting 1962 version. Production was divided almost evenly between the convertible and the new coupe—10,919 and 10,594, respectively—and more than half the convertibles were ordered with the optional lift-off hardtop. Nevertheless, the coupe wouldn't sell as well again throughout the Sting Ray years. In fact, not until 1969 (by which time the coupe came with removable T-tops) did the closed Corvette sell better than the open one.

Equipment installations for 1963 began reflecting the market's demand for more civility in sporting cars. For example, the power brake option went into 15 percent of production, power steering into 12 percent. On the other hand, only 278 buyers specified the $421.80 air conditioning; leather upholstery—a mere $80.70—was ordered on only about 400 cars. The beautiful cast aluminum knock-off wheels, manufactured for Chevy by Kelsey-Hayes, cost $322.80 a set, but few buyers checked off that option. However, almost 18,000 Sting Rays left St. Louis with the four-speed manual gearbox—better than four out of every five.

With the Sting Ray on such a roll, it was prudent for Chevrolet to make only evolutionary changes to the 1964 model. Styling modifications were mostly for the better, as Chevrolet began a clean-up campaign that would continue through the design's 1967 finale. Besides the coupe's backbone window, the two simulated air intakes were eliminated from the hood, though their indentations remained. Also, the decorative air-exhaust vent on the coupe's rear pillar was made functional, but only on the left side. The car's rocker-panel trim lost some of its ribs and gained black paint between those ribs that remained; wheel covers were simplified; and the fuel filler/deck emblem gained concentric circles around its crossed-flags insignia. Inside, the original color-keyed steering wheel rim was now done in simulated walnut.

An improved ride was among Duntov's original goals for the Sting Ray, and most reviewers judged him successful, especially compared to previous Corvettes. But the car's shock absorbers tended to weaken as the miles rolled by, and owners began complaining of deteriorating ride quality. Chevrolet solved this problem with a few suspension refinements for 1964. The front coil springs were changed from constant-rate to progressive or variable-rate and were more tightly wound at the top, while leaf thickness of the rear transverse spring was also altered. With their wider damping range, the revised springs could better absorb both large and small disturbances, thus providing a more comfortable ride with no sacrifice in handling.

Shock absorbers were reworked toward the same end. When subjected to frequent oscillation at near full vertical wheel travel, such as on very rough roads, the standard '63 shocks tended to overheat. This caused their hydraulic fluid to "cavitate" or bubble, with a consequent loss in damping efficiency. The 1964 Corvette arrived with a new standard shock containing within its fluid reservoir a small bag of Freon gas that absorbed heat to keep the fluid from bubbling.

The European press had faulted the '63 for relatively high interior noise levels; accordingly, Chevy added more sound insulation and revised body and transmission mounts for the following model year. It also fitted additional bushings to quiet the shift linkage and placed a new boot around the lever. The result was a more livable car for everyday transportation.

Drivetrain choices remained basically as before: four 327 cid V-8s,

of performance pieces were available for it. The fuelie also gained 15 horsepower, bringing its total to 375. But at a then-hefty $538, it was too rich for most buyers' budgets. For the next decade or so, the route to 'Vette power would be through the time-honored expedient of adding cubic inches and not through comparatively sophisticated means like fuel injection.

Although transmission options remained ostensibly the same for '64, the two Borg-Warner T-10 four-speeds gave way to a similar pair of gearboxes built at GM's Muncie, Indiana, transmission facility. The "Muncie" was already being used in other GM models, so its adop-

Positraction was still a bargain-priced option in 1964 at only $43.05, and it went into more than 80 percent of that year's production. The clutch-type differential was designed to send engine torque to the wheel with greater traction, as opposed to a standard open differential that transfers power to the wheel with lesser traction. Positraction naturally enhanced off-the-line adhesion as well as helping get out of mud or snow. On ice or really hard-packed snow, however, the torque transfer from one wheel to the other could induce fishtailing, which could be unnerving in such a high-powered car. Control on slippery surfaces required a deft foot.

The J56 sintered-metallic brakes were a much costlier option—a whopping $629.50—though you

This 1964 Sting Ray "styling study" was shown at the New York World's Fair. Note side-exit exhaust.

one three- and two four-speed manual transmissions and the Powerglide automatic, and six axle ratios. The two least-powerful engines returned with 250 and 300 bhp on 10.5:1 compression, but the high-performance pair received several noteworthy improvements. The solid-lifter unit was massaged with a high-lift, long-duration camshaft to produce 365 bhp and breathed through a big four-barrel Holley carburetor instead of the base engine's Carter unit. This was an advantage, since the Holley was more easily tailored to specific needs because a larger assortment

tion for the Corvette made sense for reasons of both manufacturing and cost. Originally a Chevy design, it had an aluminum case like the B-W box but came with stronger synchronizers and wider ratios for better durability and drivability. The wide-ratio version could be teamed only with the 250- and 300-bhp powerplants; gear spacings were 2.56:1, 1.91:1, 1.40:1, and 1.00:1. The close-ratio unit was for the more potent mills; its internals were 2.20:1, 1.64:1, 1.28:1, and 1.00:1. Like the B-W boxes, the Muncies had a reverse lockout trigger, but with a thicker shifter.

also got the Al-Fin drums from the previous Z06 package. Of course, the J56 brakes were also for competition, and while not as easily modulated as the disc brakes that would come in subsequent years, they provided plenty of fade-free stopping power.

If enthusiast publications liked the first Sting Ray, they loved the '64, though some writers noted the convertible's tendency to rattle and shake on rough roads. *Motor Trend* clocked a fuel-injected four-speed coupe with the 4.11:1 rear axle, aluminum knock-off wheels (perfected at last and available from the factory), the sintered-metallic brakes, and Positraction through the quarter-mile in 14.2 seconds at 100 mph and streaked from 0 to 60 mph in just 5.6 seconds. At the opposite end of the spectrum, *Road & Track* tested the tame 300-bhp Powerglide setup in a '64 coupe and recorded a 0-60-mph time of 8.0 seconds, a standing-quarter in 15.2 seconds at 85 mph, and average fuel consumption of 14.8 mpg.

Sales of the 1964 Sting Ray reached 22,229—another new Corvette record, if up only a little from banner-year 1963. Coupe volume dropped to 8304 units, but convertible sales more than compensated, rising to 13,925.

For its third season, the Sting Ray was not only further cleaned up style-wise, but was muscled up in a big way with the addition of an all-new braking system and beefier powerplants.

Styling alterations to the '65 were subtle, confined to a smoothed-out hood now devoid of scoop indentations, a trio of working vertical exhaust vents in the front fenders that replaced the previous nonfunctional horizontal "speedlines," restyled wheel covers and rocker-panel moldings, and minor interior trim revisions.

The big news for 1965 was underneath the fiberglass exterior, however. The first welcome addition was the advent of standard four-wheel disc brakes. The brakes had a four-piston design with two-piece calipers and cooling fins for the rotors. Pads were in constant contact with the rotors, but the resulting drag was negligible and didn't affect fuel economy. Further, the light touching kept the rotors clean and didn't diminish pad life, which was, in fact, quite high: a projected 57,000 miles for the front brakes (which, because of forward weight transfer, supplied most of the braking effort in all-out stops) and about twice that distance for the rear binders. Total swept area for the

new system was 461 square inches, a notable advance on the 328 square inches of the previous all-drum system. Per pending federal regulation, there was also a dual master cylinder with separate fluid reservoirs for the front and rear lines.

Road testers rightly applauded the all-disc brakes. Testers found that repeated stops from 100 mph produced no deterioration in braking efficiency, and even the most sudden stops were rock-stable. The old drum brakes remained available, however, as a $64.50 credit option, but only 316 of the 23,562 Corvettes built that year came with them.

Another mechanical addition came at midyear, with a new optional V-8: the big-block Mark IV. Originating in early 1963 with the so-called "mystery" 427 racing engine that roared onto the scene for the Daytona 500, this husky powerplant was notable for its "porcupine" valvegear. An idea of engine designer Robert P. Benzinger, the nickname referred to the way the pushrods poked through at the oddest angles. This was the result of working "backward" by starting with the ports and manifolds rather than the combustion chambers. Intake valves were set at an angle of 26 degrees to the cylinder axis, while the exhaust valves were set at 17 degrees. Moreover, both sets of valve stems were tilted in side view, one forward and the other backward, by nine degrees; this lined them up with the pushrods to avoid setting up rotation in the rocker arms. The basic head configuration was then tested, fiddled with, and honed until it provided optimal breathing. Then all the other components were designed around it.

Officially called Mark IV but marketed as the Turbo Jet, the new engine arrived in three varieties: two 396-cid versions, and a 427 (a heavy-duty 427 was also created for

marine use). The 396s were scheduled to replace Chevy's hallowed 409 in all its applications for 1965. (The 409's brief five-year existence can be blamed on basic design limitations and the fact that it had been tooled for relatively low production.) Future demand for performance cars suggested that Chevy's Tonawanda, New York, engine plant would have to be retooled, and Semon E. "Bunkie" Knudsen, then division general manager, decided that only the most modern engine could justify such a major investment. Mark IV production commenced in mid-1965.

Like the head, the Mark IV block was also new, with 4.84 inches between bore centers, a bore of 4.094 inches, and a stroke of 3.75 inches. The 409 had a deck angled at 33 degrees to allow for wedge-shaped combustion chambers with flat head faces. By contrast, the Mark IV had the usual flat deck sitting perpendicular to the cylinder axis. Main bearings were 2.75 inches in diameter, a quarter-inch larger than those of the 409. Main-bearing width was also increased, adding two full inches to the cap-clamping surface. The forged-steel crankshaft was cross-drilled to deliver oil to the rod bearings through a full 360 degrees of rotation (a feature lacking in the 409). Crankpin journals were kept at a 2.20-inch diameter.

With hydraulic lifters, a four-barrel carburetor, and 10.25:1 compression, the 396 Mark IV offered in intermediate Chevelles and full-size Chevys arrived in two states of tune: 325 and 360 bhp. For the Corvette, the engine was given 11:1 compression, impact-extruded alloy pistons with chrome rings, solid lifters, and a bigger carburetor, all helping to produce 425 bhp. Also on hand were a double-snorkel air cleaner and an oversized oil sump.

Although in short supply at the showrooms, the top Mark IV Corvette wasn't short on performance. Pulling even the moderate 3.70:1 rear axle, it could do standing quarter-miles of around 14 seconds at terminal speeds of 102–104 mph. Given enough road, it would show a top speed of nearly 140 mph. Numerically higher or lower axle ratios would respectively deliver even faster acceleration or higher top speeds (an insane 160 mph was not inconceivable).

Stiffer front springs and sway bar, a special rear sway bar, super-heavy-duty clutch, and a larger radiator and fan were included with the Mark IV option. For instant recognition of the monster at rest, there was an aggressive-looking hood bulge and (as an option) side-mounted exhaust pipes. Though the big-block engine weighed more than 650 pounds, it didn't leave the Sting Ray overly nose-heavy. In fact, weight distribution was a near-perfect 51/49 percent front/rear, a tribute to the foresight of the car's chassis planners.

GM management had initially decreed that no car line smaller than full-size should carry an engine larger than 400 cubic inches. Since the 396 squeaked in under that limit, it replaced the fuel-injected small-block V-8. But with Carroll Shelby installing Ford's impressive 427 V-8 in his sparse two-seater Cobras, Chevrolet felt it would likewise need a 427. It materialized for 1966—basically a 396 with a larger 4.25-inch bore.

For the Corvette, this bigger big-block came in two forms: 390 bhp on 10.25:1 compression, and 425 bhp via 11:1 compression, larger intake valves, a bigger Holley four-barrel carburetor on an aluminum manifold, mechanical lifters, and four- instead of two-hole main bearing caps. Though it had no more horsepower than the previous high-compression 396, the 427 packed a lot more torque—460 pound/feet vs. 415. Of course, engine outputs were sometimes deliberately under-

stated in the Sixties so as not to arouse the ire (and, subsequently the rates) of insurance companies. Here, 420 and 450 bhp would be closer to the truth.

Ordering a 427 Corvette meant you had to take it with Positraction and the close-ratio Muncie four-speed; there was no other choice. You also got an upgraded suspension, basically the same as the 396 package, as well as stouter, shot-peened halfshafts and U-joints and a higher-capacity radiator and sump.

Regardless of which axle ratio it turned, the 427 Sting Ray was an astonishing executor. With the short 4.11:1 gearing, 0–60 mph times were recorded in a nearly unbelievable 4.8 seconds, and 0–100 mph in 11.2 seconds, with a blistering top speed of 140 mph. The modest 3.36:1 ratio made things only a bit less sensational: *Car and Driver* reported 0–60 in 5.4 seconds and a standing quarter of 12.8 seconds at 112 mph.

With big-block V-8s being the order of the day, there was less demand for the 327, so small-block offerings were cut from five to two for 1966, and only the basic 300- and 350-bhp versions were retained. Arguably, these were still the best all-around engines. Both required premium fuel on compression ratios well over 10.0:1, and they didn't have the rocket-like thrust of the 427s, but their performance was impressive all the same. As before, both could be teamed with the Powerglide automatic, the standard three-speed manual, or either four-speed option.

Engine choices aside, the 1966 model year dawned quietly for the Sting Ray. Its frontal appearance was mildly altered with an eggcrate grille insert to replace the previous horizontal bars, and the coupe lost its roof-mounted extractor vents, which had proven inefficient. This relative lack of change reflected plans to bring out an all-new

Corvette for 1967. It certainly did not reflect a fall-off in the car's popularity, however. In fact, 1966 would prove another record-busting year, with volume rising to 27,720 units, up some 4200 over '65's 23,562 sales.

But initial plans to the contrary, the '67 turned out to be another carryover Sting Ray, because its intended successor was found to have some undesirable aerodynamic traits. Duntov demanded more time in the wind tunnel to devise fixes before it went into production.

Still, the 1967 Corvette was a Sting Ray refined to the limit—the very best of the five-year run and quite possibly the best Corvette ever. It was certainly the cleanest Sting Ray ever, though changes were again modest. Five smaller front fender vents replaced the three larger ones, and flat-finish rockers sans ribbing conferred a lower, less chunky appearance. New, and thus unique, was a single backup light, mounted above the

license plate. The previous models' old-fashioned wheel covers gave way to slotted six-inch Rally wheels with chrome beauty rings and lug nuts concealed behind small chrome caps. Interior alterations were likewise modest and included revised upholstery, and the handbrake moved from beneath the dash to between the seats. The convertible's optional hardtop was now dubiously offered with a black vinyl cover, which was a fad among all cars at the time.

Powertrains changed hardly at all. The two small-block V-8s returned, as did the 390-bhp big-block (hulking beneath a redesigned hood scoop). But the top two 427s now developed 400 and 435 bhp with a switch to triple two-barrel carburetors. As before, they differed in compression ratios—10.25:1 and 11.0:1, respectively—and the solid lifters and transistorized ignition that went on the 425-bhp unit. The latter, RPO

L71, was also available with special aluminum heads (instead of cast iron) and larger-diameter exhaust valves as RPO L89, though with the same grossly understated horsepower.

The ultimate 'Vette engine for '67 was coded L88, which was an even wilder L89 that was as close to a pure racing engine as Chevy had ever offered in regular production. Besides the lightweight heads and bigger ports, it came with an even hotter cam, aluminum radiator, small-diameter flywheel, stratospheric 12.5:1 compression, and a single huge Holley four-barrel carburetor. The result was no less than 560 bhp, again at 6400 rpm. Only one problem: You had to use 103-octane racing fuel, which was available only at select service stations. Clearly this was not an engine for the casual motorist. When the L88 was ordered, Chevy made several individual options mandatory, including Positraction,

the transistorized ignition, heavy-duty suspension, and power brakes, as well as RPO C48, which deleted the normal radio and heater to cut down on weight and discourage the car's use on the street. As costly as it was powerful—at an additional $1500 over the base $4240.75 price—the L88 engine and required options were sold to a mere 20 power-hungry buyers that year.

With potential buyers anticipating the car's overdue redesign, sales for the Sting Ray's final year totaled 22,940, down over 5000 units from 1966 results. Meanwhile, Chevrolet readied its third-generation Corvette for the 1968 model year. While the new model would hit the streets for the first time in five years without the Sting Ray designation, it would nonetheless retain a marine-based appellation, albeit as a nickname. Soon the "Shark" would emerge to prowl the turbulent waters that were churning in late-1960's America.

The Sting Ray won SCCA's 1963 national B-Production trophy by fending off the lighter Shelby Cobras, as this split-window coupe is doing.

GM styling chief Bill Mitchell customized a new '63 Sting Ray convertible as a gift to his predecessor, Harley Earl. Features included a leather-lined cockpit with extra gauges, a hopped-up 327 V-8 with side exhaust, plus a stock lift-off hardtop and special paint with racing stripes.

The Corvette Sting Ray bowed for 1963 with the previous year's engines in a stunning all-new package with a trimmer 98-inch wheelbase and first-time all-independent suspension. The trademark fiberglass body gained extra steel inner reinforcements and head-turning looks taken from Bill Mitchell's recent Stingray racer. Amazingly, the convertible shown here had nearly the same base price as the '62 version—$4037. Exactly 10,919 were built.

Perhaps even more stunning than the Sting Ray roadster was the first production Corvette coupe, a sleek fastback with a distinctive split rear window used only for '63. The coupe started at $4252, some $200 above the convertible, but buyers eagerly snapped up 10,594 for the model year. All Sting Rays featured a more comfortable, more driver-oriented cockpit dominated by a new "twin cowl" dashboard with a full array of instruments. Some critics chided styling details like the simulated hood air vents, but the Sting Ray design has come to be regarded as a modern classic, with the split-window coupe now among the most valuable Corvettes of all.

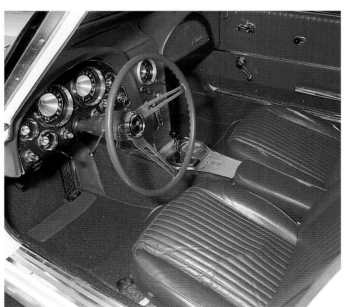

The Sting Ray boosted Corvette sales by no less than 48 percent from the model-year '62 total, itself a record. Road testers praised the new car's styling, but also its new-found handling prowess. The Sting Ray was also a some-what lighter Corvette, so acceleration improved despite unchanged horsepower. This car carries the top 360-hp fuel-injected 327 V-8 (announced by front-fender badges) and the equally desirable four-speed manual gearbox option. Carbureted 327s were again available in 250-, 300-, and 340-bhp versions.

The Sting Ray design omitted an external-opening trunk. Chevy omitted the dummy hood vents for '64. Coupes also lost their distinctive rear-window divider bar but gained functional air-extractor vents in the roof. Horsepower swelled to 365 on the top carbureted engine and to 375 for the "fuelie" version. Sales improved, too, reaching 22,229, though coupe production dropped to 8304. This coupe wears the multi-spoke aluminum wheels with genuine knock-off hubs that were available throughout the Sting Ray generation and are now highly prized by collectors.

Further refinements marked the '65 Sting Rays. Immediately apparent were the new trio of functional air vents in the front fenders, a smoothed-out hood, and more legible instruments. Small-block V-8 power was unchanged, but four-wheel disc brakes were newly standard to rein it in more effectively. A wood-rim steering wheel and telescopic steering column were among several new options. The convertible's base price now stood at $4106.

Sting Rays became ferocious with the mid-1965 debut of a big-block V-8 option, the 396 Turbo Jet. A product of Chevy's recent NASCAR racing efforts, it delivered 425 bhp and a thumping 415 pound-feet of torque. It also added some 200 pounds, but reduced 0–60 to well under six seconds. The option included side exhaust pipes and a bulged hood but saw relatively few installations. The small-block "fuelie" vanished when the 396 arrived.

A bigger big-block option was the big news for 1966, as the 396 became a 427 offering 390 bhp or a stout 425, versus 350 for the year's top 327. Side exhaust pipes were again included and remained available for small-block Sting Rays like the coupes shown here (the convertible is a '65). Corvette sales kept climbing, reaching 27,720 for the model year, up 4158 units from the '65 total.

The Sting Ray's grille switched from thin horizontal bars to a crosshatch pattern for '66, one of only a handful of subtle appearance changes made that season. To the dismay of many 'Vette lovers, 1966 would be the last year for the factory's optional aluminum wheels, as shown on this 427-equipped convertible. Note also the two extra taillights, which are an owner modification, not factory-stock.

The Corvette was born as a convertible, which may explain why the ragtop Sting Ray outsold its coupe companion by ever wider margins as time passed. By 1966 the difference was almost two to one. This beauty sports a rear-deck luggage rack, long a popular Corvette accessory—and handy for supplementing the regular Sting Ray trunk, which is fairly spacious but reachable only from within the cockpit.

Front-fender "gills," single backup lamp above the license plate, and central handbrake identified the last-of-the-line 1967 Sting Rays. Big-block models also got a new hood treatment, as on this coupe. The burly 427 returned with a "normal" 390 bhp and in new 400- and 435-bhp versions. There was also a new racing-oriented monster called L88 with no less than 560 bhp, installed on just 20 cars.

PART 3 The Grand Sport

While the automotive industry's self-imposed ban on racing remained in effect, 1962 marked both a turning point and, inevitably, unfinished business for the Corvette's competitive fortunes. By 1961, Chrysler and Ford were defying the ban more openly than ever, and Carroll Shelby's V-8-powered Ford Cobra would soon begin to burn up the asphalt on the nation's road courses. Insiders at General Motors, including "Mr. Corvette" Zora Arkus-Duntov and newly appointed Chevrolet general manager Semon "Bunkie" Knudsen, were itching to get back in the racing game under their own employer's banner.

Duntov felt that Corvettes should be winning races openly and convincingly, regardless of the Automobile Manufacturers' Association's dictum and GM's adherence to it. The ban had kept his radical Sebring Super Sport from realizing its full potential, and Duntov felt the new production Sting Ray in the works could be a sure winner in GT competition if given the opportunity. Knudsen had recently been brought over from Pontiac, which zoomed from number six to the industry's number-three seller in just four years, and his addiction to racing was almost as pronounced as Duntov's. He was

solidly behind Duntov's quiet, competition-oriented projects like the exotic mid-engine CERV II. He also backed the Chevy "mystery" engine that would astonish the NASCAR world when it briefly appeared at Daytona in 1963.

An opportunity for Duntov and Knudsen to return to racing opened up for the 1963 season when the Federation Internationale de l'Automobile (FIA), the world's chief auto-racing governing body, announced that the World Manufacturers Championship would be open to Grand Touring cars as well as prototypes and approved sports-racing models, with no limit on engine displacement. This was virtually an open invitation to big-engined American cars, including both the Corvette and Carroll Shelby's Cobra project for Ford. All that was required was that at least 100 such cars be built to an approved ("homologated") specification within one year of certification. While the new Sting Ray Corvette was shaping up to be heavier and not as aerodynamically clean as might be desired for high-speed endurance racing, Duntov, as usual, had something up his sleeve.

This was a lightweight "Grand Sport" version of the forthcoming Sting Ray coupe powered by a considerably modified 327-cubic-inch

Corvette V-8. With Knudsen's enthusiastic backing, though appropriately muted for political reasons, Duntov's special engineering team got down to work in earnest—and under great secrecy—during the summer of '62.

While the racer was fundamentally based on stock Sting Ray engineering, the Grand Sport differed from what would be the production car in most every respect. The chassis, for example, retained the new ladder-type design but featured large tubular-steel side rails that ran straight front to rear, rather than tapering inward. Three equally large cross-members tied things together at the back; up front was a hefty single cross-member that measured a half-foot in diameter.

Suspension geometry in the racing version also followed that of the new production Corvette, but com-

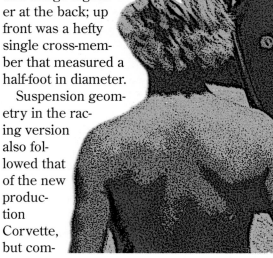

GM executives felt the potent Sting Ray should be promoted in competition despite the auto industry's self-imposed racing ban. A perfect venue appeared in 1963, when Grand Touring cars were sanctioned to compete in the World Manufacturers Championship. Due to excess weight and less-than-perfect aerodynamics, a stock Sting Ray wouldn't have been competitive, but Zora Arkus-Duntov figured a "doctored" version could be—and he set out to prove it.

The high point of the Grand Sport's brief racing career was the December 1963 Nassau Speed Week, where a three-car team scored high finishes in three contests. Driver Jim Hall drove number 65 and later purchased a GS.

1

ponents were specially fabricated and designed to save weight. The main changes were the use of thin sheet steel instead of thicker cast metal for the front A-arms, larger-diameter coil springs all around, the absence of flexible rubber bushings for the rear suspension (given that there was no need for concern about noise and vibration in the racing model), and special rear trailing arms with lightening holes. Disc brakes were installed at all four wheels; these were big 11.75-inch-diameter British-made Girling units with two-piston aluminum calipers and solid rotors. The brakes' deeply offset "hat-section" design allowed small rear drums to be incorporated at the rear as an emergency brake, operated from the cockpit by a traditional lever. The car's steering assembly was the usual recirculating-ball mechanism within a special weight-saving aluminum case, with modified gearing allowing a speedy two turns lock-to-lock.

Bodywork was closely patterned after Bill Mitchell's newly designed Sting Ray fastback and was likewise made of fiberglass, but was thicker (0.040-inch) and specially hand-laid. Dimensions were kept close to stock, though front/rear tracks were slightly wider at 56.8/57.8 inches. Duntov summarily removed Mitchell's rear-window divider bar, added a small opening panel in the rear deck for access to the spare tire, substituted fixed headlights (behind Plexiglas covers) for the production car's hidden lamps, and placed a racing-style quick-fill fuel outlet in the right rear roof quarter. A sheet-aluminum framework around the doors and windows bolstered the Sting Ray's new steel "birdcage" underbody structure. Fender wells were carefully shaped to accept the largest possible wheels and tires. Duntov chose 6.0 × 15.0 Halibrand magnesium knock-off rims able to mount 7.10-7.60 section tires up front and 8.00-8.20 rubber in back.

Inside, the GS was quite civilized for a racer, with full carpeting and the same instrument cluster and steering wheel found in the production car. An oil-pressure dial was substituted for the fuel gauge, however, and a special speedometer was calibrated to 200 mph. Seats were deep one-piece molded buckets bolstered onto tubular tracks, which allowed fore/aft adjustment, albeit with the aid of a wrench.

Power would come from a specially modified version of the versatile Chevy small-block engine. Here, however, the basic 327 production block would be fitted with new big-valve aluminum cylinder heads that offered more efficient hemispherical combustion chambers instead of the normal wedge-type and—the tricky part—two spark plugs per cylinder, activated from a single distributor by twin coils. Rochester constant-flow mechanical fuel injection was specified, which was basically the familiar "Ramjet" system but altered to feed individual, vertically situated ram pipes. The 327's normal 4.00-inch bore was retained, but stroke

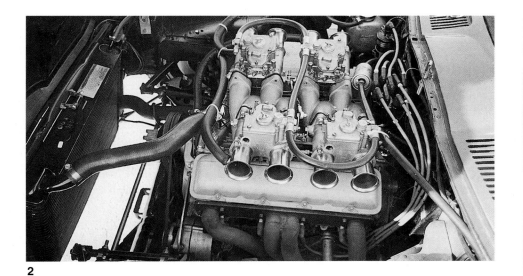

2

3

4

5

1. Though GM squashed the Grand Sport effort after Nassau '63, the cars were sold to favored racers, who ran them privately. The new owners made various changes to suit different venues and distances. The streamlined plastic headlight covers here are but one example. **2.** The GS first raced with a special all-aluminum 377-cubic-inch V-8, but this, too, was subsequently changed on most of the five cars built. **3.** As expected of a racer, the battery was relocated to the trunk to help balance weight distribution. **4-5.** GS cockpits were naturally race-car stark and functional.

lengths of up to 4.00 inches were possible for displacements of up to 402 cubic inches. Ultimately, the team settled on an intermediate 3.75-inch stroke for greater simplicity and reliability, producing a 377-cid powerhouse that could rev happily to 6500 rpm.

Duntov's engineers reportedly had been hoping for up to 600 horsepower but had to settle for 550 bhp at 6400 rpm for the 377-cid engine. However, this was more than enough to overcome the Sting Ray body's relatively high aerodynamic drag, given the car's bantam 1900–2100-pound curb weight. Torque was a massive 500 pound/feet at 5200 rpm. As the peak power and torque speeds suggest, the GS engine gave its best at the top end, which is just where you want it in a racing machine.

Completing the drivetrain was a fortified four-speed manual gearbox linked to an aluminum-case limited-slip differential supplied by Dana.

By mid-December, the first Grand Sport was complete and ready for initial testing. The test was conducted at Sebring, with drivers Masten Gregory and Corvette veteran Dick Thompson doing the honors. Excessive heat retention within the brakes proved the biggest problem in its initial runs. Slightly wider ventilated Girling discs were the solution, and were included in the Grand Sport's specification as submitted for FIA approval.

FIA policy at the time was to homologate a car even before the minimum 100 examples had been built, and so it was with the GS. An additional four Grand Sports were

built, and Duntov obtained authorization for an additional 20 cars and 40 of the 16-plug engines, all of which were deemed adequate to satisfy customer demand for the '63 season. Production of the remaining 60-plus cars would be handled by an outside firm under contract to Chevrolet and would be sold on a first-come, first-served basis.

Unfortunately, like the Super Sport that preceded it, the Grand Sport's promising racing career under Duntov and Knudsen's guidance would be thwarted by the AMA's anti-racing edict. Rumors had been circulating that some GM divisions were defying this corporate policy. Chairman Frederic Donner and president John Gordon circulated an internal memo on January 21, 1963, which affirmed that GM was still, in fact, abiding

157

by the AMA agreement and that the various divisions should thus comply accordingly. At a news conference less than a month later, Donner went public with this crackdown on his company's internal racing efforts. Only five cars had been completed by that point, and the 16-plug engine remained largely undeveloped.

Still, the GS would live to race another day, thanks to the efforts of Grady Davis and Dick Doane, both of whom had close ties to Chevrolet management. Davis (a Union Oil official) and Doane (a Chevrolet dealer) each managed to obtain a GS, allegedly delivered in unmarked Chevy Division trucks. The Davis car was given minor body modifications and fitted with a stock 360-bhp 327 fuelie for Dick Thompson to drive through the 1963 season in SCCA's C-Modified class. Under the circumstances, it did well. The highlight was an outright win at Watkins Glen in late August, as Thompson staved off a front-engine Chaparral to take the checkered flag with an average speed of 90.82 mph. Thompson also took third in class and fifth overall at Cumberland, Maryland, in May, third overall at Elkhart Lake, Wisconsin, and fourth overall at Bridgehampton, both in June. Ed Lowther also drove the Davis car, placing third in class and fourth overall in the 90-minute Governor's Cup at Danville, Virginia, in April. The Doane GS saw less action in '63, but the owner drove it to a sixth-place finish at Meadowdale, Illinois, in August.

Meanwhile, the remaining three Grand Sports had been sold to millionaire Texas oilman John Mecom, Jr. Mecom had just become a major force in motorsports by backing the best machinery money could buy and hiring stellar drivers like Roger Penske, Augie Pabst, and A.J. Foyt. Carroll Shelby's Cobras had been running wild on the tracks, and despite GM's reaf-

firmed adherence to the AMA racing ban, Chevrolet officials from Bunkie Knudsen on down were just itching to get even. They chose to do so through the Mecom Racing Team and would start with the Nassau Speed Week events early in December 1963. The scene was set for the Grand Sport's greatest triumph.

Three Grand Sports were prepared: the Davis and Doane cars, plus another GS that had been in storage at the GM Tech Center in Warren, Michigan. Again in great secrecy, Duntov's team focused on the 377 V-8, giving it a new aluminum block and discarding the original fuel injection for four big-bore Weber carburetors on a special light-alloy manifold with crossover intake pipes. Body alterations were both functional and intimidating in their appearance: They included a new hood with a pair of tall, front-facing scoops to feed the carbs, eight holes cut in between the taillamps to aid brake cooling, functional engine-compartment air vents in the front fenders (replacing the previous faux outlets), opaque shrouds for the headlights, and—most noticeable— wheel openings that had been radically flared to accommodate 11-inch-wide Halibrand wheels with low-profile Goodyear racing tires.

The Grand Sports quickly became the talk of Nassau '63. Chevy engineers—officially "on vacation"—were in Nassau to oversee the car's efforts. In qualifying for the December 1 Tourist Trophy race, Dick Thompson and Jim Hall (of Chaparral fame) blasted away from a pack of Cobras and a Ferrari GTO to capture the front-row grid positions, only to retire from the actual race with differential trouble. Insufficient cooling was the culprit, but it was rectified in time for the Governor's Cup Trophy on December 6, a 25-lap, 112-mile dash with 58 entries. To Carroll Shelby's dismay, Roger Penske led all the

way, finishing third overall and first in the prototype class. All three Grand Sports were entered in the week's longest and most important event, the 56-lap, 252-mile Nassau Trophy race on December 8. Although one GS dropped out, Thompson took fourth place overall and first in class, while newly recruited teammate John Cannon drove to eighth overall and third in class.

Elated by this showing, and having learned some valuable lessons at Nassau, the Duntov team immediately set to work on further improvements to the Grand Sport. Among these were a new timed fuel-injection system with cross-ram manifolding, a suitably redesigned hood with stronger fasteners (excessive underhood pressure had caused hoods to pop open at Nassau), and a pneumatic jacking system to speed pit-side servicing and tire changes. All this was intended for Sebring in March 1964, but the GS proved disappointing in its showing there. Delmo Johnson and co-driver Dave Morgan endured numerous mechanical breakdowns to finish only 32nd overall, while Penske and Hall put their white car across the line in 18th.

Meanwhile, the two remaining Grand Sport coupes that had been sitting around in Warren were prepped for the 2000-kilometer Daytona Continental in February 1964. This was run on the combined infield/tri-oval course used for long-distance road races at the Florida speedway. Reasoning that the coupe body's high drag would limit maximum speed on the high-banked sections, Duntov decided to reduce frontal area by converting this pair to roadster configuration. The result was a mean-looking open GS with a low racing wind screen and stylishly integrated roll bar over an integrated driver's headrest. These cars were also given the pneumatic jacking system

and even a left-side fuel filler for quickest accessibility at that particular track (versus the right-hand access required at most other venues, including Le Mans and Sebring).

But another roadblock would impede the Grand Sport's racing career. Irked by press reports that Chevy was racing again, GM management told Knudsen to cease and desist his competition efforts or risk losing an annual bonus equal to his entire yearly salary. While his resolve to race was determined, money ultimately talked and Knudsen listened, withdrawing all his previous support. The two roadsters were unceremoniously moved to a company warehouse for storage.

Yet, as it turned out, there was still some life left in the Grand Sport. Further rules changes and advancing age conspired to limit the competitiveness of the five existing racers, and some of the private parties who'd been involved with the GS in 1963 were being pulled off in other directions. This led to a rather confusing series of ownership changes among the hardy quintet. The three coupes, which Chevy had repurchased in preparation for Nassau, were sold—one to Jim Hall, the others to John Mecom, Jr.—unchanged except for the substitution of iron-block engines for the all-aluminum

powerplants. Mecom then sold one of his coupes, the original Grady Davis car, to Delmo Johnson of Dallas. Johnson entered it in the late-1964 revival of the legendary Mexican Road Race, then fitted a big-block Mark IV engine for Sebring in '65, but the car fared poorly on both occasions.

Hall's car, chassis 005, soon wound up in the hands of Roger Penske, who'd retired from driving after Nassau to build his own racing team. Penske decided to overhaul this car, with modifications to the gearbox, rear end, and wheels among the changes, intending to enter it at the Bahamas speed weeks in late 1964. With engine preparation by Traco Engineering, the Penske GS won the Tourist Trophy, beating back a prototype 427 Cobra and John Mecom's other GS, which was driven by Jack Saunders.

Penske then sold this winningest of Grand Sports to friend and fellow Philadelphian George Wintersteen, who had it prepped for Sebring '65. The one major engineering change was a stroke shortened an eighth of an inch, an adjustment that scaled displacement back to 365 cid on an engine again tweaked by Traco. Driven by Wintersteen, Peter Goetz, and Ed Diehl, the car weathered 12 rain-soaked hours to finish 14th overall and second in the prototype category despite

completing two fewer laps than the year previous. Wintersteen then sold the car, sans engine, to a New York collector.

Early in 1966, the aforementioned two roadsters were taken out of storage and sold to Penske, who engaged Californian Dick Guldstrand to prepare one of them, chassis 002, for Sebring. Guldstrand, renowned for the racing magic he works on Corvettes, fitted a 427 Mark IV engine, tried aluminum heads (iron ones were substituted for the actual race), and made minor suspension changes. He then agreed to a co-drive with Dick Thompson, but the car retired due to engine trouble after five hours.

Soon afterward, Wintersteen purchased Penske's other newly acquired roadster. With big-block power and other modifications, this car, chassis 001, appeared in several East Coast events during 1966 but never finished high enough to leave Wintersteen in contention for points. Wintersteen sold this car the following year, much to his later regret. Roadster 002 was subsequently acquired by none other than John Mecom, Jr.

With that, the Corvette Grand Sport finally and completely passed into racing history. While the battle to make the car into a competitive racer had been won, the war against GM management and its adherence to the AMA's self-imposed prohibition would remain a losing cause. Still, just seeing the car through development and watching it fare well against the likes of Ford and its Shelby Cobra proved to be a vital moral victory for Duntov and his engineers, as well as the other true believers at Chevrolet and GM who remained committed to racing.

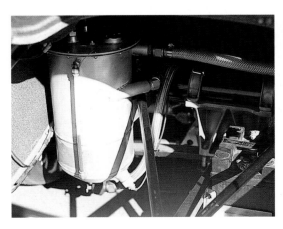

Zora Arkus-Duntov, Corvette chief engineer since 1955, defied GM's anti-racing policy in 1962 by surreptitiously building five competition Grand Sports based on the new-for-'63 Sting Ray. All survive today. This coupe is one of three (chassis no. 003). Grand Sports contested long-distance races at Watkins Glen, Sebring, and Nassau.

Two Grand Sports were built as roadsters for races requiring that body style. The GS was intended to dethrone Carroll Shelby's Cobra as king of production sports-car racing, but angry GM managers prevented that by abruptly canceling the project in 1963. The wily Duntov, however, had the cars sold to favored private owners, who raced them through 1966. Though Grand Sports looked much like showroom Sting Rays, their construction and mechanicals were far more exotic.

PART 1 1968-1977

Nineteen sixty-eight would prove to be among the most turbulent years in U.S. history: The war in Vietnam raged on, with over a half-million U.S. troops stationed in Southeast Asia. Meanwhile, protests railed against the war at home, with universities being held under siege by antiwar activists, and riots erupting at the 1968 Democratic convention in Chicago. Civil rights leader Dr. Martin Luther King, Jr. and presidential hopeful Robert F. Kennedy fell to assassins' bullets; King's death would fuel the explosive flames of racial insurrection in 100 cities across America, making for a "long hot summer." The women's rights movement was beginning to take hold, as was the budding sexual revolution. Drug experimentation exploded on the nation's campuses, and Richard Nixon edged out Hubert H. Humphrey in his bid for the presidency.

Amid all this tumult, a new Corvette was released for model year 1968 that would prove to be nearly as controversial as the times

The Sting Ray had barely hit the road when Bill Mitchell and his GM colleagues started planning its replacement. These sketches from early 1964 point the way to the eventual C3 "Shark."

The so-called Shark was spawned during one of the most troubled periods in America. Against all odds the C3 Corvette carried on through war, civil unrest, burgeoning federal safety guidelines, fuel economy and pollution regulations, oil embargoes, rising fuel and insurance costs, runaway inflation, and a lingering recession. To the credit of its corporate caretakers, the Corvette prospered through these uncertain times despite remaining in its same basic form for a whopping 15 years. The motoring press may have remained nonplussed, but America sure loved the Shark.

themselves. The so-called "Shark" generation was a very different sort of sports car than its predecessors—what was a dual-purpose race-and-ride machine had evolved into more of a plush and powerful boulevard cruiser. Critics would blast the initial C3 offering for its excessive styling, increased bulk, and carryover platform—it certainly was not the substantial leap forward 'Vette fans had hoped for.

Then again, the much-revered C2 Sting Ray was a tough act to follow. It had literally remade Corvette's image, so it was logical to expect that an all-new incarnation would be another forward-looking trendsetter. Enthusiasts were perhaps hoping for a mid-engine car, as had been rumored since 1958—or maybe a rear-engine design based on the compact Corvair, something like Bill Mitchell's exhilarating Monza GT and SS show cars. But for a variety of reasons, none of these ideas came to pass.

Though initially flawed, the '68, like earlier Corvettes, would

improve and mature into a car precisely right for its time, and would run in its basic form all the way through 1982—a full 15 model years. Though the C3 would weather these changing times and emerge victorious, it would not be without a struggle, particularly in the early-to-mid-1970's. Engineers at the time were scrambling to meet newly mandated federal regulations for auto safety, fuel economy, and tailpipe emissions. Meanwhile, skyrocketing gasoline prices and performance-car insurance premiums—along with a pronounced and prolonged economic downturn coupled with spiraling inflation—made owning such cars expensive. All this resulted in a diminishing sports-car market that certainly tested Chevrolet's marketing mettle. Yet even with these factors conspiring against it, the Corvette remained anything but dull.

Traditionally, automakers begin working on new designs even before the old ones go on sale, and so it was with the '68 Corvette. The Sting Ray's second year, 1964, was pivotal to C3 development in that it ushered in two new kinds of American performance autos: the big-engine mid-size "muscle car" exemplified by the Pontiac GTO, and the playful "ponycar" as pioneered by Lee Iacocca's Ford Mustang. Both concepts proved to be enormously popular, and they inspired a horde of imitators. By 1967, the market was awash in

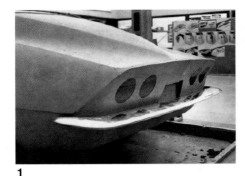

1

2

3

4

muscle machines like the Olds 4-4-2, Dodge Charger, and Mercury Cyclone, as well as Mustang clones such as the Plymouth Barracuda and Mercury Cougar.

Chevrolet offered its own pavement burners in the form of the intermediate Chevelle SS 396, turbocharged versions of the compact Corvair, and its own ponycar, the new Camaro. Even the full-size Impala could be equipped for sports-car-like 0–60-mph times. Significantly, these new Chevys offered high performance in packages that were more accommodating than the Corvette and sold for less money. Clearly a new model would have to offer more than straight-line speed to remain a solid value compared to these bargain-priced contenders.

European automakers, on the other hand, were upping the ante on the higher end of the sports-car spectrum. The Italian makes in particular were offering sports and GT cars that were considerably more sophisticated than the Corvette, albeit at higher prices. The leading-edge mechanicals and exotic style of cars like the mid-engine Lamborghini Miura made the Corvette and its traditional front-engine/rear-drive formula seem dated. To Bill Mitchell, Zora Arkus-Duntov, and the Chevrolet Engineering Center under Frank Winchell, the Miura and its ilk represented a challenge that could not go unanswered.

As a result, the division estab-

5

1-4. A Sting Ray-like "boattail" roofline was a persistent theme in early C3 clay models. These are from October 1964. **5.** Bill Mitchell established basic lower-body forms early on—purposely exaggerated in this concept sketch.

lished a friendly competition among several departments to develop the new 'Vette, all of which envisioned a far more radical car than the one that would ultimately come to pass. Introduction was targeted for 1967, and there were at least two separate lines of development. Significantly, both of these assumed the mid/rear-engine format that had fascinated Corvette planners since before the stillborn Corvair-based proposals of the early Sixties.

By 1965, when work toward a new Corvette was well underway, the Corvair had matured into a unique, well-rounded little car. Its original swing-axle rear suspension and quirky handling had given way to a more capable independent rear suspension and equally competent cornering prowess. Corvair's design similarity with the honored

Porsche 356 and 911 was obvious, and its technology intrigued Corvette stylists and engineers alike. Winchell's group conjured up an advanced, very compact design with a Lotus-type backbone frame, all-independent suspension, and a 327-cubic-inch V-8 in the rear, driving a modified version of the Pontiac Tempest's rear transaxle. But with an aft-weight bias around 70 percent, handling would prove to be perilous at best, making the concept unworkable.

A separate group under Zora Arkus-Duntov took a slightly different approach: a true mid-engine design with a big-block Mark IV motor riding just ahead of the rear

wheels. The radiator was placed in the extreme rear behind the engine; a pair of fans provided low-speed cooling via a "forced draft" effect.

Duntov's group also devised a shape for their car's fiberglass body, preparing a couple of small-scale models in 1965. These married the basic front-end theme of that year's experimental Mako Shark II concept to a curvy midsection and a long, squarish tail. Beltlines swept sharply upward to a "flying buttress" rear roofline like that found on Porsche's mid-engine 904 sports-racer, with a shallow, vertically set backlight that was flanked by long, gracefully tapered C-pillars.

1

2

3

Bill Mitchell's crew had their own ideas, producing a powerful-looking full-size mock-up that was dominated by a very pointy front, a severe "ducktail," a tapered "boat-tail" roofline along the lines of the Sting Ray fastback, and bulging, fully skirted rear fenders with vertical air slots in their leading edges. The bulky mid-mounted V-8 made a rear window useless, so a rear-facing periscope was ultimately devised, which was faired into the forward portion of the roof.

Ultimately, however, a rear- or mid-engine Corvette demanded mechanical components that just didn't exist at GM. The company had yet to produce a transaxle able to withstand the torque of a high-power V-8, and the design and tooling expenses required to develop one that would be used only in a low-volume model would

have sent Corvette prices to the moon.

But if the new Corvette couldn't entice enthusiasts with leading-edge technology, Mitchell and company would have to lure them with exotic styling. Enter Mako Shark II, one of the most famous concept cars of all time.

On the auto-show circuit, the Mako II was quickly recognized for what it was: a trial balloon for the next-generation Corvette. As if to support that view, the original static Mako II mock-up first shown in April was retired during 1965 and replaced on the show circuit by a fully operational version. Completed in October of that year, this second Mako II was less radical than the first and thus more easily produced.

Executed under Mitchell's direction by young Larry Shinoda, the

Mako II had been initiated in early 1964, more than a year before the first show model appeared. Although adaptable to either front- or rear-engine positioning, its basic design became the take-off point for a new front-engine "theme car" as an alternative to the more radical mid-engine shapes proposed by Duntov and the Advanced Design studios. Once the mid-engine format was abandoned, the Shinoda/Mitchell car was sent to Chevrolet Styling under David Holls, where Henry Haga's studio adapted it for production on the existing Sting Ray chassis.

As it turned out, the new 'Vette wouldn't be all that different beneath its skin from the Sting Ray, but Chevy was betting that a sexy new shell and higher-performance engines would be enough to keep the car on its upward sales course.

Targa convertible reflected similar thinking.

Unfortunately for Holls, Haga, and Duntov, the Mako II's basic shape proved problematic, and the production styling job didn't go as smoothly or as quickly as expected. For one thing, the new design turned out to have excessive front-end lift at high speed, which seriously compromised the car's stability. A rear spoiler was added to help keep the tail down, but this only lifted the nose more. Additional wind tunnel work produced functional front-fender louvers that relieved pressure buildup within the engine

found to be marginal in hot weather, especially with the air conditioning on—a trait that would hamper the C3 throughout its run.

One Mako II feature that survived to production virtually intact—for better or worse—was a vacuum-operated flip-up panel that concealed the windshield wipers. Hidden headlamps continued but were now simple flip-up assemblies operated via engine vacuum, rather than the Sting Ray's electric rotating hardware. An external-opening trunklid was still conspicuously absent from both body styles, but the convertible retained Corvette's

4

5

The result was much like the Mako II from the beltline down, except for softer, less extreme contours. It also adopted the "sugar scoop" roof treatment from the mid-engine models designed by the Duntov group. Chevy may simply have been seeking a different look or perhaps better rearward vision than in the Sting Ray fastback. In any case, it was intended from the beginning that the vertical backlight—as well as that portion of the roof above the seats—be removable. Though the traditional Corvette convertible would continue, Chevy felt this new coupe configuration—really a semi-convertible—would appeal just as much to the open-air crowd while offering the better weather protection and structural rigidity associated with closed body types. Porsche's 911/912

compartment at speed and also led to a small "chin" spoiler located below the grille to direct air around the car instead of beneath it.

What's more, the removable Targa-style roof had problems of its own. Originally conceived as a single piece of fiberglass, production engineers found that the resulting body/frame combination wasn't stiff enough in torsion to prevent creaks and groans in the coachwork. Accordingly, they added a longitudinal support bar between the windshield header and the roof's fixed rear section, thus creating the first T-top roof.

The most serious deficit of the Mako-inspired styling was poor engine cooling, especially with the big-block powerplants carried over from the Sting Ray. With the new version's narrow engine bay and shallow grille, radiator air flow was

traditional rear-hinged top cover, and an accessory hardtop was designed to match the new Shark styling.

Unfortunately, the C3 'Vette suffered from development problems and introduction was postponed from 1967 to 1968. It was probably just as well. Although the government's first safety and emissions standards took effect nationwide with the '68 model year, Chevy would doubtless have seen to it that the engineering of an all-new '67 model reflected the new standards. As it was, the delay took some of the pressure off of harried engineers who had to worry about government scrutiny of the five other higher-selling model lines in the 1967-68 Chevrolet fleet.

As was the case with the first Sting Ray, powertrains for the new 1968 model were largely retained from the previous generation. The one significant exception was substitution of GM's new three-speed Turbo Hydra-Matic transmission for the old two-speed Powerglide automatic. Elsewhere, the car's battery was relocated behind the seats to improve weight distribution and to provide added under-hood room. Side vent windows were eliminated in favor of a new fresh-air "Astro Ventilation" system. Shoulder belts, previously an added-cost option were included at no charge on coupes. Other new features for 1968 accentuated the Corvette's GT leanings, and included an electric rear-window defroster, speed warning indicator, AM/FM stereo radio, and a futuristic fiber-optic light monitoring system.

Higher spring rates were calculated to reduce fore/aft pitching, especially under hard acceleration. This also served to lower the rear roll center and was nicely complemented by newly standard seven-inch-wide wheels, an inch broader than before, wearing low-profile

for abandoning its sports-car purity. The car was also given low marks in the press for its scarce luggage space, awkward ingress/egress, and poor instrument placement, and reviewers found the car's new interior ventilation system to be lacking. The Corvette's fit and finish and overall build quality were judged to be abysmal, and even the new T-top was greeted with lukewarm response.

Still, the motoring press thought highly of the latest Corvette's straight-line performance, though some scribes felt the big 435-horsepower 427 was too brutish a beast, though the 300- and 350-bhp small-blocks impressed as much as ever. The Muncie four-speed manual transmission and the new Turbo Hydra-Matic also garnered praise. As for handling, the press seemed to like the skidpad and slalom numbers they got but not the way the car felt generating them. Several

reported a top speed of 128 mph, a standing quarter-mile of 15.6 seconds at 92 mph, and 0–60-mph acceleration of 7.7 seconds. Fuel economy, however, was pegged at a pitiful 11–15 mpg for a cruising range of only 220–300 miles from the 20-gallon tank. Big-block cars were even thirstier—but faster, of course. *Car and Driver,* running a 400-bhp 427 coupe, hit 60 mph in 5.7 seconds and posted a 14.1-second quarter mile at a blazing 102 mph.

The car's paltry cruising range couldn't really be considered as much of a liability, however, since with only 6.7 cubic feet of cargo space available, the car wasn't exactly outfitted for long-distance driving. Further, a newly tighter cabin included accordingly tighter seats with fixed backrests raked much farther back than in the Sting Ray to accommodate the Shark's two-inch lower roofline. The result-

1

F70 × 15 tires. With these modifications and the resulting wider track dimensions (now 58.7/59.4 inches front/rear), the '68 hugged the pavement even better than did the Sting Ray, though at the expense of a perceptibly harsher ride.

Alas, the new Corvette was welcomed with mixed reviews. To many, its styling was wretchedly excessive and bloated (its weight had ballooned by some 150 pounds), and the car was criticized

complaints were made about the harder ride, and nobody much liked the power steering and brakes.

But despite its flaws, the '68 Corvette remained an exhilarating ride. It had plenty of power even in small-block form, and its all-independent suspension, if not exactly state-of-the-art, was certainly more than adequate. Testing a 350-bhp 327 roadster with the four-speed and 3.70:1 final drive, *Road & Track*

ing laidback stance conspired with a high cowl to give the impression of being in a bathtub. A long, low nose that disappeared somewhere near the horizon made parallel parking an adventure.

Yet for all the problems and poor reviews, more people bought Corvettes than ever before; model-year sales set a new record at 28,566 units, some 5000 up on the final Sting Ray. Part of this was due to prices that remained competitive at $4320 for the ragtop and $4663 for the coupe.

Reflecting its popularity, the new Corvette was chosen Best All-Around Car in *Car and Driver*'s annual reader's poll (the '67 Sting Ray had been likewise honored), as well as Best Sports/GT Car Over 3000cc.

As they usually are the year after a major model introduction, changes for 1969 were minor, made mostly to remedy problems noted by owners and the motoring media. For starters, the steering-wheel diameter was trimmed an inch for more under-rim thigh clearance, and Duntov pushed through a $120,000 tooling change for the inner door panels to open up a half-inch per side in extra shoulder width. Interior door handles and control knobs were redesigned for safety's sake. The previous dash-

Exterior alterations were likewise minimal; the most obvious was the return of the Stingray designation (now spelled as one word) in script over the front-fender louvers. Another change involved the door handles. New single-lever door-handles replaced the conventional chrome handgrips with thumb-operated pushbuttons. A new head-light washer system was added, and windshield-washer jets were moved to the wiper arms. The already over-engineered hidden-wiper arrangement became even more complex with the addition of an override switch that allowed the vacuum-operated panel to be left up in freezing weather. At the rear, the previously separate backup lights were incorporated with the inboard taillamps. The frame was stiffened

dropped a quarter point in each case—to 10.25:1 and 11.0:1, respectively. Significantly, peak power engine speed was also lower by 200 rpm, to 4800 and 5600 rpm, respectively.

The big-block 427s returned unchanged, with ratings of 390 to 435 horsepower. The special aluminum-head L88—still rated at a modest 430 bhp—remained among them, though its towering $1032 price attracted just 116 buyers.

Two new performance options were announced for 1969: One was extremely rare—with only two installed—the other was ostensibly available but put back a year. The former was RPO ZL1, which was essentially the mighty big-block L88 with all-aluminum construction plus numerous other modifications

1. The Astro-Vette toured major auto shows in 1968, the year the C3 debuted. Designers went wild with basic Shark themes. **2-3.** They also kept tinkering with approved production styling, as on this 1967 work-out. Note the domed hood, side-exit exhausts, and extended tail.

mounted ignition switch moved to the steering column, where it combined with the newly mandated column lock for additional security. A warning light was added to advise the driver that the pop-up headlights hadn't popped up completely. Attempts were also made to increase Astro Ventilation flow volume, but the system was still judged to be inadequate. Finally, a flexible dash-mounted three-section map pocket was included to help make up for the lack of a proper glovebox.

to reduce body shake and standard rim width went up another inch—to eight—for improved handling.

Engine alterations, on the other hand, were more obvious, seeing as how carmakers were in the second year of federally mandated—and still relatively straightforward—emission controls. The famed Chevy small-block was stroked about a quarter-inch to 3.48 inches, which boosted displacement from 327 to 350 cubic inches on the same 4.00-inch bore. Corvette offered 300- and 350-bhp versions, the same ratings as their 1968 equivalents but with compression

including dry-sump lubrication. Devised for the British-built McLarens that would dominate the SCCA's Canadian-American Challenge Cup series, this engine had the same compression and carburetion as the L88 but weighed 100 pounds less. It also carried the same 430-bhp rating, but that was a joke; over-the-counter racing versions were reportedly good for 585 bhp. It lurked beneath a special domed hood shared with the L88 (RPO ZL2) incorporating an air intake at the high-pressure area near the base of the windshield.

Of course, Duntov hadn't dismissed the potential of small-block power. Listed for '69 but not available until 1970 (owing to development and manufacturing problems) was a special solid-lifter version of

1

2

the new 350. Coded LT1, it was right in line with Duntov's longtime goal of minimizing weight in a performance car growing heavier with every newly added creature comfort. Unlike tamer small blocks, the LT1 had more radical cam timing with more generous valve overlap, used the big-block engines' hefty 2.5-inch-diameter exhaust system, breathed through the same 850-cfm Holley carb fitted to the L88/ZL1, and came with transistorized ignition. The result was 370 bhp at

6000 rpm and 380 pound-feet of torque at 4000 rpm. It was offered only with a four-speed manual transmission, and a Corvette so equipped typically streaked through the standing quarter-mile in 14.2 seconds at 102 mph. Visual identification was subtle—just the special domed hood with perimeter striping and discreet "LT1" lettering—but there was no mistaking the rap-rap exhaust or the distinct tapping of those mechanical lifters.

Despite continued criticism from

the enthusiast press for its dismal build quality, styling eccentricities, and overall lack of finesse, Corvette sales took a vertical leap for '69, rising by more than 10,000 units to 38,762—a record that wouldn't be broken until 1976.

Back at the racetracks, with Ford's Cobras being retired from racing, the Corvette reasserted its SCCA dominance in 1969. Chevrolet engineer Jerry Thompson and driver Tony DeLorenzo teamed up to take that year's A-Production

1. Besides many detail improvements for 1969, the Shark became a Stingray, gaining fender namescript with the same one-word spelling Bill Mitchell had used for his 1959-60 race car. **2.** Also for '69, Miitchell's crew devised the Aero Coupe show car with integral rear spoiler and a single lift-off roof panel instead of a T-roof. "Cheese grater" front fender vents forecast a 1970 change. The domed hood and side-exit exhausts here were similar but not identical to those available with 1969 big-block V-8 options.

national championship. Meanwhile, Allan Barker captured the '69 B-Production crown and would do so for the next three seasons.

While the rumor mongers continued to speculate about a possible rear- or mid-engine model being readied for the early 1970s, forces were gathering that would preclude anything really new for some time—even a new front-engine design for that matter. Chevrolet, therefore, issued another evolutionary Stingray for 1970. A UAW strike forced a two-month extension of '69 production, which gave Chevy the time it needed to make the '70 a better-built Corvette, and was doubtless a factor in 1969's record volume. But the strike also delayed the '70s from reaching dealer showrooms until February, which pushed Corvette sales to its lowest point since 1962—a mere 17,316 units.

Cosmetic changes for the abbreviated 1970 model year were slight. The extreme bodyside tuck-under was found to be susceptible to stone damage, so Chevy flared the aft portions of each wheel opening, which helped somewhat. The grille went from horizontal bars to a fine eggcrate pattern. (The real radiator air intakes, Duntov's original slots, were on the car's underside.) The eggcrate also appeared on the front fenders in place of the previous four "gills." Front parking lamps switched from small, round units to rectangular fixtures with clear lenses and amber bulbs. The dual exhaust outlets also shifted from round to rectangular.

Inside the cabin, seats were reshaped for better lateral support, more headroom, and easier access to the trunk. Shoulder belts, still separate from the lap belts, got inertia storage reels, thus ending some cockpit clutter. A redoubtable custom trim package was added to the options list that offered full cut-pile carpeting and fake wood trim on the console and doors.

Engines were again the main Corvette news for 1970. The LT1 was now genuinely available, though at a hefty $447.50. Lesser 350s returned unchanged. The mighty L88 and ZL1 weren't even theoretically offered, though Chevy continued to sell Can-Am engines to bona fide teams. Instead, big-block buyers got a 427 stroked out to a full 4.00 inches and 454 cid. Two versions were listed, one real, the other not. The former, RPO LS5, offered hydraulic lifters, 10.25:1 compression, single four-barrel carb, 390 bhp at 4800 rpm, and a massive 500 pounds-feet of torque. Listed but never officially sold was RPO LS7, with aluminum heads, mechanical lifters, 11.25:1 compression, a higher-lift cam, and transistorized ignition. Depending on the source, output was given at either 460 or 465 bhp. *Sports Car Graphic* tested an LS7 'Vette and reported a standing quarter-mile of 13.8 seconds at 108 mph.

Like the previous year's enlarged small-block engine, a bigger big-block was offered in response to stricter emissions requirements. Also like the 350, the 454 produced less power per cubic inch than its predecessor, but a lower peak power speed gave it somewhat more torque, and thus more flexibility, at lower rpm. *Road & Track* tried an LS5 with an automatic and obtained 7.0 seconds for the 0–60-mph run, a 15.0-second quarter-mile at 93 mph, and a top speed of 144 mph. On the down side, testers found the suspension suffered from both excessive harshness over irregular surfaces and a certain floatiness at speed.

Not that these criticisms mattered much, because 1970 would mark the end for big-inch, big-power Corvettes in the traditional mold. Besides skyrocketing insurance rates and fast-falling demand for sporty cars, Chevy's top performance machines were doomed by GM president Ed Cole's desire to eliminate low-volume options. He also dictated that all engines be retuned to run on 91-octane fuel, anticipating the need for catalytic converters to meet ever-tightening emissions limits.

Still, the Corvette repeated as SCCA A-Production champ in 1970, with a young John Greenwood taking the honors. He would do so again the following year, then teamed up with comedian Dick Smothers to place first in the GT class at Sebring in 1972.

1

As the Seventies wore on and the engineers came to grips with the flurry of federal regulations before them, the Corvette would develop into a more balanced—though tamer—performer. To this end, 1971's base small-block engine ran on mild 8:5:1 compression and was down to 270 bhp at 4800 rpm; the LT1 withered to 9.0:1 and 330 bhp. These respective compression numbers also applied to a brace of 454s. The LS5 came in with 365 bhp at 4800 rpm, and a new aluminum-head big-block called LS6 boasted 425 bhp at 5600 rpm. Clearly, '71 Corvette engines weren't weak. If they seemed so at the time, it was only in relation to the prodigious power outputs enthusiasts had grown used to in the previously unregulated era of muscle cars.

The ZR1 option available exclusively with the LT1 is significant for engineering, though not many saw production. It was a special racing package that included the solid-lifter small-block engine, heavy-duty four-speed transmission, power brakes, aluminum radiator, and a revised suspension with special springs, shocks, stabilizer bar, and spindle-strut shafts. Since it was competition equipment, the ZR1 could not be ordered with power windows, power steering, air conditioning, a rear-window defogger, wheel covers, or a radio. A similar ZR2 package was listed for the big LS6 engine and was just as rare.

Otherwise, Corvette again marked time for '71. Styling and equipment changes were virtually

nonexistent, and no real tampering was called for. Prices bumped up a bit to $5259 and $5496 for the convertible and coupe, respectively. With supplies healthy again after the UAW strike, sales made a satisfying recovery, moving up to 21,801 units for the model year. The coupe had taken a slight lead over the convertible in 1969, perhaps reflecting the T-top model's greater all-weather versatility.

Nineteen seventy-two was yet another stand-pat year, except that performance was being further muted as engines bore the full brunt of emissions-lowering tuning. Furthermore, all manufacturers started quoting engine outputs in the new SAE "net" measure that year, figures that were always lower than the "gross" numbers issued

2

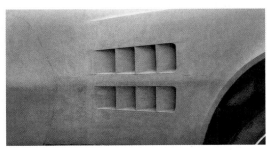

3

4

5

Corvette designers have always been passionate about their car and really sweat the details. **2-5.** As proof, consider these late-1964 workouts for the shape and placement of the Shark's front-fender vents. And these were just a few of the myriad ideas tried. **1.** Even more were needed for the 1970 model's scheduled minor facelift, though the treatment in this late-'68 photo got a pass.

previously. Net horsepower reflected power losses caused by mandatory equipment such as the water pump, alternator, power-steering pump, mufflers, and air cleaner, and were thus more realistic. (GM had begun listing both net and gross figures in 1971, possibly to dampen the blow of suddenly lower power figures that would appear for '72.) The result was that advertised engine outputs were drastically reduced, partly due to steadily decreasing compression ratios, but mostly due to the new net ratings.

There were also fewer engines offered for 1972, the casulty being the top-rated LS6 big block. The LT1 small block eased from 275 net bhp to 255 in this, its final year. At least it could finally be ordered with air conditioning. Chevy engi-

neers had been reluctant to offer this combination, fearing the LT1's high revving ability would pull the A/C belts off their pulleys; to help counter this tendency, tachometers on cars so equipped were redlined at 5600 rpm rather than 6500 rpm.

Refinements for '72 included a redesigned center console that deleted the useful but distracting fiber-optic light monitors, and the previously optional anti-theft alarm system was made standard in recognition of the 'Vette's popularity among car thieves. Sales continued crawling back upward, tacking on nearly 5200 units for a model year total of 26,994.

At that year's 24 Hours of Daytona, Tony DeLorenzo and Don Yenko scored another GT victory for the Corvette while finishing a

surprising fourth overall. John Greenwood took his 'Vette on to LeMans, where he qualified faster than any other GT contender. Unfortunately a blown engine during the race (he was leading the class at the time) forced him out of the running.

For 1973, the coupe exchanged its removable backlight for fixed glass, but a new nose treatment, shared with the convertible, was more obvious—it was the first major appearance change since the 1968 redesign. In styling at least, technology was beginning to find answers to federal mandates, and the Corvette had an ingenious solution for the new five-mile-per-hour front-impact protection rule applied

continued on page 178

1

2

3

The Shark almost had a mid-engine layout, and Chevy kept toying with the idea for many years. **1.** A smaller Camaro-like design was one of many proposed "next Corvettes" circa 1975. **2.** Project XP-882 was revealed in 1970. **3-4.** Descended from XP-882, the Aerovette came close to production for 1980.

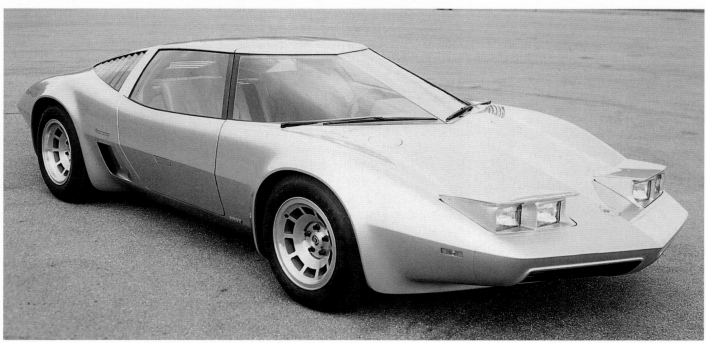

4

1

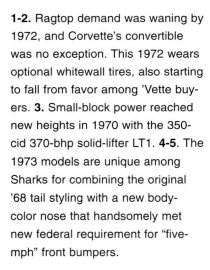

3

2

1-2. Ragtop demand was waning by 1972, and Corvette's convertible was no exception. This 1972 wears optional whitewall tires, also starting to fall from favor among 'Vette buyers. **3.** Small-block power reached new heights in 1970 with the 350-cid 370-bhp solid-lifter LT1. **4-5.** The 1973 models are unique among Sharks for combining the original '68 tail styling with a new body-color nose that handsomely met new federal requirement for "five-mph" front bumpers.

to all automobiles that year. A steel bumper was covered by deformable urethane plastic that was matched to the body color. It added only about two inches to overall length and 35 pounds to curb weight. Even better, it would bounce back to its intended shape after most any kind of parking-lot bump. Better still, it looked terrific.

Another mandated safety feature was the addition a longitudinal steel beam in each door to help protect occupants in side impacts. Standard radial-ply tires weren't yet federally mandated, but they were nevertheless included for '73. While tests

showed the new model demonstrating longer stopping distances despite unchanged brakes, lower lateral-G figures on the skidpad, and carried a maximum speed rating of "only" 120 mph versus 140 for the bias-belteds, radials did offer some real advantages for the Corvette. These included longer tread wear, better wet-weather grip, and added stability at speed.

Once again, federal regulations emasculated the car a bit more for 1973. A mechanical-lifter engine was missing from the line for the first time since 1956. This left a choice of the three hydraulic-lifter

units: the base 350, RPO L48, at a rated 190 bhp; an uprated L82 small block with 250 bhp; and a solitary 454 called LS4, which was advertised at 270 bhp. Though down on power compared to previous models, the '73 could run the quarter-mile in the mid-15-second range, virtually the same as cars costing nearly twice as much, such as the Porsche 911E or DeTomaso Pantera.

Still, if the '73 wasn't as fast and didn't handle quite as well as previous Corvettes, it was notably more civilized. Engine noise was reduced by adding extra insulation at strategic points. Body mounts were changed to a rubber/steel type that helped eliminate annoying vibrations. The problem-prone pop-up wiper panel was replaced by a simple rear-hood extension. The coupe's fixed rear window added a few inches to trunk space, since there was no longer a need for the removable panel's stowage receptacle. Handsome aluminum wheels were a new option that served both form and function, though structural problems forced a recall of the first 800 sets. A later aluminum wheel employed similar styling.

The 1974 model year proved to be a dismal year for motorists in general and auto enthusiasts in particular. This was the year the Organization of Petroleum Exporting Countries (OPEC) in the Middle East turned off its pipelines and touched off a global energy crisis. Gas prices soared as dwindling supplies had motorists waiting in long lines at the pumps; some areas even had to resort to rationing. Suddenly, big, heavy, and fuel-thirsty cars seemed out of step with the times. Fortunately, the oil embargo didn't last long, though its effects continue to be felt to this day.

Providing instant identification for the 1974 model was a new body-color rear-end treatment made to comply with a new five-mph rear-impact standard. Sheathed in urethane like last year's front-bumper revision, the new ensemble conferred a smoother, more integrated look, and though it tapered downward instead of upward like the previous Kammtype tail, it didn't seem to harm aerodynamics. The bumper was a two-piece affair with a visible seam in the middle of its plastic cover; a seamless one-piece unit would be substituted from 1975 on.

In many ways, 1974 was the end of an era for the Corvette. Engines, for example, would henceforth be tuned to run only on unleaded gas—aided by the industry's wholesale switch to catalytic converters for 1975. Genuine dual exhausts would give way to separate manifolds routed to a single catalytic converter, then on to separate pipes and mufflers. What's more, this was also the last year for the Corvette's big-block V-8.

Elsewhere, it was the same old story: detail changes, most for the better. The market's growing preference for performance automatic transmissions yielded a sturdier Turbo-Hydra-Matic designated M40. Shoulder belts, a fixture since '71, were combined with the lap belts into a single three-point harness, and the inertia-reel setup was changed somewhat. The rearview mirror became wider; radiator efficiency improved; the burglar alarm switch was moved from the rear of the car to the left front fender; and the power steering pump was made more durable via the use of magnets, added to attract fluid debris.

New for '74 was one of the all-time bargains in Corvette performance packages: the RPO FE7 Gymkhana Suspension, which cost a mere seven bucks. FE7 was little more than higher-rate springs and firmer, specially calibrated shocks—the tried-and-true formula used since the mid-Sixties in Chevy's popular F41 package—but it improved handling all out of proportion to its paltry price. The F41 itself, which had begun with the Z06 racing option back in 1963, was still around in RPO Z07 and included heavy-duty brakes.

While the Shark never seemed as nimble as the Sting Ray, and the mid-Seventies small-block cars were nowhere near as brutal as the big-block 'Vettes that came before them, the '74 remained satisfyingly quick. The 250-bhp L82 could take you from 0 to 60 mph in about 7.5 seconds and on to 125 mph while averaging about 14–15 mpg. The '74 also marked a new high for Corvette luxury, which by that point was no longer the contradiction in terms it once was. If still a bit noisy, the Corvette had evolved into a very refined grand touring car with plenty of creature comforts and far greater reliability than most of its more-exotic competition.

The '74 model defied industry sales trends by selling at or near its

1

best-ever levels at a time when it should have done anything but, given the higher cost of gasoline and insurance, the sagging economy, and emasculated powertrains. Sales were up again on the year, hitting 37,502 units. Though the energy crisis would put a temporary damper on racing activities in 1974, things were more or less back to normal on the nation's tracks the following year, and the Corvette would continue to shine in SCCA competition throughout the remainder of the Seventies.

The division stayed with the status quo again for 1975, when the only physical change was a pair of small extrusions with black pads for each bumper as additional parking-lot protection. Convertible volume continued to sink, falling to 4629 units for the model year. Convertible demand was on the wane generally, and the government accelerated the trend by threatening to enact safety standards for rollover protection that would have effectively banned fully open cars in the United States after 1975. Ironically the legislation never materialized, but it gave domestic producers the excuse they'd been waiting for to drop slow-selling ragtops, and the romantic 'Vette roadster would disappear like so many others, not to return to the lineup for another decade.

1. Like regular 'Vettes, the Aero Coupe concept got a minor facelift for 1970. Changes included high-mount mirrors, an arrow-shaped hood/nose bulge, and a roof-fairing to house a rearview TV camera. **2-3.** A "taillift" freshened looks on production '74s while meeting a new federal rule for "five-mph" *rear* bumpers. **4-5.** Appearance was all but unchanged for '75.

2

3

4

5

4

The big-block V-8 ostensibly returned, only to be dropped very early in the model run, leaving the small-block L82 as the only engine option. And its power was down as well, to 205 bhp. The base 350 also withered, detuned to a measly 165 bhp. Those ratings might have been even lower had it not been for the catalytic converter, that new and more efficient emissions cleanup device adopted for most 1975 American cars. New for '75 was a breakerless electronic ignition system, accompanied by an electronic (instead of mechanical) tachometer drive. A headlights-on warning buzzer was added per federal dictates.

Though little more was new besides the advertising, Corvette sales continued to climb. The 1975 sales tally rose to within 300 units of the '69 peak at 38,465. The car's hold on the public was such that the old record was decisively smashed the following year, despite the convertible's demise and few changes made to the remaining coupe. Dealers moved 46,558 Corvettes before closing the books on model year 1976, a reflection of the recovering economy and shrinking competition in the Corvette's price/performance class.

Style-wise, the veteran Shark looked nicer than ever for '76. The faux air-extractor vents vanished from the rear deck, rear bumper trim was slightly altered, and a new four-spoke sport steering wheel arrived, though the latter irked some diehard fans because it was borrowed from the subcompact Vega GT.

To the delight of speed freaks, however, horsepower ratings began climbing again on slightly higher compression, again courtesy of the catalytic converter. The L48 gained 15 horses for a total of 180; the L82 went up to 210 bhp. Modified induction also helped. Both engines breathed through an intake that was now in front of and above the radiator instead of at the cowl near the windshield. The change was made to remedy the noise of air being gulped in so close to the passenger compartment. To increase rigidity and reduce heat seepage from the hotter-running engines, a steel subsection was added to the forward body structure.

Unfortunately, Chevrolet had no answer for the sharp inflation that had plagued consumers since the 1973-74 energy crisis, except to

been aging, there was still nothing else quite like the Corvette. There were certainly far fewer Detroit performance cars of any kind by 1976, which was a definite factor in the car's renewed sales strength.

The C3 returned for '77 with only modest modifications. Mechanicals were carried over

leather-rim sport steering wheel was adopted (tilt/telescope adjustment remained optional), along with a new "Smart Switch" steering-column stalk that combined the headlight dimmer and wiper/washer functions with the turn signals. The steering column itself was shortened to permit a more "arms-

1

pass along the higher costs. Though the base price of the 1976 model was $7604.85, a full complement of options and the usual ancillary charges could put it just over 10 grand as delivered. Enthusiast magazines' opinions remained tepid at best. Still, though prices were rising and the Shark may have

unchanged, as the year's tweaks generally aimed for more refined cruising. Inside, the console was redesigned to accept a larger array of Delco audio decks (including an AM/FM/cassette stereo as a first-time option), its instruments were restyled for greater legibility, and climate controls were simplified. A

2

The Shark lost its convertible after 1975, the Stingray name for '77. But Corvette continued to evolve from fire-breathing muscle car to suave *grand tourismo,* abetted by the recent gas crisis, changing buyer tastes, and more federal mandates. Yet for all the change in its character, the Shark was one of the few American performance cars still left, one reason the '77 set yet another Corvette sales record.

out" driving posture; the change also eased entry/exit somewhat. A related modification lengthened the manual transmission lever for easier use of the handbrake. The alarm switch moved again and was now incorporated with the left door-lock button. The rearview mirror also shifted location slightly, and sunvisors were revamped.

Leather upholstery was now standard, and cloth seats with leather bolsters became an extra-cost item. Power steering and brakes were made newly standard, as well.

Outside, the optional rear-deck luggage carrier was reworked so that the T-tops could be carried there instead of in the lidless trunk, where they were less convenient to stow. Glass roof panels were shown

as a new option at the start of the model year, but GM canceled them in a reputed dispute with the supplier over sales rights. The vendor eventually marketed them itself, and Chevy promptly went to another source for 1978. One final exterior change for 1977 would be noted instantly by car spotters: The Stingray nameplate came off the front fenders, replaced by the traditional crossed-flags insignia. The car was again simply called Corvette.

Sales set another new record for the '77 model year at 49,213—which was (and still would be) amazing for a decade-old design. Ironically, while the Corvette was nearly pulled from Chevy's lineup during the heyday of the sports car

in prosperous post-war America, it actually thrived throughout poor economic times, during a period in which the performance-car ranks were dwindling, and despite carrying on with more-modest performance than at the beginning of its run. The increased sales spoke volumes about GM's knack for successfully updating a design to meet changing market conditions without detracting significantly from the car's fundamental appeal.

Though getting on in years, the Shark still had some miles left in it, however. The car would enter its 25th year in 1978, and Chevrolet had some special tricks up its corporate sleeve to help its many fans celebrate the car's silver anniversary with a bang.

Delayed a year by development problems, the new 1968 Corvette was not a Sting Ray, but topped its predecessor's chassis with swoopy new bodies stretching seven inches longer. The convertible returned (opposite, top left) along with a coupe (below) that now incorporated twin lift-off roof panels located by a central "T-bar." The rear window was also removable for convertible-like breeziness.

185

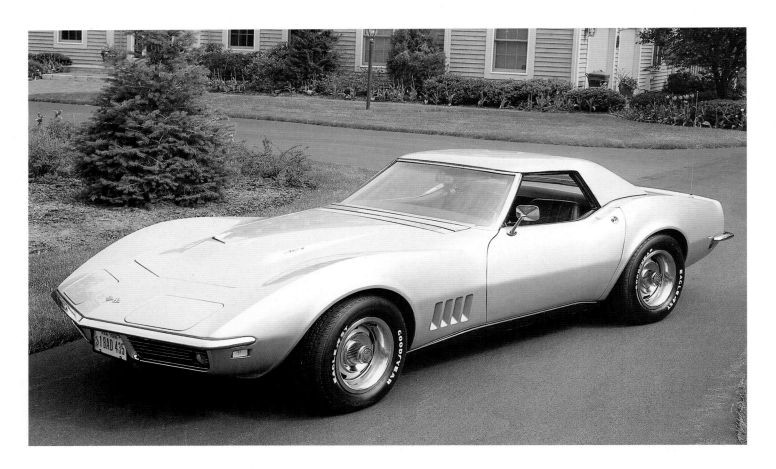

Like previous ragtop 'Vettes, the '68 offered an optional lift-off hardtop, shown here, with vinyl covering available at extra cost. Engines were a rerun of '67, including big-block 427s offering 390, 400, and 435 bhp. As ever, enthusiasts ordered four-speed manual transmission (again in close-ratio and heavy-duty versions), but the optional automatic shifted from elderly two-speed Powerglide to GM's three-speed Turbo Hydra-Matic. Corvette set another sales record as the '68s tallied 28,566 orders, with convertibles again outselling coupes.

Corvette for '69 was again a Stingray—spelled as one word on the front fenders. Optional side exhausts, also shown here, returned after a year's absence. The base small-block V-8 went to 350 cubic inches and 300 or 350 bhp. Among big-block options was a mighty new L88 version with aluminum block and a nominal 430 bhp—though only two were installed. Inside, the dashboard added map pockets to make up for lacking a glovebox, while a smaller steering wheel and thinner door panels opened up a little much-needed space.

188

"Sharks" had hidden headlamps like the earlier Sting Rays but in simple flip-up units instead of rotating pods. Newly hidden were windshield wipers, beneath a power pop-up cowl panel, and exterior door latches, beneath spring-loaded flaps. Another dream-car touch was the standard fiber-optic dashboard monitors that showed when any exterior lamp was burned out. This '69 coupe carries the 435-bhp 427 with triple two-barrel carbs mated to a four-speed manual.

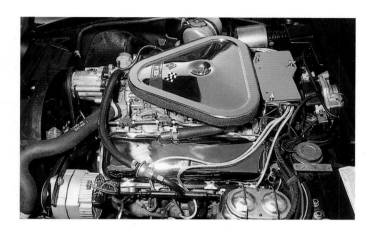

A distinctive new hood bulge was hard to miss on early big-block "Sharks" like this '69 coupe, which also sports optional side exhausts, red-stripe tires instead of whitewalls, and wire-look deluxe wheel covers. Production zoomed to 38,672 for '69, mainly because the run was extended by four months after being interrupted by a brief strike early in the season.

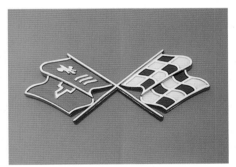

Corvette's 427 big-block became a 454 for 1970. An announced 460-bhp LS6 option was withdrawn, but the LS5 version delivered 390 bhp for just $290 extra. All models got a crosshatch-pattern grille and front-fender vents, plus deeper rear wheel-arch skirts so wheelspin in hard takeoffs wouldn't kick up so much debris. There were subtle refinements inside, too. Base prices stood at $4849 for convertibles like this, $5192 for coupes.

Small-block 1970 Corvettes, like this ragtop, offered 300 bhp standard, 350 optional. Rear-deck vents, a feature since '68, were part of the Shark's flow-through "Astro Ventilation" system, which eliminated door vent windows. Total 'Vette sales this model year were the lowest since 1962 at 17,316, reflecting a production start-up delayed to January 1970.

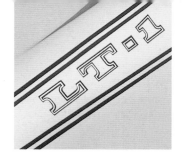

Due to a decrease in compression ratio for 1971, the potent LT1 small block dropped from 370 bhp to 330. Available with the LT1 was a ZR-1 package that included close-ratio four-speed transmission, heavy-duty brakes and cooling, uprated suspension, and big-block-style domed hood. But the ZR-1 package was quite expensive, and few Corvettes were so equipped.

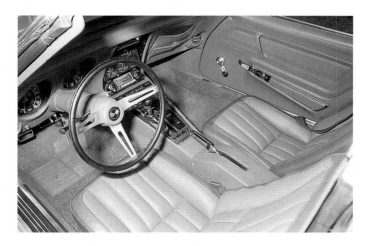

Per GM policy, 1971 'Vette engines were detuned to run on low-lead fuel—save the LS6 454, which belatedly bowed with 425 bhp on premium gas. Installations totaled just 188, including a mere 12 cars like this with a $1747 ZR2 package, basically the ZR1 option with the big-block V-8. This would be the only year for both the LS6 engine and associated ZR2 equipment.

Amber turn-signal lenses were the most noticeable exterior change for 1972, when convertibles like this started at $5296. GM now quoted horsepower in more realistic SAE net terms instead of gross numbers, so small blocks were down to 200 bhp standard, 255 for the LT1 option. Big-blocks were down to 255 bhp standard, 270 for the LS5 option. But the power losses weren't just from moving to net figures, as engines were further detuned to meet new federal emissions standards.

Fiber-optic light monitors were deleted for '72, but the optional anti-theft system was now standard in a nod to the 'Vette's high "collectibility" among thieves. Adding collector interest to this '72 small-block coupe is an air cleaner autographed by Corvette engineering guru Zora Arkus-Duntov, though many years after the car was built. The '72s drew 26,994 total sales, up from 21,801 in the previous model year.

A smart new body-color nose freshened "Shark" appearance while satisfying a new 1973 requirement for front bumpers able to withstand five-mph impacts without damage. A new hood extended back to cover the windshield wipers, thus eliminating the troublesome pop-up panel, and coupe rear windows were now fixed. Doors gained inner side-impact protection beams to meet another new federal rule. Horsepower kept sliding. The base 350 small-block withered to 190 bhp net, while a 250-bhp L82 replaced the LT1. The sole big-block option, retagged LS4, made 275 bhp net. All very disheartening, yet total sales rose again, this time to 30,464.

The Feds decreed rear "five-mph" bumpers on all 1974 cars. Corvette complied with a smart new rear-end cap covered in the same body-color plastic as the nose. Otherwise, the "Shark" changed only in detail. A $400 Z07 heavy-duty suspension and brake package returned from '73. Included with it, but also available separately for a mere $7, was a new Gymkhana Suspension with stiffer springs and front stabilizer, perfect for the increasingly popular precision-driving sport called "autocrossing." Though Corvette was much less fiery than it had been, sales kept climbing back toward the '69 record, this year totaling 37,502.

This ragtop is a '75, identified by the small black bumper pads added front and rear. Also, the rear fascia was now one piece rather than split. The convertible took an 11-year furlough after '75, mainly due to changing buyer tastes. Only 4629 were called for this model year, but total 'Vette sales rose once more, reaching 38,465. Thanks to period inflation, base prices were still rising too: now $6537 for convertibles, $6797 for coupes.

210

Despite no convertibles and few other changes, Corvette sales rose another 21 percent for '76 to 46,558 units, breaking the '69 record at last. The tally was 49,213 for 1977, when Stingray badges came off and leather upholstery became standard. Adoption of catalytic converters for '75 allowed horsepower to creep up again—now 180 net for the base V-8, 210 for the L82 option. Base prices were still creeping up, too, '77s such as this one listing at $8647.

PART 2 1978-1982

With over a half-million Corvettes on the road (the 500,000th model had rolled off the St. Louis assembly line on March 15, 1977), the C3 Corvette would celebrate its silver anniversary for 1978. It would see a decidedly different market for sports cars than did the original Motorama-born model, that's for sure. While early-

Fifties America was a time of rampant prosperity and seemingly unlimited potential, the late-1970s was a period of economic austerity and harsh realities, particularly for the automotive business.

In large part because of the 1973-74 Arab oil embargo, consumer demand for new cars had gone topsy-turvy. Buyers were now spurning the large, powerful—and gas-guzzling—autos that once ruled the road in favor of more fuel-efficient compacts and subcompacts.

The big sales winners in this changing market were the Japanese makes, which heretofore had made only a modest dent in the U.S. market. Fuel efficient cars from Toyota and Datsun did especially well as buyers sought thriftier, less expensive transportation as a practical necessity—much as the Beetle had established Volkswagen as a major competitor during the sharp recession in the late Fifties. The Japanese models also impressed consumers as being

The trouble with a long running success is how to follow it. Chevrolet faced that thorny problem in deciding what kind of Corvette should follow the durable Shark. Would it be a new car in the traditional mold—or the much-rumored, long hoped-for mid-engine Corvette? Meantime, the Shark just kept on going, as Chevy lavished it with some surprising new high-tech features.

more reliable and accommodating than traditional Detroit iron, and offered better value to boot.

Meanwhile, the higher energy prices created by the embargo started an inflationary spiral that soon pushed both interest rates and commodity prices to new highs, and cars were no exception. By the late Seventies, aggravated by the added costs of engineering and installing mandated safety and pollution-control equipment, sticker prices were heading ever upward, making new-

car ownership increasingly difficult for a growing number of Americans. Automakers were now resorting to the use of factory rebates to help reduce their dealers' burgeoning inventories.

What's more, sports cars themselves had become a dwindling commodity. The aforementioned economic and regulatory woes, not to mention sky-high insurance premiums, had chased many performance models—both domestic and import—out of the U.S. market.

Still, Corvette sales continued strong through the end of the decade. Though the 1978 tally eased by about 2500 cars from the previous year (to 47,887), 1979 brought another record: 53,807— the first 50,000-unit year in Corvette history. This was the height of acceptance for a car that General Motors once thought would never sell half as well. The Corvette was now indispensable as a high-profit personal car as well as a showroom traffic-builder. And

1-2. Shark appearance was completely transformed for 1978 as the coupe exchanged its notchback roofline for a sweeping "glassback." The change was neither cheap nor easy to effect, but it was necessary to keep the car sufficiently fresh until a truly all-new Corvette was ready. And in an echo of 1961's "ducktail" graft, the new roof blended perfectly with the familiar lower-body lines. **3.** Besides celebrating Corvette's 25th birthday in 1978, Chevy was again tapped as pace car for the Indy 500. In celebration of that, Corvette buyers were treated to this special Indy Pace Car Replica model.

though long removed from its original "dual-purpose" concept, owner loyalty was as fierce as ever. GM understandably saw no need to invest its resources to replace the Shark when it had to muster its forces so that its higher-volume models could withstand the tectonic shifts in the suddenly unstable marketplace.

Even before OPEC shut down the pipelines, GM had decided that the previous "bigger is better" approach to car design had outlived its usefulness. Thus, while Ford and Chrysler continued to focus on the big-car business after the initial crisis subsided, GM embarked on a massive, long-term program to

revamp its entire fleet. Its future cars would be smaller, lighter, and more economical. Some (eventually most) would exploit the space-saving potential of front-wheel drive to provide about as much interior room as older models but within smaller exterior packages.

Thus an all-new 1975 Cadillac Seville was the first GM car to be sliced and diced, and it successfully broke new ground as a compact (at least by the standards of the day) luxury car. It was followed by the equally popular downsized B- and

C-body sedans of 1977, which were hundreds of pounds and many inches trimmer than their behemoth predecessors, yet every bit as spacious and comfortable. The big shrink continued with the A-body intermediates for 1978, new front-drive X-body compacts for 1980, and J-body subcompacts two years after that.

Despite GM's preoccupation with downsizing, the Corvette was not forgotten. It just didn't have the highest priority at the time and, again, there was no great rush to

3

replace it when the car was still selling at or near its all-time-high volumes. Nevertheless, a spate of concept vehicles shown in the 1970s had tongues wagging about the possibility of a radical new Corvette coming down the corporate pipeline.

In particular, enthusiasts eyed the second in a series of XP-882 concepts, an experimental development program that had begun in the late Sixties. Powered by a pair of mid-mounted two-rotor Wankel-type rotary engines that were bolted together, the XP-882 was unveiled at the Paris Salon in late 1973. With an arresting new gull-wing-coupe body by Bill Mitchell, this "four-rotor car" made a mid-engine 'Vette seem closer than ever. But the Wankel suffered from relatively poor fuel economy, and when the energy crisis hit, GM abandoned its rotary engine program. However, at Mitchell's request, a 400-cubic-inch Chevy V-8 was slipped into the coupe, which was renamed Aerovette. The car again went on tour and, as before, everyone assumed it would come

to be the next Corvette.

As it turned out, GM chairman Thomas Murphy actually approved a production-version Aerovette for 1980. Ironically, Murphy's approval came about at least partly due to the threat posed by the rear-engine stainless-steel-bodied DMC-12, the soon-to-be-announced brainchild of none other than former Chevrolet general manager John Z. DeLorean.

For a time, then, the Aerovette was the long-awaited, long-rumored mid-engine Corvette that partisans had hungered for. By the end of 1976, clay models were complete and tooling orders ready to be placed. Recalling 1953, the finished product retained the Aerovette's lines virtually intact, as well as XP-882's basic steel platform chassis design, complete with Zora Arkus-Duntov's clever, transverse drivetrain. The production Corvette V-8 was a 350 by then, so that engine would likely have been used. Four-speed manual and Turbo-Hydra-Matic transmissions were planned, and suspension parts were pulled right off the Shark as per Duntov's

original, cost-cutting goal.

Meanwhile, another avenue was being explored as a possible Corvette replacement. This was a mid-engine V-6 design with running gear adapted from the forthcoming new X-body compacts. It was the same basic idea later applied to Pontiac's Fiero: a transverse front-drive power package plunked behind a two-seat cockpit to drive the rear wheels. The proposed engine was the now-familiar 60-degree 2.8-liter V-6 then in the works at Chevrolet. The Chevy Three Production Studio under Jerry Palmer sculpted clean, somewhat angular styling with Aerovette overtones.

But neither idea would come to pass. The Aerovette project lost its two most influential supporters when Duntov retired in 1974 and Mitchell followed suit three years later. Ed Cole was gone by then, too. A further blow came from Duntov's successor, David R. McLellan, who preferred the "front/mid-engine" concept, inaugurated with the '63 Sting Ray over a rear/mid layout for reasons of packaging, manufacturing ease, and performance. In the end, though, it was sales—or rather the anticipated lack of them—that proved the decisive factor. Back in the Sixties, mid-engine design had seemed the wave of the future for sports cars; by the mid-Seventies, disappointing sales had rendered that promise mere wishful thinking. Although Porsche, Fiat, and others had offered mid-engine sports cars for several years, none had sold very well. Datsun, meantime, couldn't build enough of its (admittedly less expensive) front-engine 240Z. And perhaps sounding the death knell, Porsche replaced its mid-engine 914 with a front-engine design, the 924, in 1976.

With the rear/mid-engine idea again totally abandoned—seemingly for good this time—work toward a new front-engine Corvette got underway as the press and fans celebrated its 25th birthday. Apparently there was no timetable attached to the new model. The next generation would not appear until it was completely "right," which was all the better for quality control. Of course, there was hardly any need to rush into it, with the Shark still selling so well.

Thus it was deemed that some-thing special be done to the current 'Vette, rather than introduce an all-new model, to commemorate the car's silver anniversary. But how would Chevy accomplish this on a tight budget? The answer proved as simple as trimming away the old "flying buttress" sail panels and substituting a large, compound-curve rear window. Voila! The Corvette fastback was back. Not only was this a relatively inexpensive alteration that freshened the car's appearance, it improved rear-ward visibility in the bargain. Even better, it made for a slightly larger and more accessible luggage area.

In addition to adding Silver Anniversary badges to the exterior, changes for 1978 included squared-up instrument-panel housings for the speedometer and tachometer to match the previous year's revamped console gauges, redesigned door panels with new armrests and integral door pulls, and—at last—a real glovebox. The car's fuel-tank capacity increased from 17 to 24 gallons, and the wind-shield wiper/washer control was moved from the steering column stalk back to the dashboard.

The Corvette had the dubious distinction of being one of America's most frequently stolen cars, so the standard anti-theft system was rewired on the '78 to encompass the T-tops, which were all-too-easy to pinch. To the same end, a new roller-blind security shade was added to keep would-be thieves from peering into the cargo area through the big new backlight. The glass T-tops promised for 1977 were now genuinely available from the factory, and both they and the normal fiberglass panels were mod-ified to provide more headroom and easier locking. The three-point seat belts were given a single iner-tia reel, and belt guides were elimi-nated.

Power ratings for 1978 shifted a bit in deference to emissions stan-dards, as well as to the govern-ment's new Corporate Average Fuel Economy (CAFE) mandates that took effect that year. As before, there were two basic versions of the veteran 350 small block from which to choose. The base L48 pro-duced 185 bhp in "49-state" trim, and was the only choice for cus-tomers in California and high-alti-tude areas, where it generated 175 bhp. For an extra $525, the L82 delivered 220 bhp via a dual-snorkel air intake and a revamped exhaust system designed to reduce back-pressure.

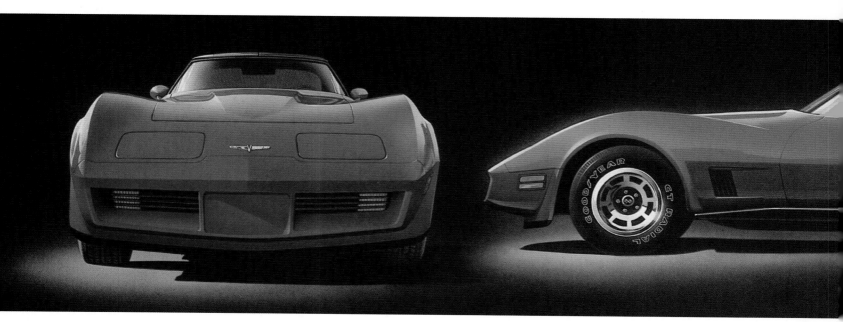

A close-ratio four-speed manual gearbox returned as an exclusive option for the L82; a 3.70:1 rear axle made this the best-performing drivetrain combination available. The same gearset was also offered for the L82 with the wide-ratio four-speed while the L48 came with a 3.36:1 axle (also available for the L82/wide-ratio setup). Also offered for the L82 was a revised Turbo-Hydra-Matic of the new, so-called "CBC" type, with a low-inertia high-stall-speed (2400 rpm) torque converter. The automatics pulled a 3.55:1 final drive, except with the L48 at low altitudes, where it was 3.08:1. Such juggling reflected the relative difficulty of balancing performance against low emissions and decent fuel economy.

The main chassis change for '78 was first-time availability of optional 60-series tires—raised-white-letter Goodyear GTs in HR60 size (225/60R-15 metric), though they necessitated some shearing of the fender liners. Aramid-belt construction contributed to a claimed improvement in ride smoothness.

The FE7 Gymkhana Suspension package was still around, though its price had gone up to $41 from the original $7 bargain. As before, it included heavy-duty shocks and higher-rate springs all around, plus a rear anti-roll bar and a thicker front stabilizer.

Cashing in on the birthday cachet, Chevy offered the '78 Corvette with "25th Anniversary paint," which was a relatively inexpensive striping package that would be viewed as a desirable option and could thus be considerably marked up. Before he retired, Bill Mitchell had suggested a Silver Anniversary model in his favorite color—silver, appropriately enough—and it appeared as the $399 B2Z option package. The first factory two-toning offered since 1961 (save for the removable hardtops for the now-discontinued roadster), it presented silver over a gray lower body with a separating pinstripe, plus aluminum wheels and dual "sport" outside mirrors as mandatory options, which added another $380 to the cost.

In another bit of anniversary schmaltz, Chevrolet had negotiated with the Indianapolis Motor Speedway to have a modified Corvette chosen as pace car for 1978's Indy 500. Initially, 2500 replica Corvette pacers—100 for each year of production—were scheduled for sale on a first-come, first-serve basis, but with Chevrolet having 6200 dealers at the time, it was decided that any such Corvette special would have to be built to a minimum order of 6200 units so that each showroom could have at least one. Thus, what was officially called the Limited Edition Indy Pace Car Replica Corvette made up some 15 percent of total production—hardly "limited" at all.

Like the Silver Anniversary model, the Pace Car Replica was actually an option package—RPO Z78—with two-tone paint as its main distinction. Here it was black over silver metallic with a bright red pinstripe in between, but a spoiler was tacked on at each end to alter appearance more dramatically. The front spoiler was similar to the one on the contemporary Firebird Trans Am, wrapped under and around to blend into the wheel wells, while the prominent rear spoiler curved down at its outboard

The 1980 Corvette brochure used these illustrations to show off that year's revised nose and tail caps with integral spoilers, which naturally changed the profile a bit. Also, "gills" returned to the front fenders, the first since '67.

ends to meet the bodysides, recalling the '69 Aero Coupe show car.

Pace Car interiors reflected Bill Mitchell's influence, with full silver leather or silver leather/gray cloth upholstery and gray carpeting. Chevrolet had scheduled new Corvette seats for '79, but the program was rushed forward so that the '78 Pace Car could have them first; these offered a new thin-shell design with more prominent (some said too prominent) lumbar support. Also, Turbo Hydra-Matic was supposedly the only transmission available, but four-speed manual showed up on quite a few models.

All replicas were equipped with the new glass T-tops, alloy wheels, power windows, rear defogger, air conditioning, sport mirrors, tilt/telescope steering wheel, heavy-duty battery, power door locks, and an AM/FM stereo with either an eight-track tape player or CB radio. The final touch was a set of regalia decals for owner installation. These included "winged wheel" Indy Speedway logos for the rear fenders and legends for the doors reading "Official Pace Car, 62nd Annual Indianapolis 500 Mile Race, May 28, 1978."

Base-priced at $13,653.21, the Pace Car Replica was quite a boost over the $9351 standard model. But because it looked like an "instant collectible," every one was sold for more than list price. This rabid interest tempted some owners of standard '78s to try and pass them off as factory Pace Cars. All anyone needed was a spray gun, a black or silver car with the right options, and a friend in your dealer's parts department willing to sell you the two spoilers and special silver cabin trim (though most counterfeiters would forget about the special seats).

If the car was now long in the Shark's tooth, its 1978 changes seemed to rejuvenate it all out of proportion to their magnitude, at least according to the auto maga-

zines. The reviewers praised the car's classic strengths to high heaven, especially an L48/automatic's 7.8-second 0–60 mph time and top speed of 123 mph, and noted its more refined, less teeth-rattling ride. On the other hand, they continued to note its weaknesses, like a rear end that tended to step out during sharp cornering maneuvers and a cabin that was still cramped and uncomfortable.

While the buff books would also speculate—as was their custom—over what form a next-generation Corvette might take, its changes were of an evolutionary nature for the 1979 model year. The base L48 gained 10 horsepower—20 in the California and high-altitude versions—by adopting the L82's more efficient twin-snorkel air cleaner; the optional engine itself tacked on five horses. Shock rates were standardized instead of varied with transmission. On cars with automatic, final drive ratio was lowered from 3.08:1 to 3.55:1.

The lightweight seats previewed in the '78 Pace Car Replica were now standard, bringing more rearward travel and different inertia seatback locks. But they still didn't include reclining seatbacks, now being found on the cheapest Japanese cars. Pace-Car-style front and rear spoilers became optional, and tungsten-halogen high-beam headlamps were phased in. The basic AM/FM radio option became standard, and the crossed-flags body insignia returned. These added features, combined with a strong inflationary spiral, pushed the car's base price over $10,000 for the first time—all the way up to $12,220.23.

While reviewers continued to be of two minds about the Shark, especially when compared to the more-nimble imports of the day, including the Mazda RX-7, Datsun 280ZX, and Porsche 924, they continued to gush over the 'Vette's impressive straight-line numbers. *Road &*

Track took an L82 to 60 mph in just 6.6 seconds, 127 mph flat out, and covered the standing quarter-mile in 15.3 seconds at 95 mph.

Weighty gas guzzlers were a dying breed, however, being victims of the new CAFE standards; this meant the Corvette would have to be put on a diet in order to survive. First-stage measures made for 1980 slimmed the car by some 250 pounds. The differential housing and front-frame crossmember were switched from steel to aluminum, and greater use was made of plastics throughout the car. The aluminum intake manifold previously used on the L82 engine was extended to the base L48, which lost five bhp to emissions tuning—back to 190 bhp at 4400 rpm and 280 lbs/ft torque at 2400 rpm. However, the L82 actually gained another five horses—up to 230 in all. California's increasingly stringent emissions standards forced buyers there to settle for a detoxed 180-bhp 305 small-block, which was available only with the automatic transmission.

Also in the interest of better mileage, the previously optional front and rear spoilers were slightly reshaped and made integral with the bodywork, and the grille was raked back slightly. As a result, the coefficient of drag (Cd) fell from 0.503 to a more respectable 0.443— still not great but an improvement none the less. Exterior chrome was now kept to a minimum, which meant removing the crossed-flags emblems from the front fenders.

Other 1980 changes included newly standardized air conditioning and tilt/telescope steering wheel, relocated power door lock buttons, and a speedometer calibrated to only 85 mph—yet another government mandate. Finally, the two behind-the-seats storage compartments were combined, though the battery remained in its separate cubbyhole directly aft of the driver.

The weight-saving measures

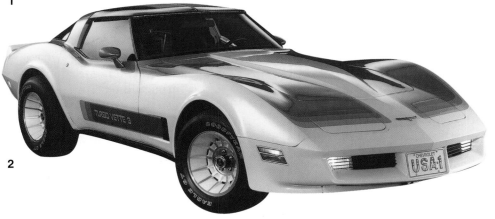

1. Corvette's crossed-flags emblem was again redrawn as a small but effective 1980 cosmetic change, and it was carried over for '81.

2. The 1981 Turbo Vette 3 "design study vehicle" packed a muscled-up 350 V-8 with Garrett turbocharger and a new type of GM fuel injection. Chevy claimed horsepower was up "by about 30 percent."

came none too soon, for early 1979 had brought another fuel crisis down upon America. This time, OPEC had less to do with the energy crisis than the overthrow of the Shah of Iran. But its effects on Americans were much the same: increasingly tight supplies of ever-more expensive fuel that sent the car market and the national economy as a whole into a tailspin. Once again the Corvette's future looked dubious, yet it continued to ride high. Although model-year volume

was down some 20 percent from 1979, the 1980 tally of 40,614 units was still quite respectable for a heavy, thirsty, specialty car that had become almost too expensive—now at a generous $13,140.24, sans options—for its target buyers.

As had been true since the very beginning of the Shark generation, press opinion of the 1980 Corvette was mixed. However, 0–60 mph times continued to be a highlight, clocked at between 7.1 and 7.7 seconds for the L82. Some scribes

took exception to Chevy's slenderizing measures—especially the "lighter-duty" rear axle—and the greater overall emphasis on fuel efficiency. Fit and finish problems were still noted, however.

Progressively rising CAFE standards dictated that the Corvette do its bit to help GM's compliance as a whole, so for 1981 the previous pair of 350 V-8s were retired in favor of a single, reworked version, designated L81. With 190 bhp at 4000 rpm and 280 lbs/ft peak torque at

221

1

1. The 1981 dashboard remained recognizably Shark, but designers had responded to changing buyers tastes and a raft of federal rules since 1968 to make it more modern and user-friendly. **2-3.** Exterior appearance was all but unchanged, but underskin improvements continued for '81. Among the most timely was a new fuel-saving lockup feature for the automatic transmission.

just 1600 rpm, it had almost exactly the same outputs as the superseded L48. Besides the aforementioned lighter components, it featured an auxiliary electric cooling fan that allowed for a smaller engine-driven fan, thereby reducing noise. But the big newsmaker was Computer Command Control (CCC). Also adopted for other '81 GM engines, CCC used electronics to integrate the emissions and fuel systems in

order to reduce smog and fuel consumption. Toward the same ends, it tied in with the automatic transmission's new lockup torque-converter clutch. This provided a direct mechanical link between flywheel and propshaft in second and third gears at steady-state speeds, thus eliminating gas-eating frictional losses through the converter.

Changes that were evident to showroom shoppers included a revised interior that now featured a standard quartz clock and optional

3

2

six-way power driver's seat (that finally reclined), plus electronic tuning for all factory radios. Prices were more eye-catching in a different way: up again, thanks to inflation, the sticker price now starting at a bit over $15,000.

Despite a generally dismal year for the industry as a whole, Corvette again showed well in 1981, as sales recovered smartly to 45,631 units.

By far the biggest Corvette news of 1981 was the announced transfer of production from the old St. Louis plant to a brand-new high-tech facility in Bowling Green, Kentucky. However, for two months during the summer of 1981, the cars were built simultaneously in both plants.

A fully up-to-date paint shop was a big plus for the new factory. St. Louis had used lacquer exclusively, but Bowling Green used more automated means to apply more durable enamels as well as the new clearcoat finishes. The Kentucky plant was also planned around much more automated manufacturing hardware than St. Louis could accommodate, reflecting the quest for tighter quality control.

With the opening of the Bowling Green facility, some observers concluded that Chevy was preparing for the arrival of an all-new Corvette. And they would be right. The existence of a new front-engine design was more or less an open secret by then. But testing new machinery and working out assembly procedures made more sense with a familiar design than with a new one, so the C3 would put in one final appearance. It also made

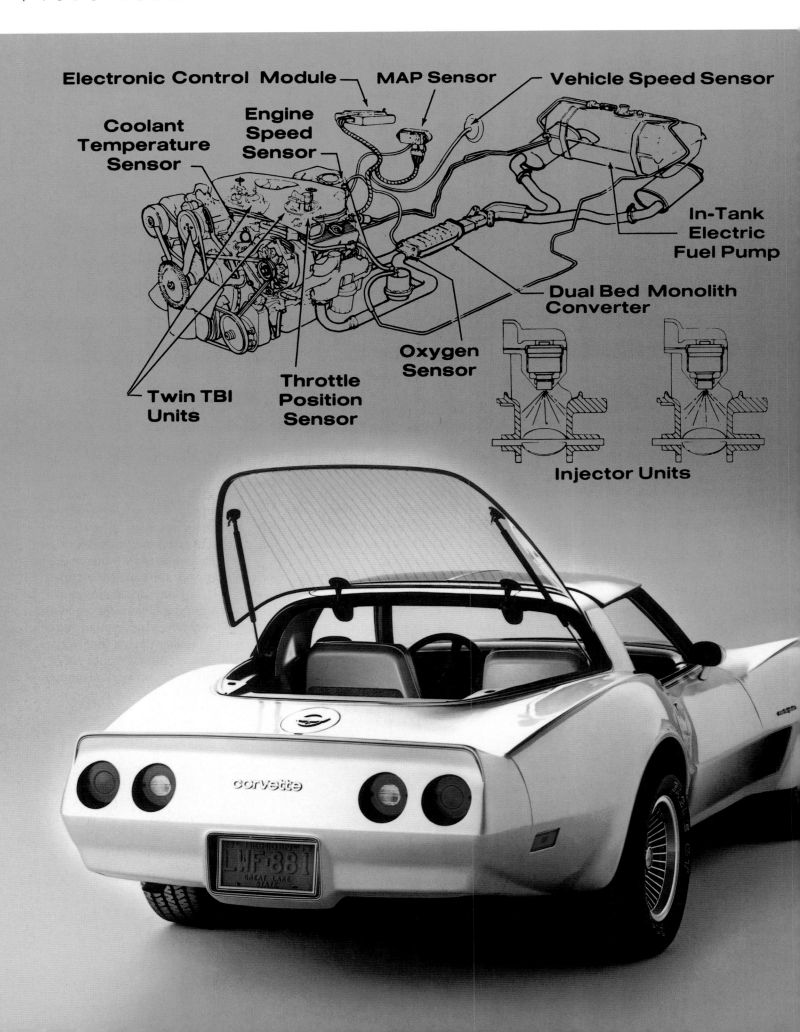

Electronic Control Module — MAP Sensor — Vehicle Speed Sensor

Coolant Temperature Sensor

Engine Speed Sensor

In-Tank Electric Fuel Pump

Twin TBI Units

Throttle Position Sensor

Oxygen Sensor

Dual Bed Monolith Converter

Injector Units

The special '82 Collector Edition hatchback was a glance into Corvette's near-term future; it was the only model that year to get an opening hatch window like the upcoming C4s. All '82s, however, got a new L83 V-8 with GM's "Cross Fire" twin throttle-body fuel injection and a more sophisticated electronic engine management system.

1

2

sense not to release a new drivetrain at the same time as a new design, so the last C3 was fitted with the revised engine and transmission destined for the C4.

While the new engine was essentially the time-proven 350 V-8, it now came with a newly developed twin throttle-body fuel-injection system instead of a carburetor—resulting in the first production Corvette "fuelie" since 1965. Dubbed "Cross-Fire Injection," an injector unit within a carb-like throttle body was used for each cylinder bank, while a crossover intake manifold fed the air/fuel mixture to the bank on its opposite side. This speeded up mixture velocity for more complete combustion and hence greater thermal efficiency and power, plus reduced emissions. Computer Command Control electronics governed the duration of injector opening in response to signals from various engine-mounted sensors. Designated L83, the Cross-Fire 350 recorded 200 bhp at 4200 rpm and peak torque of 285 lbs/ft at 2800 rpm, which were modest but satisfying gains over the L81.

In another sign of the times, the '82 was the first Corvette since 1955 to come without an available manual gearbox. Its only available

1. Signalling that the Shark would soon finally be replaced was the 1982 Collector Edition. Besides a lift-up glass hatch, this one-year-only special included multi-spoke alloy wheels recalling those of the Sting Ray era, plus unique two-toning with a fade-away color panel trailing back from the front-fender vents. 2. Shark production since 1968 totaled a smashing 542,861 units when the last of the '82s were built. No other Corvette generation had lasted so long, and it's quite likely that no future one will have the same staying power either.

transmission was a newly standard four-speed automatic, which was basically the previous three-speed Turbo-Hydra-Matic with a long-striding overdrive fourth gear tacked on. As before, there was a torque converter lockup effective on all forward gears except first, governed by the engine's electronic control unit.

Other mechanical changes for 1982 included the addition of an in-tank electric fuel pump and a new solenoid-operated trap door in the hood that opened at full throttle for better breathing. The air filter, which had previously contained charcoal, reverted to plain paper. The exhaust system was extensively redesigned around a significantly smaller and lighter catalytic converter.

Cosmetic alterations were limited to small "Cross-Fire Injection" labels above the front-fender vents and a two-tone paint option that recalled the '78 Silver Anniversary treatment: silver over a deep burgundy, separated by a red pinstripe.

For the generation's last hurrah, Chevrolet issued another commemorative "Collector's Edition" model. However, recalling its experience with bogus 1978 Pace Car Replicas, the division handled the '82 series differently, building the special model only "as needed" to satisfy customer orders (though about the same number—6759—would be built). Unique vehicle identification number plates were affixed to further deter someone from turning a standard car into the Collector's Edition.

In many ways, this was the best C3 'Vette of all. Setting it apart were cloisonné emblems on the hood, rear deck, and steering wheel; silver-beige metallic paint with graduated shadow-like contrast striping on the hood and bodysides; bronze-tint glass T-tops; and finned "turbine" alloy wheels like the ones first seen on the '63 Sting Ray. Inside were matching silver-beige

leather upholstery and door trim, leather-wrapped steering wheel, and luxury carpeting. A less obvious difference was this version's frameless lift-up glass hatch, which had been omitted from the '78 restyle because of cost considerations. Incidentally, it was not available on the base '82, though several aftermarket suppliers had turned to offering this as a conversion for "glassback" models.

What's more, the Collector Edition carried the dubious distinction of being the first Corvette to break the $20,000 price barrier, listing at $22,538—which was a far cry from the $4663 it had taken to buy a nicely equipped 1968 model.

With 10 extra horsepower and again blessed with fuel injection, the latest small-block Corvette showed definite performance gains despite being hobbled by the economy-minded automatic transmission. *Road & Track* timed it hitting the quarter-mile in 16.1 seconds at 84.5 mph and accelerating from 0 to 60 mph in 7.9 seconds.

Yet perhaps because a new model was known to be near, and aggravated by an ailing national economy, production fell to 25,407 units for '82, the lowest Corvette total since 1967.

But through its long and controversial run, the C3 would mark its place in automotive history as a true survivor. The passing years—despite the array of adversity that came with them—had been kind to the Shark, and the car never lost sight of its essential mission and character.

The challenge for the C4 development team would be to preserve and build upon that character, yet develop a new version of the venerable sports car that was—and would continue to be—right for the times. While it still would not be the futuristic and exotic machine Corvette enthusiasts had long dreamed of, it would prove to be a remarkable motorcar just the same.

227

Corvette marked its silver anniversary for '78 with a new fastback roofline that greatly increased luggage space, though the fixed glass meant you still had to load up from inside. Honoring the milestone birthday was a $399 two-tone Silver Anniversary paint package. It required optional aluminum wheels, introduced for '77 and also shown here. Horsepower rose to 175/185 base and to 220 for the L82 option. Despite all this, sales declined for the first time in seven years, easing to 46,776.

Corvette paced the 1978 Indianapolis 500, and Chevy celebrated by issuing 6502 Pace Car Replicas. Each sported special paint, glass roof panels (a new option for other '78s), front and rear spoilers, wider tires, unique high-back seats, and regalia decals. Base price was a stiff $13,653. The L82 V-8 was a separate option, but most had it. A few counterfeiters tried to make hay with bogus Replicas, causing Chevy lots of grief.

Corvette sales moved up again for '79, reaching 53,807. All models got the high-back seats from the previous year's Pace Car Replica, and its spoilers were a new option, as shown here. Improved "breathing" took the base V-8 up to 195 bhp, the L82 to 225. With inflation still galloping, base price broke the psychologically important $10,000 barrier for the first time (by $220).

The 1980 'Vette shed 150 pounds while gaining standard spoilers fully integrated with a reshaped nose and tail. The cockpit and emblems were updated too. California buyers had to take a 305 V-8, though with the same 180 bhp as this year's base "federal" 350. The L82 option gained another five bhp. A new "energy crisis" was on, which helped cut sales by 25 percent to 40,614.

234

The '81 lost a few more pounds but gained a revised rear suspension with a transverse, fiberglass-reinforced monoleaf spring. A power driver's seat was newly optional. There was now but one engine, a new 190-bhp L81, standard for all 50 states. Wood steering wheel and dashboard trim, shown here, were not. Corvette production shifted to a new plant in Bowling Green, Kentucky, for the '81 model year. Sales totaled 40,606.

The Shark reached the end of its long road for 1982 with one final round of improvements. A new L83 V-8 delivered 200 strong bhp via "Cross-Fire" fuel injection, the first "fuelie" 'Vette since 1965. However, manual transmission was no longer available. Also new was the Collector Edition, shown here, with a unique lift-up rear window and specific paint and trim. It listed for $22,537, versus $18,290 for the regular coupe. Sales plunged 37 percent this model year to 25,407, including 6759 Collector Editions.

PART 1 1984-1990

It had certainly been a long time since performance-car aficionados had seen an all-new Corvette. The Shark had held court for 15 years, undergoing only a modicum of modification—most changes being made in the name of boosting fuel economy, decreasing tailpipe emissions, or increasing safety, according to the evolving government mandates. Both big-block engine power and the convertible model had been left behind, and the car had gradually acquired a bit more in the way of sophistication and luxury with each passing year. Yet the 'Vette that bowed out at the end of the 1982 model year rode on a platform and was largely based on mechanicals that were originally designed for the inaugural 1963 Sting Ray.

Needless to say, after many years of rumors and false starts, the Corvette's rabid legions of fans were more than eager to see an all-new model roll off the Bowling Green assembly line. Few cars have been more eagerly anticipated. This would not be just another freshened carryover model, but a completely new Corvette that was recast from top to bottom as a thoroughly modern interpretation of the classic American sports car. And the faithful would finally get their wish. Sure, it wouldn't be the swoopy mid- or rear-engine "car-of-the-future-here-today" that some may have hoped for, but it was to be a brand-new 'Vette just the same, and that was reason enough to celebrate.

The car was set to debut as an early-1984 model and not an '83 as had been widely predicted. This was because the mid-model-year introduction made certifying the car as an early '84 more convenient (if tougher) in terms of meeting emissions and fuel-economy standards. Unfortunately this meant the car wouldn't technically be in production for 1983, which would have been its 30th anniversary year—thereby denying collectors and historians another special commemorative edition to mark the event.

Nevertheless, the new Corvette was finally at hand. It had been a very long time coming, so great things were expected of it.

But the automotive world had seen sweeping changes since the last generation 'Vette was born. Fuel economy standards were now a fact of life—and law—and materials, labor, and petroleum products had become much more expensive. The marketplace was now ruled by imports, such as the Porsche 928, Ferrari 308, and Lotus Esprit, along with a raft of lower-priced performance machines like the Datsun Z

The first fully redesigned Corvette in 15 years was more sophisticated and more practical than the beloved Shark, yet every inch a 'Vette for style and sizzle. And like previous generations, the new C4 only got better with time. Enthusiasts cheered when the convertible returned, while the awesome high-performance ZR-1 raised excitement to a new level. Though prices inevitably rose even as sales declined, the C4 won its own loyal following as one of the world's most desirable sports cars.

and Mazda RX-7. Critics wondered how a new Corvette would fare against not only its contemporary rivals but its illustrious predecessors as well.

Work toward the C4 had begun in earnest in mid-1978, shortly after General Motors management canceled plans to replace the existing Shark with a production version of the mid-engine Aerovette show car. This development program involved the closest cooperation between the engineering and design departments ever seen at GM. The primary collaborators were Corvette chief engineer David R. McLellan and designer Jerry Palmer, then head of Chevrolet Production Studio Three. Their close working relationship was vital if the new model was to be built with a high level of quality—which was important, because the new 'Vette would sell for considerably more money than ever before.

According to Palmer, the underlying mission statement for the 1984 design was "form follows function." While many automakers had paid only lip service to following that well-worn dictum over the years,

both Palmer and McLellan deemed it essential in order for the new Corvette to remain competitive with the latest sports cars from Japan and Europe. Specifically, their task was to eliminate the deficiencies for which prior versions had been roundly criticized, while still maintaining the traditional Corvette look and driving feel. The new car would have to cut through the air with superior aerodynamics, coddle its passengers with more interior room, and—most importantly—serve up even better handling than earlier models.

To that end, the C4 would have to be completely re-engineered—a beefed-up Shark with new styling simply would not suffice. Both design groups began their tasks with the so-called "T-point," which is the position of the driver's hip joint relative to the interior and the rest of the car. This was raised an inch and moved an inch or so rearward, which opened up more legroom and also made for a higher driving position relative to the road. Further, the change enabled the car's revised chassis to sit higher than before for more ground clearance.

This bird's-eye view from Chevy PR highlights the 1984 Corvette's single lift-off roof panel, which substituted for the Shark's twin-panel T-top design. Also evident here is the new generation's deeper, more sharply raked windshield and smooth, wind-cheating body lines.

239

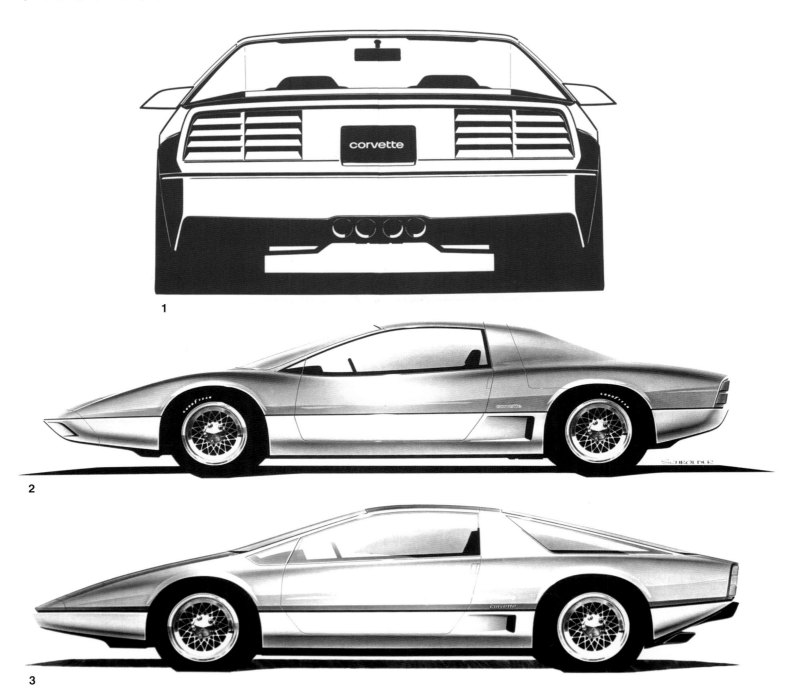

1

2

3

1-3. These mid-1970s concept sketches predate the actual C4 development program and assumed a mid-engine layout. Roof and tail treatments prefigure the styling of Chevy's 1982 Camaro. **4-5.** The C4 ultimately emerged with the traditional front-engine/rear-drive layout for cost and quality reasons. These late-1979 mockups are very close to the finished product.

The old perimeter-type ladder frame was replaced by a steel backbone design not unlike that pioneered by England's Lotus. In the Corvette, the "spine" took the form of a C-section beam rigidly connected to the differential and carrying the driveshaft. This arrangement reduced weight and opened up more cockpit room by eliminating the transmission and differential crossmembers, and by permitting the exhaust system to be run beneath the driveshaft instead of alongside it.

Welded to the backbone was what Chevy called an "integral perimeter-birdcage unitized structure" or "uniframe," making the new model the first Corvette to employ modern unit construction instead of the old body-on-frame configuration. The "birdcage" formed the windshield and door frames, lower A-pillar extensions, rocker panels, rear cockpit wall, and front subframe. It also included a "hoop" above and behind the cockpit, both for additional rigidity and as a hinge point for the lift-up

4

5

rear window. Galvanized inside and out for corrosion resistance, this structure effectively comprised a skeleton onto which the fiberglass outer panels would attach. Completing the basic assembly were an aluminized bolt-on front suspension carrier and a bolt-on extension for the back bumper.

This more rigid platform allowed McLellan's staff to rework the suspension for greater handling precision. In front remained the familiar unequal-length upper-and-lower A-arm arrangement, though with a new twist. Instead of a coil spring on each side, a single reinforced-fiberglass leaf spring was mounted transversely between the two lower arms, as at the rear. A 20-millimeter anti-roll bar was standard.

Even bigger changes occurred in the rear, where Zora Arkus-Duntov's old three-link geometry gave way to a more sophisticated five-link design. This comprised upper and lower longitudinal links between the body and hub carriers, twin lateral strut rods tying the differential to the hub carriers, another transverse plastic leaf spring (of the type used since 1981), and the customary U-jointed halfshafts and rear tie rods.

Steering was now a rack-and-pin-

1

2

As with any new car, there were hundreds of proposals for the C4 interior. **1-2.** Seats got special attention, appropriate for the most driver-focused 'Vette ever. Cloth upholstery and body-hugging side bolsters were standard. Leather was optional, as were power adjustments for bolster angle, lumbar support, and thigh cushion. **3-5.** Dashboard design was just as hotly debated, but most all workouts assumed use of the latest electronics technology for digital-graphic displays and/or readouts worthy of *Star Trek.* Continued from the Shark days was a prominent "center stack," above and ahead of the shift console, for audio and climate controls and sundry other functions.

3

4

ion design, changed from GM's usual recirculating-ball mechanism. It had a forward-mounted rack for greater precision and a standard high-effort booster for better directional control at high speeds. Normal ratio was a constant 15.5:1, which was quite fast for an American car. A tilt/telescope steering wheel was made standard.

A Z51 Performance Handling Package included heavy-duty shocks and lower-control-arm bushings, upgraded front and rear springs and stabilizer bars, plus 13.0:1 quick-ratio steering, among other features.

As before, stopping power was supplied by large ventilated disc brakes at each wheel. The brakes themselves were a new design created by Girlock, an offshoot of the British Girling company. Making extensive use of aluminum, they had large 11.5-inch-diameter rotors and featured quick-change semi-metallic pads (held by a single bolt) with audible wear indicators.

With improved handling being a major consideration, the car was originally intended to ride on larger 16-inch wheels and Pirelli's P7 performance tires, then the state of the art. But the rubber ultimately used in production was Goodyear's

Eagle VR50, specifically designed for the new Corvette and sized at P255/50VR-16. The "V-rated" tires were designed to withstand a maximum speed of over 130 miles per hour, which was a hint of the car's performance potential. These tires were notable for their "gatorback" tread design—a deep V-pattern with horizontal slots perpendicular to the sidewalls, all of which suggested the appearance of an alligator's back. Evolved from Goodyear's Formula 1 and Indy-car rain-tire program, the design was said to shed water more effectively to resist hydroplaning, which is a perpetual problem with wide, low-profile rubber. The tires were mounted on cast-alloy wheels that were 8.5-inches wide up front and 9.5-inches wide in the rear. These were among the first of the so-called "unidirectional" wheels, in which the radial fins were shaped to scoop in cooling air to the brakes only when turning forward. This, in turn, necessitated specific left and right wheels front and rear, none of which were interchangeable.

More evidence of the Design and Engineering departments' teamwork was found under a new "clamshell" hood, which was part of the design concept from the very

beginning. Recalling Jaguar's famed E-Type and various mid-engine Corvette experiments, the design integrated the hood with the front fender tops and lifted to a near-vertical position.

Residing beneath the clamshell was the 5.7-liter (350-cid) small-block V-8 carried over from 1982, with twin throttle-body electronic fuel injection and "CrossFire" manifolding with dual ram-air intakes. Though still designated L83, it now produced five more horsepower—a total of 205 at 4300 rpm—and five extra lbs/ft of torque—290 at 2800 rpm—via a more efficient radiator fan and accessory drive. It sported a flat-top die-cast magnesium air cleaner created by Palmer's crew. Separate vacuum-modulated doors molded into the underside of the hood regulated incoming air flow; the ducts mating with the air cleaner assembly when the hood was closed. A single air intake below the front bumper fed air to the underhood ducts, making the '84 a "bottom-breather" like the Shark before it. The engine compartment was color-coordinated in silver and black. Palmer even persuaded GM's AC-Delco Division to develop an appropriately styled battery.

A welcome return for the new

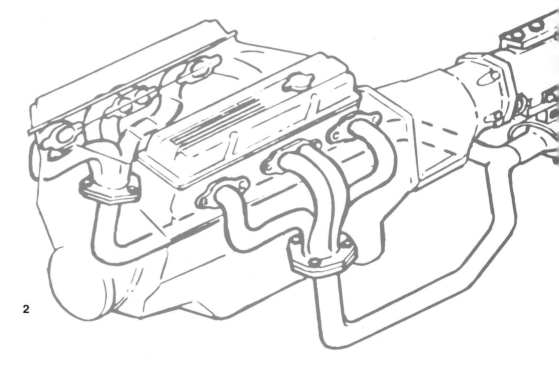

1

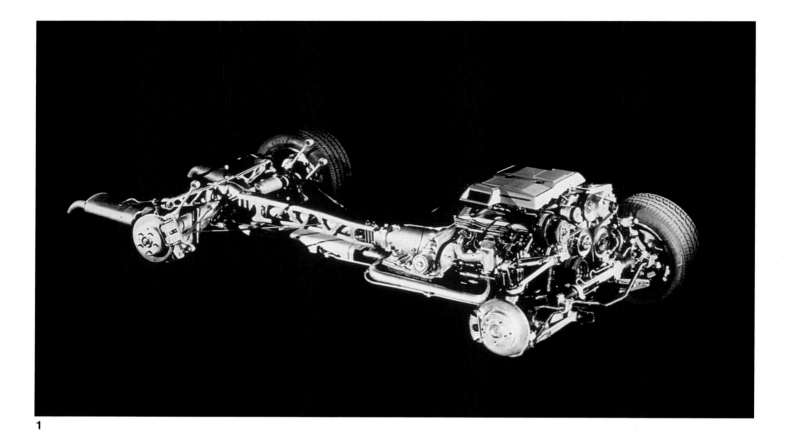

model was a four-speed manual gearbox as the Corvette's standard transmission, but it was nothing like any seen before. Called "4+3 Overdrive," it was basically an orthodox four-speed with a second set of three planetary gears attached at the rear. When signaled by the engine's Computer Command Control electronics, the auxiliary gearset engaged through a hydraulic clutch to provide a step-down or overdrive reduction of 0.67:1 in each of the top three gears. The intended result was improved part-throttle fuel economy, though in practice testers noted little difference between the manual and the automatic transmissions in that regard. For best performance, engagement was electronically inhibited at wide throttle openings, but this was quickly supplemented by a console-mounted manual override switch. Standard final drive was 3.07:1, with 3.31:1 gearing available for better standing-start performance.

Production delays postponed

2

deliveries of the 4+3 Overdrive until early calendar '84, however, so the first of the new 'Vettes were equipped only with an automatic. Returning from 1982, but as a no-cost option now, was the GM 700-R4 four-speed overdrive automatic, still with a lockup torque converter

clutch effective in all forward ratios except for first.

Despite Chevy's considerable effort to keep weight as low as possible, the new Corvette emerged heavier than expected—by a good 300 pounds—though it was 250 pounds lighter than a comparably

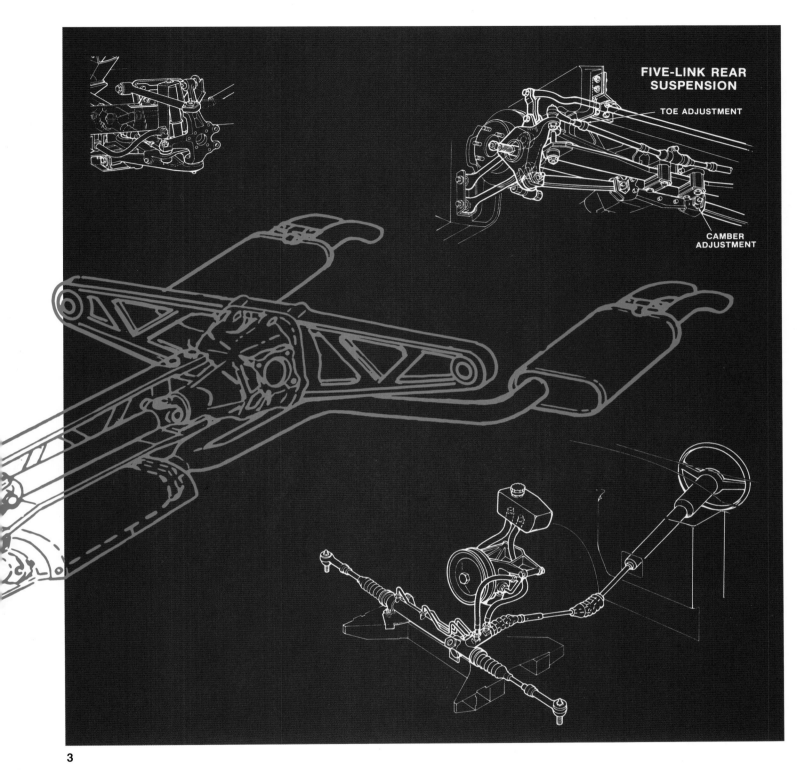

FIVE-LINK REAR SUSPENSION

TOE ADJUSTMENT

CAMBER ADJUSTMENT

3

equipped '82. Numerous subtle tricks contributed to this, not the least of which was the extensive use of lightweight materials. One of these was a driveshaft and supporting yokes made of forged aluminum, welded together. Another was a radiator support made of plastic sheet molding compound (SMC). The twin transverse reinforced-fiber-glass leaf springs weighed half as much as four steel coil springs of comparable size. (They were also claimed to be more durable, capable of withstanding five million full jounce/ rebound cycles, versus about 75,000 for the steel coils.) Plastic was also employed for the cooling system's twin expansion tanks, radiator fan, and shroud.

1-2. The C4 replaced the Shark's perimeter frame with a "backbone" chassis, so-called because of the sturdy C-section steel member connecting the powertrain to the differential. The design saved weight and provided extra cockpit space. **3.** C4 steering was updated too, switching from recirculating-ball to the more precise rack-and-pinion type.

245

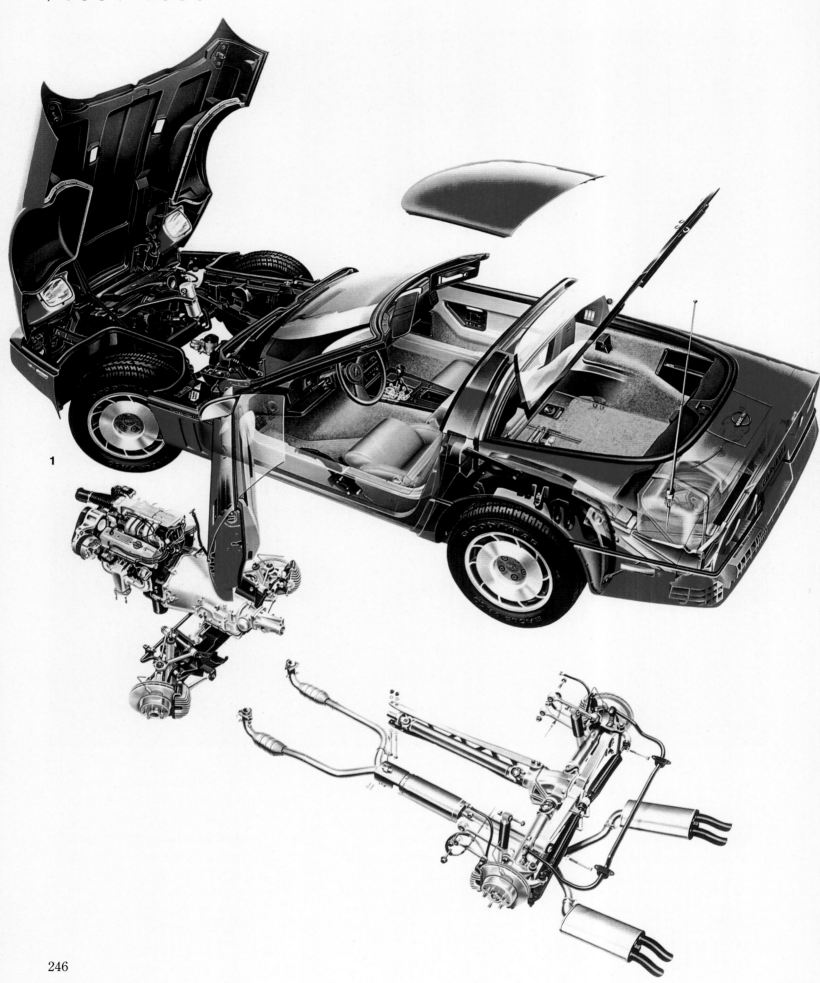

1

Aluminum figured extensively elsewhere. Front-suspension control arms and knuckles as well as the rear lateral arms were all aluminum forgings, as was the chassis' C-section "spine." The automatic transmission's torque converter housing was formed from sheet aluminum. Brake splash shields were aluminum rather than steel, and calipers were made from an iron-aluminum alloy that provided greater strength with less weight.

While McLellan's engineers busied themselves with technical intricacies, Palmer's staff was shaping the car's appearance. The design brief was imposing. First and most obviously, the new generation had to look like a Corvette; in other words, it couldn't break with the model's traditional styling cues. Drivelines would be carried over, and though the new model could be a bit smaller outside, it had to offer more interior room. Improved

than originally envisioned. By allowing the engine to ride lower in the chassis, a correspondingly lower hoodline was achieved, with better vision forward and reduced frontal area. The latter was a big contributor to reducing effective aerodynamic drag, which is not the drag coefficient (Cd) alone but the product of the Cd multiplied by the car's frontal area.

What emerged was unmistakably a Corvette from front to back. And

2

1. This "exploded" view highlights many new C4 features. Among them is a revised all-independent suspension with a transverse, fiberglass-reinforced leaf spring at the front as well as the rear, plus more sophisticated five-link rear geometry and forged aluminum front A-arms. Note, too, the meaty tires and large four-wheel disc brakes. 2. A tilt-up "clamshell" hood allowed no-strain engine and front suspension access. Out back, a glass hatch opened onto a much roomier trunk.

outward vision and less aerodynamic drag were additional goals.

Despite all the demands, the styling job went quickly. A full-scale clay model based on a Palmer sketch was completed in September 1978. By mid-November of the following year—a scant 14 months later—the design was more or less final except for taillamps, front-fender trim, and nose contour.

A key development affecting room, drag, and visibility was engineering's decision to mount the steering linkage farther forward

while its basic exterior dimensions were now slightly smaller, it still looked like a considerably large car, thanks in part to its long hood and altered proportions. Overall length was down a significant 8.8 inches despite a mere two-inch cut in wheelbase—from 98.0 to 96.0 inches—and just a 1.7-inch reduction in front overhang. The secret was the 5.2-inch chop in rear overhang, which gave the effect of a longer hood even though it was actually shorter. Another contribution was a 64-degree windshield

1

angle as measured from the vertical—then the steepest of any American production car. The base of the windshield was 1.5 inches lower and a bit farther forward than before. This, in turn, allowed the beltline to be dropped, giving the '84 a slimmer, glassier appearance.

Probably the biggest change in the car's appearance came from that increase in width. The old pinched-waist midsection was gone, along with the bulged front and rear fenderlines, replaced by a smoother, more organic contour. The car retained its predecessor's flared wheel arches, which combined with the fat tires to accentuate the hunkered-down look. Fenders no longer conflicted with the beltline, which rose uninterrupted from the windshield toward a near-vertical Kamm-style tail (a modified throwback to 1968) with the traditional quartet of lights. In

profile, the shape was a discernible wedge—which was pleasing and functional in the GM idiom.

One styling element that was new to the C4 Corvette was a full-perimeter rub strip at roughly mid-body height. This not only tied the front and rear bumpers together visually but concealed the one major seam in the new bodyshell, as well as the shutlines around the clamshell hood.

After 15 years of selling Corvettes with T-tops, Chevrolet could hardly revert to a model having a fixed roof. But this time around, the T-bar was gone, replaced by a one-piece removable panel with four attachment points—two on the windshield header and two on the rear roof hoop; this was the "targa" treatment originally planned for the C4. As on early Sharks, the panel stowed in special slots built into the top of the luggage bay. For added protection

against at least casual vandals, the top could be removed only with a special wrench. Buyers had a choice of either a body-colored panel or a tinted transparent top made of scratch-resistant acrylic, the latter an option that was delayed until well after the car's introduction. Either top was far lighter and easier to handle than the awkward glass panes that preceded them.

Chevy boasted that the '84 Corvette was partly shaped in the wind tunnel. One new wrinkle in that aspect of development was the use of a sensor to compare pressure differences at various points on the car against pressure in other parts of the tunnel as the car sat in a moving airstream. While the resulting drag coefficient was not exceptional for the day at 0.34, reduced frontal area made the new Corvette much more slippery than that often-misleading value suggest-

2

3

4

5

1. The '84 (*lower left*) posed for an introductory PR photo with the three previous Corvette generations to that point, represented by a white '53, a blue Sting Ray, and a red Shark. The C4 designation was Chevy shorthand that didn't enter common parlance until the 1990s. **2-3.** Handsome from any angle, the '84 was deliberately less flamboyant than the Shark. **4.** It was also more aerodynamically efficient, thanks to extensive wind-tunnel testing. **5.** The large "clamshell" hood looked cumbersome but moved easily on gas-filled struts.

ed. And even at that, the Cd number represented a useful 23.7 percent reduction compared to the '82 model's 0.44.

With its striking new exterior, the Corvette needed an equally arresting cockpit. Created by GM's Interior Design group under Pat Furey, it was dominated by a space-age instrument panel and the usual tall center tunnel/console. With a seating position that was slightly lower than before, the revised cabin definitely felt more spacious and open than did the prior generation's. Despite the shorter wheelbase and a 1.1-inch reduction in overall height, the '84 offered fractional gains in head and leg room, plus a welcome 6.5-inch increase in total shoulder room, an area where the old car was decidedly tight. Cargo capacity was also greater this time around, by a useful eight cubic feet or so, and this storage was more accessible thanks to the lift-up hatch window.

Instrumentation was now directly ahead of the driver; no more secondary dials in the center of the dashboard. In fact, there were now no dials at all in the usual sense; following the fashion of the times, there was a high-tech all-electronic display supplied by AC-Delco. Road and engine speeds were monitored by both graphic analog and digital displays; between them was a sub-panel with digital engine-function readouts, including a vertical-bar-graph fuel gauge. A quartet of switches, to the left of a bank of warning lights in the center of the dash, allowed the sub-panel to display up to four additional readouts. These could include instantaneous and average miles per gallon, trip odometer, fuel range, engine temperature, oil pressure and temperature, and electrical system voltage. The displays could be changed from American-standard to metric values at the flip of a switch.

The console also housed the heat/vent/air conditioning and audio-system controls. A Delco AM/FM-stereo radio was standard, while a similar unit with cassette tape player was optional. But the audiophile's choice was the $895 GM-Delco/Bose system. Similar to systems offered on other recent GM cars, it featured four speakers in special enclosures that were shaped and placed to match the interior's acoustic properties. While such audiophile systems are relatively common today, the 'Vette was the first sports car to pay such attention to the entertainment aspect of motoring.

New standard seats were specially designed highback buckets with prominent bolsters on both the cushion and backrest; they offered manual fore/aft adjustment and—at long last—reclining backrests. Full cloth trim was standard, with

249

leather upholstery optional. Also offered at extra cost was the latest in seating technology supplied by Lear-Siegler. These optional seats added electric adjustment for back-rest angle and cushion bolster in/out, plus a powered three-stage lumbar support adjuster using inflatable bladders that could be individually air-bled to achieve the proper contour.

The new Corvette was publicly unveiled in the early spring of 1983, and the general reaction from both the press and the public was a mix-ture of relief and unbridled enthusi-asm. The C4 was, thank goodness, still a Corvette in appearance and mechanical layout, yet was star-tlingly and entirely new with a full complement of high technology residing under its fiberglass skin.

Several running changes were made shortly after the new model was announced and sales began. An engine-oil cooler was made stan-dard equipment, and the originally standard 15-inch wheel/tire pack-

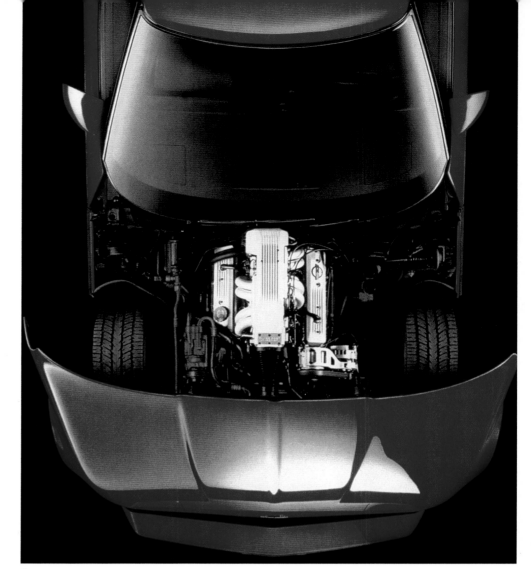

1

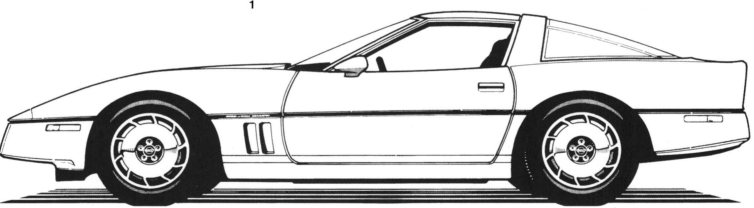

2

age was deleted, making the 16-inchers the only choice.

Meanwhile, regular production versions of the new Corvette were being subjected to their first full road tests, which cooled the initial euphoria of some reviewers in the enthusiast publications. The buff books predictably praised the car's acceleration and roadholding abili-ties, but criticized its relatively rough ride, especially with the optional Z51 suspension package;

while superior on the track, it was judged as being too harsh for daily driving. The interior earned low marks for excessive exhaust and road noise, and the digital dash-board took a sound thrashing for its "Las Vegas at night" appearance and poor legibility, particularly in bright sunlight. Most reviewers pined for a return to good-old-fash-ioned analog gauges.

The 4+3 Overdrive manual was received with mixed reviews, and

most testers agreed that it worked better with the manual override switched to the "off" position. Aside from the difficulty of trying to out-think a computer when left in auto mode, a clunky, high-effort linkage made stop-and-go driving tedious, which was aggravated by an equally unpleasant high-effort clutch. The transmission would also prove less than reliable, so it's no wonder that most Corvettes left Bowling Green with automatic in 1984—and would continue to do so through 1988, when the car would finally be given an acceptable manual gearbox.

Needless to say, the excitement of being able to buy an all-new Corvette for the first time in 15 years made the '84 a fast sellout. Helped by an extra-long model year, volume zoomed back over the 50,000 mark, the total coming to 51,547—the second highest in Corvette history. There was even another production milestone, observed in November 1983 with completion of Corvette number 750,000.

As it turned out, the C4 arrived at about the time the U.S. economy began recovering from its early-Eighties doldrums. What had been an oil shortage was unexpectedly replaced by an oil glut that caused gas prices to plunge, and buyers soon shopped for big and powerful Detroit cars once again. The Reagan Administration had also been helping out, convincing Japanese automakers to voluntarily limit their car exports to the U.S. via the Voluntary Restraint Agreement (VRA). In this new, more hospitable climate, American performance was flourishing anew by mid-decade, and Chevy wasted no time in turning up the Corvette's volume.

Thus, for 1985, the car received a new "Tuned Port Injection" system, which was basically the German Bosch fuel-injection system with a revised intake manifold. Although the time-honored Corvette small-block still measured 350 cubes, the substitution of the new multi-port fuel-injection with tuned intake runners, along with a half-point compression increase to 9.5:1, lifted output by 25 horses, to reach 230 bhp at 4000 rpm; torque improved by 40 lbs/ft, going from 290 at 2800 rpm to a meaty 330 lbs/ft at 3200. So extensive were the changes that Chevy was moved to use a new engine designation: L98.

Responding to all the complaints about the car's harsh ride, Chevy softened up both spring and shock rates on both the standard and performance Z51 suspensions for '85. The latter now came with larger-diameter fore and aft stabilizer bars

1. The C4's one carryover component was the L83 V-8 with "Cross Fire Injection" as fitted to the final Sharks. Engineers placed it slightly behind the front-axle centerline for optimum front/rear weight balance. **2-5.** Against the Shark, the C4 was a bit wider, but a whopping 8.8 inches shorter overall and two inches trimmer in wheelbase. It also boasted more glass and better outward visibility.

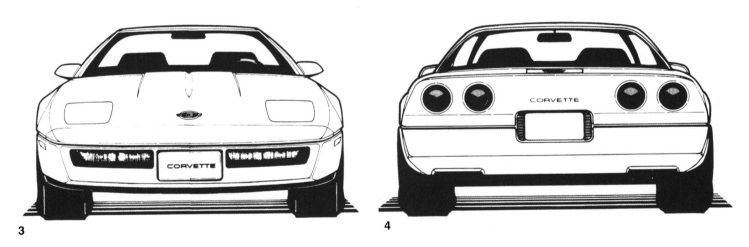

3

4

5

to maintain total roll stiffness with the softer calibrations, plus 9.5-inch-wide wheels at the front as well as the rear. Also included were Delco-Bilstein gas-pressurized shocks—available as a separate option with the base suspension—and a revised heavy-duty cooling system.

Of course, engineers were still interested in handling. The Z51 package was fine-tuned by Corvette development engineer John Heinricy to be a "showroom stock GT car," according to McLellan, referring to a hotly contested class in SCCA racing. Intriguingly, the suspension changes lowered ride height on the '85 by an imperceptible ¾ inch, which was just enough to drop the drag coefficient to 0.33 and, with the 3.07:1 axle, raise top speed to a genuine 150 mph. This year's standard axle was an even taller 2.73:1, which proved to be too tall for the car to reach 150 mph. For better straight-line stability at top speeds, the steering caster angle was increased one degree (to four). For better stopping ability from high speeds, the brake system was fortified with a larger master cylinder and booster, as well as different pads imparting more braking power and improved feel.

Transmission-wise, the 4+3 Overdrive manual received a heavy-duty 8.5-inch differential ring gear (up from 7.9 inches) for extra longevity, as well as an override button that was more conveniently placed atop the shift knob. What's more, the unit's computer was reprogrammed to make the overdrive function less intrusive. Toward the same end, the electronics governing the lockup torque converter clutch in the automatic transmission were also revised.

Cosmetic and convenience improvements included revised instrument graphics for improved legibility, and newly optional leather upholstery for the extra-cost Lear-Siegler seats. Finally,

1. More sophisticated "Tuned Port Injection" boosted Corvette power for 1985. **2, 4, 5.** Quality started taking big strides in 1981, when production moved to a new Corvette-only plant in Bowling Green, Kentucky. Extensive automation allowed workers to lavish more time and care on each car. **3.** The C4 made history as the first unit-construction 'Vette, using this sturdy "birdcage" or "uniframe" structure.

Chevy began eliminating the sources of the rattles and squeaks that had so plagued the car in its first year via an extensive series of minor structural changes.

Car and Driver was among the media celebrating the new model's added refinement. The magazine sampled two cars—an automatic with the base suspension and a Z51 manual—and found both to be "tight and solid." The former ran 0–60 mph in 5.7 seconds and the standing quarter-mile in 14.1 seconds at 97 mph. The manual version raced to 60 mph in six seconds flat and hit the quarter-mile in 14.4 seconds at

95 mph, reaching a top speed of 150 mph. Roadholding and braking characteristics for the '85 were also praised in the media, though testers still groused about an unnecessarily harsh ride with steering that was judged as being too quick for around-town use. The digital dashboard continued to be dismissed as being excessively gimmicky.

Sales for the C4's sophomore year took a steep plunge, dropping to 39,729, the lowest annual total since 1975. This downturn was at least partly due to 1985's whopping price increase—the car's base price was now $24,403.

Prices would jump even further for 1986—up to an intimidating $27,027, though this was justified in part by the inclusion of several new standard features. Primary among them was Corvette's first anti-lock braking system (ABS), which was the latest ABS II setup from Bosch in Germany. Now common among many of the least-expensive autos, ABS was still relatively new in '86, and its application was then limited mainly to high-cost luxury cars. Though the car's braking system was otherwise as before, ABS moved the C4 'Vette even closer to being the true world-class sports car Chevy said it was.

Also added as standard equipment that year for additional protection from thieves was VATS (Vehicle Anti-Theft System), a simple yet effective feature designed to augment the existing burglar alarm. A small pellet with a specific electrical resistance was imbedded in the ignition key, and it had to be read by a hidden electronic "decoder" box before the engine could be started. Use the wrong key or try and start the vehicle by other means and the decoder would shut down the starter relay and fuel pump for at least two minutes before allowing another try. VATS proved itself effective at greatly reducing drive-away theft. Indeed, figures later compiled by the Automobile Club of Michigan would show that while the theft rate for 1984 and '85 Corvettes was better than seven percent, the so-called "pass-key" system reduced it to less than one percent for 1986 models—and to near zero for 1987-88s. It was enough to prompt the Michigan AAA and other insurers to reduce their comprehensive premium rates for Corvettes so equipped by 20–25 percent.

Other changes for '86 were relatively minor. A switch from cast-iron to aluminum cylinder heads

4

5

continued on page 256

1

1. Chevy still documented Corvette "body drops" in 1985, but a C4 "chassis" was welded to the "bird-cage" body structure at this point on the assembly line. 2. Styling was unchanged on the sophomore '85 save "Tuned Port Injection" badges on the front fenders. 3. The C4 arrived with this dazzling array of digital and graphic instruments. Switches allowed the driver to change some of the displays, which included readouts for instant or average mpg and oil pressure and temperature. Some critics thought the ensemble rather too busy, though. 4. Each instrument cluster was supplied as a module and was electronically checked before installation.

2

3

4

1

plus careful weight-paring elsewhere took some 125 pounds off curb weight, making it the first 'Vette in about 20 years to weigh in at less than 3000 pounds. However, Chevy made the new heads a little too thin, and they had to be thickened again when durability testing revealed that cracks could occur around the head attachment bosses under high engine loads. Though delayed until about the middle of the model year, the new heads were worth waiting for, incorporating centrally located copper-core spark plugs for better combustion, plus larger intake ports and sintered-metal valve seats. The

exhaust system was also revised, taking on triple catalytic converters. For all this, though, output of the L98 engine was unchanged.

Elsewhere on the car, a center high-mounted stoplamp was added, per federal regulations, and wheels were given raised hub emblems and a bright brushed finish. Fuel capacity on automatic cars shriveled by two gallons to 18. LCD instruments were re-angled to aid daytime legibility (which remained

difficult all the same), and the cluster now contained an upshift indicator light that was there to help drivers achieve maximum mileage by signaling when to shift gears—it was there to help keep the car's EPA mileage figures above the gas-guzzler level. (Oddly, the indicator light also came with the automatic transmission.) Standard tires were changed to P245/VR5016s; the Z51 package continued with P255s.

However, the most significant

256

1. Far removed from showroom C4s was the racing Corvette GTP, created for the International Motor Sports Association's GT Prototype class. It ran three seasons, starting in 1985, and won two races in '86. 2-3. Wooded settings aren't exactly the Corvette's natural habitat, but the C4 dressed up the scene wherever it went.

3

news for 1986 occurred at midyear with the return of the Corvette convertible—the first such model in 11 years. Engineered with help from American Sunroof Company, it was announced just in time to be chosen as pace car for that year's Indy 500. All convertibles were designated as Pace Car Replicas, regardless of color or equipment (though the actual pace cars were painted a bright yellow).

Chevrolet stated that the C4 had been designed with a topless model in mind, so the transformation from

A crossbeam was added atop the rear torque box, and the steel riser behind the seats became a sturdier, double-wall affair. A center stop-lamp was neatly integrated into the top of the back panel.

The result was a new drop-top Corvette that weighed only around 50 pounds more than the coupe and actually proved stiffer. It had a stiffer price as well—just over $5000 more than the already costly coupe. Unfortunately for Chevrolet, the ragtop's revival didn't do much for 1986 model-year sales, which

1-2. The Bowling Green Corvette plant relied on computer-managed robots for painting, welding, and other repetitive tasks where high consistency and precision were quality musts. Better yet, the robo-workers never griped, got tired, or asked for a day off. **3.** Even so, the human touch was essential to assure best possible workmanship. **4-6.** The first 'Vette convertibles in 11 years left Bowling Green starting in early 1986, an exciting, nostalgia-filled occasion for workers and Corvette fans alike.

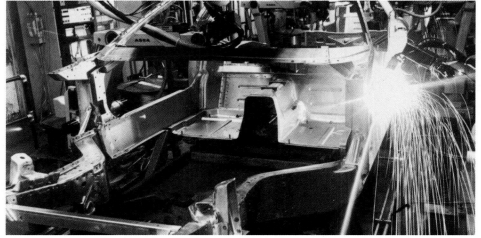

1

coupe to convertible was straight-forward. With an eye to preserving torsional stiffness in the absence of a fixed roof, reinforcement was applied to the frame crossmember ahead of the engine; larger K-shape braces were used to connect the under-engine member to the frame rails; and X-braces were added to tie door-hinge pillars to the rear chassis torque boxes. Cowl structure, including the steering column, its mounts, and the dashboard-mounting beam, were all strengthened, as was the front torque box.

2

258

3

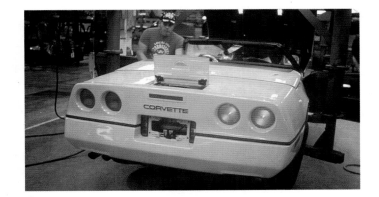

4

5

6

1. Coupe or reborn convertible? For Corvette fans in 1986, it was a tough choice. New federally mandated high-mount center stoplamp sat between the tail-lights on the ragtop and in a rear "pod" atop the coupe's roof.

2. Most '86 convertibles were sold as Indy Pace Car Replicas and finished in yellow. This is the actual car that paced that year's Memorial Day classic.

3. A gauge cluster re-angled for less glare was one of several interior improvements for 1986.

1

2

slipped to 34,937, of which just 7264 were convertibles.

United again, the coupe and convertible saw several noteworthy changes for 1987. Chevy's continuing quest for reduced engine friction in the interest of both performance and economy resulted in rollers being added to the hydraulic lifters, along with rocker-arm covers with raised rails to forestall oil leaks. Thanks chiefly to the former, horsepower went up by 10, to 240 in all, and torque improved by 15 lbs/ft, for a total of 345. A six-way power passenger's-seat option was now offered (matching the standard driver's item), and major body and mechanical components were given special identification marks to further foil thieves.

What's more, a second suspension option was made available only on manual-transmission-equipped coupes; designated Z52 and priced at $470, this was essentially a softer version of the Z51 package, with the wider (9.5-inch) wheels, plus a solid and thicker front anti-roll bar, the new gas-charged shocks, quick-ratio steering, and all but one of the chassis stiffeners developed for the convertible. A thicker-core radiator and a second electric cooling fan were also included. Spring rates and bushings were carried over from the base chassis. The racing-oriented Z51 suspension, listing at $795 for 1987, had all the Z52 hardware but much stiffer springs and front lower-control-arm bushings, plus a solid (instead of link-type) rear stabilizer. Enthusiast magazines praised the new suspension for the improved ride quality with only the most minor differences in handling characteristics.

On the acceleration side of things, *Motor Trend* timed a manual-shift 240-bhp roadster at 6.3 seconds 0–60 mph and clocked the standing quarter-mile at 15.11 seconds and 93.8 mph. With prices

continued on page 264

1

Chevy still had mid-engine dreams in the 1980s. Besides the GTP racer, it conjured the Corvette Indy to test a slew of new ideas and technologies. **1, 4.** Unveiled in early 1986, the Indy boasted all-wheel drive, four-wheel steering, a lightweight "backbone" unibody made largely of high-tech carbon fiber, and an "active suspension" without the usual springs or shock absorbers. **2-3, 6-7.** Design work began in late 1984. **5.** A full-size running car was ready less than a year later for management review. The dark suit walking off to the right is Chuck Jordan, then GM's director of design. **8.** For 1988, the Indy exchanged silver paint for red and its original 32-valve 5.7-liter V-8 for a prototype of a 2.65-liter V-8 that Chevy planned to make available for Indycar racing.

2

3

4

5

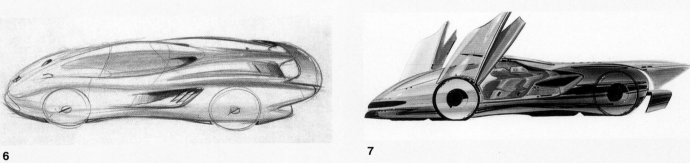

6

7

8

now starting at $27,999 for the coupe and $33,172 for the ragtop, critics felt the Corvette was becoming too pricey for its own good, though it was still perceived as being a better value than the European exotics of the time.

Though not a factory option, speed-hungry buyers could order a car with a new Callaway Twin-Turbo Engine package through participating dealers. Designated as RPO B2K, and priced at a budget-busting $19,995, the twin-turbo was rated at 345 bhp and 465 lbs/ft of torque and could reach a top speed more than three times the legal limit—all the way to 177.9 mph with .60 overdrive gearing. These were specially modified Corvette engines (except for the first four off the line, which used GM truck shortblocks); cars would be shipped from Bowling Green to Callaway Engineering in Old Lyme, Connecticut, for modification.

Corvette sales continued their downward trend on the 1987 model year, sliding to 30,632; of that fig-

1

ure, convertibles accounted for 10,625 units, which was 3400 above the '86 total. 184 well-heeled buyers opted for the Callaway twin-turbo version.

For its 35th anniversary year in 1988, the Corvette was again treated to important engine and chassis

upgrades. Freer-breathing cylinder heads and a reprofiled camshaft gave the L98 small-block another five horses—now up to 245 bhp, though torque was unchanged. Z51 and Z52 suspension packages now included 17-inch wheels; these were newly styled 17 × 9.5

2

3

"Cuisinart" rims wearing huge, P275/40ZR-17 Goodyear Eagle GTs. Enthusiasts were quick to note the tires' "Z" speed rating, indicating that they were good for sustained running at over 149 mph. The new wheel styling was also applied to the standard 16 x 8.5-inch rims, which were likewise upgraded to Z-rated rubber of 255-mm section.

To make the most of the new higher-performance tires and for better directional control in hard stops, front suspension geometry was reworked to incorporate "zero scrub radius." This means a steering axis that intersects the road at the exact center of the tire's contact patch, rather than outboard (positive scrub radius), as on previous Corvettes, or inboard of it (negative scrub radius) as on some European cars. Rear suspension was also revised, with slightly more rebound travel and reduced camber for improved straight-line and braking stability. Brakes were fortified as well, gaining two-piston front calipers, thicker rotors all around,

1. Corvette's standard 16-inch wheels were redesigned for '88; 17s remained available. **2.** Coupes continued to outsell convertibles in the C4 era. **3.** Corvette won its third straight SCCA Showroom Stock racing championship in 1988.

and a handbrake integral with the rear discs (replacing the previous small, separate drum brakes).

Like the Porsche 928 of the day, the C4 had always had its pull-up handbrake mounted outboard of

the driver's seat, with a lever that could be folded down after engagement so as not to interfere with entry/exit. This was retained for 1988, but the assembly was moved a bit lower and farther back to be a

bit less intrusive. In addition, interior air extractors in coupes were modified to increase the flow rate as an improvement to the climate-control system, which was now offered with the extra-cost automat-

All Corvettes look like they're going fast even when standing still, but we doubt any car would be showing 55 mph with the doors open and no driver aboard. Of course, this is an advertising shot, and perhaps the art director responsible felt that "0" readings wouldn't look right. The C4 cockpit was comfortable once one was settled in, though low-set seats and the wide tunnel-top console made for a cozy feel. Doors sills were relatively tall, so entry/exit wasn't that easy even for a sports car. But such practical considerations were quickly forgotten behind the wheel. Speaking of practicality, the C4 convertible top was always a manual affair, but was easy to put up or down.

ic temperature control that was phased in toward the end of 1987 production.

With total Corvette production nearing 900,000 units sold over a span of 35 years, it was time to mark another anniversary with a special-edition Corvette. Recalling the Waldorf debut of the original '53 Motorama car, the anniversary car bowed at the New York Auto Show on April 1, 1988, with announced production of only 2000 units (actually, 2050 were sold). Offered only as a coupe, the 35th Anniversary edition—officially, the $4795 option package Z01—offered a bright white lower body (includ-

1

ing color-matched door handles, mirrors, bodyside moldings, and 17-inch wheels) set off by a black roof hoop and transparent black acrylic roof panel. Special commemorative badges appeared above the front-fender "gills," and as embroidery on the seatbacks in an all-white leather-upholstered interior. Other standard features included dual six-way power sport seats, automatic climate control, the GM-Delco/Bose audio system, and heated door mirrors.

While the 35th Anniversary car was a sellout, it wasn't enough to lift the Corvette's fortunes at dealerships. The sales downturn continued for 1988, with production slipping to just under 23,000 units, the lowest model-year total since 1972.

Meanwhile, the C4 was continuing Corvette's winning ways on the track—it was the undefeated class champion in SCCA Showroom Stock racing for three straight years. Fifty-six street-legal cars were built for the 1998 SCCA Corvette Challenge series. Stock engines would come from the CPC engine plant in Flint, Michigan, shipped to Bowling Green for installation, and the cars would then be trucked back to Wixom, Michigan, for roll cages and other racing modifications. During the course of the year, Chevy would replace most engines, however, swapping them for motors having more evenly calibrated power output.

Closing out the decade, the Corvette's previously optional Z52

package was made standard for '89, with all models now including its fast-ratio steering, 17-inch wheels and tires (the 16-inch wheels were dropped entirely), Delco/Bilstein gas-charged shocks, and fortified front-end structure. The heavy-duty engine oil cooler, heavy-duty radiator, and auxiliary radiator fan were also now included on cars equipped with the six-speed gearbox. Also new for 1989 was an optional tire-pressure monitoring system (actually it was delayed from '87) that could detect a drop of as little as one psi below the preset limit via a pressure sensor within each wheel; the sensor was combined with a small radio transmitter that in turn activated a dashboard light. Also, the new Multec fuel injectors designed for the coming LT5 ZR-1

2

1. The 1988 was the last C4 available with the interesting "4+3" manual transmission. **2-3.** A nostalgic removable hardtop was a new convertible option for 1989. It included an electrically heated rear window and fit earlier rag-roof C4s.

3

powerplant were applied to an otherwise unchanged L98 engine.

The six-speed manual transmission that was new for 1998—and available as a no-cost option—was designed jointly by Chevrolet and Germany's ZF (Zandfabrik Friedrichshafen). A computer-aided gear-selection system automatically forced the driver to bypass second and third gears and lock out fifth and sixth gears under low-throttle conditions. This feature was designed to help improve fuel economy, and, once again, keep the car from attaining gas guzzler status. Annoying to most testers, the transmission's lock-out function could easily be defeated by "clipping a single red wire," according to Chevy engineers.

Inside, both the standard cloth seats and the extra-cost leather-covered sport versions had been restyled; the latter were restricted to cars with the Z51 option. Overhead, a bolt-on hardtop was newly available. Made of fiberglass-reinforced polyester resin over rigid urethane, it was molded around a steel/aluminum "cage" and coated with polyurethane inside and out. A cloth headliner and window weather-stripping were included, as well as an electrically heated rear window (which plugged into a special rear-deck socket). On soft-top models, the convertible mechanism was simplified for easier operation.

Nineteen eighty-nine would be the last year for the SCCA's Corvette Challenge, and Chevy would build 60 cars for the series. Thirty of them would have their stock engines swapped with higher-output motors from the CPC engine plant in Flint, Michigan.

Sales for 1989 would rise for the first time in years, now totaling 26,412, of which nearly 10,000 were convertibles. The Callaway twin-turbo option, now priced at $25,895,

was ordered for a mere 69 cars.

For 1990, all Corvettes benefited from a standard driver's-side airbag, installed to meet the first phase of the federal government's "passive restraint" crash-protection regulations. Also for safety's sake, the car's antilock braking system was upgraded with improved yaw control that allowed for more-secure handling. The base engine received a slight bump up to 245 bhp through an added air-intake speed density control system, a revised camshaft and increased compression ratio (this was 250 bhp in coupes with the 3.07:1 or 3.33:1 axle ratios). A newly efficient sloped radiator design precluded the need for an auxillary fan, which was no longer available for 1990.

A revised instrument display now combined a digital speedometer with an analog tachometer and other gauges. An engine-oil monitor now calculated the useful oil life

remaining in miles and alerted drivers when an oil-change was needed via a dashboard indicator. A compact disc player was newly available with the optional Delco-Bose audio system, and it now included a security lockout feature to discourage theft; if removed, a special code had to be entered or the head unit would remain inoperative.

Twenty-three Corvettes with heavy-duty suspensions were built during 1990 for the new World Challenge racing series and could be obtained via regular dealer channels. Buyers could choose a Chevy engine or provide one of their own, though any further modifications were left to the racers.

Though overall alterations would be minor, 1990 would prove to be a major model year for the Corvette because it marked the introduction of the high-performance ZR-1 version, which was actually a $27,016 option package. Originally intended

1. This 1990 convertible wears the optional hardtop and rear-deck luggage rack. **2.** A sweeping new dashboard improved control ergonomics for 1990 and replaced the digigraphic tach and speedometer with large analog gauges.

1

as a midyear 1989 model and previewed with a massive media campaign, the ZR-1 was eventually postponed until 1990 due to "insufficient availability of engines." Based around an all-new 32-valve 375-bhp V-8 called the LT5 (developed in conjunction with Lotus and built by Mercury Marine), the ZR-1 was a true production supercar that could run with even the most exotic imports. (We'll examine the ZR-1's development in the following chapter.) The Callaway twin-turbo was still available at an extra $26,895, but it languished in favor of the new ZR-1, selling just 58 units. Overall sales dropped a bit for the year, down to 23,646.

Still, of that number, 3049 ZR-1-equipped models were sold to buyers who had long saved a place on a waiting list. Many gladly paid well in excess of list price to be among the first to own what was the new epitome of American muscle, and a true Corvette classic.

2

271

All-new except for its L83 engine, the 1984 C4 was a vast advance on the "Shark": lighter yet stronger, roomier and more practical, and a better handler. Rear glass lifted hatchback style. Twin T-tops gave way to a single lift-off roof panel. Cockpit was chockablock with "high tech," including jazzy digi-graphic instruments. An extra-long model year, starting in early '83, yielded 51,547 sales, a new model-year Corvette record.

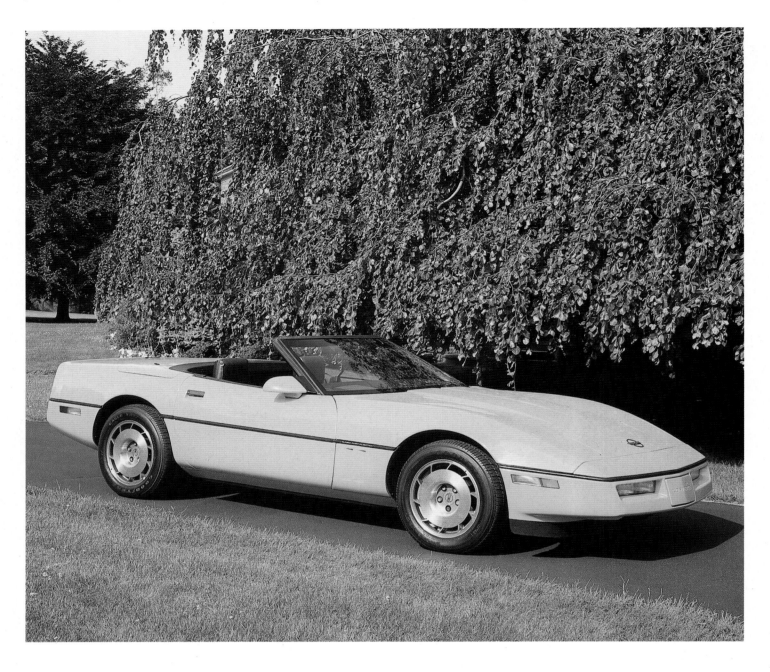

A new convertible made major Corvette news for 1986. All were sold as "Pace Car Replicas" honoring Corvette's role at that year's Indy 500. Most were painted Indy Yellow, as here. Base price was $32,032 versus $27,027 for the coupe. Both '86s benefited from standard antilock brakes. Sales totaled 35,109, including 7315 of the reborn ragtops.

Horsepower was up to 240 for 1987 via a revised exhaust system and low-friction roller-type valve lifters for the aluminum-head L98 V-8, new for '86. Automatic transmission remained C4 standard, with an innovative "4+3" manual gearbox optional. A new comfort-biased Z52 suspension package joined the handling-oriented Z51 option. The convertible's base price rose about $1100 to $33,172. Ragtop sales improved for the model year to 10,625, but coupe orders fell to 20,007.

Corvette had to skip 1983 and thus missed its 30th birthday, but Chevy tried to make amends with a special 35th Anniversary package for 1988. Limited to just 2050 coupes like this, the $4795 Z01 option included a black roof with dark-tint glass panel, white lower body with matching wheels, and a color-keyed leather-upholstered interior.

PART 2 King of the Hill

Originally slated for a midyear-1989 introduction but delayed until the 1990 model year to facilitate "additional development," the ZR-1 marked a return to the glory days of Detroit muscle. Only the ZR-1 would neither be built in Detroit nor would it rely on sheer engine displacement to provide its rocket-like thrust. This would be a thoroughly modern vehicle that would utilize the latest in technology to not only make it blindingly quick when the open road stretched endlessly ahead but remain relatively compliant and accommodating in around-town driving.

In fact, the ZR-1 wasn't even a separate model in the Corvette line; it was technically an option package, and a costly one at that. Available only for coupes (a convertible version was considered, but never produced), RPO ZR1 added a whopping $27,016 to the base price of a 1990 Corvette, making the final list price a then-staggering $58,995. While this placed it up in the range of a Mercedes SL, it was still priced far less than a comparable-performing Ferrari or Lamborghini. Nevertheless, the ZR-1 was a true, flat-out, take-no-prisoners, dual-purpose sports car in the traditional mode, though there was little about the car that could be considered traditional.

ZR-1s differed from regular 1989-90 Corvettes with a wider convex tail panel and squarish taillights.

Although blessed with a world-class chassis, the C4 Corvette that debuted in 1984 inherited a relatively low-tech overhead-valve V-8 from its Shark predecessor. Though fast enough in its own right, it had been outclassed by the more sophisticated and powerful engines of European GTs of the day, like the Porsche 928S, Lamborghini Countach, and Ferrari Testarossa. Chevrolet chief engineer Fred Schaafsma and Corvette engineering chief Dave McLellan weren't at all happy with this state of affairs, but given General Motors' corporate policies, politics, and finances, getting the green light to build a high-tech powerplant that would enable the 'Vette to run with those venerable marques didn't seem likely.

Years before "King of the Hill" became the title of an animated television program, it was the nickname given to one of the fastest production autos ever. It was a true supercar that could run with some of the most exotic sports cars in the world—and do so for less than half their stratospheric sticker prices.

Not that the Corvette staff had been lacking for ideas, mind you. Earlier in the decade, Chevrolet solicited outside firms for engineering concepts that would take small-block performance a quantum leap ahead. These efforts would include an array of V-6s and V-8s with twin turbochargers, and a naturally aspirated V-8 capable of up to 600 horsepower. None would be put into production, however. The turbo V-6 was dismissed as being too noisy, harsh, and vibration-prone, convincing McLellan that a V-8, with its inherently greater smoothness and tractability, was the only answer. The twin-turbo V-8 garnered considerable internal support, and though 14 such cars were built and tested (leading Chevy to approve Reeves Callaway's twin-turbo conversion option for 1987), the concept was ultimately rejected. Not only wasn't it the high-tech alternative the company had been hoping for, but the twin-turbo V-8's emissions and fuel consumption were both unacceptably high.

The development team finally came to the notion that any new higher-output Corvette should be "Bi-Modal," meaning it had to be quiet, docile, smooth, unobtrusive, and undemanding in routine driving, yet be able to summon race-car speed and handling at a moment's notice. This was to be a refined sports car that would mind its manners in traffic, yet be ready to cut loose whenever the circumstances warranted bad behavior.

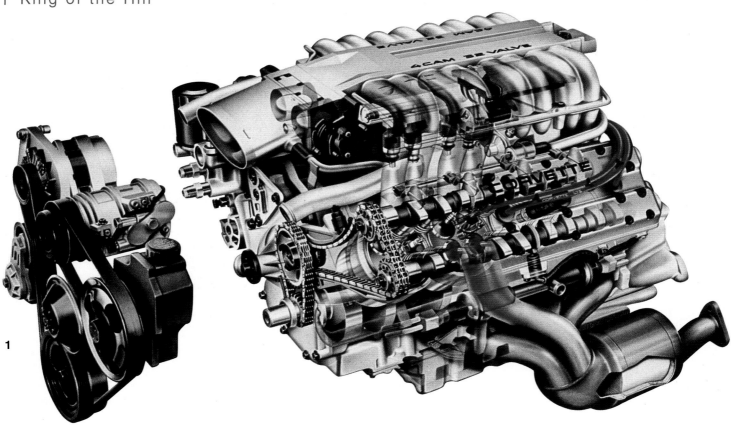

1

Among the consultants Chevy had called in during this period was England's Group Lotus, the world-renowned builder of championship Formula 1 cars and a leader in high-output engine technology. Chevy had, in fact, been talking with Lotus about co-development projects for years. But it wasn't until the spring of 1985, when GM began negotiations to purchase the British firm, that the Corvette Group met with Lotus Managing Director Tony Rudd to discuss adapting Lotus's four-valve head technology to the 'Vette's 350-cubic-inch V-8. Somewhat surprisingly, Rudd proposed building an all-new engine that would meet Chevrolet's performance, emissions, and fuel-economy targets.

With continued prodding from Chevrolet Engineering, and with the takeover of Lotus concluded in 1986, GM management approved a brand-new no-holds-barred V-8.

The goals for this singular new engine were exacting: It should provide acceleration second to

2

1-2, 5-6. The ZR-1's new all-aluminum LT5 V-8 was the same physical size as the iron-block L98 and was just 39 pounds heavier despite producing some 60 percent more power. **3-4.** LT5 manufacturing was contracted to Mercury Marine, which took extra special care in producing the sophisticated, high-tech powerplant.

3

4

5

6

none while maintaining superior driveability at all speeds, fuel economy comparable with the existing L98 engine, and be compatible with the existing body/chassis structure (i.e., no structural modifications should be required for installation). Specifically, engineers desired power and torque gains of at least 50 percent over the L98, and wanted this to come from a modern engine having four valves per cylinder and twin overhead camshafts

per cylinder bank for superior breathing and reduced valvetrain mass. They mandated electronic control of ignition, fuel delivery, and throttle actuation to ensure good driveability, with overall fuel economy of at least 22.5 mpg and the ability to meet all U.S. emissions requirements. What's more, they deemed this new motor should have a pleasing underhood appearance, with no compromise in reliability or durability.

Fortunately, Lotus and the Chevrolet-Pontiac-GM Canada engineering groups were up to the challenge. Thus was born the powerplant Chevy labeled "LT5," the latest in the long and storied line of L-badged Corvette performance engines. Like the L98, the LT5 was a 5.7-liter/350-cid 90-degree V-8 with 4.4 inches between bore centers. Beyond that, the LT5 was sig-

continued on page 286

283

Profile: David R. McLellan

David R. McLellan succeeded Zora Arkus-Duntov as the head of Corvette engineering in 1975. Like so many others who have been involved with the car over the years, McLellan is a unique personality. The 1984 was the first Corvette to fully reflect that personality—and his considerable expertise.

McLellan was born on Michigan's Upper Peninsula in the mid-Thirties, soon after Harley Earl had designed his first LaSalles and Cadillacs. McLellan grew up in Detroit, where he later attended Wayne State University, majoring in mechanical engineering. Fresh out of school, he went to work for General Motors in 1959 at the corporation's Milford proving grounds. McLellan spent the better part of a decade there, during which he earned a master's degree in engineering mechanics from Wayne State.

In 1968, McLellan was transferred to Chevrolet Division, where he worked on the second-generation Camaro. He was also involved with John DeLorean's proposal for a common chassis shared by Camaro, the compact Nova, and possibly, McLellan says, the Corvette (though it never came to pass).

Next came a year's sojourn at MIT in 1973 as a Sloan Fellow. He returned to Chevrolet in 1974, at which time he was given his first Corvette assignment as a staff engineer under Duntov. Just six months later, Duntov retired and McLellan was named chief Corvette engineer.

Though the proposed mid-engine production car derived from Bill Mitchell's Aerovette design was nearly ready at that point, McLellan favored the traditional front-engine/rear-drive configuration, and he carried the day with what ultimately became the C4 Corvette. Significantly, a series of owner surveys supported his position. Also by that point, McLellan had established himself as a clever, capable designer—which he had to be. The challenge of engineering and overseeing development of the first all-new Corvette in some 20 years was formidable, to say the least.

The editors had several interviews with McLellan soon after the 1984 model was unveiled. What follows are excerpts from those conversations.

Q: What was the first Corvette you worked on?

David R. McLellan: The first program I had any impact on was the '78. As chief engineer there are some aspects that are under my direct control, some things not under control. The engine and transmission were not under direct control. The '78 program involved many things besides moving on emissions and fuel economy. From a design standpoint, we had devised a hatchback Corvette, which was never approved. That was a hatch with a large frame around it. For '78 we reassessed why we were having problems getting stuff like that approved. The '78 design was originally conceived as a frameless hatch design. This was the one that appeared in the Collector Edition in 1982, its first production appearance.

Q: When did you realize you would be able to build a new Corvette?

McLellan: We realized in that 1977–78 time frame [that] we had to do

a new Corvette or the product would be in serious jeopardy. There was general recognition it was time to take a major step with the Corvette. The big issue was what should that step be? The options ranged from carrying out the midships V-8 Aerovette-based design to doing a V-6 midships car to taking the front/mid-engine design we had and doing a thorough reassessment of it. We started the process with the midships variation as our mainstream. It occurred to us only as we got into detailed assessment to look into the front/mid-engine design again. About that time, Porsche came out with the 928—a front-engine V-8 sports car. We looked again at the benefits, and it emerged as a very strong candidate and . . . ultimately emerged.

Q: What was the mid-engine design's downfall?

McLellan: When you get to a high-performance-engined car that carries two people and has some kind of creature comforts, the mid-engine gets very tough to deal with. There is a certain amount of cubic volume that is consumed by all those functions to transport two people and achieve a level of creature comfort. To make the midships cars look so slick, we had been ignoring the people issue. There was no utility or luggage space at all in those cars. That's where you get into trouble with the larger engine. The front/mid-engine design offers more benefits at that point. Then it comes down to what can we do to reconfigure [it].

So we set about doing that by repackaging the details: putting the front suspension around the engine, putting the engine in at a completely different attitude, designing the rear suspension to configure it around the occupant requirements. Generally, we were able to make the car a little bit shorter and lower, though a little bit wider.

Q: What changes did you deem most important?

McLellan: As we analyzed the old car, a lot of things, we felt, were right.... That was reflected in its performance in the marketplace. We really look at this new Corvette as an ultimate performance statement by Chevrolet. What I mean by that is, in all respects that are important to a Corvette, the car needs to be king of the hill. If it's worth doing, it's worth doing better than anybody else. With the old Corvette, we had kind of let things slip a little bit. We had not been pounding the table with our management as hard as we should have.

Q: What changes in automotive technology have affected the Corvette?

McLellan: It has been updated year by year. It progressed dramatically in '81 and '82 when we moved production from St. Louis to Bowling Green. It was Jerry Palmer and the design team who worked closely together. One of the first things we laid down [for the '84 model] was the tire size. For the kind of performance we wanted, the only tire available in that size was a Pirelli P7. Much of the design was done around that tire. We brought Goodyear in early in [the program] and gave them the specifications, and they worked hard on it. We're very pleased with the results. The tires have been trouble-free. [Even with the wider footprint] they have better hydroplaning performance than previous tires. Goodyear is X-raying 100 percent of the tires for quality control and is testing a sampling using a holographic technique.

Q: Why the unidirectional wheels on the '84?

McLellan: Basically for aesthetics.

It's kind of a non-issue. If that is what the designer wanted and it's reasonable to give it to him, then we'll give it to him.

Q: Is your relationship with Design Staff much like it was between Bill Mitchell and Zora Arkus-Duntov? Mitchell told us that he thinks Engineering is running the show more now than he let them when he was in charge.

McLellan: Certainly Bill Mitchell was a very flamboyant guy. The only way we really got our act together on this car was by waiting until Bill Mitchell retired. The previous car was never really accepted outside the U.S. The new car carries the cues that make people recognize it as a Corvette, but [are] not so exaggerated. As we got into the aero aspect of it, this car was really designed in the tunnel. [It] has a coefficient of drag of 0.34, and we know how to get it down to a 0.31 or even 0.30 in honest production trim.

Q: How did the wind tunnel affect the '84 styling?

McLellan: Top speed and fuel economy have a lot to do with aero design. Probably the most critical piece of the car from an aero design standpoint was the backlight and the way the taillights were formed. We looked at a variety of ways to terminate the rear of the car.

I can't think of any great disagreements we had with Palmer. The only thing I recall was that we had to redo the taillamps without visible screws. Once we laid down where the engine and people were, it was Jerry fine-tuning the design. I think Jerry was very satisfied with the design, and so were we.

Q: Why is the Corvette still as heavy as it is?

McLellan: I can't tell you how many pounds are tied up in open [Targa-roof body] design, but it's a lot. Structural integrity is important.

Q: Was anything other than fiberglass considered for the C4 body?

McLellan: We never considered anything other than reinforced plastic. It has the ability to absorb minor impacts and is nearly as light as aluminum.

Q: Will the Corvette continue to employ plastic or fiberglass construction?

McLellan: Yes! I see the plastic family of materials evolving themselves. There's a great revolution going on in composites.

Q: The 1984 Corvette took a lot of criticism for being a hard-riding car. Why did you do it that way?

McLellan: There are two schools of thought in the press, and we obviously don't side with those who say the car is too harsh. It is a "tough" car. It was never intended as anything else. It was intended to allow you to get out on a race track and not wallow all over the place. It was intended to enable you to get out and set lap records, and the car has set a number of production lap records at various race tracks. That's one aspect of the car we wanted to optimize and—no question about it—we did.

When you get onto some of the terrible concrete we have in the frost zone, the car gets kind of tough. In response to those kind of inputs, we are looking into softening up the ride [accomplished starting with the '85 model]. But we're doing it very carefully so as not to jeopardize the handling performance that is inherent there. It's going to be evolutionary, and it's going to be done without degrading the handling performance we've already demonstrated.

Q: What's the rationale in having a separate export model for the first time?

McLellan: The car was designed not just for Canada and the U.S. market, but for the export market from the ground up. The export requirements were taken into consideration very early in design, so changes were kept to a minimum. We're producing the export car in the Bowling Green plant so it doesn't have to be retrofitted at point of sale. The car is export-certified for—(and I think I'll get all the countries here, but I may miss a few)—Germany, France, Switzerland, Austria, the low countries, Sweden, England, Spain, Italy, Saudi Arabia and that whole Middle East area, and Japan.

Q: Will we see much factory support of Corvette racing?

McLellan: Our support of racing is a technical support, a position we have taken for a long time. We won't be out there racing the car ourselves.

Q: Is racing still important to maintaining Corvette sales?

McLellan: I think it's a very important adjunct to it. There's the overall statement on Chevrolet performance we're making with the Lola turbo V-6 GTP car project. That's a joint venture between ourselves and Ryan Faulkner, who is doing the turbocharged V-6 motors. We did the aero work. That car...will be a test-bed development tool to wring out the vehicle system as a competitive prototype vehicle. Then it's up to various private racers to take replicas of that car and turn them into successful racing cars. We're doing the part of that venture that we do best, which is supporting engine development and doing the aerodynamic development.

Q: Will we see twin-turbocharged, aluminum-block V-6s in racing 'Vettes?

McLellan: That's certainly a possibility. But that's up to [the private racers] given the rules of the series. We really feel the production car is itself a viable competitor.

Q: Will we see a different engine such as a V-6 anytime?

McLellan: Probably not. We're not going to see them in the short run, period. We'll see them only if we see a benefit. If we can see a V-6 turbo that would outgun the V-8 and had fuel economy and what other benefits it would need to have to be viable, we would consider it. Part of it is that we have such a damn good engine in the small-block V-8. Its evolutionary progress outstrips anything we can demonstrate in a competing alternative. That engine in NASCAR form is putting out over 600 horsepower. We are continuing to evolve the engine. You'll see an evolutionary process over the next few years where you'll look back and say, step by step, "they radically changed that engine."

Q: What sort of Corvettes do you see further down the road?

McLellan: There may be turbine powerplants by then that are viable. That would open up dramatic new opportunities in terms of vehicle design.

Q: Several manufacturers are looking at four-wheel drive for road cars. Is there a four-wheel-drive Corvette in the future?

McLellan: Duntov did a four-wheel-drive Corvette back in the Sixties [CERV II]. In fact, the first of the mid-engine production designs [XP-882] was conceived such that it could have a four-wheel-drive variation. It's not out of the question, [but] it's not very pertinent to the short term.

Q: Why was the first C4 Corvette designated a 1984 model and not an '83, leaving out a 30th anniversary model?

McLellan: Well, [then Chevrolet general manager Robert C.] Stempel said it. He had two choices: He could have the last '83 into the marketplace or the first '84. Everything we built [on an experimental basis] we called an '83. Bob made the decision that, nope, it's going to be the first '84. The government rule is that you can have only one January 1 in your model year. Since we were not going to sell the cars to the public until March 24, we fell within that criterion.

nificantly different than any Corvette engine that preceded it. All-aluminum construction was mandatory to minimize weight and promote rapid heat dissipation in the interest of operating efficiency and fuel economy. Because the existing front frame rails could not be altered, to allow production on the regular Corvette assembly line engineers chose an included valve angle of 22 degrees to make the four-valve V-8 as narrow as possible. At just 26.6 inches across at its widest point, the LT5 took up no more space in the C4 Corvette engine bay than did the L98.

While the ZR-1's contemporary, the Porsche 928, employed an aluminum V-8 in which the pistons ran in linerless silicone-etched bores, the LT5 employed separate, "wet" cylinder liners, also constructed of aluminum. These reduced bore by 0.1 inch compared to the L98 (3.90 versus 4.00 inches), thereby increasing stroke from 3.48 to 3.66 inches to maintain the 5.7-liter displacement. The liners were special-

ly matched to their bores, into which they locked via a simple slip-fit. Interior surfaces were coated with Nikasil, a nickel-silicon alloy that provided an extremely tough wearing surface for the specified lightweight cast-aluminum Mahle pistons. For strength and durability, forged steel was chosen for the connecting rods and crankshaft (the latter were also nitrided), and the block was heavily ribbed and gusseted. The usual five main crankshaft bearings were supported by a special one-piece aluminum cradle that attached to the block by no fewer than 28 bolts. The bearings were oversized at 70 mm, which was deemed necessary for reliable. sustained operation at 7000 rpm.

Proper lubrication is essential for any high-performance engine, so the LT5 crankshaft was cross-drilled for internal centrifugal oiling from the front of the crank to the conrod pin bearings and main bearing journals. The engine included a separate oil cooler with thermostatic control, and the crankcase was a two-piece aluminum assembly with an integral pickup that assured proper feed and bottom-end oiling during hard cornering (when sloshing might otherwise leave part of the sump momentarily dry).

One of the most intricate and intriguing aspects of the LT5 was its unique three-stage induction system. This took advantage of advances in integrated electronic

1

engine controls and also the well-known dynamics of "natural super-charging" or pulsed "ram-effect" tuning (much like the Tuned Port Injection used in the C4 since 1985). A large forward-mounted air cleaner would feed a cast-aluminum throttle-body assembly with three throttle blades—a primary blade of 0.87-inch diameter and two larger, secondary blades measuring 2.32 inches across. The throttle body, in turn, connected to an aluminum plenum chamber that branched into no fewer than 16 individual runners, one for each intake port. Eight of these would feed the so-called primary ports and function full-time; the remaining eight had individual throttles for supplying the secondary ports under certain conditions. Each runner was given its own fuel injector that was sup-plied by twin tank-mounted electric fuel pumps and activated in sequence by the engine control module (ECM).

Air would first be drawn into the throttle body and past the primary throttle blade to the plenum, from which it was distributed to the eight primary ports. In this "first stage" mode, the secondary throttle blades remained closed below roughly 80 degrees of primary blade opening, which corresponded to about 70 miles an hour on the road. Above that, they would open to add air to the eight secondary runners and ports—the full-power "second-stage" mode—provided that certain conditions were met, as calculated by the ECM. Only when the ECM was satisfied that full power would be required did it trig-ger the vacuum actuator that opened the secondary-runner throt-tles.

What's more, the lengths and diameter of the 16 runners were individually selected ("tuned") to take maximum advantage of the high-pressure internal air pulses created by the opening and closing of the intake valves. The pulses increased the density of air in the fuel/air charge by forcing more air into the combustion chamber—this is the "natural supercharging" effect that improves cylinder filling and hence volumetric efficiency.

One handy byproduct of this unique engine-management system was that second-stage performance could be locked out—literally, with a key. The actuator could be manu-ally disabled via a mechanism in the center console; engaging this so-called "valet" mode inhibited full-power operation when handing the

1. Available only for coupes, the ZR-1 option cost a bundle. One reason was the flared rear body-work needed to house wider wheels and tires measuring some 11 inch-es across. Suspension upgrades also included new "Selective Ride Control" shock absorbers. 2. ZR-1s came only with a new six-speed manual gearbox from Germany's ZF, optional for regular '89 'Vettes.

2

1

2

car over to parking-lot attendants or other drivers who could not otherwise be entrusted with the fastest vehicle of its time.

Like the L98 a year earlier, the LT5 was fitted with the new Multec (for Multiple Technology) fuel injectors from GM's Rochester Products Division. Besides improved fuel atomizing and spray control, this design was claimed to need less operating voltage for improved cold-weather cranking performance and be less susceptible to clogging than earlier designs. An ECM-governed fuel shutoff limited maximum rpm to 7200.

The LT5 came with four camshafts in all, two per cylinder bank, one for each set of intake and exhaust valves. Each bank's pair of

288

3

1-4. ZR-1s went together on the same assembly line as "everyday" L98 Corvettes, but volume was much lower. Yearly production was first pegged at 4000–5000, but just 3940 were built for 1990, 2044 for '91, and 500 or less per year thereafter.

4

camshafts was driven by a steel duplex roller chain with a hydraulic tensioner. Valves were actuated directly from the cam lobes, and the intake cams featured distinct primary and secondary lobe profiles to match the valve operation of the staged induction system.

Valves were canted at 11 degrees to their respective ports in a classic cross-flow cylinder head. Essentially a modified pentroof type, it allowed the spark plugs to be centrally placed for good flame propagation and thus faster, more complete combustion, for better efficiency and emissions control. With this combustion-chamber shape and slightly dished pistons, compression ratio was a high 11.25:1. Yet the fast-burn design coupled with the new injection system, the Corvette's first electronic ignition, and staged induction, enabled the LT5 to run happily on regular unleaded (87 octane) fuel.

Chevrolet contracted with Stillwater, Oklahoma-based Mercury Marine to build the LT5, and ultimately a marine version of the new powerplant (which was appropriate, since many of the firm's "Mercruiser" engines had originated as GM designs). This also made sense given the low production anticipated for the ZR-1 model—a maximum of only 4000–8000 units per year. As shipped to the Corvette assembly plant in Bowling Green, Kentucky, the LT5 weighed in at a mere 39 pounds more than the L98—which was amazing since it accounted for a 60 percent increase in power. For the record, the LT5 produced a blazing 375 bhp, compared to 245 in the base Corvette (power was limited to 250 bhp with the valet function engaged). Yet for all its power, the LT5 garnered respectable fuel economy—around 22 mpg combined city/highway.

For a time, whenever an LT5 needed certain repairs, a Chevy dealer's service department would have to remove the engine and ship it back to Mercury Marine; an owner would then have the choice of either receiving a new engine or having the original one fixed, if possible. This practice would continue through the end of calendar-year 1993, after which Chevrolet assumed all service responsibilities for the powerplant.

Linking the engine to the ZR-1's beefy rear wheels and tires was a new six-speed transmission, designed in collaboration with and supplied by the renowned German transmission company Zandfabrik Friedrichshafen—better known as ZF. (In standard Corvette models it replaced the awkward "4+3 Overdrive" unit.)

The ZF gearbox offered two significant new features over the previous Corvette manual. First, its gears were arranged to minimize synchronizer loads. Second was the inclusion of Computer-Aided Gear Selection (CAGS), included to help improve fuel economy. The CAGS system was used not only on the Corvette, but also on the Chevrolet Camaro and Pontiac Firebird six-speeds. It employed an integral-rail shift linkage with a solenoid actuator that guided the lever from first gear directly to fourth whenever the car was running at 12–19 mph, with at least a partly warm engine and a throttle opening of no more than a third. Though it could be intrusive and irritating, particularly when driving in traffic, this feature helped enable the ZR-1 to avoid the dreaded gas-guzzler tax. Ironically, it may have had the opposite effect in real world driving, since many drivers tended to accelerate harder in first gear than they otherwise might in order to avoid locking out second and third. Still, the shift quality afforded by the new ZF gearbox was a big improvement

1

over the stiff, clunky linkage of the old 4+3.

As could be expected, motoring journalists were absolutely effusive in their praise of the ZR-1's added muscle, and their published reviews featured acceleration figures that looked more like typographical errors than bona fide test results. The buff books recorded uncanny 0–60 mph times ranging from 4.5 to 4.9 seconds, reaching the quarter-mile in 12.8 seconds at 111 mph to 13.4 seconds at 108.5 mph. Testers reached top speeds as high as 175 mph.

Elsewhere around the ZR-1, differences with the standard coupe were much more subtle. For starters, the car's rear fenders bulged three inches wider than on L98 models. This was done to accommodate the car's massive 315/35ZR17 rear tires; at 11 inches wide they offered an added 1.5 inches of "footprint" compared to the standard-issue 275/40ZR17s

The ZR-1 looked much like any other 1990 Corvette coupe, something that disappointed many fans.

(which were still used up front, as on L98 models).

The package also included a beefier differential, the 13-inch twin-caliper front disc brakes introduced optionally for the 1988 Z51 package, and a reinforced front-end structure designed to help counter cowl shake on rough roads. The race-oriented Z51 handling package was likewise standard, as well as the Selective Ride Control suspension option that was added elsewhere in the line as optional equipment for 1989.

Aside from the more-muscular rear haunches, the only visual differences Chevrolet offered for the ZR-1 were square (instead of round) taillamps in a convex (rather than concave) back panel that Chevy claimed would benefit aerodynamics. More subtle was a small ZR-1 badge on the rear bumper at the extreme right, below the perimeter rub strip. To be sure, only the most rabid Corvette followers could discern a ZR-1 from a conventional 1990 model at a casual glance.

Not only was the ZR-1 eagerly anticipated, it created an instant

sensation in the marketplace. A total of 3049 well-heeled fanatics paid well in excess of the 1990's already stiff price tag for the privilege of owning the fastest car in town. It's been reported that some dealers initially asked for—and received—as much as $100,000 for early ZR-1s.

While reviewers gushed about the car's uncanny acceleration, the ZR-1 was criticized for its high sticker price, the manual transmission's dubious skip-shift feature, and especially its dearth of unique bodywork. Most writers felt buyers were owed more tangible evidence to show the world that they'd paid the additional $27,000.

Out on the track, a stock ZR-1 would set 12 FIA world records for speed and endurance in March 1990, at Stockton, Texas. Three of these records were set regardless of classification—the first time in 50 years they had been claimed by a regular production car. The ZR-1's FIA records would stand until 2001, eventually being surpassed by a specially built 600-bhp "W-12" Volkswagen prototype.

Alas, its freshman year would prove to be the high-water mark for the ZR-1. Its subsequent slide in sales was likely due in part to the

fact that the rest of the Corvette line would adopt the ZR-1's convex rear fascia design with four rectangular taillamps for 1991. (However, the ZR-1 would continue to use a roof-mounted, center stoplamp, rather than the fascia-mounted version now featured on standard coupes and convertibles). Thus the package, the price of which had risen to $31,683, offered even less identifiable exterior exclusivity. Sales would slip to 2044 for '91, and it's not likely many of them commanded in excess of the sticker price.

Additional ZR-1 emblems would be added above the side-fender vents for 1992, along with more-aggressive-looking twin exhaust tips at the rear, for a bit easier identification. Unfortunately, this was also the year the just-introduced Shelby Cobra-inspired Dodge Viper and its ferocious 400-bhp V-10 engine would lay claim to the ZR-1's sports-car supremacy. Probably more damaging to ZR-1 sales was a revised small-block V-8 that was added to the standard 1992 coupe and convertible—the LT1. This new engine would offer

300 bhp, 50 more than the L98 it replaced, which rendered the exorbitant cost of the ZR-1 package, still $31,683, superfluous to most potential buyers. As a result, ZR-1 sales would plummet to a mere 502 units for '92.

In the great Detroit tradition, horsepower was added to the LT5 for 1993 to help bolster the ZR-1's fortunes—it was now up to a rambunctious Viper-matching 405 bhp. The additional 30 horses were obtained via modifications to the valvetrain and cylinder head, platinum-tipped 100,000-mile spark plugs, and the use of synthetic oil. The ZR-1 package also dropped slightly in price, to $31,258. But the changes would be for naught, as sales slipped to a miniscule 448 units.

The ZR-1 would soldier on for 1994 and 1995, with production again limited to 448 cars each year, before Chevrolet management would finally dethrone the "King of the Hill." (Mercury Marine had actually built its last LT5 back in November 1993; the remaining inventory of engines and the tooling

used to build them had been sent to the Corvette assembly plant for storage.) The final ZR-1 out of a total of 6939 built during its six-year reign would roll off the Bowling Green assembly line on April 28, 1995.

Ultimately, the car's high price, continued lack of physical distinction, stiff competition from the faster and flashier Dodge Viper, and its pallid performance premium over a beefed-up standard Corvette would be named as co-conspirators in its downfall. Adding to its demise, an all-new Corvette was already in the works, and Chevrolet couldn't justify the expense of retooling the low-volume LT5 to meet the EPA's coming rule changes.

Fortunately, however, the ZR-1 wouldn't be the last ultra-high-performance 'Vette Chevy would build; the C5's Z01 variant would help fill the void seven years later. Still, for one brief and shining moment in the annals of automotive history, the ZR-1 Corvette was indeed the King of the Hill, ruling America's highways with an iron fist and an aluminum engine.

This Chevy PR photo emphasizes the ZR-1's convex, three-inch wider tail versus that of the standard 1990 coupe (*background*).

Profile: Chuck Jordan

Charles M. "Chuck" Jordan was one of the most likeable and enthusiastic design executives in all Detroit. He was 59 years old when he succeeded Irwin W. Rybicki in October 1986 as only the fourth design vice president in GM history. He was certainly well prepared to assume the job once held by Harley Earl and Bill Mitchell, having worked for both of his illustrious predecessors. Jordan joined GM in 1949 after earning a degree in mechanical engineering from MIT. He served early on in the Advanced Styling section, where he first became enamored of Corvettes when the original 1953 Motorama show car was being developed under Earl. Jordan's first major assignment came in 1957 as chief designer for Cadillac. Five years later he was put in charge of all GM car and truck exteriors. Then, in 1967, he was named design director at Opel, GM's German subsidiary, where he spearheaded the 1970–75 Manta coupe.

Jordan was brought back to Detroit in 1970 to take charge of exteriors for Buick, Olds, and Cadillac, while Rybicki was given the same responsibilities for Chevrolet, Pontiac, and commercial vehicles. The two then switched jobs in 1972. When Rybicki succeeded Mitchell as corporate vice-president for design in 1977, Jordan became his second-in-command as director of design, a position he held until Rybicki's 1986 retirement. Jordan himself retired in 1992, as per company policy, upon reaching age 65.

Blessed with a delightful "down home" manner that quickly put guests at ease, Chuck Jordan was always eager to talk cars—especially high-performance cars. He was also surprisingly candid for a high-ranking executive of the world's largest automaker, as you'll see in the following excerpts from a 1989 interview with the editors.

Q: You're a well-known admirer of Ferraris. How does this influence design work on the Corvette?

Chuck Jordan: As we move forward with the Corvette, which we're doing right now, we're starting from the inside out. We're taking care of all the things that we and our loyal customers—the people who love Corvettes—feel should be improved. Our own feelings are influenced somewhat by our experience with Ferraris. [Chevy designer] Jerry Palmer has a Ferrari. I've got a Ferrari—a Testarossa

that, for example, I can get in and out of very easily. I've also got a Corvette convertible that I've driven for about 10,000 miles—and it's a lot more difficult to get in and out of. So there are some things that we learn both from driving our own product and the experience with other cars that we drive and that some of us own, like Porsches, Ferraris, and Lotuses—high-performance cars, which is what the Corvette is. All this influences what we're doing as we move ahead.

One thing I've experienced in my Corvette is that it feels and looks "plastic" inside. I'm used to the Testarossa. Wherever you touch that car, there's something soft. Whether it's vinyl or leather is not the point. The point is, it's soft. So I retrimmed my Corvette to show our guys and management what we ought to be doing in a car of this caliber—a world-class sports car.

I love Ferraris, but I sold my Lusso, my Daytona, and my Boxer because I'm not a collector. I just always want to drive the current car, the state of the art, because that's the jumping-off point for us.

Q: The late Bill Mitchell once told us that the current Corvette lacks the character and excitement of the ones he did. How do you respond to that?

Jordan: Well, you know I worked with Bill for many, many years. I really admired him. He was our leader—he was almost a god to us. He was a hard taskmaster and raised a lot of hell with us, but we learned well and learned clearly under Mitchell. The Corvette was his preoccupation, it really was. I know, because I was Mitchell's assistant for a long time. I saw all these things

happening: the Stingray race car, the split-window Sting Ray, the show cars he did. He really ate and slept Corvettes, and he had a profound influence on the car. Now the last one he designed was after he left GM—his own personal car. He thought that our design was too tame or too conservative. But his car was a throwback to what he was doing 10 years earlier with the show cars, and that wasn't an answer either.

It wouldn't be constructive to go into how we got the car that's on the street today [the C4]. It's there, it's a good design, and it's going to be at least 10 years old before we replace it. But when we do replace it, I can guarantee you that the next Corvette is going to be a great design. Its proportions will be striking. Its interior will look like performance and feel like performance. The shape of the car will make you drool. But you're still going to know it's a Corvette—even from a block away.

Q: What do you think of the ZR-1?

Jordan: The ZR-1 is fantastic—just a wonderful car! The 6-speed gearbox is smooth. The engine is unbelievable, and driving the car is a real pleasure. It's very civilized to just tool around in, but underneath your foot you've got all that potential—when you punch it, it really, really goes.

Q: How does it compare to your Ferrari in that respect?

Jordan: Both the ZR-1 and the Testarossa have outstanding performance. The ZR-1 reminds me more of a [Porsche] 928 in sound and feel—very smooth, quiet, and silky—whereas the Ferrari is a Ferrari with all that goes with it—it's a different deal. But one thing is for sure: The ZR-1 is a world-class sports car—right up there with the "big boys."

Q: Why wasn't the ZR-1 made visually different from the regular Corvette other than in the tail? Were there any plans to set it more apart from other 'Vettes?

Jordan: We [Design Staff] had a long discussion about that, and marketing had something to say about it. We had to change the rear because the rubber is wider, so we had to kick the body out over the rear wheels. That even got into the doors, so there was a change in the door as well as the rear quarter. We also wanted a different front fascia, but marketing felt strongly that that wasn't important. And maybe they're right. We, as designers, would always like to do a whole new car. We're always impatient to do more, so they kind of keep a

balance. But really, a Corvette's a Corvette. We don't want a "standard" model and a "deluxe" model. We want to make sure that the image of the Corvette is not diluted, that it's clear. Whether you've got a ZR-1 or not, the image is going to be just one image.

Q: So you wouldn't want to follow Ferrari by having two entirely different Corvettes the way they have the 328 and the Testarossa?

Jordan: No. To follow Ferrari we'd have to have two separate cars—a Corvette like we have now and something like the Corvette Indy [a late-'80s concept car], a mid-engine supercar. Maybe someday that'll happen. But right now, the ZR-1 and the regular Corvette aren't like that. They're different in their performance characteristics, but not in their basic character.

Q: Out of all the Corvettes built since 1953, what's your personal favorite?

Jordan: There are two that stand out for me. One is the '53, because I was a kid here then, as a designer, and I was working on the floor above where the original Corvette was being designed for the Motorama. When we'd work overtime, which we did almost all the time, we used to sneak down there at night and look at that car. We weren't supposed to, but we did. That was Harley Earl's car, and it had the most profound influence on me. I couldn't believe it. Wow! You know, it was the time of the Jag XK-120 and Austin-Healey, cars like that. It was hard to

Among the many famous designs in Jordan's portfolio is the '59 Cadillac, which he spearheaded as chief designer for that GM division.

believe this was really happening.

But the most exciting [Corvette] to me was the split-window Sting Ray [from 1963]. We couldn't believe when we were doing that car that it would actually be on the street. That's how different it seemed in those days, how exciting it was. And it's still an exciting-looking car. We got everything right on that one.

Q: What's your least favorite?

Jordan: My least favorite is the '58 Corvette with dual headlights and all that chrome. I was chief designer on that one. and I guarantee it was the result of the era we were in. Fifty-eight was not a vintage year.

Q: Of the many Corvette-inspired show cars and experimentals built over the years, such as the Two-Rotor car and the Aerovette, are there any you think should have been produced for sale?

Jordan: There's been a lot of great Corvette show cars—all interesting cars. Many of them had big pipes, made a lot of noise, and went like a banshee. They were Mitchell's toys. They were wonderful—and we all loved them. But, I suppose I felt strongest about the

Aerovette as a candidate for production. I believe the strongest Corvette statement yet [circa 1989], is the Corvette Indy. Now there's a car I'd really like to see in production!

Q: What would you have had to do to the Corvette Indy to make it a production car?

Jordan: We'd already done it. We started with the static show model, then made a running version, [and then] a productionized version. It meets all the conditions [federal requirements], and it's sensational! But keep in mind, because of its layout and sophistication, if the Corvette Indy were to be produced, it would fall in the supercar category—very expensive. So don't expect a Corvette Indy type of car to replace the front-engine/rear-drive car any time soon.

Q: Where are you right now with the C5 Corvette design?

Jordan: We're in the fun part—the search stage where anything goes. It doesn't get better than this—designing a new Corvette with no holds barred. We set up a studio in the far end of the basement—nobody can find us. We call it the "Corvette skunk works," and that's where we're working on the new Corvette.

But our isolated studio location doesn't mean we're designing in a vacuum. Our Advanced Packaging group is right next door. We've had many discussions already with Dave McLellan [Corvette chief engineer] and his guys.

1

2

3

And the marketing group has been over to give us the "voice of the customer"—how sports-car people feel and what they like and dislike about today's cars. And these discussions will continue. In the meantime, behind the locked doors of the skunk works, a small family of our best designers, sculptors, and technical people are at work in a free, creative atmosphere. This is "bubble up" time—the time to explore, to reach. Walking through the door of that studio is like walking into a new era. The collection of ideas—the sketches, scale models, fullsize drawings, and the interior buck—give you a "smell" of the new car.

Now it may sound like this is a "play pen" where we're just having fun—and it is to a degree, but it's also serious business. This free atmosphere produces some wild, imaginative design directions—but they have to be tempered with good judgment. In the end, we're only looking for one design—the right design for the next Corvette.

Q: What about your Advanced Concepts Center in California?

Jordan: Yeah, they're working on the new Corvette design, too. Their first proposals look great—but we're going to keep them independent from our work here. It's basically the same approach we took with the California IROC concept car, where we asked the team in California to design a Camaro that would be a significant car in that market. We figure a car that can make a

strong impact in California will be fine in, say, Wichita, Kansas. You know, they're pretty hard-nosed out there in California, and you've got to do some things differently from what you do in Warren, Michigan. So we're going to use their designs as another input for the final production design.

Q: You've declared that the era of look-alike styling is over at GM and that you want to establish greater brand identity among the five car divisions. How will this affect the Corvette, and what do you see as the biggest challenge in designing the next one?

Jordan: Part of our new design philosophy has to do with strong images on the road. There's a pot full of car brands running around out there. An awful lot of them are just plain bland, dull, and boring design-wise. I think it's time to bring the excitement back—to make a bold statement and focus the image of the cars and trucks we produce. When you see a Buick, you've got to know it's a Buick. Not from some loud graphics or strange design elements but from its proportions, its shape—the "feel" of the car. And you shouldn't need 20/20 vision to recognize this.

The same thing applies to the Corvette. I suppose it's a little easier with the Corvette. It already has a strong image. We're going to make it stronger. There's a lot of competition out there in the sports car area and more coming. So we're not going to be timid.

Other Jordan efforts included GM's Impact electric-car concept (**1**) and the Stingray III concept (**2**). Another noteworthy production Cadillac done during his tenure was the first front-drive Eldorado of 1967 (**3**).

You know, people don't buy Corvettes for basic transportation. It's an emotional car. Some people love it for its ride, handling, and performance. Others are attracted by its image—the excitement of driving a distinctive sports car. We're dealing with a "total car" here—one that will perform the way it looks. And that's the exciting part for us, as designers. From our standpoint, our design will be new in proportion and shape—and beautiful from any angle. Our goal is to make the next Corvette as significant, designwise, as the split-window Sting Ray when it came out.

Now that's easy for me to say—not so easy to do. I'm not talking about doing another split-window design. I'm talking about the feeling I had when I was younger, and we were designing the split-window coupe. I just couldn't believe that car would actually be on the road—it was so wild! We're doing it again right now in our basement studio.

PART 3 1991-1996

Nineteen-ninety had been a banner year of sorts for the Corvette: The long-awaited ZR-1 was truly the "King of the Hill," and it had created a buzz the likes of which 'Vette fans hadn't known for some time (and wouldn't see again for several years). The ZR-1 had met or exceeded most reviewers' performance expectations, and eager buyers gleefully paid well in excess of the car's $58,995 list price to be among the first drivers to command the car's awesome acceleration.

Unfortunately, if the motoring public had worked itself into an absolute frenzy over the ZR-1's debut, its enthusiasm was rapidly

beginning to wane during the 1991 model year. While there was no faulting the car's high-tech approach to hitting triple-digit speeds on command, critics now began to harp on its most obvious flaws. True, it was considerably more affordable than most exotic European sports cars, but there was no avoiding the fact that the 1991 ZR-1 package added a lofty $31,683 premium to the $32,455 base coupe, yet offered little in the way of styling enhancements to go along with the 125 added horsepower. While there was no mistaking, say, a Porsche 911 from a 924,

it took a trained eye to discern a pricey ZR-1 from the otherwise "entry-level" Corvette.

And for 1991, Chevrolet made the "King of the Hill" look even more like a commoner. While the ZR-1 retained unique doors and rear fenders to accommodate its 11-inch-wide rear wheels and tires, the standard Corvette coupe and convertible received a ZR-1-type tail, with similar convex styling and four rectangular taillamps. This left only

"The King" may have been the ultimate C4, but other models weren't ignored, gaining yet another improved version of their classic small-block V-8, plus more new high-tech features. A rougher-than-ever market and new corporate troubles had GM again wondering about Corvette's future in the 1990s—but not for long. Meantime, the C4 just kept on getting better and better.

the slightly wider rear flanks, a roof-mounted center stop-lamp (other models now integrated it into the rear fascia) and a single badge to distinguish a ZR-1 from a base coupe.

Further stealing the ZR-1's thunder, Dodge had announced that its all-new Viper would debut for 1992, offering some of the most aggressive race-car looks to date (inspired by Carroll Shelby's famed Ford Cobras of the 1960s), wrapped around a mammoth V-10 engine that produced a stunning 400 bhp. To be priced roughly on a par with the ZR-1, the Viper promised well-heeled sports-car enthusiasts a considerably more expressive way to

Chevy PR mailed out this sketch to announce that a new Corvette would be pace car for the 1995 Indy 500—the 10th time a Chevrolet had been so honored and the third time for a 'Vette. The car itself was publicly unveiled a few days after Christmas 1994, fittingly at the annual Indianapolis Auto Show.

spend their performance-car dollars.

As a result, ZR-1 sales would fall by a third for 1991, down to 2044 units; nowhere near the planned maximum capacity of 4000–8000 cars per year Chevrolet had hoped for. Buyers were finally paying more-realistic prices, as dealers were losing their ability to command a hefty premium for the ZR-1.

What's more, it was determined that an all-new Corvette, originally anticipated for 1995, would still be several years away. GM brass delayed the program until as late as 1998 due to the automaker's flaccid financial situation. At one point, Chevrolet General Manager Jim Perkins was even brought before GM brass to defend whether the division should continue to build the car at all. Though it was agreed that the 'Vette would and should continue as the division's flagship, it had become painfully evident that Chevrolet still wouldn't have the financial wherewithal to produce a flashy mid-engine model. After all, sales were still a fraction of their all-time highs from the mid-1980s, and even the ZR-1's heady introduction hadn't lifted the car's fortunes.

It was not all bad news for the Corvette in 1991, however. All models received a smoother, slimmer nose with wraparound parking/cornering/fog lights, wider bodyside moldings that were now body col-

ored, and horizontal front-fender strakes that replaced the previous gill-like louvers. Though they remained the same size (9.5 inches wide) as before, aluminum wheels on the standard coupes and convertibles were restyled for '91.

Inside, a new power-delay feature allowed the audio system and power windows to operate after the ignition key was switched off until the driver's door was opened, up to a maximum of 15 minutes. In addition, a "low oil" indicator was added to the driver information center, and all models were pre-wired to accommodate a cellular telephone or other 12-volt accessory. On ZR-1s, the "full power" indicator light was relocated to alongside the valet-selection key.

Effectively combining the previous Z51 performance handling package with the FX3 selective ride and handling option was the new RPO Z07. At $2155, the new package included all heavy-duty suspension components to offer a choice between a "firm" and "very firm" ride; previously, if the Z51 and FX3 were combined some standard suspension components were retained, allowing a choice between a "soft" and "firm" ride. Limited to coupes

only, the Z07 package was intended for enthusiasts and racers.

Exhaust systems were also revised for '91, and included larger muffler sections with a more finely tuned exhaust note and lower back pressure; though this was intended to boost performance, power ratings for the L98 engine remained the same as before.

1991 was the final year for the dealer-installed Callaway Twin-Turbo package, which was ordered by 62 hearty individuals at an additional $33,000 a copy. Meanwhile, Reeves Callaway introduced a Corvette conversion of his own for '91, the twin-turbo Callaway Speedster convertible. Its front-end design was reminiscent of Callaway's 1998 Sledgehammer but with an overall more aerodynamic profile. Its L98 used two turbochargers to produce 450 hp and 600 lbs/ft of torque. O.Z. brand racing wheels dressed up the exterior, and Connolly leather was applied to the cabin. Prices started at $107,000, and a grand total of 10 would be built.

The World Challenge racing series would continue for 1991, though Chevrolet would no longer build specially modified Corvettes

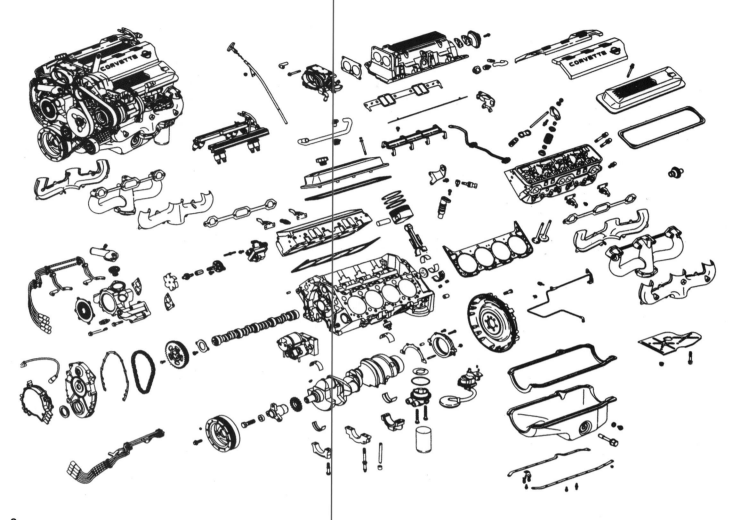

2

3

to run in the series; all performance modifications were now the responsibilities of the individual race teams.

Sales for the 1991 model year followed the ZR-1's downward trend, and declined to 20,639 units, with coupes outselling convertibles by about a three-to-one ratio.

While Chevrolet would unveil a concept car called the Stingray III at the North American International Auto Show in January 1992, it was announced that the C4 generation would have to remain in production at least until 1997. Fortunately, it would continue with added power for 1992—a boost of 50 bhp to be exact—thanks to a new version of the standard pushrod small-block engine, dubbed LT1.

1. A subtle 1991 facelift ushered in a smoother nose and front-fender "strakes" instead of gills. **2-3.** Base horsepower jumped by 50 for '92 as the L98 V-8 gave way to a much-modified version called LT1.

Rated at a healthy 300 bhp at 5000 rpm, and with 330 lb/ft of torque at 4000 rpm, the LT1's new-found power came from a number of improvements and refinements to the workhorse 5.7-liter V-8. These included the introduction of computer-controlled engine timing, a new low-restriction exhaust system that used two catalytic converters and oxygen sensors (one for each cylinder bank), a new camshaft profile, a higher compression ratio, free-flow cylinder heads, and a revised multiport fuel-injection system. The LT1 weighed 21 pounds more than the L98 it replaced, however, primarily due to the use of cast-iron, rather than stainless-steel exhaust manifolds.

The LT1 was also the first Chevrolet powerplant to use

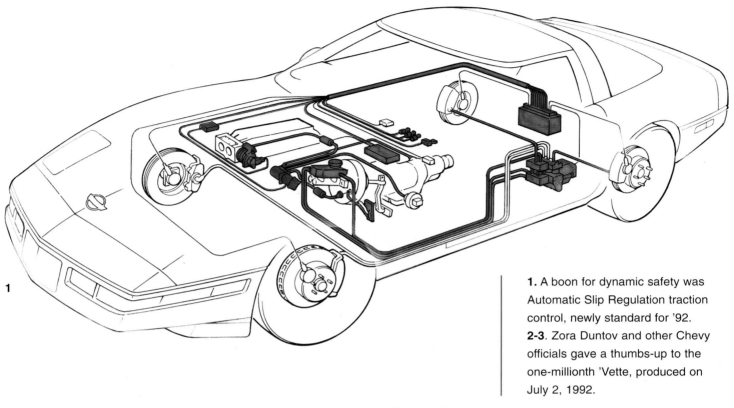

1. A boon for dynamic safety was Automatic Slip Regulation traction control, newly standard for '92.
2-3. Zora Duntov and other Chevy officials gave a thumbs-up to the one-millionth 'Vette, produced on July 2, 1992.

"reverse flow cooling," in which the engine routed coolant directly to the cylinder heads, rather than sending it through the block first. This was said to allow higher bore temperatures and reduced ring friction, and also help cooling at key points. Mobil 1 synthetic oil was now used at the factory and was recommended for subsequent changes; the use of synthetic oil precluded the need for an engine-oil cooler, which was no longer offered as an option.

As could be expected, the motoring press greeted the new standard engine with gusto. Perhaps what Chevrolet did not expect was that most reviewers would also conclude that the LT1 and its 300 bhp tended to make the ZR-1 with its 75 extra horsepower—not to mention its steep sticker price—somewhat irrelevant. *Car and Driver*, for example, found that while the ZR-1 could hit 60 mph from a standing start in 4.7 seconds, the LT1 could reach it in just 5.1 seconds. While the magazine's top speed of 179 mph for the King of the Hill still reigned supreme, few rational

motorists could argue that the 161 mph top-end the LT1 reached wasn't enough. On paper and in buyers' minds, the extra $31,683 tariff for the ZR-1's dwindling performance premium hardly seemed worth it, and only a scant 502 buyers ordered RPO ZR1.

All 1992 Corvettes benefited from a new standard traction-control system called Acceleration Slip Regulation, which was developed in conjunction with Germany's Bosch. It used the ABS sensors to detect rear-wheel slip and apply the brakes to the affected wheels and/or throttle back power to maintain traction. A dashboard switch could be activated to disable the system. Further helping the car hug the road to match the LT1 powerplant's added muscle were standard new directional/asymmetrical-tread Goodyear GS-C tires.

Otherwise, physical changes were nominal at best for '92. The car's twin exhaust outlets were now rectangular in shape, and the ZR-1 acquired additional identifying emblems on its side fenders.

The 1-millionth Corvette, a white

convertible with specially stitched headrests, rolled off the Bowling Green assembly line on July 2, 1992. Ironically, 'Vette production withered to just 20,479 for the '92 model year, its lowest output since 1962.

With the Dodge Viper outpacing Chevy's "King of the Hill" ZR-1, and the standard LT1 engine nipping at its heels, the LT5 was appropriately beefed up for 1993. Modifications to the valvetrain and cylinder heads—along with the use of platinum-tipped spark plugs and synthetic oil—enabled the engine to produce 405 bhp (up from 375 bhp), while a new exhaust gas recirculation system also improved emissions control.

Not to be ignored, the standard LT1 engine gained 10 lbs/ft of torque, now up to 340 lbs/ft, and ran more smoothly and quietly, thanks to a host of internal improvements.

To aid handling, base models followed the ZR-1's lead by adopting different width tires at the front and rear. The front tires were narrowed slightly to 255/45ZR17 and their rims slimmed by one inch, to 8.5 inches. The rear tires were widened slightly, to 285/40ZR17, on the same 9.5-inch wheels as before.

A newly optional passive keyless entry system that was unique to the Corvette automatically locked or unlocked the doors as the driver left or approached the car. The proximity-based system engaged or disengaged when a specially encoded keyfob sensor entered or left a magnetic field that surrounded the vehicle. In addition to unlocking the doors when in range, the system would also turn on the interior lights and disengage the alarm system, and it could be programmed to unlock either just the driver's door or the passenger's as well.

With the Corvette reaching yet another milestone in 1993, another special edition was prepared: The 40th Anniversary Edition, RPO Z25, cost $1455 and included Ruby Red paint, matching leather seats and wheel centers, and special badges; it was ordered on 6749 cars. In addition, all cars equipped with leather seats came with 40th Anniversary embroidery on the headrests, while standard black cloth seats remained unadorned.

Florida-based Greenwood Automotive Performance offered its ultra-high-performance G572 for '93, which was a souped-up Corvette coupe with functional aero body panels and a reinforced chassis. Under the hood was an aluminum-block-and-head 9.4-liter (572 cid) Chevy V-8 rated at 575 bhp at 5400 rpm; it was mated to a GM four-speed automatic transmission. The modified 'Vette could reach 60 mph in 3.4 seconds, the quarter-mile in 11.5 at 135 mph, and a top speed of 218, all for $179,333.

Despite the added oomph to its LT5 engine, ZR-1 sales remained at

2

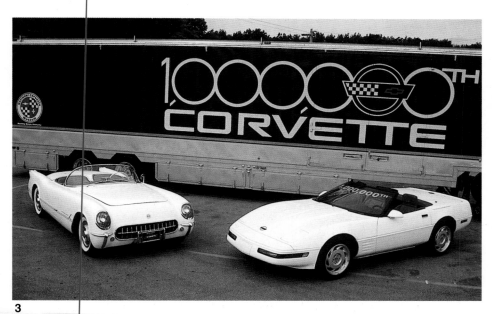

3

a mere trickle, with only 448 produced for 1993. Overall, however, Corvette sales rose for the first time in four years, to a final tally of 21,590 units.

For 1994, revisions to the base LT1 engine included a more powerful ignition for shorter starting times (especially in cold weather), and a new sequential fuel-injection system for better throttle response, idle quality, overall driveability, and lower tailpipe emissions. Matching

the engine's refinements was the Corvette's first electronically controlled automatic transmission, offering smoother and more consistent shifting than the previous all-mechanical four-speed. Also, in light of industry concerns regarding so-called "unintended acceleration" episodes, a lockout switch on the new automatic gearbox required a driver to depress and hold the brake pedal before shifting out of "park."

1

2

3

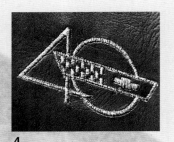

4

5

1-2. The 1992 Stingray III concept showcased that year's new LT1 V-8. A rear-mounted transmission—but little else—previewed the next-generation 'Vette. **3-4.** Honoring Corvette's 40th birthday was a special 1993 package with the expected logos inside and out. **5.** Internal modifications for 1993 boosted ZR-1 horsepower to 405, a gain of 30 that finally exceeded Chevy's original target. **6,8.** A "passive keyless entry" system was new option for '93 'Vettes, including the base convertible and coupe. **7,9.** Newly available for '94s, ZR-1s included, were five-spoke wheels wearing Goodyear "run-flat" tires.

6

So-called "run-flat" or "extended mobility" tires were newly added to the options list for 1994. Designed by Goodyear, these low-profile tires were among the first available on a production car. They featured a special bead construction that could maintain its shape, even with a complete loss of air pressure. The tires were advertised as being able to hold up for a range of at least 50 miles after losing air without a noticeable loss of ride and handling quality. The optional low-tire-pressure warning system was mandatory when buyers ordered the run-flat tires, however, since a driver might not be able to otherwise tell when one of them was "flat."

Also for 1994, spring rates on the RPO FX3 selective ride and handling package were softened a bit to improve ride comfort, and tire pressures on standard models were reduced from 35 psi to 30 psi.

7

8

9

1

Cosmetic changes for the model year were limited to the addition of two new colors, Admiral Blue and Copper Metallic (though only 116 cars were sold with the latter due to limited availability) and unique non-directional five-spoke wheels included with the ZR-1 package. Inside, a passenger-side airbag and knee bolster were made standard, complying with the second phase of the federal government's "passive restraint" safety requirements. Leather seats were made standard, and were available in base and "sport" versions. Less-restrictive bolsters were now included to accommodate larger passengers and to facilitate entry and exit. Also new was a redesigned two-spoke steering wheel that, to most reviewers, was a functional step down from the one it replaced (there were no longer spokes at the convenient "10 and 2" positions, for example). A one-touch "express down" driver's side power window was likewise added for '94, and new

dashboard instrumentation now changed colors—from white to tangerine—at night. Also, the car's air-conditioning system now used an environmentally friendly refrigerant, R-134a, instead of the ozone-layer-unfriendly R-12 Freon. What's more, rear windows on convertibles were now made of glass instead of plastic and came standard with a defogger.

Reeves Callaway would continue massaging Corvettes, and ran a modified 'Vette at LeMans in May, 1994—the first time in nearly 20 years Chevy had appeared there. While the car qualified for pole position in the GT-2 class, and would lead the pack at the six-hour mark (running 8th overall)—it would run out of gas an hour later due to a fuel-consumption miscalculation. The 'Vette's racing fortunes would be more favorable in July, as a Callaway SuperNatural Corvette driven by Andreas Fuchs and Enrico Bertaggia finished first in GT-2 class and second overall at

the four-hour endurance race at Vallelunga, Italy. The same month, a Callaway SuperNatural driven by Boris Said and Halmut Reis would finish first in GT-2 class and third overall at the Spa/Francorchamps four-hour race.

Surprisingly, 1994 Corvette sales rose to 23,330 despite few noteworthy changes and a modest price increase to $36,185. The $31,258 ZR-1 package managed only 448 orders, however. It was subsequently announced that 1995 would be the last model year for the King of the Hill. The package was being continued in order to make use of the several hundred LT5 engines built by Mercury Marine that remained in storage (Mercury had completed production of the LT5 back in November 1993).

On a happier note, after years of planning and fund-raising with support from both Chevrolet and private contributors, the National Corvette Museum would open in Bowling Green, Kentucky, not far

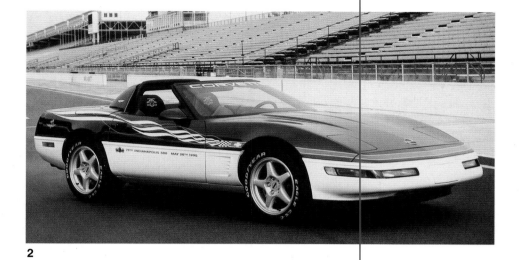

2

3

4

1. Besides improved ergonomics, a prime reason for the redesigned dashboard on post-1989 C4s was to provide space for a passenger-side airbag, which ended up beneath a panel on the upper right. **2-4.** Like past Indy Pace Car Chevys, the 1995 Corvette (*top*) was available as a replica, actually a $2816 option package. Buyers got the same special paint and graphics, but not the actual pacer's roof "hoop," light bar, and other track-required features. Mechanically, though, all were basically stock LT1 ragtops. Orders for the replica package totaled a mere 527.

from the assembly plant, on September 2, 1994. Four-thousand Corvettes from virtually every state in the union would be on hand for the opening ceremonies, and 118,000 visitors would tour the museum over the course of the three-day festivities; the gift shop alone would ring up $1 million in sales.

It was announced that an all-new C5 Corvette was on track for the 1997 model year, and with testing already underway on the new model, changes for the 1995 Corvette would remain incremental at best. Revised "gill" air vents now graced the car's front fenders. Inside, seats carried stronger "French" seam stitching, the CD player was given stronger mounting to prevent skipping, and several adhesive-fabric straps were installed in key places around the cabin to help reduce rattles.

The standard LT1 engine's refinement process continued, though power remained at 300 bhp. Connecting rods were revised to improve strength and weight uniformity, the engine fan was made quieter, and the fuel-injection system was improved to account for the use of alcohol-blend fuels and to reduce fuel dripping when the engine was turned off. Likewise, enhancements to the electronically controlled four-speed automatic transmission afforded even smoother shifting, and the unit's torque converter was made lighter but stronger. Heavy-duty ZR-1 brakes were made standard across the board, and all models now included a new ABS/traction-control system (ABS/ASR-5). Models equipped with the base suspension now had lower front/rear spring rates.

Since the available extended-mobility tires effectively did away with the need for a spare, buyers who chose the optional run-flat rubber could delete the spare tire (in the name of weight reduction as well as a lower price) via RPO N84 for a $100 credit.

A near-stock LTI convertible paced the Indy 500 in 1995, and Chevy marked the occasion with the RPO Z4Z Pace Car Replica. This $2816 package was limited to convertibles, and included Dark Purple Metallic over Arctic White paint, a white top, and unique graphics and trim. Of the 527 replicas built, 87 were sent to the Indy 500 and/or used for public relations purposes, 20 were exported, and the remaining 415 were doled out to Chevrolet's top-performing U.S. dealers.

Though the Corvette had been around in its basic form for 11 years, the media still found good things to say about it, particularly regarding its traditional strong suits, like neck-snapping acceleration and ultra-grippy handling. And thanks to Chevy's ongoing improvements, the buff books were now also praising the car for its much-improved finish and build quality.

The successful C4 era ended with 1996 and two special option packages offered only that year. The tellingly named Collectors Edition was more popular, but the Grand Sport (*shown*) packed more excitement with its included LT4 V-8, vivid Admiral Blue paint, broad Sixties-style dorsal striping, and unique interior trim. Orders totaled exactly 1000, with coupes likely in the majority.

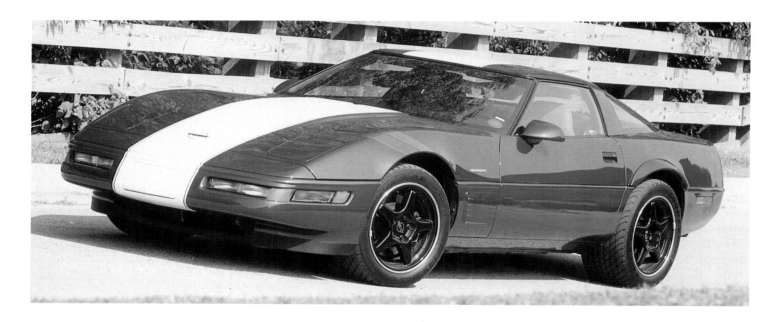

Prices had risen by a small amount and were now up to $36,875 for the coupe and $43,665 for the ragtop—and dealers were discounting. Sales slid by several thousand units, however, and were down to 20,742 for the model year. Only 448 ZR-1s were sold for 1995, marking a total of 6939 built during its six-year run. The last model was built on April 28, 1995.

With a brand-new Corvette only a year away, Chevrolet marked the end of the C4 generation with two special 1996 models: The first of them was the Collectors Edition, which included Sebring Silver paint, 5-spoke matching alloy wheels, and special trim. The $1250 option package, RPO Z15, was ordered on 5412 coupes and convertibles.

More exciting was the limited-edition Grand Sport. Priced at $3250 for the coupe or $2880 for the convertible, the package included exclusive Admiral Blue paint with a large white stripe and red accents to pay visual homage to the classic Corvette-based racer of the 1960s. The coupe used ZR-1 wheels and tires—P275/40ZR17s in front and P315/35ZR17s in the rear— while convertibles rode on P255/45ZR17s in the front and P285/40ZR17s at the back; rear fender flares were added to cover the wider back tires. The only interior upholstery treatments offered were black or a vivid red/black combination, and the GS was available only with the six-speed manual transmission. Chevy built 1000 Grand Sports, each having a special sequential serial number.

Required on the GS and optional on manual-transmission-equipped coupes and convertibles (at an additional $1450) was a taste of the next-generation Corvette: a revised 5.7 small-block V-8 called the LT4. The new powerplant came with newly designed aluminum heads, a new throttle body (shared with the '96 LT1), revised camshaft and roller rocker arms, and higher compression, now 10.8:1 compared to 10.4:1 for the LT1. These and other improvements allowed the LT4 to produce 330 bhp, 30 more than the LT1. Since the new engine redlined at 6300 rpm (700 more revs than the LT1), models equipped with the LT4 were fitted with 8000-rpm tachometers instead of the standard 6000-rpm gauges. When ordered with Grand Sport models, the engine was dressed up with bright red paint and red ignition wires.

Reviewers, however, didn't find that the LT4 added noticeably to the Corvette equation for '96 (clocking similar 0–60 mph times as the LT1), and noted that the beefier tires and revised torque curve made the GS more difficult to launch quickly from a standing start. The tires were also cited for improving cornering abilities, but at the expense of excessive oversteer during extreme handling situations at speed. While the press did appreciate the new engine's higher-revving ability, they also noted that the LT4, lacking an engine oil cooler, tended to overheat at sustained top speeds of around 186 mph. And the GS's garish graphics, especially the optional bright-red upholstery, were considered excessive.

Elsewhere in the line, the standard four-speed automatic transmission was treated to a variety of minor revisions for 1996—implemented to further improve shift quality—and new torque converters promised better durability.

Selective Real Time Damping, RPO F45, replaced the previous Selective Ride suspension option. Similarly priced as the former configuration at $1695, the F45 suspension calculated the optimal damping mode for its custom shock absorbers to maintain ride and handling quality via data gathered from sensors at all four wheels. The system could alter each shock individually (the former unit governed all four shocks simultaneously) at a rate of once every 10 to 15 milliseconds, or about every foot of roadway traversed at a speed of 60 mph.

What's more, the Z51 Handling Package returned to the options list for coupes after a five-year absence, offering Bilstein shocks, unique front and rear springs, bushings and stabilizers, and 9.5-inch-wide 17-inch wheels with P275/40ZR17 tires. If the $350 package was ordered with the automatic transmission, a 3.07:1 axle ratio was specified. While journalists found that the Z51 package indeed boosted the car's grip and would be ideal for autocross racers, they also judged it to be much too harsh for daily driving, especially in potholed urban areas.

With not one, but two special editions to help bring buyers into dealers' showrooms, Corvette sales rose somewhat for 1996, totaling 21,536. Still, this was a far cry from the C4's 1984 introductory model year, when it racked up sales of more than 51,000 units. But then the Corvette's price had risen by over 70 percent during the C4's run, from $21,800 in 1984 to $37,225 in 1996, which certainly helped to maintain the car's profitability despite the lower volume.

In its 43-year history, the Corvette had evolved from its origins as a garish plastic-bodied toy in the early 1950s into a bona fide sports car in the '60s and '70s. In the '80s and '90s it would become a well-equipped and increasingly sophisticated—and costly—gran touring car epitomized by the final 1996 C4.

And the car would follow that script even more closely for the C5 generation, which was set to debut as a 1997 model. While fans would yet again be denied a cutting-edge flight of automotive fancy—with the coming edition retaining a front-engine configuration and a pushrod V-8—the C5 would prove to be the most sophisticated and civilized Corvette ever.

Beginning with the 1984 model, the Corvette's future would be entirely in the hands of a younger, yet no less capable generation of General Motors professionals. Jerry Palmer is one of the most important of the new breed. In 1974 he became head of Chevrolet's Production Studio Three, where the 1984 Corvette would take shape. Though he has since been appointed executive head of GM's Advanced Design Studios under vice-president Charles M. Jordan, Palmer still has overall responsibility for the Corvette's exterior in the manner of his illustrious predecessor, William L. Mitchell.

When Mitchell retired as GM design chief in 1977, Palmer inherited an exciting yet formidable job, much as Dave McLellan did in taking over for Zora Arkus-Duntov on the engineering side. Both men and their respective teams faced the challenge of not only maintaining the tradition of America's sports car, but improving on it.

Though admirably suited for the job, Palmer did not find it easy. For one thing, this articulate, thoughtful, soft-spoken man took over for one of the most flamboyant and outspoken designers in the industry. Moreover, Mitchell had been the sole arbiter of Corvette styling for more than 20 years, itself a tough act to follow. And though the C3 had remained quite popular through its extraordinarily long production run, it was also quite dated by the mid-Seventies. Clearly, its replacement had to be more modern both in appearance and in function. Yet as development work proceeded on what would become the 1984 model, it was equally clear that any new Corvette would still have to be instantly recognizable as a Corvette. Palmer also faced the problem of providing a look that would remain fresh well in the 1990s.

Finally, Palmer faced the thorny matter of "updating the future." GM had tantalized enthusiasts with numerous Corvette dreams over the years, notably the mid-engine experiments of the late Sixties and early Seventies, exemplified by the shapely Aerovette. In fact, Mitchell's stunning Aerovette was actually readied for 1980 production, only to be canceled at the last minute. Palmer's challenge was to come up with styling that would be just as eye-grabbing within the 'Vette's traditional format, yet practical for production.

Jerry Palmer claims to be one of the few designers in the domestic auto industry who is a native Detroiter. His experience with GM Design goes back

Profile: Jerry P. Palmer

to 1964, when he spent a summer there as a student. The following year, he graduated from Detroit's Center for Creative Studies, then joined GM permanently, completing the company's internship program before serving briefly in the Advanced Studios he would later head. After a hitch in the Army during 1966–67, he worked for Chevrolet except for brief tours at GM subsidiaries in Europe and Japan. His first Corvette assignment came in 1969, when he assisted Mitchell in creating several show models.

Palmer's affable, easy-going personality belies an intense enthusiasm for his work, about which he is uncharacteristically modest for such a high-ranking executive. He's always eager to talk Corvettes despite an always-hectic schedule. What follows are excerpts from several conversations the editors have had with him since the introduction of the 1984 model.

Q: When did you first become involved with the Corvette?

Jerry P. Palmer: My first production involvement came in the '73 and '74 cars. I was the assistant chief designer, and we were doing only the front and rear of the car.

Q: What did you think of the 1968 generation?

Palmer: I thought it was an exciting car. I was really enamored by the show cars, such as the Mako Shark, that led into that body style.

Q: When did you start work on the '84?

Palmer: We're always working on new Corvettes. We started on [the C4] in 1977, but there were designs before

that, which were part of the program. We literally laid out the package starting with a clean sheet of paper. The only thing that was a given was the engine and transmission and need for additional ground clearance. We really started with a package. There's a lot of time and effort spent finalizing the rest of the architecture.

Q: At that point, were there any more thoughts of a mid-engine design?

Palmer: When the decision was made to go front-engine, the mid-engine responsibility went downstairs to the Advanced Studio. [Chevy Production Studio Three] had mid-engine responsibility until that time. We are the production studio, so when the decision to go front-engine was made, the mid-engine design went downstairs to an Advanced studio.

Q: Would you have preferred the mid-engine format?

Palmer: A mid-engine design offers different proportions, more unfamiliar proportions. Based on the components available at that time, we made the right decision. The P-car [1984–1988 Pontiac Fiero] was essentially what we were looking at—V-6 powered. I also had [1982] Camaro responsibility, and we were going to come out with a pretty wild Z28 package. There's no way that a 60-degree V-6 Corvette in the form we were working on could compete with the Z28 we were working on. Then Porsche came out with their front/mid-engine [928] design. All those decisions made back in that late-Seventies time frame fortified Chevrolet's direction.

The mid-engine car is an exciting car, but the [C4] Corvette is a fantastic car for the money in handling, braking, performance. It's right there. We didn't have to apologize for anything. The car is very forgiving. It's hard to screw up in a Corvette. You can screw up in a Ferrari or a rear-engine Porsche very easily. Those considerations were very strong on the engineering side. Plus, the mid-engine car offers less packaging flexibility.

Q: Tell us about your working relationship with Dave McLellan.

Palmer: We have a very good relationship. Dave knows enough about what we do to understand our challenge. We are very knowledgeable about each other's bailiwick and can challenge each other. I would say Chevrolet was very creative in helping us achieve the package we wanted.

To come up with the idea and make it look good is one thing; to make it work is another. There is more integration between the two [disciplines] than there was . . . years ago. We have a better understanding of what has to be done to make the product people are demanding out there. We're getting closer together.

Q: The late Bill Mitchell criticized the 1984 Corvette in some respects. What was your reaction?

Palmer: We talked about it. Bill and I were still good friends. He really didn't like the car at first and said so. Then, after he saw the car out in the real world and saw it in motion, he called me up and said, "I gotta tell ya, that thing really looks aggressive. I still don't quite like the back end, but it looks like a Corvette." It doesn't have the exaggerated statement that the previous Corvettes had, but I'm sure if Bill were running the studio . . . the Corvette would be a lot different than it is today. The shapes are Corvette, but the shapes are also aerodynamically tuned. We didn't conceive the design to aero, but we certainly had aero in mind. We had to meet targets.

Q: Mitchell once told us he thought the '84 was more an engineer's car, not a stylist's car.

Palmer: I was not controlled at all by Engineering. In fact, Engineering bent over backwards to give us what we wanted. I think Bill would have probably done things a little differently. However, I don't think it would be a lot

different. The 16-inch wheels, the 65-degree windshield—those things are all designers' wants, like the flip-open front end, the T-less T-top. Engineering didn't make those things. They made them happen, but the concepts originated here at Design Staff. For some of those design features we paid penalties . . . in cost and in mass. But the appearance or aura of that car is the thing we wanted. Engineering didn't back off. In fact, I can't think of anything Engineering demanded we have that we're not happy with. I think the days [are gone when Engineering compromises] what we want. They want as exciting a car as we do.

Q: What is the limiting factor in production numbers with the current car?

Palmer: It gets down to how many people you want to employ at Bowling Green and how many shifts. We are very reluctant to go into a double shift until we are satisfied the demand is there, not an artificial demand because of the newness of the car. If the demand

In addition to the 1984 Corvette, Palmer's talents influenced the 1984 Pontiac Fiero (*top*) and 1982 Chevrolet Camaro (*bottom*).

is there, I'm sure Chevrolet will consider another shift. I feel with a double shift we can make 60,000 cars with the quality the car has to have. We will not pump out cars and detract from the quality. We are still gaining on the quality of the car. I see the car leveling out at around 40,000 units a year. That's a gut reaction.

Q: The C3 design lasted 15 years. How long do you think the current one will be around?

Palmer: I don't think it's going to last anywhere near that long. But I think it will take us into the Nineties; in fact, I know it'll take us into the Nineties. That's not to say the car will not be injected with new technology wherever possible or [if] we discover something better appearance-wise or function-wise. We'll implement that, but it won't be a total new design.

Q: Do you have a favorite Corvette?

Palmer: Several. The 1956 [and] '57 are favorites of mine. Of course, the '63 split-window coupe has been identified as the classic Corvette, and I have to agree with that. The '65 convertible, '68, [and] '69 cars. Didn't like the rounded-off rear end [on] the '61. I think the '80 car was an improvement over the 1974–79 car.

Q: Do you keep an eye on the after-market to see what other people do with the Corvette?

Palmer: Sure, but there hasn't been anything that's gotten me to say, "Hey, look at what they've done here. Let's try that." We've been through this thing for so many years [and] we've tried a lot of things. I really get a kick out of seeing the competition cars, because [altering the design] becomes functional.

Q: Do you foresee a V-6 Corvette?

Palmer: It's an interesting package. I'm sure it's one of the options we'll be looking at in the Nineties if the gas-guzzler problem stays with us and we have to maintain or achieve higher performance levels.

Q: Would a V-6 work in the current chassis, and what kind of styling options would that offer you?

Palmer: I really don't know, because when you get the V-6 to put out the kind of power needed to match or surpass the performance levels we know now, all that room vacated by the two cylinders will be absorbed by intercoolers. The secret to the V-6, obviously, is turbocharging. I don't think there's any question the V-6 is going to be the performance engine of the future. But we're not planning any styling changes around that possibility now.

A 1991 facelift gave C4 'Vettes a smoother, more rounded nose, plus small front-fender "strakes" and a back panel with squared-up taillights *a la* the high-power ZR-1. Workmanship progressively improved as part of the C4 series' considered evolution over what would turn out to be a 13-season career. This convertible is one of 5692 built for 1993. Price before options was up to $41,195 versus $34,595 for that year's coupe.

All 1993 Corvettes were "40th Anniversary" models, including coupes with the hot ZR-1 package, added four years before. This one has option Z25, a special $1455 birthday package available for any '93, featuring Ruby Red paint and matching leather-lined cockpit. ZR-1's unique twincam 32-valve LT5 V-8 went from 375 to 405 bhp, versus 300 for other models' year-old LT1, the newest version of Chevy's famed pushrod small-block. Model-year sales totaled 21,590, including just 448 ZR-1s.

You needed a good deal of "discretionary income" to upgrade an early-Nineties 'Vette coupe to ZR-1 status. The 1993 price was a towering $31,683—on top of the cost of the regular coupe. Why so much? A special wide-body tail accommodating much broader wheels and tires, plus numerous features that cost extra on other 'Vettes and an exclusive, exotic all-aluminum LT5 V-8 made virtually by hand.

The C4 convertible top was manual, not power-operated, but was quick and easy to put up or down. And as this '93 attests, it did little harm to the car's racy looks when raised. Available from dealers since 1989 was a removable hardtop, complete with an electrically defrosted glass window, that allowed the convertible to be true "four-seasons" transport. The sweeping dashboard here was part of the C4's 1991-model update.

High price and low sales helped kill the mighty ZR-1 after 1995. Total production over six model years was 6939, with exactly 448 built in each of the final three seasons. The option's best year was inaugural 1990, when installations numbered 3049. Needless to say, the rare, potent ZR-1 is already a bona fide collector car.

Two 1996 options signaled the C4 series' imminent retirement. Shown here is the Z15 Collectors Edition group, installed on just 5412 cars. Priced at $1250, it included Sebring Silver paint, special emblems and wheels, and perforated-leather sports seats. More exciting was the Grand Sport, offered only this year. A sort of stand-in for the departed ZR-1, option Z16 featured a 330-bhp LT4 V-8, Admiral Blue paint with white dorsal stripes, and other unique features. Only 1000 were built.

1997-2004

While the 1984-96 Corvette, the C4, didn't continue in its basic form for quite as long as its 1968-82, C3, predecessor, 12 years was still a long time in an era when some high-volume cars would undergo complete makeovers as often as every four years. The C3 "Shark" had carried on for 15 years simply because it was selling well and GM executives saw little need to invest in an all-new model, particularly at a time when the company was investing its resources to meet a myriad of new federal regulations. The C4, however, was another, less successful story.

The mid-to-late 1980s were not kind to General Motors. The automotive juggernaut was rapidly losing market share, the economy was rubber-legged, and manufacturing and engineering problems plagued GM's model lines. Furthermore, American motorists were paying in excess of list price for import-controlled Japanese cars they perceived to be more appropriately designed and of better quality than those from domestic automakers.

Every program at GM was subject to scrutiny during this period, and many new development programs were delayed or scrapped altogether as the company was getting its corporate house in order.

The Corvette would be no exception. The long-running sports car was facing serious competition from import rivals like the Mazda RX-7, Datsun/Nissan Z, and Porsche 924 and 928. A new generation of enthusiasts had come to appreciate such cars for their more-balanced approach to performance, trading simple straight-line speed for docile handling and a relative degree of comfort. Corvette sales were plummeting to their lowest level in years. While higher prices helped recoup in profits what was otherwise lost in volume, there was some doubt as to whether Chevrolet would continue building the Corvette at all.

While planning for the fifth generation began in earnest in the late 1980s, with drawings that tried to capture the essence of a 21st Century Corvette, the final product would ultimately be delayed until 1997. In between were years of turmoil, as GM brass wavered on killing the car while Corvette engineers and designers fought valiantly to save it.

The opening salvo in this internal power struggle came in October 1989 at GM's annual executive conference in Traverse City, Michigan, where it was decided that the C5 development program would be placed on indefinite status. The following year, GM brass debated whether the slow-selling Corvette should be taken away from Chevy and sold under another brand or killed altogether. Chevrolet general manager Jim Perkins, a true "car guy" in the traditional sense, successfully convinced GM brass that not only should the Corvette program continue, but that it must remain as the division's flagship. GM president Lloyd Reuss later agreed to cancel a proposed 1995 "reskin" and revive the $250-million program to create an all-new Corvette for the 1996 (later delayed to 1997) model year.

At the 1992 North American International Auto Show in Detroit, held in January, GM debuted a show car called the Stingray III, a styling preview then being considered for the next generation Corvette. Developed at GM's Advanced Concept Center in California, the concept was much smaller than the C4 Corvette and was powered by a V-6 engine. While it never got much farther than the auto-show circuit, the same swept-back styling would eventually become the basis for Chevy's Cavalier convertible.

Meanwhile, work on a new model continued, and in December 1992, the Corvette design group secretly contracted with TDM, Inc., to build a prototype of the proposed C5. The test car was officially called CERV-4 (Corvette Engineering Research Vehicle). GM management was not

America's sports car became more exciting than ever with the C5, the first truly all-new Corvette since the original. A new generation of designers and engineers went all out to achieve higher levels of performance, sophistication, and quality. No wonder the C5 was hailed as the best Corvette in history.

C5 "beta" prototypes began real-world testing in 1995, ultimately covering more than a half-million miles over every road and climate condition imaginable. All were lightly camouflaged to fool magazine "spy" photographers.

told about the project, however, in the fear that they would cancel it. The following May, Corvette chief engineer Dave Hill, a former Cadillac engineer who had recently replaced Dave McLellan in that position, unveiled the CERV-4 at GM's Technical Center in Warren, Michigan. Up until that point, most of the hundreds of people in attendance didn't have a clue that the $1.2-million test car was being built.

In June 1993, Dave Hill (who would later be re-titled as the car's Vehicle Line Executive) and Corvette program manager Russ McLean met with the General Motors Strategy Board, including then president Jack Smith. The goal of the meeting was to seek approval for Concept Initiation of the 1997 Corvette program. The plan was endorsed, and Jim Perkins proudly announced that a fifth-generation Corvette would be produced, with

its introduction slated for the 1997 model year.

At about this time, design head Chuck Jordan had retired and was replaced by John Cafaro, who was also chief designer for the 1993 Camaro. Likewise, John Heinricy was named assistant chief engineer. Not only were the parties involved in developing the car different this time around, the project was also being conducted according to a dramatically new corporate mandate.

To help counter the existing version's moribund sales trend, GM decreed that the C5 must cater to a broader audience than had any previous 'Vette. So, where towering personalities like Bill Mitchell and Zora Arkus-Duntov once ruled, customer

clinics and market research now held sway. Nearly 1600 owners of Corvettes and competitive vehicles were surveyed. Scores passed judgment on styling, design, and features. This unprecedented "voice of the customer," as Chevy executives called it, preferred a front-engine, rear-drive layout, and ranked other desired attributes in this order: 1) quality construction, 2) performance, 3) safety, 4) appearance, 5) comfort, and 6) value. Handling and maneuverability were favored over sheer acceleration. Easy ingress and egress and additional luggage space were deemed essential attributes to any new Corvette.

continued on page 328

1

2

3

4

5

6

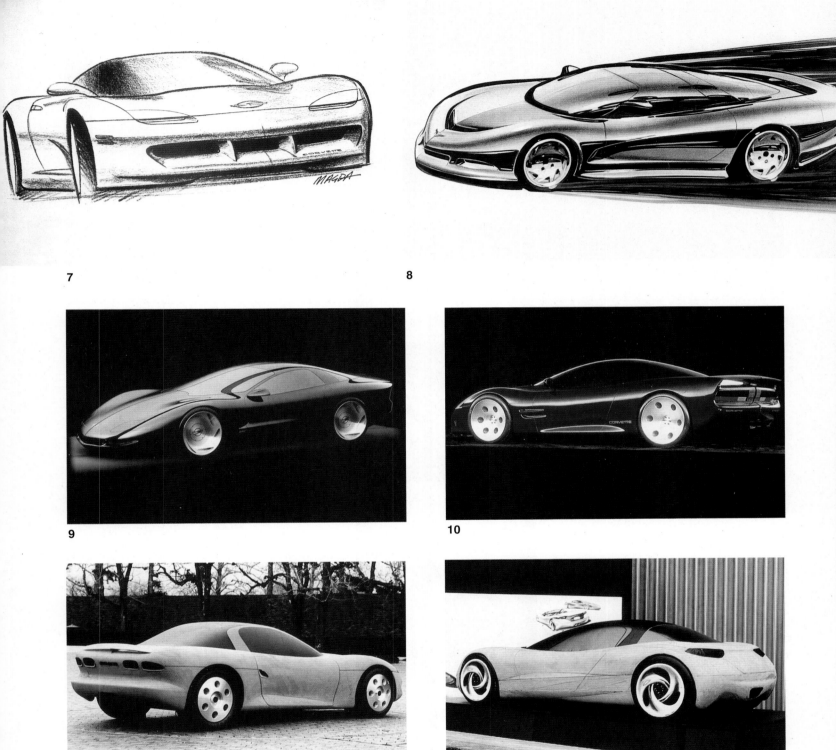

7   **8**

9

10

11

12

1, 7-8. Early C5 design work envisioned a C4 package size and swoopy, dramatic lines *a la* the mid-engine Corvette Indy and later CERV III concepts. **2-6, 9-12.** A smaller, lighter car like the concept Stingray III, perhaps even V-6-powered, was also in contention for a time, but was ultimately scrapped as not in keeping with what 'Vette buyers wanted.

1

1-3. A plunging arrow-shaped nose theme persisted for some time, as these proposals attest, but ended up (in muted form) on Chevrolet's new 1993 Camaro ponycar. **4-5, 7-9.** The C5's flowing lines begin to emerge. The "double-bubble" roof visible on some of these scale workouts was an interesting but dead-end idea. **6.** Designers were almost finished by mid-1993, when Chevy general manager Jim Perkins dropped by for a look. The clay scale-model notchback coupe on the left indicates that a third body style was planned early in the C5 program.

2

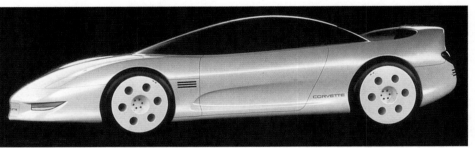

3

4

5

6

7

8

9

By May 1993, the car had progressed to a form that appeared suitable for production. The exterior styling was being influenced by aerodynamics and the aforementioned (and unprecedented) customer input. "They told us, 'Don't make it look like a Ferrari or an [Acura] NSX. We want it took look like a Corvette,'" said chief designer Cafaro. "That's a dilemma for a designer. If I had been working in my basement on my own, I might have done something different."

That August, the C5 program was subjected to what GM calls its "Concept Alternatives Selection," in which virtually every component, procedure, and design aspect is presented, defended, and decided on. The program passed its most critical test to date, though perhaps an even more important review was yet to come, considering GM's newfound attention to the "voice of the customer."

Chevy held a marketing clinic in Los Angeles in May 1994, to determine how well the new model might ultimately sell. Even those who were leery of the company's market-research-driven approach to the car's design couldn't argue with the results: Sixty percent of the respondents interviewed said they'd buy the C5 Corvette over the competition, a level of acceptance no GM car had ever before garnered in prelaunch testing.

On June 26, 1994, the first alpha test car was completed, with build chief John Fehlberg having the honor of being the first C5 driver. GM would start building the first C5 beta test cars the following April and begin road-testing them under substantial camouflage. In August '96, the first pre-pilot '97 Corvettes rolled off the assembly line, and the first production 1997 Corvette was completed on October 1. The C5 Corvette was unveiled to the press in November, with an official

continued on page 333

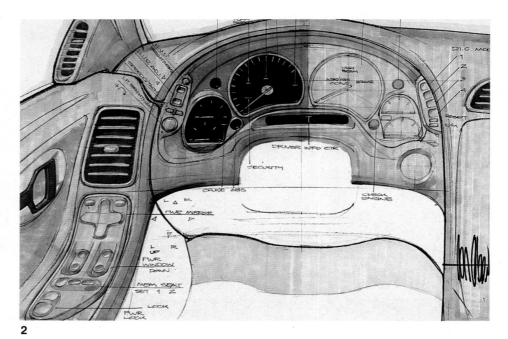

1

2

1-2. Chevrolet found that buyers wanted more room, comfort, and convenience in a new Corvette cockpit, and designers worked hard to comply. A revived "dual cowl" interior theme surfaced early and persisted to production. **3-8.** These full-size clay models preview ultimate C5 styling in their proportions, overall nose and tail treatments, and prominent C-shape bodyside sculpting. Other elements here, including the lower fascias and door window shape, would be changed.

3

4

5

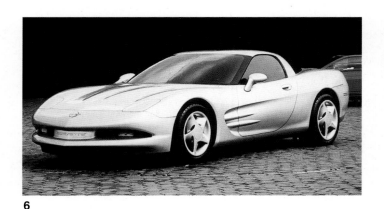

6

7

8

Profile: John A. Cafaro

John A. Cafaro is best known as the chief designer for the C5 Corvette, as well as for all production Corvette styling from 1991 to 2002. From '92 to '99, John worked on the C5-R Corvette race program, managing all bodywork design and graphic design for the Chevrolet Raceshop and GM Motorsports.

Soon after beginning his career at General Motors in 1977 as an associate designer, he moved to Chevrolet where he began work on the '82 Camaro Z-28 and the '84 Corvette. Cafaro became a senior designer in the Pontiac Studio in '82, where he helped craft the mid-engine Fiero, and was made assistant chief designer in '84.

In 1986, Cafaro became Chevrolet's chief designer with responsibility for the '93 Camaro, '95 Cavalier, Impala SS, and Corvette. After his C5 experience, Cafaro functioned as chief designer for the Chevy Avalanche and Hummer H-2, and was appointed Director of GM's Full-Size Truck and H2 in February 2002.

A native of Camden, N.J., Cafaro received a Bachelor of Arts degree in industrial design from the Pratt Institute. He has also earned degrees from the University of Michigan and the Center for Creative Leadership in Brussels, Belgium. Cafaro has been a Corvette enthusiast since first laying eyes on the Mako Shark concept car as a wide-eyed youth at the 1965 New York Auto Show.

Possessed with an energetic spirit and continued enthusiasm for automotive design, Cafaro joined an elite group of his esteemed predecessors in the Corvette Hall of Fame on Aug. 30, 2002. He graciously agreed to sit down with the editors for the following interview just prior to his induction.

Q: Which is your favorite Corvette?
John A. Cafaro: Up until the C5, which I obviously had a hand in creating, it would have to be Bill Mitchell's Stingray racer, which was driven by Dr.

Dick Thompson. The fact that it was the forerunner of the 1963 production car, that it was an open-top speedster, really appeals to me. If I could buy any vehicle past or present, I'd have that one. It's on display outside of the design studio and it still looks fabulous. I also love the Mako Shark concept car that I saw at the New York Auto Show as a kid. I find as I get older my appreciation of "classic" cars is growing. As a young designer I was fascinated by futuristic designs, but now I'm more interested in some of the older models I grew up with.

Q: How did you feel following in such illustrious footsteps as the champion of Corvette's fifth generation?
Cafaro: When I was made head of Chevy's Studio Three it was a great feeling—I was on cloud nine. Then I began to realize all the pressure I would be under, from both the company and the Corvette's faithful fans, and knew I would have to approach the task very seriously. The C5 was a great departure from the way previous Corvettes had been designed, and I was concerned about getting it "right." There were times I was having great fun and felt confident in what we were doing, and there were other times I was worried that the final product wasn't headed in the right direction. When we flashed some slides of what was close to our final design to our peers at GM and received a collective "wow" from the room, I finally knew we had something and that the project would be successful.

Q: What unique challenges did you encounter in recasting the car that your predecessors didn't have to face?
Cafaro: First there was the uncertain state of the corporation at the time, and the questioning of whether we should be doing a new Corvette at all. Plus, we were feeling the pressure from import competitors in terms of quality and performance. We literally had to change the way we thought about a Corvette. Previous models had been designed around the powertrain or a specific exterior design. Interior ergonomics, passenger comfort, and cargo capacities were largely afterthoughts in the process, and it showed. We spent a lot of time with the car's "packaging" to make it more comfortable to a wider range of body types—frankly, larger people. We also knew we had to raise the bar on quality to meet the formidable, mainly Japanese, competition. These are factors previous Corvette chief designers never had to consider, at least not as seriously.

I truly believe that cars are reflections of the people who design them. For example, Harley Earl was a golfer, so the first Corvette had a trunk. Bill Mitchell, on the other hand, hated golf, so he got rid of the trunk. I golf and play ice hockey and want to be able to carry my gear, so I made sure the C5 would have substantial cargo room.

Also, we placed more emphasis on aerodynamics than any design team that came before us. No Corvette had ever spent more time in the wind tunnel during its development—we clocked over 1000 hours in wind-tunnel testing to refine the car's slippery shape. This was especially helpful when we went on to develop the C5-R racer. The production car's already excellent aerodynamic qualities enabled the C5-R to compete with some of the best cars in the world with few exterior modifications.

Q: Given decades of speculation about a mid- or rear-engine model, such as the Corvette Indy and Aerovette, was there ever any question that the C5 would be a front-engine car?
Cafaro: No, not really. Once the C5 project got underway we knew it would be a front-engine, rear-drive design. We didn't have a second design studio concurrently exploring different configurations, as might have been done in the past. There was some discussion that there could be two Corvettes, the current model and a limited-edition mid-engine exotic version that might sell something like 200 units a year, but that idea was never taken too seriously.

Q: Is a mid-engine sports car prohibitive cost-wise for GM to design?
Cafaro: The reality is that it takes as much money to design a model that might sell 200 cars a year as it does to create one that would sell 200,000, and GM is just not set up to produce exotic cars that don't have a solid business case. Some companies, like Porsche, can afford to create a "supercar" for the sake of corporate image, but not us.

Having said that, I've been interested in mid-engine cars since I was a kid, and I did work on the Fiero, which was the last mid-engine vehicle we created here. A mid-engine configuration has long been the hallmark of sports-car design, and I'd like to see GM do another one someday. But in terms of the Corvette, it's not likely if only from a heritage standpoint. The 'Vette has always been a powered by a front-engine small-block V-8 with rear-drive. Adherence to tradition and a certain continuity has had a lot to do with the Corvette's success and longevity over the last 50 years.

Q: How did you approach the C5, from both a designer and an enthusiast standpoint?

Cafaro: My approach, which I learned from my predecessor Jerry Palmer, was that I had to be in lockstep with the chief engineer as much as possible if I wanted to create a "total" car. To that end, we took a holistic approach to creating the C5. We wanted to improve its overall quality, accommodations, and already-excellent performance, not create a vehicle based purely on styling cues. Yes, we had to make sure that the final product looked like a Corvette, but we didn't want any one styling cue to jump out at you. I actually approached the C5 as a race car first—I tend to get my inspiration from racing cars. There's a certain beauty and functionality to racers that excites me. Race car design tends to be more of a team approach than was taken with previous Corvettes. I don't like to be thought of as an egotistic "stylist," which I think implies a certain flakiness. I want to be regarded as the leader of a design team who puts motion and passion into his products and remains very focused on them.

Q: The C4 design is said to have started from the driver's hip joint, and worked its way outward. Did you have a similar focal point for the C5?

Cafaro: We started from the occupants' packaging—made it more generous with better visibility and added luggage space, but without taking the easy way out and simply turning the car into a larger hatchback. Instead, we created additional space in nontraditional ways, such as the placement of the fuel tank and rear transaxle, and the unique oil pan that allows the engine to sit lower, and created a lower hood to provide better sight lines—all our efforts were very driver-focused. We had a wooden seating buck that we'd put people into, including some very big guys, and designed the car around them. Big guys, as they say, can have big wallets, and we couldn't risk losing them as potential customers.

Our subsequent buyer feedback says we hit the target right on center. A lot of C5 owners had never owned a Corvette before, and a lot of it had to do with the former models' lack of passenger comfort. We literally shut down three import brands when we came out with the C5—the Toyota Supra, Nissan 300ZX, and the Acura NSX. When you take 50 years of history and add world-class performance, engineering, and comfort, the Corvette is pretty hard to beat. And especially with the addition of the Z06, the car is certainly not a poseur in any

sense—the Z06 can go up against anything Ferrari has to offer for one-quarter the price.

Q: What lessons learned from the C4 generation helped shape the C5?

Cafaro: The C4 was the first break in what had become an established Corvette look in many years. With the 1963 Sting Ray, Bill Mitchell created the shark-like appearance that carried all the way to 1984. The C4 started off in a different direction. Jerry Palmer loved Ferraris and he helped the car became more contemporary and "global" in its design. The 1984 model was the first version to incorporate a clear European influence with the inherent Corvette styling elements. I wanted to retain the idea of a "world car" with the C5 and create a car that would look as good and at home on the streets of Europe as it does here in the U.S.

Q: How did computer-aided design affect the car's development?

Cafaro: When we started working on the C5, the level of technology was nowhere near where it is today. So, we used computer-aided design mainly to help speed up the design process, but we didn't use it as a creative tool. We still worked in the old-fashioned way—we used a lot of pencil power to make sketches on real paper, not a computer screen, had sculptors meticulously creating clay models, and so forth. The computer tools came more into play from a quality standpoint—we were able to quickly see how different components like doors, headlamps, and fascias would fit. Since we did the C5, the technology has become more sophisticated. People now come out of design school with higher levels of training on the latest equipment, so we're using computers much more now to create the next generation than we did with the present car. We still have sculptors creating hands-on models, but those people are also trained to use computers to help in their efforts. I'm glad I had the chance to work the old way, sort of straddling the fence between the pencil and the PC.

Q: The C5 was the first Corvette to utilize extensive market research throughout its development, How did you feel about subjecting your work-in-progress to focus groups?

Cafaro: I can still hear the sound of Harley Earl spinning in his grave, but you have to remember GM had just gone through two styling disasters at the time—the Chevy Caprice and the "Dust-buster" minivans—and wasn't about to

repeat its mistakes on a new Corvette. The clinics certainly created a lot of extra work for the design studio. The process tests your strengths as a chief designer and forces you to question where and when to take styling risks and struggle to maintain a unified approach to the program. Whether it's a comment made at a focus group or one from some guy who just wanders into the studio, you can't just go ahead and change any part of your design based on one person's opinion. We had focus groups with everyone from potential customers and current owners, to members of the media and the top-selling Corvette dealers from around the country. It could certainly test your patience at times, but I made a lot of new friends.

Q: Was the Z06 planned from the beginning of the C5 project?

Cafaro: Actually, the Z06 wasn't part of the original C5 plan. We knew we wanted to do a "club racer" version, which eventually became the hardtop, but hadn't yet considered a high-performance model. The Z06 came about sometime after the C5 was finished. It was very circumstantial—mostly a case of the powertrain engineers coming up with an engine that someone in planning felt we should drop into the Corvette. We found that the LS6 engine really transformed the previous hardtop and gave it a completely new identity. Now we find some Corvette hardtop owners modifying their cars to look and run more like a new Z06.

Q: Where do you see the Corvette headed in the next 20 years?

Cafaro: Since the C6 is scheduled to run for at least seven years, we'd be looking ahead to the C7, which might be smaller and could possibly come with all-wheel drive or a high-tech dual-power hybrid design. Neither of these is on the drawing board at this time, but they are possibilities. In general, future Corvettes will need to get lighter, probably from using new materials that have yet to be perfected. Power could come from a smaller-displacement V-8 engine, say 3.0 liters, or one that's packaged more efficiently but retains tremendous power. The car will also likely be more aerodynamic. All these changes will likely come in the name of fuel-efficiency. Gasoline won't continue to sell for $1.50 much longer, I'm afraid. Regardless, I think people will still to want to own and drive a high-performance personal sports car 20 years from now, and I'm sure the Corvette will continue to be around in one form or another.

1

1. The Corvette design team poses with a near-final C5 mockup, though they would later revise its wheels, lower-bodyside forms, and the small air ducts in the lower front fascia. 2. Workers at the Bowling Green Corvette plant inspect the handbuilt C5 "alpha" prototype to prepare for building a small run of "beta" test cars. 3-4. On-road test prototypes are typically disguised to foil magazine spy photographers, who seem to know all the places they might go and lie in wait, hoping for a scoop. Adding various soft and hard body pieces helped make the "beta" C5s look like something other than Corvettes, but most shutterbugs weren't fooled. Drive routes encompassed mountains, deserts, snowy back roads, and more, often with GM's Mesa, Arizona, proving grounds as home base.

2

3

4

It was slightly larger than its predecessor, but with its wheels pulled out to the corners, the new 'Vette was distinctly more modern in its appearance. Wheelbase was stretched by 8.3 inches (to 104.5) on a body longer by just 1.2 inches. The car's track was significantly wider as well, by 4.3 inches in front and 3.0 in back, making the rear width equal to that of the former ZR-1. The body was broader by 2.9 inches and taller by 1.4. Thanks to weight-saving materials, the 3218-lb C5 weighed 80 lbs less than the C4.

Some journalists felt that the car's styling was the uninspired result of too many voices and too much attention paid to wind-tunnel testing. But the shape was semi-exotic, with a suggestion of mid-engine proportions. It was fresh, yet unmistakably a true Corvette.

Tradition called for a body made of composite plastics, with hidden headlights and quad taillamps. Bodyside coves extracted engine heat and evoked the 1956-62 car. Front-fascia intakes cooled the brakes, while rear valance slots vented the exhaust system. The razor-edged tail wasn't necessarily graceful in its appearance, but it was sufficiently aerodynamic and

on-sale date set for March 7, 1997.

What the press discovered in the course of that momentous introduction flat-out floored them. There was a fresh air of sophistication and purpose about the 1997 Corvette. A driver could sense this version was unlike any other before it from the first turn of the key, and not just because the ignition switch was off the steering column and back on the dashboard, where it belonged.

A lower hood and cowl allowed for greater visibility. This revealed 18 more feet of road in front of the car than before, thus dramatically

heightening the driver's sense of control. A new rear suspension kept the tail on course through washboard corners, and the body-work no longer groaned and creaked over bumps.

The drivetrain was isolated from the chassis, so the new small-block V-8 rumbled from four central tailpipes rather than reverberating through the car's structure. Low doorsills confirmed a clever new chassis design, and accommodatingly wider footwells verified that the transmission had been relocated to the rear axle.

1

2

tall enough to help double the previous Corvette's luggage space to a full 25 cubic feet. A less intriguing but easier-to-open front-hinged hood replaced the C4's clamshell design.

The cockpit was now bigger, brighter, and more thoughtfully designed. A new frame eliminated the C4's four-inch-tall doorsills, so ingress and egress were now a breeze. There was nearly 1.5 inches more head and shoulder room than before, and 3.4 inches more hip room, which added a welcome degree of comfort to what was never before considered a user-friendly interior. The dual-cove dashboard updated the classic 1963-67 design and came replete with a passenger's grab handle. Full-analog instrumentation replaced the oft-criticized former model's digital/analog array, with circular gauges marked with ultra-violet-lit "day glo" paint and set on different planes for a three-dimensional effect. Soft-touch pads replaced cheap plastic switchgear throughout the compartment. The parking brake was activated by a proper center console arm instead of an inconvenient lever placed to the left of the driver's seat, and

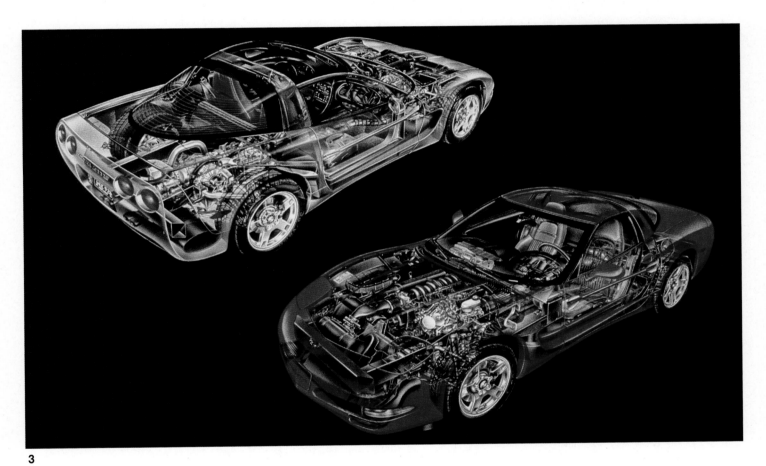

3

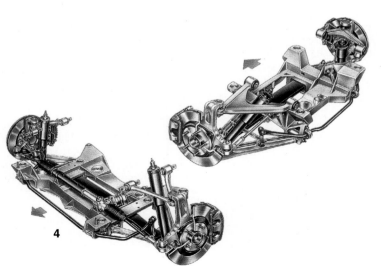

4

1. C5 was the first production 'Vette with a rear-mounted transmission linked to the engine via a stout aluminum tube. **2.** Chassis design was C4 in concept, but thicker, one-piece hydroformed members achieved greater rigidity with less weight. **3.** The new chassis design also gave the C5 more passenger and cargo room. **4.** The suspension was updated with double-A-arm rear-end geometry (*above right in diagram*).

Profile: David C. Hill

Only the third Chief Engineer in the Corvette's 50-year history, Dave Hill admittedly had big shoes to fill when he took over the tumultuous C5 program from his successor Dave McLellan in 1992. A life-long auto enthusiast with over a quarter-century of experience at General Motors, Hill has parlayed his love of cars and motorsports into a successful and satisfying career.

Fresh out of Michigan Technological University with an undergraduate degree in mechanical engineering, Hill joined Cadillac in 1965 to work in the engine lab and was soon named senior project engineer. Hill subsequently earned a master's degree in mechanical engineering from the University of Michigan in 1970 and became staff project engineer for Cadillac engine design in '73. Hill became general supervisor of Cadillac's body and chassis lab in '76, and was promoted to staff engineer for Cadillac development in '78, and for emissions and transmissions in '82. Later that year he was handed the keys to the Cadillac Allante roadster as the car's chief engineer. In 1988, he assumed responsibility for the DeVille and Concours models. Early in '92 he was promoted to engineering program manager for Cadillac.

As a longtime owner—and racer—of sports cars (he drove a Lotus Super 7 in SCCA competition from 1968 to '72), Hill stretched his engineering muscles in a different direction in November 1992 when he was named the Corvette's chief engineer. Assuming responsibility for the long overdue, oft-delayed, and nearly canceled C5 project was no easy task. His first step upon accepting the new position was to learn as much as possible about the legendary sports car's heritage and its fiercely loyal owner body. Given added responsibilities as vehicle line executive for all GM performance cars in 1995, Hill was also placed in charge of the Chevrolet Camaro and Pontiac Firebird lines.

Hill launched the fifth-generation Corvette in 1997, and it quickly became considered to be the best Corvette ever. For 2001, he one-upped himself with the release of the acclaimed Z06 high-performance version. By all accounts, he has succeeded in ways his revered predecessors could only imagine.

We sat down with Mr. Hill in August 2002 to talk about the C5. As you'll read, the conversation also touched on the then-forthcoming 2004 Cadillac XLR and the sixth-generation Corvette.

Q: How did you feel about taking over as Corvette Chief Engineer from Dave McLellan, and following in the footsteps of Zora Arkus-Duntov?

David C. Hill: It was a daunting challenge to become the third chief engineer of the Corvette. Actually, Dave McLellan and all of the Corvette team went out of their way to give me a "deep immersion" into Corvette lore, the Corvette customer, and the technology they had been developing. There was an enormous amount to learn in assuming these responsibilities, and I had excellent help. I did not have the privilege to know Mr. Duntov very well, but I knew he was very hopeful for my success and the future of the Corvette.

Q: How did you approach working on the Corvette after spending so much time engineering plush and soft-riding vehicles like the DeVille and Concours?

Hill: Before I became a Cadillac employee, I was a sports car enthusiast, even prior to the day I saw my first Corvette in 1953. The Cadillac development lab contained many automobile hobbyists, and I was in with a group of SCCA racers there. The first new car I purchased was a 1970 Corvette coupe, and I own it still. The similarity to Cadillac is in the effort to create the best car America has to offer, and although the products are diverse, the means to achieve results are the same. My Cadillac background prepared me well to emphasize the refinement Corvette needed to achieve world-class status.

Q: How did your experience as a race-car driver affect your work as an engineer in general and on the Corvette in particular?

Hill: Amateur racing was one of the most challenging elements in my life. Preparing a car for racing disciplines one to strict deadlines, handling emergencies requires instantaneous problem solving, and driving it in competition requires intense concentration. These characteristics are all beneficial in the world of work. Upon joining the Corvette team, I brought the ability to evaluate the car's performance at its limit.

Q: What challenges did you confront approaching the C5 project that your predecessors didn't have to face?

Hill: Although not unprecedented, two especially significant challenges for us were to upgrade the totality of the car to meet increasingly stringent, world-class quality standards—to take the Corvette's weaknesses and turn them into strengths. The other was to create a business plan to win the right to even do the C5 program in the first place, and then to maintain the plan successfully so the company would want to keep investing its money in us.

Q: What "legacies" carried over into the C5 from an engineering standpoint?

Hill: Corvette does have engineering legacies, and fortunately, they enable us to keep improving on a very successful formula. The large-displacement V-8 engine, located behind the front wheel centerline, provides immediate acceleration response, together with excellent handling and a high degree of passive safety, in a layout that achieves high utility for daily transportation for two people and a significant amount of cargo. Composite body materials are also favored, along with other advanced, mass-savings materials. We were not governed by any other technical constraints.

Q: Was there ever a point in the C5's development that an alternative to the small-block pushrod V-8 was considered, like the twin-turbo V-6s in various concept Corvettes over the years?

Hill: Other V-8s were considered, even other layouts, and fortunately the V-8s were improved enough in their performance, cleanliness, and economy that we did not need to consider a V-6. The LS1 and LS6 engines are beautifully suited to the Corvette, and are a great part of its value.

Q: Were any lessons from the C4 passed along to you that helped drive the C5's engineering?

Hill: The team had a thorough knowledge of what the customers wanted that the C4 lacked, and this made up a "must-do" list. We had amassed a substantial knowledge of competition loads and stresses from the Corvette Challenge racing program that enabled us to engineer for competition success right from the start of the C5 program.

Q: What were your original engineering objectives for the C5? Did any of them change over time?

Hill: The engineering objectives were to exceed the customers' expectations for a passionate, technically sophisticated, high-value sports car. The customers' top priority was for the car to be well-built, and their second priority was performance. These were foremost in setting our quantitative engineering objectives. Throughout the program, product content was rebalanced to optimize the value to the customer. We take great pride in Corvette's tremendous value—it's an exotic car that many people can aspire to own, and that's because we do our best to skillfully balance the trade-offs to maximize value to the customer. Advancements that could not be kept on time for the start of the C5 came along later in its life cycle, such as active handling in the '98 and a higher output [LS6] engine in 2001.

Q: How did the extensive efforts with various focus groups impact the C5's engineering? Do you feel it ultimately was a worthwhile process?

Hill: We give a great deal of importance to customer input when designing and engineering a new Corvette. Initially, focus groups were instrumental in guiding the design and prioritizing the engineering efforts. The dilemma is that Corvette folks enjoy their cars so much, they'll tell you to not change a thing, which is impossible because they also expect it to be at the cutting edge when it comes on the market. I think we do a good job of delighting customers because we know them well enough to understand how they think and how they feel about cars, enabling us to make aesthetic and technical choices for them, and to delight them several years into the future.

Q: By the late 1980s, computers were beginning to change the way cars were being crafted, and the process was becoming a far cry from the pen-and-paper techniques of old. Obviously, unlike Zora Duntov, you didn't have to personally build a new cam by hand to boost the car's performance. How did new technology affect the car's engineering development?

Hill: The C5 was engineered with the industry's most powerful computer systems, operated by some of its most clever people. It has revolutionary structural effectiveness and excellent crashworthiness, all of which was achieved with very competitive mass, accomplished with the help of Finite Element Modeling. Computer Aided Design enabled designers to create more solutions quicker, thus arriving at better solutions than would otherwise be possible.

Q: The LS1 was the first Corvette V-8 to use an aluminum block—how difficult was this to accomplish?

Hill: An aluminum engine was a necessity to enable the Corvette to progress to the next level of total performance, and our engine guys were up for the challenge of reinventing the pushrod V-8. It is a marvel, that in spite of progress since 1955, we were able to make such large steps beyond where the small block had been before. This layout is so space-efficient that it enables us to achieve a relatively large displacement in quite a small, light package, so the vehicle has an excellent layout and excellent performance. The fuel efficiency still surprises people, but you must remember that this engine has very low friction, due to lots of torque at low engine speed and few moving parts.

Q: How difficult was it to engineer the C5's new, more rigid structure?

Hill: The C5's patented structure is the car's single most significant upgrade, because it creates the foundation upon which everything is built. The car feels solid and substantial, even with the lower roofline, yet it is lighter than its predecessor, and therefore feels more agile. People notice this from their very first drive, and the car's structural durability makes it hold up very well. Numerous structural solutions were considered, but the best one emerged for C5 production. It looks simple today, but it was daunting to design a vehicle that complied with the simple primary structure. The team "bet the whole car" on the success of large-scale hydroforming, because it was a terrific enabler for the structural and manufacturing efficiency needed for the new Corvette.

Q: The hardtop and Z06 are noted for their extreme weight-saving measures. How slavish were you to reducing unnecessary bulk on those cars?

Hill: The Z06 has many innovative mass-conserving strategies to improve its total performance, like the titanium exhaust system. It shows that Corvette continues to push the envelope in the development of performance technologies. The Z06 performs excellently on the racetrack, but it is a very complete road car for the extreme performance enthusiast, so it does not sacrifice its overall goodness by casting off high value features like radio, air conditioning, and power windows

Q: What can you tell us about the Z06 development? Why wasn't the 2002's extra 20 hp in the original '01 version?

Hill: As soon as the decision was made to forgo the price leader hardtop, the enthusiasts in Team Corvette began creating the Z06. The LS6 engine was in response to the need for more power for the Z06. The 2001 version was the quickest Corvette ever produced when it was introduced, and had all the power we could produce in that year. By 2002, a new catalyst formulation had been validated, and it enabled us to delete the warm-up converters, lower the backpressure, allowing a lighter, higher lift valvetrain to produce 20 more horsepower. Today the Z06 model represents about 25 percent of sales, and it is being purchased by the extreme performance enthusiasts for which it was designed.

Q: How do you feel about the upcoming C6 sharing platforms and components with another GM vehicle for the first time, namely the 2004 Cadillac XLR?

Hill: We did strive to have the [C5] architecture support another product, to increase our success as a business and as a contributor to GM's bottom line. We are quite proud about how the Cadillac XLR is shaping up, and believe it will be very credible in relation to its competitors, the Mercedes Benz SL, Jaguar XK8, and Lexus SC 430. We believe the Cadillac challenges will enable our team to deliver a better Corvette, and by having the heart of a performance car, the Cadillac XLR will represent a very exciting entry into the luxury-sports class.

Q: Early reports suggest the coming C6 will be evolutionary in nature, with less-radical changes than were made to the C5 over the C4. How then do you foresee the Corvette evolving in its seventh generation and beyond?

Hill: The C6 will be every bit a Corvette for the 21st century, but the C5 will be much "younger" than was the C4 when it was replaced. Some changes will be less radical, while others will be more so. We're feeling very good about the car's passion, technology, and value. The future will certainly include more and more change, and the engineering staff will be challenged to keep upgrading the car to meet societal needs.

Q: Which is your favorite Corvette over the last 50 years?

Hill: I can't even think about a favorite Corvette without thinking C6. It's where all my energy is being focused right now. Among existing Corvettes, I love the 2003 50th Anniversary Edition convertible I'm driving. I think it represents a high point in the evolution of the Corvette. Among oldies, I'm partial to the '57 fuelie and the '67 small block.

Q: Is there anything in your personal garage you're working on right now?

Hill: The garage still contains my original one-owner 1970 Corvette coupe, but it is not receiving any attention these days. A '48 MG TC is in the same predicament. My '86 El Camino and my three motorcycles get regular driving, but with my work schedule such as it is, coming home to work on a car doesn't add up. Maybe after we're done with the C6....

drilled cast-aluminum brake and clutch pedals burnished the sporting ambiance.

Power for the C5 came from a clean-sheet redesign of the pushrod small-block V-8. Called the LS1, it delivered 345 bhp at 5600 rpm and 350 lb-ft of torque at 4400 rpm. Displacement rounded off to a familiar 5.7 liters, but the block was rendered in aluminum, not iron, and was of a stouter, deep-skirt design. Premium fuel was recommended and synthetic oil was filled at the factory. Fitting the LS1 beneath the C5's newly lowered hood required an oil pan that was hardly thicker than a briefcase, yet offered increased capacity and the ability to supply lubricant during even the most extreme cornering maneuvers. Fully dressed, the LS1 weighed 45 pounds less than the LT4 engine it replaced.

As before, the V-8 used a four-speed automatic transmission as its standard gearbox. A revised ver-

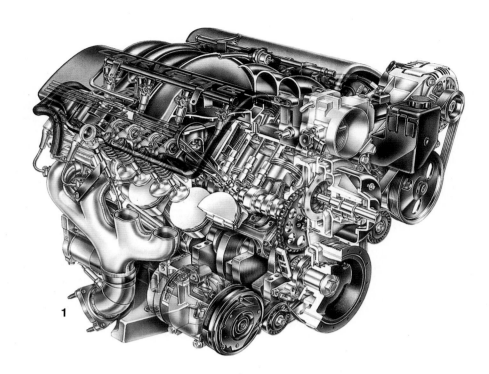

1. A clean-sheet redesign of Chevy's classic small block, C5's new all-aluminum LS1 V-8 was lighter yet more potent than the iron-block LT1/LT4 engines it replaced. Output was up considerably, to 345 bhp and 350 lb-ft of torque. **2.** The C5 was birthed by Dave Hill (*pictured*), who took over from Dave McLellan as Corvette chief engineer as the new-model program got underway.

The rear suspension no longer relied on the axle half shafts for its upper control arms, an arrangement that had transmitted powertrain vibration through the chassis. It was now a true short/long-arm double-wishbone design with geometry and bushings tuned for optimal ride and handling. Rear driveline componentry, meanwhile, was segregated from the structure. Transverse plastic leaf springs returned but, thanks to the stiffer structure, had lower spring rates for a softer ride. There were two suspension options: the autocross-ready (but tooth-rattling) Z51; and the high-tech F45 Selective Real Time Damping system that allowed driver-selectable "Tour," "Sport," and "Performance" modes.

Quick and offering good road feel, GM's second-generation electro-magnetic variable-assist steering automatically increased wheel effort as the car's speed increased. The brakes featured vented discs and aluminum calipers as before, but were treated to thicker rotors, and, since the ABS was integrated with the aforementioned traction-control system, the pedal no longer pulsed to signal antilock activation.

The ability of new Goodyear Eagle F1 GS Extended Mobility Tires to run airless for 200 miles convinced Chevy to eliminate the spare tire and jack altogether, which was another boon to reduced curb weight and increased cargo space. Inflation levels were monitored constantly and could be called up on an instrument-panel display. Wheel diameter was again 17 inches in front but grew to 18 in back. At

sion of the Borg-Warner six-speed manual remained optional at an additional $815, and again came with a first-to-fourth Computer-Aided Gear Selection skip shifter. Despite the more complex linkage, the transmission's shift effort and feel were similar to that of the C4.

So-called "drive-by-wire" technology provided precise throttle modulation and integrated cruise- and traction-control systems, the latter losing its pedal feedback in the process. Linking the engine and transmission was an aluminum tube, which ran through an enclosed tunnel that formed a chassis backbone strong enough to reduce structural loads on the outboard frame rails.

The C5's 'Vette's chassis design and powertrain layout were astute responses to the customers' call for friendly handling, roominess, and solidity. Relocating the transmission to the rear axle created a near-ideal 51/49 percent weight distribution for better-balanced road manners. It also eliminated bulk behind the engine, so footwells were no longer toe-pinching tunnels; the driver's side was even wide enough to accommodate a proper dead pedal.

Instead of 28 welded pieces like the C4's, the new model's frame rails were seamless one-piece steel tubes that had been "inflated" into shape by hydraulic pressure. They defined a new perimeter-frame chassis that was vastly stronger than any previous Corvette structure. Tying it together was a chassis floor of composite plastic sheets sandwiching Ecuadorian balsa wood. Balsa proved lighter than synthetic fillers and better at absorbing noise and vibration. Mounting the fuel tank ahead of the rear axle instead of behind it enhanced the car's weight balance and cargo room.

1

2

1. Only a hatchback coupe was offered for 1997, here posed with four of its grandfathers. 2. Even the Corvette's traditional crossed-flags emblem was redone for the C5.

245/45ZR-17 and 275/40ZR-18, respectively, the unidirectional all-season tires were slightly narrower than the 1996 model's base tires and didn't nibble and trammel nearly as much, which made for outstanding directional stability.

The car came packed with the same complement of comfort and convenience features as before, including a removable body color roof panel (a blue-tint panel could be substituted for $650 while dual panels remained available for $950), power accessories, the proximity based keyless-entry system, a Bose audio system with an AM/FM/cassette head unit by Delco, and leather seats. All this came in at an introductory price of $37,945, just $720 more than the 1996 coupe. Newly offered options included electronic dual-zone air conditioning for $365, a $600 remote 12-disc changer, and a $150 Memory Package that recalled the driver's settings for the outside mirrors, radio, climate-control system, and power seat.

Exceptional braking, handling, ride, comfort, roominess, ergonomics, and value—the C5 had it all.

And it was one of the fastest cars in the world to boot. The six-speed went from 0 to 60 mph in 4.7 seconds, a half-second less than an LT4 and just as quickly as the 405-bhp ZR-1. A 172 mph top speed put it about two mph in front of the fastest C4 and just seven mph shy of the ZR-1. On the skid pad, its .93g was the best number ever achieved by a production Corvette, while braking from 60 mph was a supercar-short 125 feet.

The automotive press was enthusiastic about the C5, comparing its performance favorably to exotic Ferraris and Porsches that were priced on a par with new homes. This was clearly a Corvette that satisfied both the emotions and the intellect, a car without excuses. Reviewers agreed that this was the quickest and most agile 'Vette ever, yet they praised it for being the most-civilized iteration, as well.

1

2

3

While the C4 was routinely slammed for its omnipresent squeaks, rattles, vibrations, and all-pervasive lack of sophistication, the C5 was credited for its newfound rigidity, feeling of precision, and overall quality. The new Corvette earned high marks for departing from the age-old philosophy that held that a car needed to trade off ride quality to achieve better handling; this car, they felt, offered both attributes in ample amounts. Seat comfort was lauded as much as the car's ride comfort, and the much-improved instrumentation, interior ergonomics, and outward visibility were welcome changes, said the scribes. Niggling criticisms involved poor side-window seals, unwelcome air currents with the removable top off, and a tendency for the vehicle's low-slung nose to scrape dips, driveways, and parking-lot barriers.

Total sales for the foreshortened and production-constrained 1997 model year accounted for a mere 9752 units. Even so, the new Corvette was selling briskly for the first time in more than a decade.

With a car that apparently hit a bull's-eye right from the start, it might have seemed difficult to broaden the C5's appeal. But Chevy did just that by introducing an all-new convertible version for 1998.

Chevrolet had planned to build a convertible companion to the coupe literally from day one of the C5 project. In fact, the vehicle was engineered to accommodate a ragtop without adding the heavy structural reinforcements most open cars require. As a result, the convertible weighed just one pound more than the coupe and was only slightly less rigid. What's more, it weighed 114 pounds less and was four times more torsionally sound than its C4 equivalent. It also came

1

with a traditional trunk, the first one to be included on a convertible Corvette since 1962. And this was no mere cubbyhole, either—at 13.9 cubic feet, its cargo area was larger than that of any other contemporary convertible.

The design team also revived the convertible's "waterfall," a body panel that continued down from the tonneau, flowing between the seats as it did on 1953 to '62 versions. A glass rear window with electric defroster was standard, but the top still had to be raised or lowered manually. (A power top would have reduced trunk space and added almost 15 pounds to the package.) Still, the double-lined folding top was lighter and easier to operate than the C4's; it could be raised or lowered in about 20 seconds, though the system's weight and release points precluded that this be accomplished from outside the car. The new design eliminated the

unsightly tonneau anchor holes and roof locator pins of previous Corvettes. The ragtop now used the tension of its raised framework to hold the bottom in place.

The 1998 convertible's price was set at $44,425, compared to $37,495 for the coupe—approximately the same price spread as the C4 models (though it was still a far cry from the Sixties and early Seventies, when ragtop 'Vettes actually cost less than base coupes).

A 1998 C5 convertible was chosen to be the fourth Corvette to pace the Indianapolis 500. Modifications from stock were few: The pace car's LS1 engine got a freer-flowing intake manifold and exhaust system that boosted horsepower by 25, to 370; its ride height was lowered slightly; a roll bar was mounted behind each seat; and rear-facing strobe lights were integrated in the tonneau's fairings.

To mark the occasion, Chevy built

1158 pace-car replica convertibles for public sale at an option-package price of $5039 ($5804 for cars with the manual transmission). While the replicas included none of the actual pace car's mechanical tweaks or safety equipment, they did carry its exclusive radar blue paint, decals, two-tone upholstery, and yellow wheels. They also came with a full ensemble of otherwise-optional features, including a new Corvette performance option introduced at midyear: an antiskid system.

The new Active Handling System (RPO JL4), available for $500, was designed to sense an impending skid during a turn and guide the car back on line by selectively applying individual brakes and activating the standard traction-control system; throttle control remained unaffected. Unlike other such antiskid systems, and keeping in character with the vehicle's sporting nature, this one added a "Competition mode."

2

3

Corvette's highest production total in 12 years—with the new convertible accounting for about 38 percent of the volume.

Early in the C5's development, Chevrolet product planners pondered the idea of creating a lower-cost "stripper" model with fewer amenities, roll-down windows, cloth-covered seats, and smaller wheels and tires. A few prototypes were built and submitted to market-research clinics, but Chevy was surprised to find that few potential customers were interested in a budget-minded Corvette. Furthermore, GM executives were hesitant to approve a substantially lower-priced base model that might lure buyers away from higher-profit versions. Still, the idea of a no-frills 'Vette remained intriguing to the car's managers, if only for the sake of eliminating otherwise unnecessary features in the name of performance-enhancing weight reduction.

Thus, for 1999, Chevy introduced a C5 hardtop, casting it as the Corvette for serious performance enthusiasts. Essentially a convertible with a fixed fiberglass roof, the hardtop's beefier structure made its body 12 percent more rigid than the coupe with the targa panels in place, and the car weighed some 92 pounds less. Plus, it retained the convertible's external trunk.

Activated by a console button, it deactivated the traction-control portion of the system for extreme cornering situations in which some rear-wheel spin was desirable.

Optional magnesium wheels were also introduced for 1998, but the $3000 rims proved unexpectedly popular and had to be discontinued when supplies ran out.

Incremental improvements across the board for 1998 included a number of noise-reduction efforts; these included a modified accessory drive tensioner, the removal of an alternator brace that was found to produce a high-rev "whine," improved window seals, and, later in the production run, a quieter electric fuel pump. In addition, the power-steering system's caster angle was increased for better tracking, and the optional Real-Time Damping suspension now afforded better wheel control. A second-gear start mode was added to the standard four-speed automatic transmission to help limit wheel spin from a standing start on slick roads. Finally, the transmission cooler was now made of stainless steel instead of a copper-nickel alloy.

Sales for the C5's first full model year roared to 31,084 units—the

1. A new 1998 convertible was the 11th Chevrolet and the fourth Corvette to pace the Memorial Day Indianapolis 500. Chevrolet public relations issued a "heritage" photo for the occasion. **2.** Pro golfer Greg Norman was originally tapped as the pace car driver but he had to give way to Parnelli Jones due to shoulder surgery. **3.** This is the actual 1998 pace car, but Chevy sold 1163 replicas that were virtually identical in appearance.

While not exactly inexpensive, the hardtop did cost $394 less than the coupe. Yet it came with the 345-hp LS1 small-block V-8 under the hood and was fitted with the six-speed manual transmission (its only available gearbox) and the Z51 Performance Handling suspension, which otherwise added $1165 to coupes and convertibles. Exterior colors were limited to blue, pewter, red, and white; and only the base black leather seats were offered—without power adjustments. Several weight-increasing options were unavailable on the hardtop, such as the Real-Time Damping suspension. Likewise, a number of comfort-and-convenience items were restricted only to the coupe and convertible.

Enthusiast-publication reviews of the slimmer 1999 hardtop were generally quite positive, though their actual road tests showed only slight improvements in performance. *Car and Driver,* for example, reported a 0–60 mph time of

4.8 seconds for the hardtop compared to 4.9 seconds for the coupe, and a quarter-mile clocking of 13.2 seconds at 110 mph versus 13.3 seconds at 109 mph. What's more, the hardtop's exterior was slightly less aerodynamic than the targa-top's version. Therefore, it reached a lower maximum speed of 169 mph in *C/D*'s tests, while the coupe was able to make it all the way to 171 mph. Still, every tenth of a second apparently counted to die-hard enthusiasts and weekend racers; Chevy was able to sell 4031 hardtops for 1999.

One new feature offered for 1999 coupes and convertibles was borrowed from high-tech fighter-jets: The $375 RPO UV8 was a sophisticated "Head-Up Display" system that projected instrument readouts onto the windshield so the driver could keep his or her eyes fixed on the road. Appearing in the lower left-hand area of the windshield, the driver could customize the display to include the full complement of

For the first time, Corvette offered three separate models with the 1999 debut of a notchback hardtop coupe. Essentially a convertible with a fixed roof made of reinforced fiberglass, it was stiffer than other C5s and, with fewer standard and optional features, lighter and less expensive. Even so, the hatchback remained the most popular model.

readings, or just the speed, rpm, and/or other selected information. A "check gauges" warning would indicate times the driver needed to pay attention to a dashboard gauge or warning not duplicated on the head-up array.

Also added for 1999, and limited to coupes and convertibles at an extra cost of $350, was a power telescoping steering column that offered plus or minus 20 mm of travel over the fixed-shaft version; the wheel's standard tilt function remained manually operated, however. Likewise, newly optional automatic-engaging "Twilight Sentinel" headlamps, priced at $60, were also excluded from hardtops. The $3000 magnesium wheels returned to the options list and were also offered only on coupes and convertibles.

All 1999 Corvettes benefited from modifications to the car's magnetically variable power-steering system, implemented to make steering more sensitive and with less of a tendency to "wander" at highway speeds. So-called "next generation" airbags were designed to deploy with less force than before to help reduce airbag-induced injuries sustained in collisions.

The $38,197 hardtop helped lift sales to 33,270 units, with the coupe now selling for $38,591 and the convertible for $44,999.

In a serious performance statement, Corvette returned to factory-backed racing in 1999. Competing as a production-based sports car, the new C5-R was designed as a GTS-class racer that maintained the integrity of the production Corvette and shared a number of standard-issue components. These included the stock Corvette frame, engine block, windshield, taillights and marker lights, power steering pump, steering rack, alternator, water pump, and assorted suspension components. But it was almost four inches wider, had a carbon-fiber body that was loosely based on the production car's exterior, and its engine produced 255 more horse-power than a conventional Corvette.

The C5-R quickly established itself by finishing third in its GTS-class debut at the Rolex 24 Hours of Daytona and claiming third place in the GT2 class.

Corvette thus began the new millennium with renewed momentum on the track, where it did battle with Vipers and Porsches; and on the street, where sales were healthy and performance unquestioned. America's legendary sports car was thriving.

Production Corvettes for 2000 continued with limited styling changes, though the five-spoke standard aluminum wheels were revised; despite their thinner spokes, they were now fully forged with a flow-formed rim for greater durability. A polished finish for the alloy wheels was newly optional; at $2000, the optional magnesium wheels, which were now also available on the hardtop, cost a third less than before. A new body color, Millennium Yellow, was available for an additional $500.

The proximity-based keyless-entry system, which was reported to be perplexing to many buyers, was discontinued for 2000 in favor of a more-conventional keyfob-button-controlled configuration. What's more, the passenger-side outside door lock was now deleted, leaving the driver-side key cylinder the only mechanical way to unlock the

1. The performance-oriented notchback hardtop coupe came only with the Z51 suspension and six-speed manual transmission. **2-5.** General Motors announced the C5-R racing program in 1998, the first "official" effort for Corvette "production-based" race cars. The C5-R team first saw action at the 1999 Rolex 24 Hours of Daytona, where it took an impressive third place in the SCCA's United States Road Racing Championship GT2 class. The majority of the C5-R's subsequent race action came in the American LeMans Series' (ALMS) GTS class.

2

3

4

5

car from the outside in the case of a dead battery.

The Z51 Performance Handling Package added larger stabilizer bars at the front and rear, along with revised shock-absorber damping; these changes increased roll stiffness for added cornering stability without resulting in a noticeably harsher ride. Also for 2000, quality and engineering improvements were made to the manual-transmission shifter, Selective Real-Time Damping suspension, windshield seals, dual-zone climate control, seat belts, and seat materials and construction.

With fairly negligible price increases for 2000 boosting the hardtop to $38,705, the coupe to $39,280, and the convertible to $45,705, sales ticked up slightly, to 33,659 units on the year.

Encouraged by the C5-R's performance in 1999, Chevrolet replaced the race car's 6.0-liter engine with a 7.0-liter V-8 in 2000, gaining 20 horsepower. The car went on to place third and fourth in its class (10th and 11th overall) at the 24 Hours of LeMans in June 2000. It then racked up its first victory at the American LeMans Series race when Ron Fellows and Andy Pilgrim drove it at Ft. Worth, Texas, that September.

While the lean-and-mean hardtop model promised slightly higher performance via a lower curb weight, its replacement for 2001, the Z06, brought ZR-1-like muscle to the Corvette, and at $46,855, did so for far less money. The name was chosen to honor Zora Arkus-Duntov and the original race-ready Z06 package that was introduced in 1963. At the heart of the new flagship was a newly engineered powerplant, called the LS6. The name LS6 was likewise an homage to Duntov and his famed 425-bhp (gross) big-block V-8 of the same designation that was offered, briefly, in 1971.

Exclusive to the Z06, the LS6

1

2

1-2. The hardtop was an artifact of an aborted plan for a "stripper" C5 aimed at all-out performance enthusiasts. The follow-up 2000 boasted many detail improvements but looked little different. The same was true of its linemates. The hardtop body style remained for 2001, but was only available as the high-performance Z06.

delivered a lusty 385 bhp and 385 lb-ft of torque. Based on the standard 5.7-liter LT1 powerplant, the LS6's higher-compression aluminum heads (10.5:1 versus 10.1:1) were modified for better management of crankcase pressures and speedier return of oil from the upper part of the engine during high-speed runs. A more-aggressive camshaft profile was added to take advantage of a new intake manifold that provided higher-

volume breathing and worked with improved porting to get the added air into the combustion chambers as smoothly as possible. Larger fuel injectors were in place to match the added air volume, and a unique titanium exhaust system that was 50 percent lighter than the standard stainless-steel array was included to help relieve exhaust-gas back-pressure. Finally, stronger valve springs were added to manage the higher rpm.

1. From the start, the C5's front license plate box created a split lower fascia that was criticized as being too Pontiaclike. **2.** Despite the Corvette's obvious performance character, the majority of buyers chose the four-speed automatic transmission. **3.** Power for 2000 remained unchanged at 345 bhp. **4.** In their second season, the C5-Rs entered the 2000 running of the fabled 24 Hours of LeMans, finishing third and fourth in the GTS class, 10th and 11th overall—impressive for such a new race car.

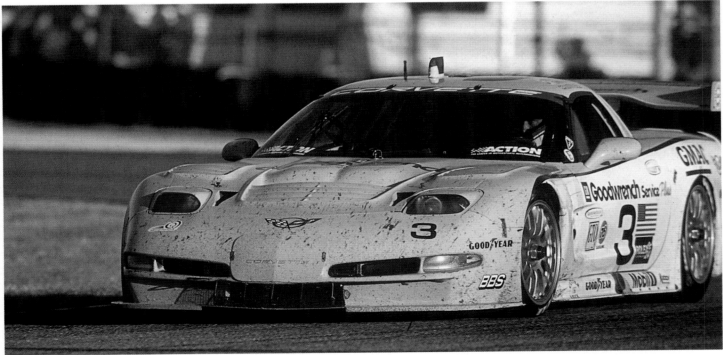

A new six-speed manual transmission, the only available Z06 gearbox, came with more-aggressive gearing. With an impressive power-to-weight ratio of 8.09 pounds per horsepower, this was clearly the fastest Corvette ever produced, able to outrun even the venerable big-block V-8s that ruled the road in the 1960s. Chevy boasted (and exuberant magazine testers confirmed) 0–60 mph times for the Z06 of around four seconds, reaching the quarter-mile in just over 12 ticks of the clock. Clearly, the Corvette could again run unashamedly with the likes of some of the fastest production cars in the world.

Added to help handle the Z06's extra go-power was an exclusive suspension, named FE4, that came with a larger front stabilizer bar, stiffer rear leaf spring, and revised camber settings, all calibrated to deliver maximum high-speed control. Wider and grippier Goodyear

Eagle F1 Supercar tires, created specifically for the car, weighed less than the standard rubber and came with an asymmetrical tread design to better hold onto both dry and wet roads. The new tires also had more compliant sidewalls and improved wear characteristics. P265/40ZR-17s rode in front, with P295/35ZR-18s in the rear. They were mounted on unique lightweight forged-aluminum wheels. An inch wider front and back than those offered on standard Corvettes, the new wheels were painted in a light-gray metallic color.

The Z06 was also put on a weight-reduction program that, in addition to the aforementioned exhaust system and wheels/tires, included a compact lead-acid battery and a thinner windshield and backlight than standard models. All told, it weighed in at 36 pounds less than the already slimmed-down hardtop it replaced and was 117 pounds

lighter than the coupe.

As with the ZR-1, unique styling cues added to differentiate the Z06 were minimal. These included the addition of purposeful grilles to the center air inlets on the front fascia, and air scoops added to the rear rocker panels to feed air to the rear brakes for better cooling. Finally, both the disc-brake calipers and the engine cover were painted bright red, and Z06 emblems were added to the front fenders.

Inside, the Z06 sported an exclusive instrument cluster with stylized graphics that helped to accentuate the model's higher 6500 rpm redline. Seats were leather-trimmed in solid black (with Torch Red accents optional) and included additional side bolstering to help occupants remain firmly planted no matter how high the g-forces became during cornering; headrests were embroidered with Z06 logos. A Bose audio system with

Like previous Corvettes, the C5 steadily improved each year. For instance, the 2001 convertible got a smoother-looking soft top with better sealing and sound insulation. It's stowed here because that's where it should be when skies are clear. Interestingly, the ragtop narrowed the hatchback's sales lead for 2001 to a mere 1508 units.

CD player was also included.

Needless to say, the buff books were wildly enthusiastic about the Z06. They heralded it as race-ready out of the box, a bona fide bargain among high-performance sports cars, and a new Corvette legend.

Elsewhere in the line, the 2001 coupe and convertible benefited from the LS6's new intake and exhaust manifolds and received a slight bump in power—now 350 bhp instead of 345. They real boost, however, came in low-end torque, now up to 360 lb-ft at 4000 rpm on automatic-transmission-equipped models, and 375 lb-ft at 4400 rpm on those with the six-speed manual.

The additional power was found at lower engine speeds. For example, 340 lb-ft now came at 2500 rpm, which was 1400 revs earlier than before. This meant that the "slowest" Corvette (a base model with the automatic, which Chevy said was ordered by 60 percent of buyers)

racked up a 0–60 mph time that was a full quarter second quicker than the 2000 model. When fitted with the performance axle, the automatic could now run as fast as the previous year's manual-gearbox version.

What's more, LT1 fuel economy improved by one mpg, and all Corvettes were now certified as National Low-Emission Vehicles (NLEV). The LT1 engine also received a stronger, larger-diameter aluminum driveshaft, and base manual-gearbox versions received a revised clutch that required less pedal pressure to engage.

Chevrolet introduced a version of the Corvette's Active Handling system for 2001 and made it standard across the line. It featured a new brake-pressure modulator supplied by Bosch and a number of new or revised system calibrations. The new stability control system was programmed to be less "intrusive" than the previous version. Also

included for the first time on the coupe and convertible was an absorbent glass mat battery, which was lighter and more durable than the cell it replaced. A revised alternator included a new clutch pulley that helped eliminate "idle creep" on automatic transmission models.

Added sound insulation made for a quieter ride, and auto-dimming "electrochromic" side and rearview mirrors were newly added to the options list for '01. Convertibles received a new top that offered a tighter seal, improved noise isolation, and a smoother look. Chrome-flashed exhaust tips were also new.

Meanwhile, the Corvette C5-R racer dominated its competition during 2001. Among its victories, the C5-R notched an overall win at the 24 Hours of Daytona, a double-podium finish at the 12 Hours of Sebring, first and second places in the GTS class at the 24 Hours of LeMans, and class victories in

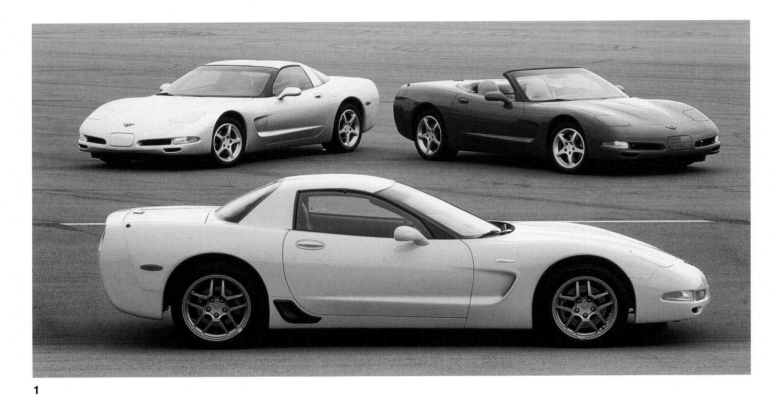

1

1. The hardtop (foreground) realized its performance potential in 2001 as Chevrolet transformed it into the Z06 with a new LS6 V-8 making 35 more horses than the parent LS1. Revised suspension, red brake calipers, and rear brake cooling ducts were among many other Z06 exclusives. **2.** The number 4 C5-R finished second in the GTS class at the 2001 12 Hours of Sebring. Note the glowing front brake rotors.

2

American LeMans Series runs at Portland, Sears Point, and Texas Motor Speedway. In August 2001, Chevrolet announced it would sell as many as five track-ready versions of the C5-R GTS-class racer to private teams, much as it had done with previous specially modified Corvettes. The engine and related electronics had to be purchased separately through Katech and fitted to the chassis by Pratt and Miller, both Chevrolet partners in the C5-R project.

Prices nudged upward for 2001: $39,830 for the coupe and $46,355 for the ragtop. Buoyed by 5798

units of the new Z06, 2001 Corvette sales leaped ahead to 35,537, its highest volume since 1985.

Chevrolet and the Z06 wouldn't rest on their laurels after an impressive freshman year, either. For 2002, the 5.7-liter LS6 engine received an additional 20 horses, bringing the small-block V-8 up to a mighty 405 bhp (a healthy 71 bhp per liter). Torque was also up by another 15 lb-ft, now rated at 400 lb-ft at 4800 rpm. These improvements came about as a result of modifications to make the LS6 breathe more freely, including a new cam profile that allowed the

engine's intake and exhaust valves to open .7 mm further than before. New hollow-stem valves, a low-restriction mass-airflow sensor, and a new low-restriction air cleaner also contributed to the power boost.

Significantly, the LS6 now matched the rated output of the highest-powered LT5 from the fabled ZR-1, but because of a higher power-to-weight ratio, the Z06 was a quicker car. Chevy claimed 0–60-mph times of a mere 3.9 seconds and a run to the quarter mile in just 12.4 seconds at 114 mph. By comparison, the fastest recorded times for the ZR-1 were 0–60 mph in 4.5

1

2

3

1. Buyers of 2001 Corvettes could opt to take delivery at the National Corvette Museum, near the Bowling Green, Kentucky, factory. This new option, R8C, was chosen by only 457 of that year's 35,627 customers. The $490 price included Museum admission and a plant tour. **2.** The C5-R scored its first victory in a world-class long-distance race at Daytona's 2001 Rolex 24 Hours. The number 2 C5-R romped home eight laps ahead of the second-place number 3 C5-R. **3-4.** The C5-Rs competed in their second 24 Hours of LeMans in 2001 and claimed a 1-2 finish in the GTS class. It was the first LeMans win in Corvette history. Drivers Ron Fellows, Johnny O'Connell, and Scott Pruett drove the number 63 car to victory, while Andy Pilgrim, Kelly Collins, and Franck Freon took second in the number 64.

4

1

1. In the 2001 American LeMans Series' 12 Hours of Sebring, the numbers 4 and 3 Corvette C5-Rs finished second and third, respectively, in the GTS class. 2. Afterward, drivers Kelly Collins (*left*), Andy Pilgrim (*center*), and Franck Freon celebrated their second-place effort. All told, the two C5-Rs were dominant, winning eight of the ten races they entered in 2001. The C5-R also claimed its first of four consecutive ALMS GTS Manufacturer's Championships in 2001.

2

seconds and the quarter mile in 12.8 seconds at 111 mph.

To withstand the additional torque from the newly revised LS6, the Z06's clutch was likewise redesigned: The flange-plate thickness was increased by 20 percent, damper springs were revised to increase wind-up rate, and premium alloy steel wire was now used for the damper springs. All told, the improvements purported to offer better overall performance and added durability.

The Z06's FE4 suspension also received several minor improvements for 2002. Among these was revised rear-shock damper valving for improved handling on the track and a less-punishing ride on city streets. Also benefiting the suspension were the use of lighter-weight cast-aluminum stabilizer links (instead of rolled rod steel links)

and cast-spun aluminum wheels (replacing the previous forged aluminum set) for an additional weight reduction of nearly two pounds. In addition, new higher-performance brake pads were added in front for improved lining durability and better high-performance fade resistance.

As if that wasn't enough, Chevy also made the Corvette's optional Head-Up Display standard on the Z06. These revisions contributed significantly to the $2850 price increase for 2002, meaning thrill-seekers now needed to pony up $49,705 to command the Z06's hair-raising abilities. Nevertheless, the car was selling at a rapid pace.

Otherwise, changes were minor for 2002: An in-dash AM/FM/CD player was made standard on coupes and convertibles, making the AM/FM/cassette head unit

The convertible and hatchback again saw only detail updates for 2002, including a lighter automatic transmission case.

only available with the optional 12-disc CD changer. Automatic transmission models received a lighter-weight cooler case that was now made out of cast aluminum instead of stainless steel. Finally, the cast-aluminum stabilizer links added to the Z06 were now included with the optional Z51 Performance Handling Package.

Tearing up the track, a Corvette C5-R, driven by Ron Fellows, Johnny O'Connell, and British driver Oliver Gavin, was victorious in the GTS class at the 2002 12 Hours of Sebring, the Corvette's 14th class win in the event's 50-year history and the first win in four tries for the specially

1

1-2. The Z06 got the most attention for 2002, with its LS6 engine muscled up to 405 horsepower, the same as in the great ZR-1 of 1990-95. The '02 Z06 also boasted a retuned suspension and new "spun-cast" aluminum wheels. 3. The hatchback was once again the most affordable Corvette for 2002 at $41,005 plus a $645 destination charge. The standard roof panel was body color, but for $1200 customers could also get transparent roof panels.

2

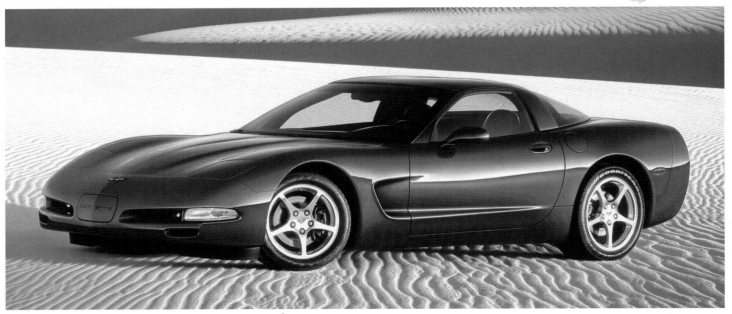

3

1

modified C5-R. The same team also dominated its class in the 24 Hours of LeMans for the second straight year, completing 335 laps around the legendary 8.5-mile circuit and besting the likes of the Dodge Viper, Saleen S7, and Ferrari 550 racers. The team of Andy Pilgrim and Kelly Collins took their C5-R to first in class and fifth place overall at the Road America 500 in Elkhart Lake, Wisconsin. Fellows and O'Connell placed first in class in the inaugural

running of the Cadillac Grand Prix of Washington, D.C., while Pilgrim and Collins finished second.

Base prices again rose by about $1000 each for the 2002 coupe and convertible, now selling for $41,005 and $47,530, respectively.

To mark the Corvette's first half-century of production in 2003, Chevrolet offered a 50th Anniversary Special Edition. Available only on coupes and convertibles, the package included a handsome

1. The passenger-side grab handle was a nod to Sixties Sting Rays and a welcome plus for passengers during spirited driving. 2. Echoing Fifties Corvettes was the convertible's between-seats "waterfall" panel extending down from the top cover. 3. Z06s came with more heavily bolstered seats with headrest logos. Upholstery was black leather only, but red cloth seat inserts were available.

2

3

1-3. A ghost view reveals engine placement within the stout frame rails of the Z06. Astute tuning wrung 405 horsepower from the Z06's 5.7-liter V-8, an impressive feat considering its "antiquated" pushrod design.

1

2

3

1

2

1-2. The numbers 63 and 64 C5-Rs returned to the 24 Hours of LeMans in 2002 and posted their second consecutive 1-2 finish. The number 63 car driven by Ron Fellows, Johnny O'Connell, and Oliver Gavin claimed the GTS class win, also finishing 11th overall. The number 64 car placed 13th overall, completing 331 laps around the 13.9-kilometer circuit, four less than its teammate. For the season, the C5-Rs won 10 of 11 races and marched to their second straight Manufacturer's Championship.

metallic-burgundy Anniversary Red exterior with champagne-painted wheels and specific badges; a shale interior was highlighted with embroidered emblems on the seats and floor mats, armrests, and grips. The 50th Anniversary convertible also had a shale-hued top. As many as 10,000 Anniversary cars would be built, based on customer demand, and the package—RPO 1SC

Preferred Equipment Group 2— added $5000 to the cost of a base coupe or convertible.

Also standard with the golden-anniversary model, and optional on 2003 coupes and convertibles for $1695, was a new F55 Magnetic Selective Ride Control suspension. Similar to the system GM introduced on the 2002 Cadillac STS, the system used a unique damper

design to govern wheel and body motion via "Magneto-Rheological" fluid in each shock absorber. Simply put, this is synthetic oil permeated with millions of minute iron balls that float uniformly within the shock fluid. Adjusting the current fed to an electromagnetic coil causes the ball-imbued fluid to change viscosity—and thus the shock absorber's damping—with

1

2

3

4

5

1. Corvette's Golden Anniversary celebration began in April 2002 with word that a 2003 Corvette C5 hatchback would pace the 2002 Indy 500. **2.** Chevrolet had a great day all around, as Team Penske driver Helio Castroneves (*on roof*) scored his second straight Indy 500 win, piloting a Chevy-powered Dallara. **3-5.** Chevrolet said the pace car was virtually identical to a 50th Anniversary Edition package planned for 2003 models, though with more graphics. **6.** Film star Jim Caviezel drove the C5 pace car driver for the 86th running of the Memorial Day classic.

6

the ability to go from no damping to virtually solid damping.

The F55 suspension was designed to make such adjustments at the blinding rate of about 1000 times per second, governed by a dual-processor computer chip and based on the car's speed, steering-wheel angle, wheel travel, lateral acceleration, braking, and even the outside temperature. The system was designed to isolate and smooth the action of each tire to help minimize bouncing, vibration, and noise. The result was a quieter, flatter ride with more responsive and precise handling, especially during sudden high-speed maneuvers. The system worked in tandem with both the 'Vette's traction-control and antilock braking systems to afford maximum balance and stability over a full range of road conditions. For the heartiest motorists willing to trade some ride

361

comfort for additional road feel, a console-mounted switch afforded a change from "Tour" to "Sport" mode.

Enthusiast-magazine testers came away duly impressed by the F55 system's ability to maintain control and reduce ride harshness when traversing large bumps or dips at speed, and its ability to absorb pavement imperfections and eschew superfluous suspension

travel without sacrificing road feel. The alternate "Sport" mode was appreciated, but its greater degree of control and subsequently harsher ride was noted to be more appropriate for running hot laps on a race track than it was in daily driving. The Magnetic Selective Ride Control's added heft, just over 13 pounds, precluded the new system from being offered on the high-performance Z06, however, where every ounce of added weight was looked upon with disdain.

A host of equipment was made newly standard on coupes and convertibles for 2003, including fog lamps, sport seats, a power passenger's seat, and dual-zone auto climate control. Coupes received a standard parcel net and privacy

shade for the hatch area. To accommodate future enthusiasts, special hooks were installed on the passenger's seat to facilitate connection of a specially equipped child seat (which was recommended only to be used in conjunction with a passenger-side airbag-cutoff switch engaged for added safety). All '03 'Vettes came with special silver 50th Anniversary emblems at the front and rear that featured the number "50" along with the car's signature crossed-flags logo.

Prices went up again for 2003, partly due to the birthday trimmings and other added features. The coupe now started at $43,255, the ragtop at $49,700, the Z06 at $50,485. Despite the hikes, sales held steady on model-year produc-

1

3

2

1. To commemorate its two consecutive wins at the 24 Hours of LeMans, Chevrolet eschewed its regular yellow paint scheme for the 2003 race in favor of LeMans Blue paint with silver and red stripes. The C5-Rs placed second and third. The cars won five of ten races for the year. **2-3.** The C5-Rs won all ten of the races held during the 2004 season, kicking off with the March 20 12 Hours of Sebring (*shown at left*).

1

tion of 36,026, a slim 88-unit gain over the '02 tally.

The C5 did well to hold its own, because 2003 ushered in a raft of new competitors, all hot off the drawing board and bracketing Corvette's price range. A redesigned V-10-powered Dodge Viper roadster tempted those with $80,000 to spare. A more serious threat was Nissan's head-turning V-6 350Z, which grabbed much enthusiast

attention with its slick looks, 'Vette-like handling, and prices starting at just $26,269. Mazda would up the ante for 2004 with the RX-8, a new-generation rotary-powered sports car pitched in the mid- to high-$20,000s. And Porsche's mid-engine Boxster, though just as old as the C5 in design terms, was still a formidable rival at prices that almost exactly duplicated the 'Vette's.

But by this time, everyone knew the C5 was heading for retirement. Indeed, the motoring press in 2003 was filled with rabid rumors and spy photos of the replacement C6. Sure enough, Chevrolet signaled another changing of the guard with the 2004 Corvettes, which were virtual '03 carryovers except for the addition of tellingly named "Commemorative Edition" packages.

The commemoration celebrated a sterling 2003 season for the racing C5-Rs, which notched a third straight manufacturer's title in the American LeMans Series after just missing a GTS-class three-peat at the LeMans 24 Hours. The Commemorative packages must have been good-luck charms, because C5-Rs won every race they entered

in 2004, notching a fourth ALMS championship and a third double victory in France.

All the Commemorative Edition 2004s were finished in vivid LeMans Blue paint with wide red-edged silver stripes adorning the hood, roof, and rear deck. Special "LeMans 24-hours" crossed-flags emblems appeared on the nose and tail, and as embroidered logos on the headrests within a specific shale-colored interior. Polished alloy wheels completed the coupe and convertible ensembles, which cost $3700 and included all features of the regular 1SB Preferred Equipment Group.

The Commemorative option for the Z06 cost $4335, but included a unique (and costly) carbon-fiber hood that took a useful 10.6 pounds off the nose. Also featured were special clear-coat wheels with hubs reading "Commemorative 24:00 Heures du Mans." In addition, testing at Germany's famed Nürburgring track produced revised damping for the Sachs gas-pressure shock absorbers, stiffer bushings for the front upper-control arms, and softer bushings for the rear antiroll bar. Together, these tweaks

2

3

4

5

aimed to "settle" the Z06 more quickly in fast transient maneuvers—and they did. As Frank Markus enthused in *Car and Driver*'s September 2003 review: "[The Z06's] steering response is [now] so much quicker it's hard to believe the ratio is the same [as in other 'Vettes]. Its weight is within 141 pounds of [other models], yet it feels like hundreds less. Its structure also feels twice as rigid. Yes, it filters out less road noise and harshness, but at least each bump is felt *just* once.... Grip is astonishing"—Markus reported a leech-like 0.98g—"but these wide paws tend to wander a bit along pavement ruts. This chassis is also exceptionally well tuned to the active handling system's competitive-driving mode.... The [Commemorative] Z06 is clearly the [Corvette] that best rewards expert driving."

Or just good ol' pedal-to-the-metal driving, for that matter. *Motor Trend* lauded the Commemorative Z06 as the fastest showroom 'Vette it had ever tested, timing just 4.2 seconds 0–60 and a standing quarter mile of 12.4 seconds at 117 mph. All this, plus GM's usual three-year/36,000-mile bumper-to-bumper warranty.

The one sour note to the tasty Commemorative confections was deliberately limited production: a mere 2000 Z06s, perhaps twice that many coupes and convertibles. But whatever one may think about "factory collector cars," this was a fine sendoff for a highly successful Corvette generation.

Of course, success can be defined in many ways, but consider that nearly a quarter-million C5s were built over eight model years. That averages out to some 34,000

yearly sales, the best 'Vette performance since the mid Eighties. What's more, the C5 added a slew of awards to the Corvette's bulging trophy case—besides all those racing cups. An independent panel of automotive journalists named the 1998 Corvette the North American Car of the Year. The C5 was also *Motor Trend*'s Car of the Year in 1998, *Automobile* magazine's "Automobile of the Year" in 2001, and on *Car and Driver*'s annual 10 Best List in 1998, 1999, 2002, 2003, and 2004. Last but not least, the C5 was a perennial *Consumer Guide*® "Best Buy" among sports cars.

No doubt about it. The C5 had lifted the bar to lofty new heights, not only for Corvette but for sports cars all over the world. It would definitely be one tough act to follow. Could the replacement C6 possibly be better? Read on.

Corvette was transformed with 1997's all-new C5 series. Sold only as a hatchback coupe that year, C5 boasted swoopier styling than the C4, Detroit's lowest air-drag factor, and the longest wheelbase in Corvette history at 104.5 inches. A more sophisticated new all-aluminum 350-cid LS1 V-8 sent 345 bhp to a standard six-speed manual gearbox mounted at the rear, another 'Vette first. A more driver-friendly dashboard dominated a roomier, well-equipped cockpit with lower door sills for easier entry/exit. Priced from $37,945, the C5 coupe found only 9752 buyers in its debut year due to a deliberately slow production ramp-up.

After a year off, the convertible returned for 1998 with the new C5 design and the first external trunklid on a 'Vette roadster in 36 years. The top remained manual. Despite weighing slightly less than its C4 predecessor, the ragtop C5 was much stiffer, sharing the coupe's strong new "hydroformed" chassis with frame rails measuring a stout six inches across. Corvette was again the Indianapolis 500 pace car in '98, and 1163 convertibles were sold with the $5039 Pace Car Replica package, shown here. Total 'Vette sales were 31,084 for '98, of which 11,849 were convertibles.

369

Consumer Guide® tested this 1998 convertible and praised its power, structural strength, day-to-day livability, and what the editors saw as the best Corvette workmanship ever. Colleagues agreed, naming Corvette the 1998 North American Car of the Year. Base prices this year were $44,425 for the ragtop, $37,495 for the hatchback, making the C5 a bona fide high-performance bargain. Even the ragtop could do 0–60 mph in close to five seconds flat.

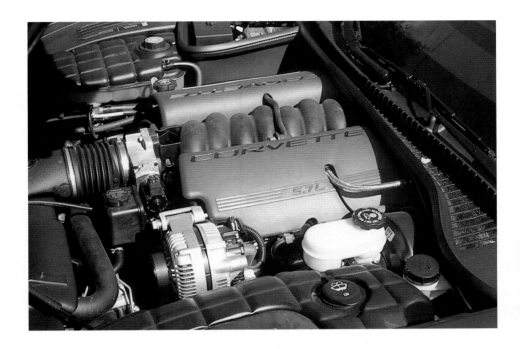

A convertible-based fixed-roof hardtop model expanded C5 offerings for 1999. Two years later, it was muscled-up into a separate, all-out enthusiast's delight called Z06. The 2002 edition, shown, was stronger still. Its unique LS6 V-8 went from 385 to 405 bhp this year, as proclaimed by the discreet front-fender badges.

In celebration of its 50th birthday, any 2003 Corvette coupe or convertible could be ordered with the 1SC package that included special anniversary paint and trim. Oddly, it was not available on the Z06 hardtop. The package brought monogrammed headrests, special champagne-colored wheels, additional 50th-anniversary emblems, and "Anniversary Red" paint, actually a deep metallic burgundy. Also included was Corvette's new-for-'03 F55 Magnetic Selective Ride Control suspension with variable-damping shock absorbers. Production was limited only by the number of orders for the $5000 package, a small price to pay for such a fitting tribute to the 50th anniversary of "America's only true sports car."

2005-2006

An exciting chapter in Corvette history began in January 2004 when the C6 met the public at the North American International Auto Show in Detroit. Sales commenced that summer. The new 2005 coupe and convertible were quickly hailed as the best Corvettes ever, yet they somehow weren't new enough to satisfy a few critics. Indeed, *Car and Driver* first described the C6 as a "C5 and 11/16ths.... Like the '68 Vette, the 2005 is a profound evolution of the existing car. It's one long stride on the road of continual improvement."

Well, Porsche's vaunted 911 has been evolving for 40 years, and no one minds that. Besides, the C5 was as revolutionary a Corvette as the C2 Sting Ray was in its day. And even after eight model years, the C5 remained not only a strong seller but unparalleled for sports-car performance and value. So why start over when you have the talent, funds, and drive to make a world-beater even more so?

That's precisely what the Corvette team did. The result is like a C5 that's been given an extreme makeover, gaining a trimmer, more chiseled physique; more muscle; and noticeably buffed-up levels of quality and refinement. Still not new enough for you? Then consider the 2006 Z06, the fastest, most exotic production 'Vette yet.

Significantly, the C6 is the first Corvette developed in tandem with another GM car. That, of course, is the Cadillac XLR, the suave two-seat retractable-hardtop convertible launched for 2004 as the for-sale version of the striking 1999 Evoq concept. From the outset, both the XLR and the three C6 models were planned for the GM Performance Vehicle Architecture introduced with the C5. Sensibly, senior managers assigned the Corvette design and engineering group to do them all. The Cadillac was given priority because it would launch first and would stand as a symbol of an emerging renaissance for GM's luxury brand. Only after the XLR was finished could the Corvette team turn full attention to C6 work, which was under way in earnest by mid 2000—yet another reason why the C6 could not be totally new in concept.

It is, however, very new in content—85 percent by weight, says group chief engineer Dave Hill. Much of that newness stems from having XLR in the mix. As assistant chief engineer Tadge Juechter told us: "We had to engineer that car first and yet not allow it to compromise our vision for what the C6 needed to be. Because [Corvette] customers would see through that right away. But we intentionally let the Cadillac rub off in areas where we thought it was important to improve the Corvette." Chief among those were the fit and finish of the composite-plastic exterior body panels; powertrain and road-noise isolation; and interior design, materials, and assembly.

As a Cadillac, the XLR had to be world-class in every respect. And that neatly dovetailed with the overarching goal for C6. "We had really stretched to upgrade the C5 each year," Hill told us. "Now we wanted to stretch again and annihilate the compromises we had been living with. We went at the new one with the idea of 'more exciting,' but with a surprising amount of refine-

More an evolution of the C5 than an all-new car, the C6 took giant steps forward in performance and refinement. Smaller, more nimble, and more precise than its predecessor, the C6 carried a design that, while not retro, tipped its hat to the beloved 1963-67 Sting Rays. Then came the next-generation Z06, a race-bred beast unlike any Corvette in the history of America's favorite sports car.

ment that people wouldn't believe possible at Corvette's performance level. We wanted once again to exceed expectations, even if not in a clean-sheet way. But we knew customer expectations would be real high, and we set out to beat 'em all." In fact, the team identified some 100 "dissatisfiers," as Hill calls them—things to be changed and/or improved based on complaints from C5 owners.

Certain items on that long to-do list posed special challenges for chief designer Tom Peters and lead exterior designer Kirk Bennion. From the beginning, the team accepted widespread criticism that the C5 was a bit large for a high-power sports car. Shedding bulk would shed pounds to the benefit of performance, but would also make the 'Vette easier to live with in crowded urban conditions—an important consideration for Europe, where GM wanted to boost Corvette sales. "Up front, we wanted to

1

2

3

1. General Motors' chairman and CEO Rick Wagoner unveiled the 2005 Chevrolet Corvette on Jan. 4, 2004, at the Detroit Opera House, in conjunction with the North American International Auto Show. 2. In 1999, Cadillac introduced the Evoq luxury roadster concept. 3-4. The Evoq was realized as the 2003 Cadillac XLR, and also became the first car ever to share the Corvette's space-frame architecture.

4

make it smaller, a tighter package," Peters told us. "Then we drove some C5s in Europe. That further emphasized it....The numbers I remember were three inches off the front, two off the rear, and an inch off the sides. And those kind of stuck."

Complicating matters was the desire for improved aerodynamics, which had great implications for a new C6.R racer. "We had the race team come in and really work with us on the development on the base [model], more so on the Z06," Peters recalls. "What were the real-world elements that would translate back into production—and get back into the race car, too. So things were developed like the center-port opening in the front end. The C5 was kind of split-grilled, and we realized there was criticism of that as being too Pontiac-like. Looking at older Corvettes, they all had a center-port opening, and I wanted to get back to that. Lo and behold, that worked out great for the race team."

So did a decision made early on to abandon pop-up headlamps for Corvette's first exposed beams since 1962. Besides reducing drag—Hill likened the pop-ups to

continued on page 383

378

Profile: Tom Peters, Chief Designer, Chevrolet C6 Corvette

Tom had a passion for art and design at a very young age. He developed a love of cars and industrial design. After his second year of college in Louisiana, Tom left his home state for the West Coast in 1976. After graduating in Transportation Design, from the Art Center College of Design in 1980, he went to work for General Motors. He left GM and accepted a position at Texas Instruments in the later part of 1980, designing consumer electronics including children's learning aids and first-generation laptop computers.

By 1982, Tom returned to GM. He was promoted through the ranks in Advanced and Production Studios for Pontiac and Chevrolet. Designing concepts for the first Saturn, Tom also worked on production Camaros and Corvettes including the Corvette Indy show vehicle and the 1988 Pontiac Banshee prototype.

He transferred to California in 1992 as director of GM's Advanced Concept Center. Programs at ACC ranged from full-size trucks to alternative-drive vehicles and championed progressive-math development processes. In addition, Tom was invited by Forms and Surfaces to freelance design proposals for architectural door and cabinet hardware.

In 1995, Tom returned to Detroit managing programs in Portfolio Development and Pontiac Production Studios.

Tom was vehicle chief designer for the Cadillac XLR roadster and the C6 next-generation Corvette. Upon completing these two programs he was named advanced design director for General Motors, Michigan. In this position, he reconstructed the Advanced Design Department, directing various projects that included the V-16 Cadillac and Buick Velite concept vehicles. Tom is, at present, the director of design for Production Midsize Trucks and Corvette, where his responsibilities range from releasing the new Z06 Corvette to contributing to the Hummer programs.

Tom lives in the Detroit area with his wife and their three children. He enjoys family activities, rollerblading, and tennis, and is a muscle car enthusiast.

Q: When did you get involved with the C6 Corvette program?

Tom Peters: I think it was spring or summer of 2000. Before then I was focusing on the Advanced area. Just previous to that, I was really involved with the [Cadillac] XLR—about a year and a half before that. We knew that the XLR was going to be built off the Corvette,

so we knew that we had to understand both vehicles preliminarily and understand the tradeoffs and the balancing between the vehicles. They had to be unique in terms of their performance, and, obviously, the customers were quite different.

I talked to [executive director of design] Jerry Palmer and [vice president of design] Wayne Cherry when I heard that the Corvette was coming on line to be redone. I said, "I would love to have the opportunity to do this Corvette. I'll give you a hot Corvette." They said that they were planning on having me be the Corvette guy anyway. "And, oh, by the way," [they said], "you have to do the XLR project as well—and first." I said OK, that's cool. Because I remember the whole concept car which served as the impetus for the XLR, the Evoq. I did not realize at the time the tiger I had by the tail.

Q: What sort of "tiger" do you mean?

Peters: I didn't realize how challenging doing the XLR would be. You say, "Well, OK, we'll just interpret the Evoq into a production format or architecture. But it proved to be extremely challenging. The Evoq was an incredible show vehicle, super-expressive. The decision was made to put it on the Y-architecture, which is the Corvette architecture. And where the Evoq had basically complete freedom in terms of its expression—the proportion, the packaging, not only the components but how the people fit into it, the top, how that folding-hardtop mechanism would work. Now when you get into dealing with the realities, the Y-platform has certain characteristics that you have to work around: the real-

life packaging of the engine, the performance requirements related to it, real-world usage relative to the driver and passenger in terms of entry/egress, visibility, comfort, luxury.

When translating the theme over to the Corvette architecture, it required different proportions. Imagine packaging a real-world hardtop stack that had to work every time and would be reliable and easy to use. The interior had to be completely reworked from a theme standpoint from the original Evoq for a lot of different reasons. And then we added Bulgari as a codeveloper in the instrumentation. Because this was meant to be not only Cadillac's flagship but a flagship for the corporation, [there were] high expectations.

Q: Did the C6 Corvette play a role in the development of the XLR?

Peters: We had to comprehend the impact to the C6 as we were doing the XLR. I'll give you an example. On the wheelbase, we slid the centerline of the rear wheels back an inch over the C5. We had to understand what impact that would have performancewise and aesthetically on the C6 Corvette without any designs yet. Since we knew on the Corvette we wanted to shorten the rear, pushing the rear wheel rearward just helped the proportion. And thus we felt what was good for the XLR would be great for the Corvette, too. And it was pushed back because of the XLR's transmission requirements.

Another example is a lot was learned relative to quietness of drivetrain. On the C5, one of the big issues was road noise from the rear tires coming into the passenger compartment. Because of the

higher price and luxury-sport area that the XLR had to play in, the noise level had to be reduced quite a bit. Not that we implied the same noise requirements for the Corvette, but we benefited from the knowledge and the development that we did on the XLR.

Q: When did you begin working in earnest on the C6? Was it before or after you had finished the XLR?

Peters: They overlapped a little bit. One of the first things we did was have a lot of discussion around fixed head-lamps. We brought a C5 into the studio, took pieces of paper, and mocked up three projector headlamps where we thought they may be located, just to get an idea what this graphic may look like on a Corvette-like body. Plus there were sketches going on. There was a cross-over right around 2000-2001.

Q: What did you start with for the C6? What was the brief for the design?

Peters: It's just not a matter of cor-recting problems on a current car. It's gotta be more than that. You have to make a statement. It's a Corvette. If it's going to be a next-generation Corvette, albeit with carryover architecture, how different can you make it? And with the Corvette, there has to be a lineage to it. Obviously there are a lot of functional factors that affect Corvette design. It's more than just a pure aesthetic state-ment. As an example, aerodynamics play a huge role in driving the aesthetic. Every square millimeter of that vehicle is affected by what's discovered in the tunnel. This is a very serious high-per-formance vehicle, and you can't just blow that stuff off for a pure styling statement. To me, that's what true design is. It's not styling. It's a holistic execution of a product.

Q: Did you use any past or present designs as inspiration for the C6?

Peters: In terms of inspiration, I used three areas as drivers to help the team focus. One was Corvette history relative to style, design, and character. There are certain cues that make it Corvette. Obviously, the '63 always comes to mind. It's the most powerful Corvette Sting Ray statement in history.

I am not an aficionado of retro design. But I analyzed Corvettes over the years, focusing primarily on that '63-67 vintage.

The 1963 Corvette Sting Ray and Lockheed Martin F/A-22 (the pro-duction version of the YF-22 proto-type) served as design inspiration for the C6 Corvette.

What were the elements that made that car powerful and a strong statement back then? What makes that car so attractive now?

You have those peaked fender shapes. You've got the way that upper sits on the body, like a jet-fighter canopy cockpit. It isn't like a monocoque bodyside following into pillars. It's separate. The wheel orientation of the fenders. The simplicity of the body. It's expressive but it's integrated; it's singular in nature in terms of its sculpting character. But upon closer inspection, you see some very sophisticated surface transitions and forms that are quite wonderful. It doesn't slam you in the face with some of the details. It doesn't rely on add-on wings or add-on spoilers or things like that. There are very beautiful transitions. But when you stand back and look at it, it's one overall cohesive, bold statement.

We looked at all those elements, and my assignment to my team was to take those elements and translate them in a fresh new way. It doesn't look retro like a Volkswagen Bug does or a [Ford] Thunderbird. It isn't retro. I think the Corvette is a sign of the times.

My second area of inspiration was aircraft design. Designers always look to aircraft. And why is that? One reason is aircraft have always expressed state-of-the-art technology. They're usually singular in function or singular in purpose. The function does affect the aesthetic. They do what they look like they can do. They're very directional. And the one we used as kind of a guiding star was the YF-22 Raptor. We thought, "What are those areas that you can translate into automotive vernacular that aren't literal but kind of give the context of that?"

One of the areas on the C6 I like to refer to is the upper portion. It is a modification of the C5, but it has lot more taper, it's a lot more pointed in the rear, and it is more jet fighterlike in profile. There are also some sheer surfaces on the C6 that flow into these more organic or more muscular surfaces. If you look on the YF-22, you see these very angular, sheer surfaces, and where the engine is, it bulges up very soft and goes over the engine shapes. Those elements I think play a key role in creating a very unique and expressive design, so it isn't all angular or all organic. It's just a neat combination of angular and organic surfaces.

The third element in terms of inspiration was Corvette's racing heritage. We all know the success of the C5-R. How can we translate a little bit of that? We had the race team come in and really work with us on the development on the base [model], more so on the Z06. What were the real-world elements that would translate back into production—and get back into the race car, too. So things were developed like the center-port opening in the front end. The C5 was kind of split-grilled, and we realized there was criticism of that as being too Pontiac-like. Looking at older Corvettes, they all had a center-port opening, and I wanted to get back to that. Lo and behold, that worked out great for the race team.

Q: The racing team spent a lot of time with you in the wind tunnel because they knew that anything you could do to the production car would give them a better race car.

Peters: That was more focused on the Z06. But, aerodynamically, the goal on the base car was to reduce the amount of drag. The Z06 was different in that we were trying to get the best downforce or decrease the lift as much as we could.

Out of the box, as I understand it, the C6.R was way superior to the C5-R. That was due in part to the collaboration between design and the race team. On Corvette, the elements that are on it and the way it looks are really driven by a specific, functional purpose. But at the same time, it makes a beautiful statement. It's functionally beautiful. On the Z06, the moniker was "functional brutality."

Q: You spent some time in Europe with the C5 and came to the decision that the C6 had to be a little trimmer. Can you talk about that?

Peters: Up front, we wanted to make it smaller, a tighter package. Then we drove some C5s in Europe. That further emphasized it. I had never been to Germany. But when I was over there and I drove a Corvette around urban areas, it seemed kind of ungainly—not a bull in a china shop—but just a big guy walking down a narrow street. The Porsche 911 seemed to be much more in tune with that kind of environment.

There's not too many places you can drive pedal-to-the-metal in sixth gear for 15 minutes like you can on the autobahn. That's just what I did. And I preferred the Corvette, because it just seemed more stable, more assured in its steering characteristics. Where the 911, I felt, was much more twitchy and you had to stay on top of it to manage it. It just seemed a lot less predictable, a lot less stable at high speeds.

Q: Let's move to the interior. What, if any, special highlights or features do we need to know about?

Peters: The C5 was criticized for looking too plasticky, too much black, not uplevel, and poor-quality fit and finish. We wanted to improve all that. But from a design standpoint, we felt there was a lot of opportunity to simplify it. We felt that the analog-gauge approach rather than going full electronic was straightforward and keeping with an honest sports vehicle. So we felt that the C5 was a pretty wonderful execution. How could we improve on that?

We made the graphics bigger and bolder, but still maintained the round motif. We then enhanced that with an improved head-up display as an electronic, hi-tech counterpart to the analog graphics. And we simplified the theme. The twin cockpit—Corvette's had that twin space—we opened it up. The materials are much more refined, but we also kept in mind the functionality. The C5 was pretty good ergonomically. We felt that it had to be a "serious" interior, very straightforward.

Q: You've actually found a little bit more interior space in some dimensions, have you not?

Peters: Oh yes, we have. In head room there's more space. One of the objectives I had was, knowing the body was narrower, could we take any more cove? The doors are coved out deeper. We found storage space in the doors, which we didn't have before. Between the seats, the console, there's more room. Those are all functional aspects.

Q: The idea of a midengine Corvette has persisted for more than 30 years. Can you ever see a time when the Corvette might go to a midengine format?

Peters: Sure. I think you can do that. I can see that. However, I would say I could see it being an addition to the Corvette lineup. Because when you look at the front-engine/rear-wheel-drive setup, this vehicle is a 50/50 perfect balance from a weight-distribution standpoint. And from a usability, functionality standpoint, the Corvette is probably one of the first "crossover" vehicles. The space in the rear holds just a ton of cargo. It's surprising to most. If you haven't been near a Corvette and haven't experienced one, you can't believe the usability of it. The fact that you can take the top off and store it in the back. It's so beneficial from a customer standpoint. To me—I think you can't just make a shift like that. I think you could add to the marque with, say, a supercar version of the Corvette. I was involved with the Corvette Indy in the late Eighties, and they worked with that around the Ilmor engine, but again, just in concept. My perspective is, I think you can add to the lineup, but you couldn't replace it.

1

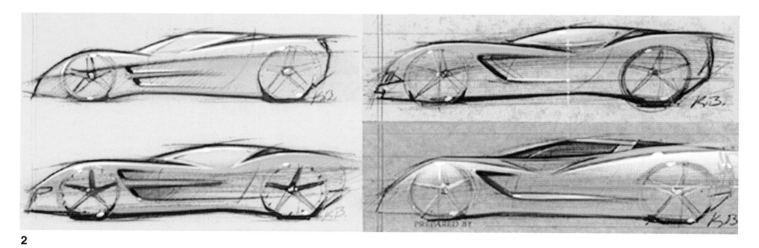

2

3

1. Corvette designer Sang Yup Lee made this drawing in early 2000 to study how first-generation Corvette influences could be incorporated into the C6. Note the grille and side cove designs. **2.** Corvette lead exterior designer Kirk Bennion experimented with side treatments and fender shapes in these early thumbnails. The pronounced, peaked fenders are reminiscent of the 1963 Corvette Sting Ray. **3.** Sang Yup Lee drew this convertible once the coupe styling was basically complete. The tonneau and decklid were especially important to study at this stage.

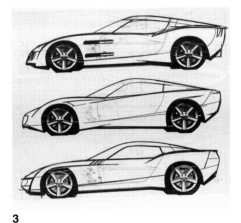

1

2

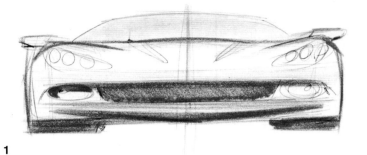

3

4

5

6

continued from page 378

"air brakes"—the fixed lamps take "some good little weight" off the front, punctuate the new C6 face, and lower cost and complexity. As Hill told *Automobile* magazine's Joe Lorio: "With the Corvette, when we make a decision that's technically correct, then it's right for the car."

Even so, as Peters says, "It's just not a matter of correcting problems on a current car.... You have to make a statement. It's a Corvette.... There are a lot of functional factors that affect Corvette design. It's more than just a pure aesthetic statement. As an example, aerodynamics play a huge role in driving the aesthetic. Every square millimeter of that vehicle is affected by what's discovered in the [wind] tunnel." The team's aero target, a 0.28 drag coefficient, was met, yielding a small but important 0.01 Cd improvement over the production C5.

Beyond competition needs, C6 styling was influenced by the C2

1-2. Corvette lead designer Tom Peters did these sketches in late 2000 to develop the taillamp shape and the integration of the fog lamps into the grille opening. **3-4.** These ⅓-scale tape drawings were made as model proposals. The team was investigating side covers, fender designs, and how the theme sat over the wheels. **5-6.** Peters' vision of a twenty-first century Sting Ray was first realized in ⅓-scale model form in September 1999. Note the fender creases and crisp side covers.

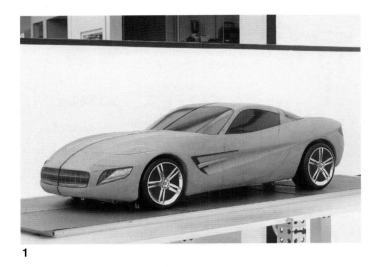

1

2

3

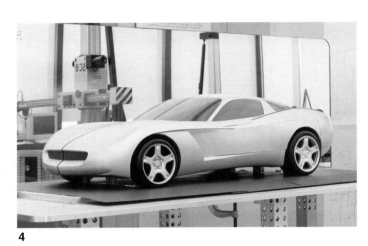

4

5

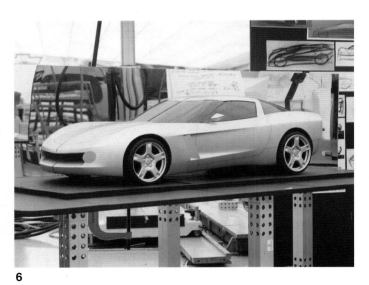

6

1-14. General Motors' designer Kirk Bennion calls side coves "the art of a Corvette's bodyside." As shown on these models built between March and May of 2000, the design team experimented with several ideas early on, including sharklike gills (Photo 12), coveless body sides, and scoops mounted in the fender tops (Photo 2). Also note the various roof treatments with body-color and blacked-out A-pillars; a modern, spinelike take on the split-window concept (Photo 10); and a fastback look with raised sail panels (Photo 3). Of course front ends, headlights, and grilles varied, too. Note the 1957 Corvette SS-inspired grille in Photo 7 and the

7

8

9

10

11

12

13

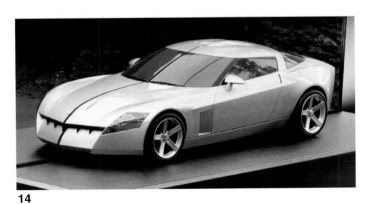

14

more modern interpretation of that same idea in Photo 14. Photo 11 features a Pontiac-like nose that is also reminiscent of Formula One styling. The beltline dip tried in Photo 8 was meant to improve sightlines for performance driving. An early problem for the design team was the balance between the front and rear fenders. To study the problem, the designers built some models with a short-front, long-rear approach, others with a long-front, short-rear design, and still others with a more-balanced "camelback" appearance. The camelback design would win out in the end, teaming with the wheel flares and fender peaks to provide a muscular look.

1

2

3

4

5

6

1-3. By June 2000, the design team was ready to see how their models' designs would play out full size. Two ideas were applied to one full-scale clay, a common design trick. **4.** The design in Photos 1 and 3, was further developed two weeks later as shown in Photo 6 (Photos 2, 4, and 5 go together, too). Ultimately, the designers felt the grille in Photo 1 was too round, but they liked the angular side cove and fender shapes in Photo 4.

Sting Ray. "I am not an aficionado of retro design," Peters says. "But I analyzed Corvettes over the years, focusing primarily on that '63-67 vintage. What were the elements that made that car powerful and a strong statement back then?

"You have those peaked fender shapes. You've got the way that upper sits on the body, like a jet-fighter canopy cockpit....The wheel orientation of the fenders. The simplicity of the body. It's expressive but it's integrated; it's

singular in nature....It's one overall cohesive, bold statement.

"We looked at all those elements, and my assignment to my team was to take those elements and translate them in a fresh new way."

Another styling influence was Peters love of aircraft, especially the YF-22 jet fighter. "Designers always look to aircraft," he says. "They're usually singular in function or singular in purpose. The function does affect the aesthetic. They do what they look like they

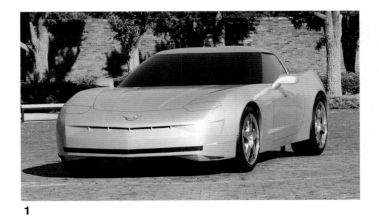

1

2

3

4

can do. They're very directional.... We thought, 'What are those areas that you can translate into automotive vernacular.'

"One of the areas on the C6 I like to refer to is the upper portion. It is a modification of the C5, but it has lot more taper, it's a lot more pointed in the rear, and it is more jet-fighter-like in profile. There are also some sheer surfaces on the C6 that flow into these more organic or more muscular surfaces."

The C6 has plenty of other details to appreciate. Rear decks, for example, gain a "boattail" character line swept neatly back from the belt, a touch of split-window Sting Ray coupe. Corvette's trademark four taillamps are almost perfectly round again, and nestle in a more-sculpted back panel that's still rather wide yet contrives to look lighter. Bodysides gain visual interest from a deft blend of creases and

curves, especially around the indented "coves." And the "double-bubble" contouring of the coupe's lift-off roof panel is slightly more pronounced. As Hill told *Car and Driver,* "The more you look, the more you see." He's right.

The C6 measures 5.1 inches shorter and an inch narrower than the C5, but is 1.2 inches longer in wheelbase at 106. That wheelbase was dictated by packaging requirements for the Cadillac XLR, but it adds to the Corvette's purposeful new "wheels at the corners" stance. Helping the cause, the wheels themselves are larger, growing an inch at each end to 18 front and 19 rear. The one downside to the downsizing is slightly less cargo space: now 22 cubic feet for coupes (previously 24.8), and 10.5 max for convertibles (vs. 13.9).

Matching the more-sophisticated exterior is an all-new cockpit created

1. The Corvette design team tried this front-end-treatment idea with thin air intakes, but they found it couldn't breathe enough for proper cooling. **2.** The designers experimented with taillamp shapes. In the end, a 60-degree ellipse would be used. **3.** This clay shows the team's first attempts to integrate the fog lamps into the grille and experiment with bodyside moldings. **4.** By August 2000, fiberglass versions of the wheels that would make it to production were ready for inspection. This car's rear vertical side markers would not be used on the final car.

by Peters and lead interior designer Eric Clough. "The C5 was criticized for looking too plasticky, too much black, and not uplevel in fit and finish," Peters admits. "We wanted to improve all that, but we also felt there was a lot of opportunity to

1

2

3

Most clay models are covered with a silver material called Dinoc that looks like paint. Silver works well for studying shapes. Sometimes, however, designers want to look at a car in different colors. **1-2.** This red clay sports the first attempt at carving out the headlight shapes. The team set camera lenses in place (inset) to preview the final design. Note the heat extractor scoops tried in the hood. **3.** An exaggerated version of what would become the C6's double-bubble top is evident here.

simplify it."

That they have. The most obvious change is the dashboard. It's laid out like the C5's, but the sculpted "twin cowl" theme gives way to a clean, vertical, passenger-side panel with newly hidden airbag door. New seats offer longer cushions and more prominent side bolsters. A sprinkling of aluminum and metal-look accents provides a tasteful touch of modern "hi tech." Gauges look much the same, but audio and climate panels have fewer buttons and clearer mark-

ings. The center stack can also house a navigation system, yours for $1400 as a first-time 'Vette option. A reworked console provides proper twin cupholders beneath a sliding cover and a larger armrest/ storage bin. Designers also found space for small but useful door map pockets. The doors themselves gain electric latches with pushbutton interior releases and exterior press pads; a mechanical release outboard of each seat lets you escape in case power fails. The ignition key is gone, replaced by a large

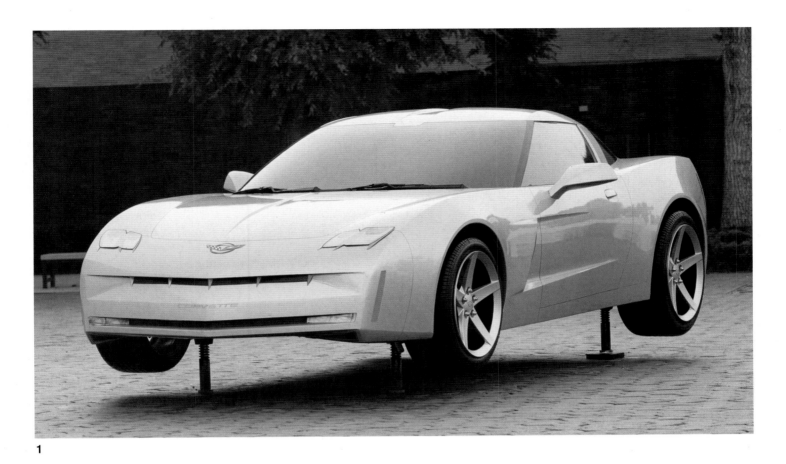

2

4

1. Paper headlights were placed on this clay as a design alternative. 2. The first attempts at a rear diffuser design were tried on this clay from September 2000. 3. The first full-scale interior clays showed the C6 would use the dual-cowl design that had become a Corvette trademark. Also shown is a motor-cycle-inspired curved gauge cluster that couldn't be used due to reflection issues. 4. Straight, virtually equal-length side strakes marked this clay. The final design would imply more motion than this one.

1

2

3

1. The final hand-formed design was complete by June 2001. Designers prepped it in black to do a final surface check and study how light would play off the body panels. Note the reflection of the ceiling lights in the bodyside. From here, the surfaces were scanned to make body tooling. The stylized stingray emblem the design team experimented with (inset) may be a clue of things to come. Insiders say a Sting Ray model could be offered at a premium above the Z06. 2. A detailed clay mock-up of the interior was also ready by June 2001. Here, chief engineer Dave Hill tests the C6 driving position. 3. The final interior theme featured a bright metal center stack with the familiar dual-pod design. 4. This full-scale fiberglass model was built in October 2003. The interior is only modeled above the beltline. The ten-spoke wheels are early versions of those offered through Genuine Corvette Accessories.

4

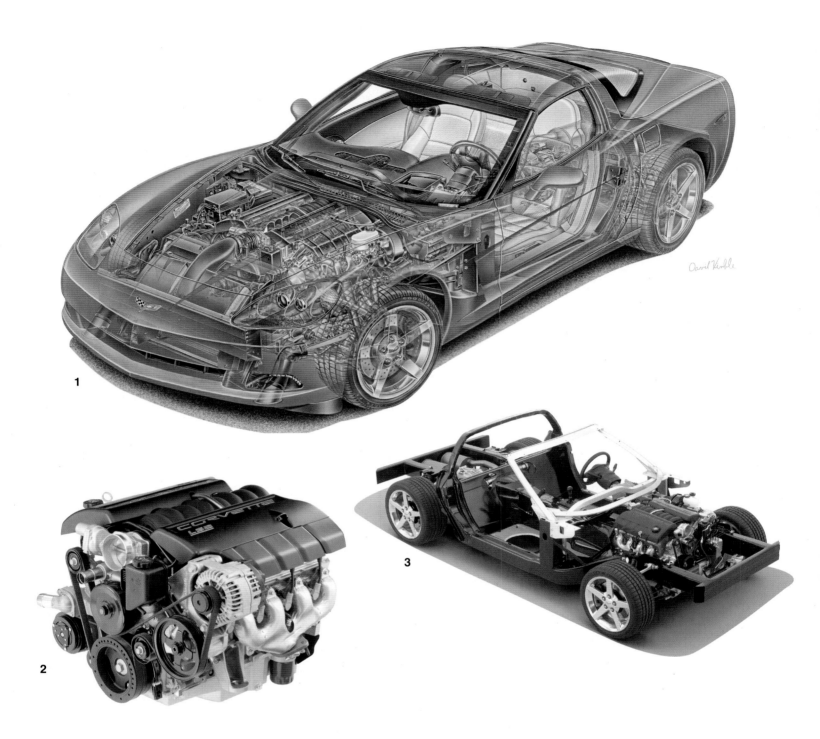

engine-start rocker switch, part of a standard keyless entry system with secret decoder ring...er, pocket transmitter, another "gift" from XLR.

Pushing that switch unleashes a mannerly bellow from a Chevy small-block V-8 that's sufficiently revised to warrant the new designation LS2. Changes begin with a 2.6-mm bore stretch to 101.6 mm, which ups total displacement to 6.0 liters (precisely 5967 cc) or 364 cubic inches on the same 92-mm stroke. Compression goes from

10.1:1 to 10.9:1. A revamped intake system takes in 15 percent more air. The exhaust system gains a lightweight thin-wall manifold with 20 percent higher outflow, plus straight-through pipes and new mufflers that reduce back pressure 10 percent. Various internal mods decrease pumping losses.

With all this and more, standard horsepower jumps from 350 at 5200 rpm to a beefy 400 at 6000. Torque swells from 360/375 pound-feet at 4000 revs to a stout 400 at 4400. To

1. According to chief engineer Dave Hill, the C6 was 85 percent new. Note the front brake-cooling air ducts behind the front fascia. **2.** The aluminum-block 5.7-liter LS1 V-8 made its debut in 1997. A revised version, bored out to 6.0 liters and called LS2, boosted output from 350 to 400 bhp for the C6. **3.** The C6 shares its hydroformed frame rails with the Cadillac XLR. A reinforced windshield frame and a crossbar mounted at the bottom of the dash added rigidity.

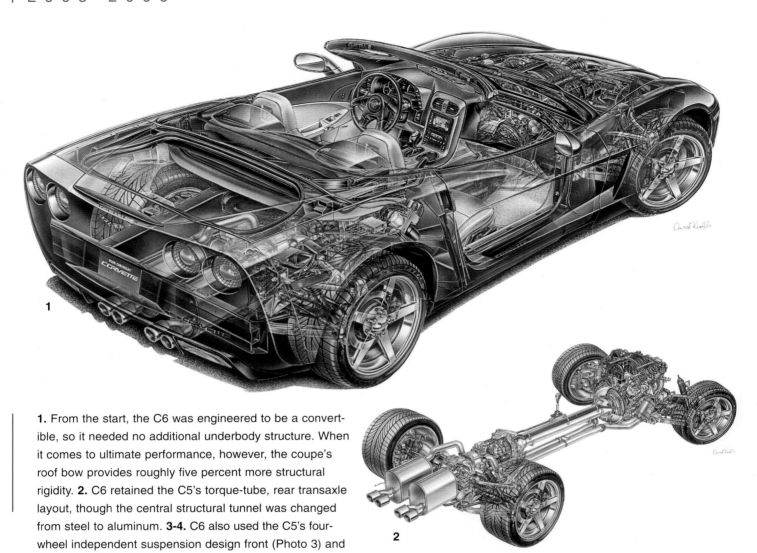

1

2

1. From the start, the C6 was engineered to be a convertible, so it needed no additional underbody structure. When it comes to ultimate performance, however, the coupe's roof bow provides roughly five percent more structural rigidity. **2.** C6 retained the C5's torque-tube, rear transaxle layout, though the central structural tunnel was changed from steel to aluminum. **3-4.** C6 also used the C5's four-wheel independent suspension design front (Photo 3) and rear (Photo 4), but no components carried over.

3

4

1

2

3

4

1, 3. Using an in-car data-recording device and laptop computer, the "Track Rats" engineering team of Jim Mero, Richard Quinn, Tony Rifici, and Luke Sewell conducted extensive testing at Germany's Nürburgring road course. The goal was to fine-tune the C6's brakes, suspension, powertrain, cooling system, and electronic chassis controls. **2.** Engineers also ran at top speed for hours on the autobahn to evaluate high-speed stability. **4.** A developmental C6 was fitted with a towing dynamometer at the GM Desert Proving Ground in Mesa, Arizona. The towing "dyno" has internal braking and is used to apply a parasitic load to the vehicle towing it. Loads simulating steep grades help engineers develop cooling systems for severe hot weather conditions.

put that in perspective, the LS2 is only five horses down on the previous Z06's LS6 engine and makes the same torque at slightly lower revs. That's why there's the new 500-bhp Z06—more on that shortly. Icing the cake, the LS2 weighs 15 pounds less than the predecessor LS1, helped by a smaller water pump and a new, specially designed aluminum oil pan that takes a quart less to fill yet ensures superior lubrication at high cornering forces.

As before, the convertible and base coupe offer a choice of six-speed manual or four-speed automatic transaxles. An XLR-style five-

speed automatic would be nice, but GM doesn't yet have one that's up to the C6's torque. But the veteran four-speed does get Cadillac-style Performance Shift Algorithm programming, while the Tremec T56 manual boasts a revised linkage with more positive action and a shorter shift lever. And where C5s offered a manual at extra cost, C6s have it standard and offer the automatic at no charge.

Chassis changes abound. The all-independent suspension, for example, is basically the C5 setup, but all components are new, highlighted by increased wheel travel from

longer-stroke shock absorbers, plus stiffer antiroll-bar mounts and revised bushings. Spring and shock rates are recalibrated too, and the front caster angle is increased one degree for more stable tracking. The base FE1 suspension adopts Goodyear's new-generation Eagle F1 GS run-flat tires. So does the $1695 Magnetic Selective Ride Control option, which goes from three firmness modes to two, but is otherwise unchanged. The $1495 Z51 Performance Package substitutes asymmetric-tread Eagle F1 Supercar shoes in the same EEE sizes—P245/40ZR18 front,

P285/35ZR19 rear—plus the usual upgraded springs, shocks, and antiroll bars. All C6s have slightly larger all-disc antilock brakes than C5s, with standard diameters up 0.2 inch to 12.8 front and 12 rear. Z51 cars get 13.4/13.0-inch cross-drilled rotors with high-performance pads. Among the few carryover chassis bits are GM's Magnasteer power rack-and-pinion steering and standard Active Handling antiskid/traction control.

The C5 "Uniframe" was already quite light and plenty stiff, but the C6 structure benefits from welded extruded-aluminum members that are bolted and bonded to strengthen the door-hinge pillars. Also added is an under-dash hydroformed brace that tie those pillars firmly to the center chassis tunnel. Ragtops gain rigidity from a new fiberglass tub that forms the trunk as well as a rear cockpit wall. This not only reduces noise and body shake, but

protects trunk contents. The C5 droptop had no rear bulkhead.

It also offered no power-top option, but the C6 does. Priced at $1995, it takes up no more trunk space than the manual roof, scales at a mere 15 pounds, and goes from full on to full off (or vice versa) in under 20 seconds. Powered or not, the C6 top—available in black, gray, or beige—is shaped to generate less wind noise and is fully lined. As on some German convertibles,

1. Corvette designers decided the area surrounding the headlights should be body color to ease the pain that enthusiasts might feel due to the loss of pop-up headlamps. **2.** The headlamps were positioned as low and wide as possible, but were limited by the front-bumper beam and wheelwells. **3.** The rear end was designed to reduce aerodynamic lift, keeping the car planted and balanced at all speeds.

1

2

1

2

3

4

5

the side windows power down slightly when opening a door, then snug up against the top to form a firm seal.

Other first-time 'Vette options include GM's useful OnStar system ($695) and XM satellite radio ($325). Standard equipment is as plentiful as ever. Convertibles, however, add torso side airbags, which are available for coupes in a 1SA Preferred Equipment Package ($1405) that also includes perforated leather upholstery (replacing unholey standard wear), a six-way power passenger seat, and a cargo net and cover.

An upgraded 1SB group ($4360 for coupes, $2955 for ragtops) adds heated seats, seat memory system, power telescopic steering-wheel adjustment, Bose audio with six-disc in-dash CD/MP3 player, auto-dimming mirrors, and a new three-mode head-up display.

Considering all the improvements, it's amazing that the C6 coupe bowed with a base price of $43,710. That's $125 lighter than the final price for the last C5 coupe. The 2005 convertible started at $51,445, little more than $600 above its '04 counterpart. Talk about value!

1. Corvette engineers made it easier to stow the targa top in the C6 than in the C5. **2.** The C6's narrower and shorter dimensions made it more nimble and more attractive to overseas customers. **3.** Corvette designers identified a list of "dissatisfiers" with the C5 and strove to correct them in the C6. Chief among them was interior quality. **4.** All C6s came with GM's Keyless Access system, which replaced a key with a start button. **5.** The C6's LS2 engine boasted a 6500-rpm redline, 500 revs higher than the C5's LS1.

1

"Buff" magazines talked about that a lot in the C6's first year. It's a big reason why the new 'Vette made *Car and Driver*'s "10 Best Cars" list for 2005—and eked out a one-point win over the redesigned 2005 Porsche 911 Carrera in a *C/D* comparison test. Over at *Road & Track*, the C6 came in first in a nine-way sports-car showdown, even though most of those editors picked Porsche's similarly priced Boxster S as their personal favorite. Nevertheless, *R&T* concluded, "[The C6] has no real weaknesses and many strengths. It possesses world-class performance, a high level of comfort and dashing good looks. And it's available for nearly

2

half the price of a Porsche Carrera S.... America's sports car is now back in its rightful place atop the sports-car mountain."

We couldn't agree more. In fact, the C6 continues the C5's perennial place on *Consumer Guide* magazine's "Best Buy" list. As we noted in our review: "Corvette delivers thrilling acceleration, handling, and braking ... and costs tens of thousands less than rivals with similar performance. If you like your sports cars bold and brawny, there's no better high-performance value and no stronger Best Buy in this class." All the more curious, then, that the C5 was passed over as 2005 North American Car of the Year in favor of Chrysler's new 300 sedan. Oh well, there's always 2006.

Enthusiasts always want to know performance stats. The C6 posts mighty impressive numbers, but keep in mind that most all published road tests so far have involved manual-transmission Z51s, which share a 3:42:1 final drive with non-package six-speeds but have slightly shorter second- and third-gear

1. With the release of the 2005 C6, a navigation system became available in the Corvette for the first time. 2. The C6's side scoops are functional in that they relieve hot air pressure from under the hood. Their forward rake is reminiscent of the C5, and the side coves recall the original Corvette of 1953. 3. Chevy blacked out the front pillars to play off the black convertible top and the coupe's optional black-tinted targa roof.

3

1

2

3

1. Sang Yup Lee drew this Z06 in late 2001 as an early front-end proposal. The diagonal grille mesh would be used. Note the distinctive "reverse mohawk" roof treatment meant to play off the dual-cowl cockpit. **2.** C6.R and Z06 were developed together from the first sketches. The designers wanted the Z06 to mimic the race car as much as possible. **3-4.** The first ⅓-scale clay models of the Z06 began in June 2001. The design team experimented with an exposed carbon-fiber hood and different side-cove treatments on these two models. The large rear spoiler in Photo 3 didn't make it into production, but may become a Genuine Corvette Accessory.

4

1

2

3

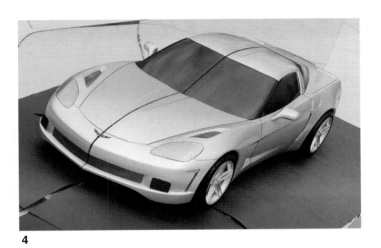

4

5

1-3. These hood and fascia treatments were ultimately scrapped, but they demonstrate the "touch of anger" designers wanted in the Z06 face. **4.** Vents, or "extractors," situated atop the front fenders were tried, but couldn't be used because they would kick water and grime onto the windshield of a production car. **5.** The black rear end was inspired by a paint scheme used on the C5-R race car.

ratios. (Automatics use a 2.73:1 axle or an optional 3:15:1.) Also note that C6s are indeed lighter than C5s, but not by much: 67 pounds for coupes, 49 for convertibles. Still, Hill's team deserves credit for paring any heft in view of the added structural reinforcements and some extra soundproofing.

First, the benchmark 0-60-mph

time. Among coupes, *Car and Driver*'s 4.1 seconds is the best reported so far. *Road & Track* timed 4.5. Chevy claims 4.2. *R&T* got 4.8 with a manual Z51 convertible, which seems subpar given the ragtop's mere 20-pound penalty in official base curb weight. For standing quarter-miles, *Car and Driver* clocked a blazing 12.6 seconds at

114 mph. That compares with 12.8 at 114.5 for *R&T*'s similar coupe and 13.2 seconds at 107.9 mph for its convertible. Top speed, though ever academic in America, is a Chevy-claimed, air-drag-limited 186 mph. Skidpad pull? Coupe or convertible, the Z51 package serves up an easy 0.98g, which you can have fun checking with the g-meter in

the available head-up display. Last but not least in our book: fuel economy. The EPA rates city/highway mpg at 19/28 with manual transmission and 18/25 with automatic. Published overall averages are running 18-20 mpg, more than respectable for the sizzle on tap and sufficient for a comfortable touring range of nearly 350 miles.

But numbers never fully describe the driving experience, and especially with Corvettes. Having spent a week with an automatic Z51 convertible, we can confirm several consensus opinions about the C6. For starters, it's a flat-out blast. As you'd expect, go-power is tremendous, but so is stopping power. Cornering is almost race-car flat. The antiskid/traction control doesn't spoil the fun by intervening too soon, and you can turn it off completely for even more fun. Of course, all that low-end torque demands a skillful, respectful driver. Even with the stability system engaged, the tail will come unstuck over sharp midcorner bumps or on smooth pavement should you mash the throttle at the wrong moment. The only real dynamic flaw is the steering, which is quick but suffers weak self-centering action.

More impressive perhaps, the C6 doesn't beat up its occupants like C4s and some C5s we remember. Even the Z51 setup, which is slightly softer now, furnishes a civilized ride on most roads, abetted by a rock-solid structure with very few squeaks or rattles, even in the ragtop. And the interior is a major miracle by 'Vette standards: comfortable, logically organized, pleasing to the eyes and fingers.

We could go on, but you get the point. The C6 may not be the huge conceptual leap that the C5 was, but it is a major Corvette advance in ways anyone can appreciate. The "dissatisfiers" are dead, the newfound refinement is indeed a pleasant surprise, and performance is more satisfying than ever. Mission

1

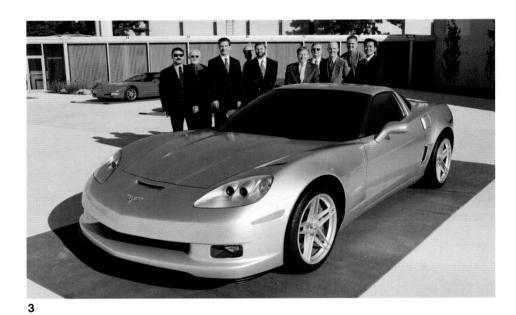

2

3

1. The Corvette team found that brake-cooling scoops placed this low would catch stones that would ruin the surface finish. Placing them higher avoided this problem and achieved as much airflow. **2.** The completed full-scale clay was ready by September 2001. **3.** Tom Peters (third from right) and his staff became the first Corvette design team to head up all interior and exterior styling and develop all three models (coupe, convertible, and Z06) simultaneously.

1

2

3

1. Corvette team engineers used computational fluid dynamics to compute the Z06's front-end-cooling airflow and identify regions of high pressure and flow separation on the frontal surfaces. The next step was to try a variety of surface changes on a detailed ⅓-scale clay model. Wind tunnel testing of the clay model revealed what could be done to reduce lift and drag, and to optimize airflow into the grille and below the front splitter. **2.** Next, a detailed full-scale clay model was employed to further develop front-end-cooling airflow and to fine-tune aerodynamics. **3.** Finally, a full-scale "Integration Vehicle" built with production-intended parts was run through the wind tunnel. It demonstrated that the team had met all of the aerodynamic targets.

accomplished.

But wait. There's more! Mr. Hill and company have really outdone themselves with the C6-based Z06. No published tests existed in time for publication, but we'll bet writers will use a lot of superlatives.

That's because the new Z06 reflects lessons learned from the all-conquering C5-R racer and is the starting point for the C6.R. Three big things to note first. It's based on the hatchback coupe for better high-speed aero, with a fixed roof panel for race carlike rigidity. Second, its Uniframe structure is reengineered in aluminum, which more than offsets the fastback body's added weight vs. the former notchback. "It's like a whole different car," says Dave Hill. "It was an extremely large stretch to take 136 pounds out of something that only weighed about 350 to begin with—a revolutionary improvement." Chev-

rolet says the Z06 scales at 3130 pounds, 49 less than the base coupe.

But the really big news here is the 500-bhp V-8. Dubbed LS7, it's sized like the fabled big-blocks of yore—7011.3 cc, 428 cubes—but uses the LS2's new "Gen IV" small-block architecture. Even so, the LS7 differs in almost every respect from the LS2—and the old LS6. Handcrafted at GM Powertrain's new Performance Build Center in Wixom, Mich., it uses a unique block with thin pressed-in liners that allow a larger bore and stroke of 104.8 × 101.6 mm (4.13 × 4.00 inches). Pistons are forged, not cast, and are flat-topped for a high 11.0:1 compression ratio. A forged-steel crankshaft with forged-steel main-bearing caps works connecting rods made of costly, lightweight titanium. Titanium is also the material of choice for the intake valves (replacing stainless steel), pushrods,

and all valve springs. The intakes also grow to 2.2 inches across, while new 1.61-inch exhaust valves are sodium filled to improve heat dissipation and durability. For optimal breathing, valve angles narrow from 15 to 12 degrees, valve lift rises to a lofty 0.591 inch, and a specific low-restriction air cleaner feeds a new intake manifold with a 3.5-inch-wide throttle body. All ports are CNC-machined, a premium step that contributes to smooth airflow. On the exhaust side are new hydroformed "four into one" headers feeding big three-inch pipes, two for each of the new "bimodal" mufflers. Below 3500 rpm, a single pipe per side handles all exhaust flow to minimize noise; above that, a vacuum-operated bypass routes the gases through a second, nearly straight pipe for max power in the time-honored way. Last but not least, a racing-inspired dry-sump oiling sys-

403

1

2

1. At 7.0 liters, the LS7 is still a small block due its physical size.
2. Wider tires and flared fenders added aerodynamic drag to the Z06, but front and rear lift characteristics were much improved over C6. **3.** All C6 models' windshield headers sat slightly higher than the C5's, and the basket-handle targa bar slightly lower. This provided a more aero-dynamic teardrop shape that would be especially beneficial to the C6.R.

tem with eight-quart reservoir replaces the base 'Vette's oil pan.

With all this, the LS7 delivers its peak 500 bhp at 6200 rpm, but can rev to 7100, one of the few pushrod engines able to do so, says Chevrolet engineers. Torque peaks at 4800 rpm with a thumping 475 pound-feet, with 385 pound-feet available from just 1600 rpm.

Like earlier Z06s, the 2006 model comes only with a beefed-up six-speed manual transaxle. The clutch, halfshafts, U-joints, and limited-slip differential are beefier, too. One neat touch, again racing-inspired, is a transmission-oil pump that sends fluid to the main radiator, a second-ary heat exchanger, and then back to the gearbox, where it can help cool the differential oil.

Besides its lighter inner structure, the Z06 saves weight with a magne-sium front engine cradle (replacing aluminum) and carbon fiber-skinned floorboards. The front fenders are also made of carbon fiber—and

3

1. The C6.R's front-fender louvers provide improved brake cooling.
2. CNC-ported cylinder heads and titanium valves and connecting rods help the C6.R's 7.0-liter V-8 produce approximately 700 bhp.
3. The C6.R race team helped develop the Z06. Items such as the front splitter, fascia deflector, rear-brake-cooling ducts, central front scoop, and taller front-grille opening were added to aid road and racing applications.

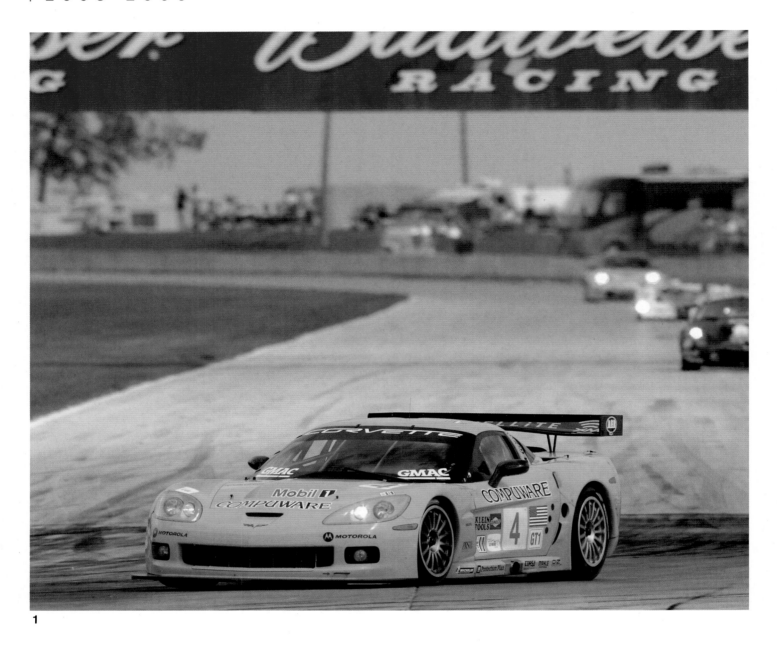

1

visibly bulged to accept inch-wider wheels wearing P275/35ZR18 Eagle F1 Supercar run-flats. The rear fenders are radiused to snug around massive P325/30ZR19 rubber on 12-inch-wide rims—three inches wider than stock. Naturally, the springs and shocks are retuned to maximize the extra power. And the brakes are predictably larger— 14 inches fore, 13 aft—and all have cross-drilled rotors clamped by one-piece calipers with six front pistons and four rear pots, plus that many brake pads. As another exclusive Z06 visual, those calipers are painted bright "Corvette Red."

The remaining visuals comprise a cold-air scoop in the nose; a wider grille opening with an air "splitter" below it; a small brake-cooling duct ahead of each rear wheel; and deeper, aero-shaped perimeter skirting. The interior changes are confined to a two-tone color scheme, a slightly smaller steering wheel, and unique seats with larger, non-adjustable side bolsters.

With a bit less weight and a lot more power than other C6s, the newest Z06 will certainly take production-Corvette performance to a whole new level. Official numbers weren't available at the time of this writing, but Chevrolet talks of 0-60 times in under four seconds, quar-ter-miles in the mid 11s, and a top speed of well over 190 mph. Pricing was also unavailable, but you can bet this thrill ride won't be cheap. Still, various sources are estimating $60,000-$65,000 base and mid $70,000s loaded, so the new Z06 should cost far less than other high-power, low-production exotics, even the midengine Ford GT.

Chevrolet introduced the C6.R race car to the media in January 2005 at Detroit's North American International Auto Show. The newest racing Corvette made its first racing appearance at the famed 12 Hours of Sebring in March 2005, where the two factory entries

406

2

1-3. The Corvette C6.R made its competition debut on March 19, 2005, at the Mobil 1 12 Hours of Sebring. The two C6.R entries dominated the first eight hours, but both were involved in late-race accidents. The number 3 Corvette of Ron Fellows, Johnny O'Connell, and Max Papis finished one lap behind the GT1 class-winning Aston Martin DBR9, while the number 4 car of Oliver Gavin, Olivier Beretta, and Jan Magnussen placed third despite missing extended action for repairs.

placed second and third. The C6.R had large shoes to fill, as it was defending the C5-R's lock on the American LeMans Series' GT1 (formerly GTS) class.

The most important point about the C6.R is how much it builds on the new Z06, as photos suggest. Even after all these years, racing can improve the breed—certainly the Corvette breed. In fact, C6.Rs are crafted using Z06 structures sourced from the Bowling Green Corvette factory. As Harry Turner, GM's group manager for road racing, noted in a press release, the C6.R is, "the best [competition Corvette] we've ever built, and it has been our privilege to develop it alongside the new Corvette Z06. History will remember the C5-R as one of the [most successful] sports racing cars of all time, and we've set the bar high for the C6.R. With the new C6 chassis and body structure as our starting point, we're already ahead."

That's the story so far, but there will be many 'Vettes to come, as future editions of this book will doubtless record. In the fast-changing automotive world, we can think of no happier way to close.

3

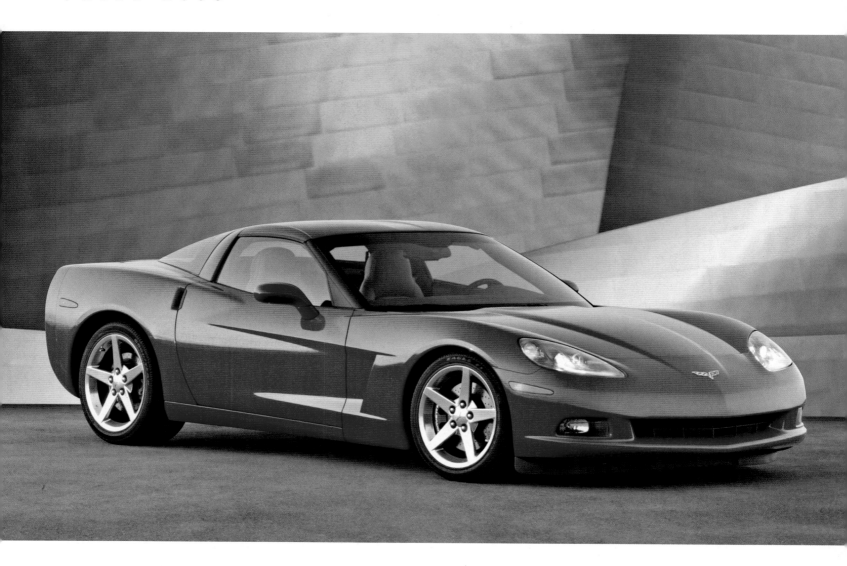

Starting at $44,245 with destination, the 2005 C6 targa top coupe actually cost $400 less than the final price of its C5 counterpart. The new car was 5.1 inches shorter than the C5, but its wheelbase was 1.2 inches longer. The result was a nimble, more "tossable" car, especially when equipped with the $1695 Z51 Performance Handling Package. The Z51 package included larger brakes with cross-drilled rotors, a power-steering-fluid cooler, engine- and transmission-oil coolers, stiffer springs and stabilizer bars, and a performance axle ratio when ordered with the automatic transmission. Chevrolet claimed a Z51 C6 could almost equal the lap times of the C5 Z06 model. *Motor Trend* magazine posted a 4.3-second 0-60-mph run in a Z51-equipped coupe, and ate up the quarter mile in 12.7 seconds.

With the release of the 2005 models, the Corvette convertible offered a power-folding top for the first time since 1962. It folded down in 18 seconds and cost $1995. Initially, black, beige, and gray tops were offered, but beige and gray were dropped midyear. Interior colors options for coupes and rag-tops were Cashmere, Ebony, Steel Gray, or Red.

The C6 Z06 Corvette was unveiled in January 2005 at Detroit's North American International Auto Show, but it didn't hit the streets until that fall as an '06 model. After a one-model-year hiatus, the fixed-roof coupe Z06 now boasted Dodge Viper-like numbers, with a thumping 500 bhp, 475 pound-feet of torque, and a promised 0-60-mph time of less than four clicks. Several unique design cues delineated the Z06 from base C6s, including the central front scoop, slightly longer nose with a taller grille opening, flared fenders, wider tires, rear brake ducts, square fog lamps, and taller CHMSL spoiler. All of these modifications were made to increase performance.

1953

Vehicle Specifications

	convertible
Wheelbase, in.	102.0
Length, in.	167.0
Width, in.	72.2
Track, in.	front: 57.0 rear: 59.0
Height, in.	51.3
Curb weight, lb	2850

Mechanical Specifications 2-door convertible

Suspension	**front:** Independent; upper and lower A-arms, coil springs, antiroll bar, tubular hydraulic shock absorbers **rear:** Live axle on semi-elliptic leaf springs, tubular hydraulic shock absorbers
Wheels/Tires	6.0×15
Brakes	front: 11-inch drum rear: 11-inch drum
Transmission	2-speed Powerglide
Standard axle ratio	3.55:1

Engine Specifications

Type	ohv I-6
Displacement, liters/cu in.	3.85/235.5
Bore × Stroke, in. × in.	3.56 × 3.95
Fuel management	3 Carter sidedraft
Horsepower @ rpm	150 @ 4200
Torque @ rpm, lb-ft	223 @ 2400

Published Performance Numbers   150 hp, 2-sp automatic

0-60 mph, sec	11.0
0-100 mph, sec	41.0
1/4-mile, sec	17.9
source	*Road & Track*

Base Prices & Production

	Production	Price
2-door convertible	300	$3498.00

Options & Production

	Production	Price
AM radio, signal seeking	300	$145.15
Heater	300	91.40

Color Choices & Production

	Production
Polo White	300

1954

Vehicle Specifications

	convertible
Wheelbase, in.	102.0
Length, in.	167.0
Width, in.	72.2
Track, in.	front: 57.0 rear: 59.0
Height, in.	51.3
Curb weight, lb	2890

Mechanical Specifications 2-door convertible

Suspension	**front:** Independent; upper and lower A-arms, coil springs, antiroll bar, tubular hydraulic shock absorbers **rear:** Live axle on semi-elliptic leaf springs, tubular hydraulic shock absorbers
Wheels/Tires	6.70×15
Brakes	front: 11-inch drum rear: 11-inch drum
Transmission	2-speed Powerglide
Standard axle ratio	3.55:1

Engine Specifications

Type	ohv I-6
Displacement, liters/cu in.	3.85/235.5
Bore × Stroke, in. × in.	3.56 × 3.95
Fuel management	3 Carter sidedraft
Horsepower @ rpm	150 @ 4200
Torque @ rpm, lb-ft	223 @ 2400

Base Prices & Production

	Production	Price
2-door convertible	3640	$2774.00

Options & Production

	Production	Price
Directional Signal	3640	$16.75
Heater	3640	91.40
AM Radio, signal seeking	3640	145.15
Whitewall Tires, 6.70×15	3640	26.90
Powerglide Automatic Transmission	3640	178.35
Parking Brake Alarm	3640	5.65
Courtesy Lights	3640	4.50
Windshield Washer	3640	11.85

Color Choices & Production

	Production		Production
Polo White	3230	Pennant Blue	300
Sportsman Red	100	Black	4

1955

Vehicle Specifications

	convertible
Wheelbase, in.	102.0
Length, in.	167.0
Width, in.	72.2
Track, in.	front: 57.0 rear: 59.0
Height, in.	51.3
Curb weight, lb	2910

Mechanical Specifications 2-door convertible

Suspension	**front:** Independent; upper and lower A-arms, coil springs, antiroll bar, tubular hydraulic shock absorbers **rear:** Live axle on semi-elliptic leaf springs, tubular hydraulic shock absorbers
Wheels/Tires	6.70×15
Brakes	front: 11-inch drum rear: 11-inch drum
Transmission	3-speed manual (std) 2-speed Powerglide (opt)
Standard axle ratio	3.55:1

Engine Specifications

Type	ohv I-6	ohv V-8
Displacement, liters/cu in.	3.85/235.5	4.34/265.0
Bore × Stroke, in. × in.	3.56 × 3.95	3.75 × 3.00
Fuel management	3 Carter sidedraft	Carter 4-bbl.
Horsepower @ rpm	150 @ 4200	195 @ 5000
Torque @ rpm, lb-ft	223 @ 2400	260 @ 3000

Published Performance Numbers   195 hp, Powerglide

0-60 mph, sec	8.7
0-100 mph, sec	24.7
1/4-mile, sec	16.5
source	*Road & Track*

Base Prices & Production

Base Prices & Production	Production	Price
2-door convertible, six-cylinder	700*	$2774.00
2-door convertible, V-8		2909.00

*700 combined production.

Options & Production

Options & Production	Production	Price
Directional Signal	700	$16.75
Heater	700	91.40
AM Radio, signal seeking	700	145.15
Whitewall Tires, 6.70×15	700	26.90
Powerglide Automatic Transmission	625	178.35
Parking Brake Alarm	700	5.65
Courtesy Lights	700	4.05
Windshield Washer	700	11.85

Color Choices & Production

	Production		Production
Polo White	325	Pennant Blue	45
Corvette Copper	15	Gypsy Red	180
Harvest Gold	120		

1956

Vehicle Specifications

	convertible
Wheelbase, in.	102.0
Length, in.	168.0
Width, in.	70.5
Track, in.	front: 57.0 rear: 59.0
Height, in.	51.9
Curb weight, lb	3020

Mechanical Specifications — 2-door convertible

Suspension	**front:** Independent; unequal-length A-arms, coil springs, antiroll bar, tubular hydraulic shock absorbers **rear:** Live axle on semi-elliptic leaf springs, antiroll bar, tubular hydraulic shock absorbers
Wheels/Tires	6.70×15
Brakes	front: 11-inch drum rear: 11-inch drum
Transmission	3-speed manual (std) 2-speed Powerglide (opt)
Standard axle ratio	3.70:1

Engine Specifications

Type	ohv V-8	ohv V-8	ohv V-8
Displacement, liters/cu in.	4.34/265.0	4.34/265.0	4.34/265.0
Bore × Stroke, in. × in.	3.75 × 3.00	3.75 × 3.00	3.75 × 3.00
Fuel management	1 × 4-bbl.	2 × 4-bbl.	2 × 4-bbl.
Horsepower @ rpm	210 @ 5600	225 @ 5600	240 @ 5600
Torque @ rpm, lb-ft	270 @ 3200	270 @ 3600	270 @ 5200

Published Performance Numbers

	225 hp, 3-sp manual
0-60 mph, sec	7.3
0-100 mph, sec	20.7
1/4-mile, sec	15.8
source	*Road & Track*

Base Prices & Production

Base Prices & Production	Production	Price
2-door convertible	3467	$3120.00

Options & Production

Options & Production	Production	Price
Heater	NA	$123.65
AM Radio, signal seeking	2717	198.90
Parking Brake Alarm	2685	5.40
Courtesy Lights	2775	8.65
Windshield Washer	2815	11.85
Whitewall Tires, 6.70×15	NA	32.30
Powerglide Automatic Transmission	NA	188.50
Auxiliary Hardtop	2076	215.20
Power Windows	547	64.60
Two-Tone Paint	1259	19.40
High-Lift Camshaft	111	188.30
225 hp Engine	3080	172.20
Rear Axle, 3.27:1	NA	0.00
Power Operated Folding Top	2682	107.60

Color Choices & Production

	Production		Production
Onyx Black	810	Aztec Copper	402
Cascade Green	290	Arctic Blue	390
Venetian Red	1043	Polo White	532

1957

Vehicle Specifications

	convertible
Wheelbase, in.	102.0
Length, in.	168.0
Width, in.	70.5
Track, in.	front: 57.0 rear: 59.0
Height, in.	51.1
Curb weight, lb	2985

Mechanical Specifications — 2-door convertible

Suspension	**front:** Independent; unequal-length A-arms, coil springs, antiroll bar, tubular hydraulic shock absorbers **rear:** Live axle on semi-elliptic leaf springs, antiroll bar, tubular hydraulic shock absorbers
Wheels/Tires	6.70×15
Brakes	front: 11-inch drum rear: 11-inch drum
Transmission	3-speed manual (std) 4-speed manual (opt) 2-speed Powerglide (opt)
Standard axle ratio	3.70:1

Engine Specifications

Type	ohv V-8	ohv V-8	ohv V-8
Displacement, liters/cu in.	4.6/283	4.6/283	4.6/283
Bore × Stroke, in. × in.	3.875 × 3.00	3.875 × 3.00	3.875 × 3.00
Fuel management	1 × 4-bbl.	2 × 4-bbl.	fuel injection
Horsepower @ rpm	220 @ 4800	245 @ 5800	250 @ 4800
Torque @ rpm, lb-ft	300 @ 3000	300 @ 3000	305 @ 3800

Type	ohv V-8	ohv V-8
Displacement, liters/cu in.	4.6/283	4.6/283
Bore × Stroke, in. × in.	3.875 × 3.00	3.875 × 3.00
Fuel management	2 × 4-bbl.	fuel injection
Horsepower @ rpm	250 @ 4800	283 @ 6200
Torque @ rpm, lb-ft	305 @ 3800	290 @ 4400

Published Performance Numbers

	250 hp, 4-sp manual
0-60 mph, sec	5.7
0-100 mph, sec	NA
1/4-mile, sec	14.3
source	*Road & Track*

Base Prices & Production

Base Prices & Production	Production	Price
2-door convertible	6339	$3176.32

NA= Not Available

(1957 cont.)

Options & Production

	Production	Price
Heater	5373	$118.40
AM Radio, signal seeking	3635	199.10
Parking Brake Alarm	1873	5.40
Courtesy Lights	2489	8.65
Windshield Washer	2555	11.85
Wheels, 15×5.5	51	15.10
Whitewall Tires, 6.70×15	5019	31.60
Powerglide Automatic Transmission	1393	188.30
Auxiliary Hardtop	4055	215.20
Power Windows	379	59.20
Two-Tone Paint	2794	19.40
245 hp Engine	2045	150.65
270 hp Engine	1621	182.95
Power Operated Folding Top	1336	139.90
250 hp Engine FI (579A)	182	484.20
283 hp Engine FI (579B)	713	484.20
250 hp Engine FI (579C)	102	484.20
283 hp Engine FI (579E)	43	726.30
Positraction Rear Axle, 3.70:1	327	48.45
Positraction Rear Axle, 4.11:1	1772	48.45
Positraction Rear Axle, 4.56:1	NA	48.45
Heavy Duty Racing Suspension	51	780.10
4-speed Manual Transmission	664	188.30

Color Choices & Production

	Production		Production
Onyx Black	2189	Aztec Copper	452
Cascade Green	550	Arctic Blue	487
Venetian Red	1320	Polo White	1273
Inca Silver	65		

1958

Vehicle Specifications

	convertible	
Wheelbase, in.	102.0	
Length, in.	177.2	
Width, in.	72.8	
Track, in.	front: 57.0	rear: 59.0
Height, in.	51.1	
Curb weight, lb	3050	

Mechanical Specifications 2-door convertible

Suspension	**front:** Independent; upper and lower A-arms, unequal-length wishbones, coil springs, antiroll bar, tubular hydraulic shock absorbers **rear:** Live axle on semi-elliptic leaf springs, tubular hydraulic shock absorbers
Wheels/Tires	6.70×15
Brakes	front: 11-inch drum rear: 11-inch drum
Transmission	3-speed manual (std) 4-speed manual (opt) 2-speed Powerglide (opt)
Standard axle ratio	3.70:1

Engine Specifications

Type	ohv V-8	ohv V-8	ohv V-8
Displacement, liters/cu in.	4.6/283	4.6/283	4.6/283
Bore × Stroke, in. × in.	3.875 × 3.00	3.875 × 3.00	3.875 × 3.00
Fuel management	1 × 4-bbl.	2 × 4-bbl.	fuel injection
Horsepower @ rpm	230 @ 4800	245 @ 5000	250 @ 5000
Torque @ rpm, lb-ft	300 @ 3000	300 @ 3800	305 @ 3800

Type	ohv V-8	ohv V-8
Displacement, liters/cu in.	4.6/283	4.6/283
Bore × Stroke, in. × in.	3.875 × 3.00	3.875 × 3.00
Fuel management	2 × 4-bbl.	fuel injection
Horsepower @ rpm	270 @ 6000	290 @ 6200
Torque @ rpm, lb-ft	285 @ 4200	290 @ 4400

Published Performance Numbers

	230 hp, 4-sp man.	250 hp, 4-sp man.
0-60 mph, sec	9.2	7.6
0-100 mph, sec	NA	21.4
1/4-mile, sec @ mph	17.4 @ 83	15.7 @ 90
source		*Sports Car Illustrated*

Base Prices & Production

	Production	Price
2-door convertible	9168	$3591.00

Options & Production

	Production	Price
Heater	8014	$96.85
AM Radio, signal seeking	6142	144.45
Parking Brake Alarm	2883	5.40
Courtesy Lights	4600	6.50
Windshield Washer	3834	16.15
Wheels, 15×5.5	404	0.00
Whitewall Tires, 6.70×15	7428	31.55
Powerglide Automatic Transmission	2057	188.30
Auxiliary Hardtop	5607	215.20
Power Windows	649	59.20
Two-Tone Paint	3422	16.15
245 hp Engine	2436	150.65
270 hp Engine	978	182.95
Power Operated Folding Top	1090	139.90
250 hp Engine FI	504	484.20
290 hp Engine FI	1007	484.20
Positraction Rear Axle, 3.70:1	1123	48.45
Positraction Rear Axle, 4.11:1	2518	48.45
Positraction Rear Axle, 4.56:1	370	48.45
Heavy Duty Racing Suspension	144	780.10
4-speed Manual Transmission	3764	215.20

Color Choices & Production

	Production		Production
Charcoal	1631	Snowcrest White	2477
Silver Blue	2006	Regal Turquoise	510
Panama Yellow	455	Signet Red	1399
Tuxedo Black	493	Inca Silver	193

1959

Vehicle Specifications

	convertible	
Wheelbase, in.	102.0	
Length, in.	177.0	
Width, in.	73.0	
Track, in.	front: 57.0	rear: 59.0
Height, in.	52.0	
Curb weight, lb	3080	

Mechanical Specifications 2-door convertible

Suspension	**front:** Independent; upper and lower A-arms, unequal-length wishbones, coil springs, antiroll bar, tubular hydraulic shock absorbers **rear:** Live axle on semi-elliptic leaf springs, tubular hydraulic shock absorbers, trailing radius rods
Wheels/Tires	6.70×15

Brakes	front: 11-inch drum
	rear: 11-inch drum
Transmission	3-speed manual (std)
	4-speed manual (opt)
	2-speed Powerglide (opt)
Standard axle ratio	3.70:1

Engine Specifications

Type	ohv V-8	ohv V-8	ohv V-8
Displacement, liters/cu in.	4.6/283	4.6/283	4.6/283
Bore × Stroke, in. × in.	3.875 × 3.00	3.875 × 3.00	3.875 × 3.00
Fuel management	1 × 4-bbl.	2 × 4-bbl.	fuel injection
Horsepower @ rpm	230 @ 4800	245 @ 5000	250 @ 5000
Torque @ rpm, lb-ft	300 @ 3000	300 @ 3800	305 @ 3800

Type	ohv V-8	ohv V-8
Displacement, liters/cu in.	4.6/283 4.6/283	
Bore × Stroke, in. × in.	3.875 × 3.00	3.875 × 3.00
Fuel management	2 × 4-bbl.	fuel injection
Horsepower @ rpm	270 @ 6000	290 @ 6200
Torque @ rpm, lb-ft	285 @ 4200	290 @ 4400

Published Performance Numbers

	250 hp, 4-sp man.	290 hp, 4-sp man.
0-60 mph, sec	7.8	6.8
0-100 mph, sec	NA	15.5
1/4-mile, sec @ mph	15.7 @ 90	14.9 @ 96
source		Road & Track

Base Prices & Production

	Production	Price
2-door convertible	9670	$3875.00

Options & Production

	Production	Price
Heater	8909	$102.25
AM Radio, signal seeking	7001	149.80
Parking Brake Alarm	3601	5.40
Courtesy Lights	3601	6.50
Windshield Washer	7909	16.15
Radiator Fan Clutch	67	21.55
Sunshades	3722	10.80
Wheels, 15×5.5	214	0.00
Whitewall Tires, 6.70×15	8173	31.55
Powerglide Automatic Transmission	1878	199.10
Auxiliary Hardtop	5481	236.75
Power Windows	587	59.20
Two-Tone Paint	2931	16.15
245 hp Engine	1417	150.65
270 hp Engine	1846	182.95
Power Operated Folding Top	661	139.90
250 hp Engine FI	175	484.20
290 hp Engine FI	745	484.20
Positraction Rear Axle	4170	48.45
Heavy Duty Brakes and Suspension	142	425.05
4-speed Manual Transmission	4175	188.30
Metallic Brakes	333	26.90
Blackwall Tires, 6.70×15 nylon	NA	NA
24 Gallon Fuel Tank	NA	NA

Color Choices & Production

	Production		Production
Tuxedo Black	1594	Classic Cream	223
Frost Blue	1024	Crown Sapphire	888
Roman Red	1542	Snowcrest White	3354
Inca Silver	957		

1960

Vehicle Specifications	convertible	
Wheelbase, in.	102.0	
Length, in.	177.2	
Width, in.	72.8	
Track, in.	front: 57.0	rear: 59.0
Height, in.	52.3	
Curb weight, lb	3080	

Mechanical Specifications — 2-door convertible

Suspension	**front:** Independent; upper and lower A-arms, unequal-length wishbones, coil springs, antiroll bar, tubular hydraulic shock absorbers
	rear: Live axle on semi-elliptic leaf springs, tubular hydraulic shock absorbers, trailing radius rods
Wheels/Tires	6.70×15
Brakes	front: 11-inch drum
	rear: 11-inch drum
Transmission	3-speed manual (std)
	4-speed manual (opt)
	2-speed Powerglide (opt)
Standard axle ratio	3.70:1

Engine Specifications

Type	ohv V-8	ohv V-8	ohv V-8
Displacement, liters/cu in.	4.6/283	4.6/283	4.6/283
Bore × Stroke, in. × in.	3.875 × 3.00	3.875 × 3.00	3.875 × 3.00
Fuel management	1 × 4-bbl.	2 × 4-bbl.	2 × 4-bbl.
Horsepower @ rpm	230 @ 4800	245 @ 5000	270 @ 6000
Torque @ rpm, lb-ft	300 @ 3000	300 @ 3800	285 @ 4200

Type	ohv V-8	ohv V-8
Displacement, liters/cu in.	4.6/283	4.6/283
Bore × Stroke, in. × in.	3.875 × 3.00	3.875 × 3.00
Fuel management	2 × 4-bbl.	fuel injection
Horsepower @ rpm	270 @ 6000	290 @ 6200
Torque @ rpm, lb-ft	285 @ 4200	290 @ 4400

Published Performance Numbers

	270 hp, 4-speed manual
0-60 mph, sec	8.3
0-100 mph, sec	NA
1/4-mile, sec @ mph	16.1 @ 89

Base Prices & Production

	Production	Price
2-door convertible	10,261	$3872.00

Options & Production

	Production	Price
Heater	9808	$102.25
AM Radio, signal seeking	8166	137.75
Parking Brake Alarm	4051	5.40
Courtesy Lights	6774	6.50
Windshield Washer	7205	16.15
Temperature Controlled Radiator Fan	2711	21.55
Sunshades	5276	10.80
Wheels, 15×5.5	246	0.00
Whitewall Tires, 6.70×15	9104	31.55
Powerglide Automatic Transmission	1766	199.10
Auxiliary Hardtop	5147	236.75
Power Windows	544	59.20
Two-Tone Paint	3312	16.15
245 hp Engine	1211	150.65
270 hp Engine	2364	182.95
Power Operated Folding Top	512	139.90
250 hp Engine FI	100	484.20

NA= Not Available

(1960 cont.)

290 hp Engine FI	759	484.20
Positraction Rear Axle	5231	43.05
4-speed Manual Transmission	5328	188.30
Metallic Brakes	920	26.90
Heavy Duty Brakes and Suspension	119	333.60
Blackwall Tires, 6.70×15 nylon	NA	NA
24 Gallon Fuel Tank	NA	NA

Color Choices & Production

	Production		Production
Tuxedo Black	1268	Tasco Turquoise	635
Horizon Blue	766	Honduras Maroon	1202
Roman Red	1529	Ermine White	3717
Sateen Silver	989	Cascade Green	140

1961

Vehicle Specifications — convertible

Wheelbase, in.	102.0
Length, in.	176.7
Width, in.	70.4
Track, in.	front: 57.0 rear: 59.0
Height, in.	52.9
Curb weight, lb	3108

Mechanical Specifications — 2-door convertible

Suspension	**front:** Independent; upper and lower A-arms, unequal-length wishbones, coil springs, antiroll bar, tubular hydraulic shock absorbers **rear:** Live axle on semi-elliptic leaf springs, tubular hydraulic shock absorbers, trailing radius rods
Wheels/Tires	6.70×15
Brakes	front: 11-inch drum rear: 11-inch drum
Transmission	3-speed manual (std) 4-speed manual (opt) 2-speed Powerglide (opt)
Standard axle ratio	3.70:1

Engine Specifications

Type	ohv V-8	ohv V-8	ohv V-8
Displacement, liters/cu in.	4.6/283	4.6/283	4.6/283
Bore × Stroke, in. × in.	3.875 × 3.00	3.875 × 3.00	3.875 × 3.00
Fuel management	1 × 4-bbl.	2 × 4-bbl.	2 × 4-bbl.
Horsepower @ rpm	230 @ 4800	245 @ 5000	270 @ 6000
Torque @ rpm, lb-ft	300 @ 3000	300 @ 3800	285 @ 4200

Type	ohv V-8	ohv V-8
Displacement, liters/cu in.	4.6/283	4.6/283
Bore × Stroke, in. × in.	3.875 × 3.00	3.875 × 3.00
Fuel management	fuel injection	fuel injection
Horsepower @ rpm	275 @ 5200	315 @ 6200
Torque @ rpm, lb-ft	290 @ 4200	295 @ 5100

Published Performance Numbers

	230 hp, 4-sp man.	315 hp, 4-sp man.
0-60 mph, sec	8.3	6.0
0-100 mph, sec	NA	14.2
1/4-mile, sec @ mph	NA	15.5 @ 106

Base Prices & Production

	Production	Price
2-door convertible	10,934	$3934.00

Options & Production

	Production	Price
Heater	10,671	$102.25
AM Radio, signal seeking	9316	137.75
Positive Crankcase Ventilation	NA	5.40
Wheels, 15×5.5	337	0.00
Whitewall Tires, 6.70×15	9780	31.55
Powerglide Automatic Transmission	1458	199.10
Auxiliary Hardtop	5680	236.75
Power Windows	698	59.20
Two-Tone Paint	3351	16.15
245 hp Engine	1175	150.65
270 hp Engine	2827	182.95
275 hp Engine FI	118	484.20
315 hp Engine FI	1462	484.20
Power Operated Folding Top	442	161.40
Positraction Rear Axle	6915	43.05
4-speed Manual Transmission	7013	188.30
Metallic Brakes	1402	37.70
Heavy Duty Brakes and Suspension	233	333.60
Blackwall Tires, 6.70×15 nylon	NA	15.75
24 Gallon Fuel Tank	NA	161.40

Color Choices & Production

	Production		Production
Tuxedo Black	1340	Fawn Beige	1363
Honduras Maroon	1645	Roman Red	1794
Ermine White	3178	Sateen Silver	747
Jewel Blue	855		

1962

Vehicle Specifications — convertible

Wheelbase, in.	102.0
Length, in.	176.7
Width, in.	70.4
Track, in.	front: 57.0 rear: 59.0
Height, in.	52.9
Curb weight, lb	3137

Mechanical Specifications — 2-door convertible

Suspension	**front:** Independent; upper and lower A-arms, unequal-length wishbones, coil springs, antiroll bar, tubular hydraulic shock absorbers **rear:** Live axle on semi-elliptic leaf springs, tubular hydraulic shock absorbers, trailing radius rods
Wheels/Tires	6.70×15
Brakes	front: 11-inch drum rear: 11-inch drum
Transmission	3-speed manual (std) 4-speed manual (opt) 2-speed Powerglide (opt)
Standard axle ratio	3.70:1

Engine Specifications

Type	ohv V-8	ohv V-8
Displacement, liters/cu in.	5.35/327	5.35/327
Bore × Stroke, in. × in.	4.00 × 3.25	4.00 × 3.25
Fuel management	1 × 4-bbl.	1 × 4-bbl. (AFB)
Horsepower @ rpm	240 @ 4400	300 @ 5000
Torque @ rpm, lb-ft	350 @ 2800	360 @ 3200

Type	ohv V-8	ohv V-8
Displacement, liters/cu in.	5.35/327	5.35/327
Bore × Stroke, in. × in.	4.00 × 3.25	4.00 × 3.25

Fuel management	1 × 4-bbl. (AFB)	fuel injection
Horsepower @ rpm	340 @ 6000	360 @ 6000
Torque @ rpm, lb-ft	344 @ 4000	352 @ 4000

Published Performance Numbers
360 hp, 4-speed manual

0-60 mph, sec	5.9
0-100 mph, sec	13.5
1/4-mile, sec @ mph	14.5 @ 104

Base Prices & Production

	Production	Price
2-door convertible	14,531	$4038.00

Options & Production

	Production	Price
AM Radio, signal seeking	13,076	$137.75
Rear Axle, 3.08:1	NA	0.00
Positive Crankcase Ventilation	NA	5.40
Wheels, 15×5.5	561	0.00
Powerglide Automatic Transmission	1532	199.10
Auxiliary Hardtop	8074	236.75
Power Windows	995	59.20
Direct Flow Exhaust System	2934	0.00
340 hp Engine	4412	107.60
360 hp Engine	1918	484.20
300 hp Engine FI	3294	53.80
Power Operated Folding Top	350	139.90
Positraction Rear Axle	14,232	43.05
4-speed Manual Transmission	11,318	188.30
Metallic Brakes	2799	37.70
Heavy Duty Brakes and Suspension	246	333.60
Blackwall Tires, 6.70×15 nylon	NA	31.55
Whitewall Tires, 6.70×15	NA	15.70
24 Gallon Fuel Tank	65	118.40

Color Choices & Production

	Production		Production
Tuxedo Black	NA	Fawn Beige	1851
Roman Red	NA	Ermine White	NA
Almond Beige	820	Sateen Silver	NA
Honduras Maroon	NA		

1963

Vehicle Specifications

	convertible	coupe
Wheelbase, in.	98.0	98.0
Length, in.	175.3	175.3
Width, in.	69.6	69.6
Track, in.	front: 56.3	front: 56.3
	rear: 57.0	rear: 57.0
Height, in.	49.8	NA
Curb weight, lb	3150	3150

Mechanical Specifications
2-door convertible/coupe

Suspension	**front:** Independent; upper and lower A-arms, coil springs, antiroll bar, tubular hydraulic shock absorbers **rear:** fixed differential, U-jointed half shafts, lateral struts, radius rods, transverse leaf spring, tubular hydraulic shock absorbers, antiroll bar w/big block engines
Wheels/Tires	6.70×15
Brakes	front: 11-inch drum rear: 11-inch drum
Transmission	3-speed manual (std) 4-speed manual (opt) 2-speed Powerglide (opt)
Standard axle ratio	3.70:1

Engine Specifications

Type	ohv V-8	ohv V-8
Displacement, liters/cu in.	5.35/327	5.35/327
Bore × Stroke, in. × in.	4.00 × 3.25	4.00 × 3.25
Fuel management	1 × 4-bbl.	1 × 4-bbl. (AFB)
Horsepower @ rpm	250 @ 4400	300 @ 5000
Torque @ rpm, lb-ft	350 @ 2800	360 @ 3200

Type	ohv V-8	ohv V-8
Displacement, liters/cu in.	5.35/327	5.35/327
Bore × Stroke, in. × in.	4.00 × 3.25	4.00 × 3.25
Fuel management	1 × 4-bbl. (AFB)	fuel injection
Horsepower @ rpm	340 @ 6000	360 @ 6000
Torque @ rpm, lb-ft	344 @ 4000	352 @ 4000

Published Performance Numbers
300 hp, 4-sp manual

0-60 mph, sec	6.1
0-100 mph, sec	14.5
1/4-mile, sec @ mph	14.5 @ 100

Base Prices & Production

	Production	Price
2-door convertible	10,919	$4037.00
2-door coupe	10,594	4252.00

Options & Production

	Production	Price
Leather Seats	1114	$80.70
Sebring Silver Exterior Paint	3516	80.70
Soft Ray Tinted Glass, all	629	16.15
Soft Ray Tinted Glass, windshield	470	10.80
Power Windows	3742	59.20
Auxiliary Hardtop	5739	236.75
Heater and Defroster Delete (credit)	124	100.00
Air Conditioning	278	421.80
Positraction Rear Axle, all ratios	17,554	43.05
Highway Rear Axle, 3.08:1	211	2.20
Power Brakes	3336	43.05
Sintered Metallic Brakes	5310	37.70
300 hp Engine	8033	53.80
340 hp Engine	6978	107.60
360 hp Engine FI	2610	430.40
4-speed Manual Transmission	17,973	188.30
Powerglide Automatic Transmission	2621	199.10
36 Gallon Fuel Tank (coupe)	63	202.30
Off Road Exhaust System	NA	37.70
Woodgrained Steering Wheel	3063	16.15
Cast Aluminum Knock-Off Wheels	NA	322.80
Blackwall Tires, 6.70×15 nylon	412	15.70
Whitewall Tires, 6.70×15	19,383	31.55
Back Up Lamps	318	10.80
AM Radio, signal seeking	11,368	137.75
AM/FM Radio	9178	174.35
Special Performance Equipment	199	1818.45

Color Choices & Production

	Production		Production
Tuxedo Black	NA	Silver Blue	NA
Daytona Blue	3475	Riverside Red	4612
Saddle Tan	NA	Ermine White	NA
Sebring Silver	3516		

NA= Not Available

1964

Vehicle Specifications

	convertible	coupe
Wheelbase, in.	98.0	98.0
Length, in.	175.3	175.3
Width, in.	69.6	69.6
Track, in.	front: 56.3	front: 56.3
	rear: 57.0	rear: 57.0
Height, in.	49.8	49.8
Curb weight, lb	3180	3180

Mechanical Specifications — 2-door convertible/coupe

Suspension	**front:** Independent; upper and lower A-arms, coil springs, antiroll bar, tubular hydraulic shock absorbers **rear:** fixed differential, U-jointed half shafts, lateral struts, radius rods, transverse leaf spring, tubular hydraulic shock absorbers, anti-roll bar w/big block engines
Wheels/Tires	6.70×15
Brakes	front: 11-inch drum rear: 11-inch drum
Transmission	3-speed manual (std) 4-speed manual (opt) 2-speed Powerglide (opt)
Standard axle ratio	3.70:1

Engine Specifications

Type	ohv V-8	ohv V-8
Displacement, liters/cu in.	5.35/327	5.35/327
Bore × Stroke, in. × in.	4.00 × 3.25	4.00 × 3.25
Fuel management	1 × 4-bbl.	1 × 4-bbl. (AFB)
Horsepower @ rpm	250 @ 4400	300 @ 5000
Torque @ rpm, lb-ft	350 @ 2800	360 @ 3200

Type	ohv V-8	ohv V-8
Displacement, liters/cu in.	5.35/327	5.35/327
Bore × Stroke, in. × in.	4.00 × 3.25	4.00 × 3.25
Fuel management	1 × 4-bbl. (AFB)	fuel injection
Horsepower @ rpm	365 @ 6200	375 @ 6200
Torque @ rpm, lb-ft	350 @ 4000	350 @ 4400

Published Performance Numbers

	300 hp, 3-sp automatic
0-60 mph, sec	8.0
0-100 mph, sec	20.2
1/4-mile, sec @ mph	15.2 @ 85

Base Prices & Production

	Production	Price
2-door convertible	13,925	$4037.00
2-door coupe	8304	4252.00

Options & Production

	Production	Price
Leather Seats	1334	$80.70
Soft Ray Tinted Glass, all	6031	16.15
Soft Ray Tinted Glass, windshield	6387	10.80
Power Windows	3706	59.20
Auxiliary Hardtop	7023	236.75
Heater and Defroster Delete (credit)	60	100.00
Air Conditioning	1998	421.80
Special Front and Rear Suspension	82	37.70
Positraction Rear Axle, all ratios	18,279	43.05
Highway Rear Axle, 3.08:1	2310	2.20
Power Brakes	2270	43.05
Sintered Metallic Brake Package	29	629.50
Sintered Metallic Brakes, power	4780	53.80
Transistor Ignition System	552	75.35
300 hp Engine	10,471	53.80
365 hp Engine	7171	107.60
375 hp Engine FI	1325	538.00
4-speed Manual Transmission	19,034	188.30
Powerglide Automatic Transmission	2480	199.10
36 Gallon Fuel Tank (coupe)	38	202.30
Off Road Exhaust System	1953	37.70
Power Steering	3126	75.35
Cast Aluminum Knock-Off Wheels	806	322.80
Blackwall Tires, 6.70×15 nylon	372	15.70
Whitewall Tires, 6.70×15	19,977	31.85
Back Up Lamps	11,085	10.80
AM/FM Radio	20,934	176.50

Color Choices & Production

	Production		Production
Tuxedo Black	1897	Silver Blue	3121
Daytona Blue	3454	Riverside Red	5274
Saddle Tan	1765	Ermine White	3909
Sebring Silver	2785		

1965

Vehicle Specifications

	convertible	coupe
Wheelbase, in.	98.0	98.0
Length, in.	175.3	175.3
Width, in.	69.6	69.6
Track, in.	front: 56.3	front: 56.3
	rear: 57.0	rear: 57.0
Height, in.	49.8	49.8
Curb weight, lb	3230	3230

Mechanical Specifications — 2-door convertible/coupe

Suspension	**front:** Independent; upper and lower A-arms, coil springs, antiroll bar, tubular hydraulic shock absorbers **rear:** fixed differential, U-jointed half shafts, lateral struts, radius rods, transverse leaf spring, tubular hydraulic shock absorbers, antiroll bar w/big block engines
Wheels/Tires	7.75×15
Brakes	front: 11.75-inch disc rear: 11.75-inch disc
Transmission	3-speed manual (std) 4-speed manual (opt) 2-speed Powerglide (opt)
Standard axle ratio	3.36:1

Engine Specifications

Type	ohv V-8	ohv V-8
Displacement, liters/cu in.	5.35/327	5.35/327
Bore × Stroke, in. × in.	4.00 × 3.25	4.00 × 3.25
Fuel management	1 × 4-bbl.	1 × 4-bbl. (AFB)
Horsepower @ rpm	300 @ 5000	350 @ 5800
Torque @ rpm, lb-ft	360 @ 3200	360 @ 3600

Type	ohv V-8	ohv V-8	ohv V-8
Displacement, liters/cu in.	5.35/327	5.35/327	6.5/396
Bore × Stroke, in. × in.	4.00 × 3.25	4.00 × 3.25	4.25 × 3.76
Fuel management	1 × 4-bbl.	fuel injection	1 × 4-bbl.
Horsepower @ rpm	365 @ 6200	375 @ 6200	425 @ 6400
Torque @ rpm, lb-ft	350 @ 4000	350 @ 4400	415 @ 4000

Published Performance Numbers

	375 hp, 4-sp man.	425 hp, 4-sp man.
0-60 mph, sec	6.3	5.7
0-100 mph, sec	14.7	13.4
1/4-mile, sec @ mph	14.4 @ 99	14.1 @ 103

Base Prices & Production

	Production	Price
2-door coupe	8186	$4321.00
2-door convertible	15,378	4106.00

Options & Production

	Production	Price
Leather Seats	2128	$80.70
Soft Ray Tinted Glass, all	8752	16.15
Soft Ray Tinted Glass, windshield	7624	10.80
Power Windows	3809	59.20
Auxiliary Hardtop	7787	236.75
Heater and Defroster Delete (credit)	39	100.00
Air Conditioning	2423	421.80
Special Front and Rear Suspension	975	37.70
Positraction Rear Axle, all ratios	19,965	43.05
Highway Rear Axle, 3.08:1	1886	2.20
Power Brakes	4044	43.05
Drum Brakes (substitution credit)	316	64.50
Transistor Ignition System	3686	75.35
300 hp Engine	8358	53.80
365 hp Engine	5011	129.15
425 hp Engine	2157	292.70
350 hp Engine	4716	107.60
375 hp Engine FI	771	538.00
4-speed Manual Transmission	21,107	188.30
Powerglide Automatic Transmission	2468	199.10
36 Gallon Fuel Tank (coupe)	41	202.30
Off Road Exhaust System	2468	37.70
Side Mount Exhaust System	759	134.50
Teakwood Steering Wheel	2259	48.45
Teakwood Steering Column	3917	43.05
Power Steering	3236	96.85
Cast Aluminum Knock-Off Wheels	1116	322.80
Blackwall Tires, 7.75×15 nylon	168	15.70
Whitewall Tires, 7.75×15 rayon	19,300	31.85
Goldwall Tires, 7.75×15 nylon	989	50.05
AM/FM Radio	22,113	203.40
Comfort and Convenience Group	15,397	16.15

Color Choices & Production

	Production		Production
Tuxedo Black	1191	Ermine White	2216
Nassau Blue	6022	Glen Green	3782
Milano Maroon	2831	Silver Pearl	2552
Rally Red	3688	Goldwood Yellow	1275

1966

Vehicle Specifications

	convertible	coupe
Wheelbase, in.	98.0	98.0
Length, in.	175.2	175.2
Width, in.	69.6	69.6
Track, in.	front: 56.3	front: 56.3
	rear: 57.0	rear: 57.0
Height, in.	49.8	49.8
Curb weight, lb	3230	3230

Mechanical Specifications 2-door convertible/coupe

Suspension — **front:** Independent; upper and lower A-arms, coil springs, antiroll bar, tubular hydraulic shock absorbers

rear: fixed differential, U-jointed half shafts, lateral struts, radius rods, transverse leaf spring, tubular hydraulic shock absorbers, antiroll bar w/big block engines

Wheels/Tires	7.75×15
Brakes	front: 11.75-inch disc
	rear: 11.75-inch disc
Transmission	3-speed manual (std)
	4-speed manual (opt)
	2-speed Powerglide (opt)
Standard axle ratio	3.55:1

Engine Specifications

Type	ohv V-8	ohv V-8
Displacement, liters/cu in.	5.35/327	5.35/327
Bore × Stroke, in. × in.	4.00 × 3.25	4.00 × 3.25
Fuel management	1 × 4-bbl.	1 × 4-bbl. (AFB)
Horsepower @ rpm	300 @ 5000	350 @ 5800
Torque @ rpm, lb-ft	360 @ 3200	360 @ 3600

Type	ohv V-8	ohv V-8
Displacement, liters/cu in.	7.0/427	7.0/427
Bore × Stroke, in. × in.	4.25 × 3.76	4.25 × 3.76
Fuel management	1 × 4-bbl.	1 × 4-bbl
Horsepower @ rpm	390 @ 5400	425 @ 5600
Torque @ rpm, lb-ft	460 @ 3600	460 @ 4000

Published Performance Numbers

	425 hp, 4-speed manual
0-60 mph, sec	5.6
0-100 mph, sec	NA
1/4-mile, sec @ mph	13.4 @ 105

Base Prices & Production

	Production	Price
2-door coupe	9958	$4295.00
2-door convertible	17,762	4084.00

Options & Production

	Production	Price
Leather Seats	2002	$79.00
Soft Ray Tinted Glass, all	11,859	15.80
Soft Ray Tinted Glass, windshield	9270	10.55
Power Windows	4562	57.95
Headrests	1033	42.15
Shoulder Belts	37	26.35
Auxiliary Hardtop	8463	231.75
Heater and Defroster Delete (credit)	54	97.85
Air Conditioning	3520	412.90
Special Front and Rear Suspension	2705	36.90
Positraction Rear Axle, all ratios	24,056	42.15
Power Brakes	5464	42.15
Special Heavy Duty Brakes	382	342.30
Air Injection Reactor	2380	44.75
Transistor Ignition System	7146	73.75
390 hp Engine	5116	181.20
425 hp Engine	5258	312.85
350 hp Engine FI	7591	105.35
4-Speed Manual Transmission	10,837	184.35
4-Speed Manual Transmission, close ratio	13,903	184.35
4-Speed Manual Transmission, close ratio, heavy duty	15	237.00
Powerglide Automatic Transmission	2401	194.85
36 Gallon Fuel Tank (coupe)	66	198.05
Off Road Exhaust System	2795	36.90
Side Mount Exhaust System	3617	131.65
Teakwood Steering Wheel	3941	47.40
Telescopic Steering Column	3670	42.15

NA= Not Available

(1966 cont.)

Power Steering	5611	94.80
Cast Aluminum Knock-Off Wheels	1194	316.00
Whitewall Tires, 7.75×15 rayon	17,969	31.30
Goldwall Tires, 7.75×15 nylon	5557	46.55
AM/FM Radio	26,363	199.10
Traffic Hazard Lamp Switch	5764	11.60

Color Choices & Production

	Production		Production
Tuxedo Black	1190	Ermine White	2120
Rally Red	3366	Nassau Blue	6100
Laguna Blue	2054	Trophy Blue	1463
Mosport Green	2311	Sunfire Yellow	2339
Silver Pearl	2967	Milano Maroon	3799

1967

Vehicle Specifications	convertible	coupe
Wheelbase, in.	98.0	98.0
Length, in.	175.1	175.1
Width, in.	69.6	69.6
Track, in.	front: 56.3	front: 56.3
	rear: 57.0	rear: 57.0
Height, in.	49.8	49.8
Curb weight, lb	3360	3360

Mechanical Specifications	2-door convertible/coupe
Suspension	**front:** Independent; upper and lower A-arms, coil springs, antiroll bar, tubular hydraulic shock absorbers
	rear: fixed differential, U-jointed half shafts, lateral struts, radius rods, transverse leaf spring, tubular hydraulic shock absorbers, antiroll bar w/big block engines
Wheels/Tires	7.75×15
Brakes	front: 11-inch disc
	rear: 11-inch disc
Transmission	3-speed manual (std)
	4-speed manual (opt)
	2-speed Powerglide (opt)
Standard axle ratio	3.55:1

Engine Specifications

Type	ohv V-8	ohv V-8	ohv V-8
Displacement, liters/cu in.	5.35/327	5.35/327	7.0/427
Bore × Stroke, in. × in.	4.00 × 3.25	4.00 × 3.25	4.25 × 3.76
Fuel management	1 × 4-bbl.	1 × 4-bbl.	1 × 4-bbl.
Horsepower @ rpm	300 @ 5000	350 @ 5800	390 @ 5400
Torque @ rpm, lb-ft	360 @ 3200	360 @ 3600	460 @ 3600

Type	ohv V-8	ohv V-8	ohv V-8
Displacement, liters/cu in.	7.0/427	7.0/427	7.0/427
Bore × Stroke, in. × in.	4.25 × 3.76	4.25 × 3.76	4.25 × 3.76
Fuel management	3 × 2-bbl.	3 × 2-bbl.	1 × 4bbl.
Horsepower @ rpm	400 @ 5400	435 @ 5800	430 @ 5200
Torque @ rpm, lb-ft	460 @ 3600	460 @ 4000	450 @ 4400

Published Performance Numbers

300 hp, 4-speed manual

0-60 mph, sec	7.8
0-100 mph, sec	23.1
1/4-mile, sec @ mph	16.0 @ 87

Base Prices & Production

	Production	Price
2-door coupe	8504	$4388.75
2-door convertible	14,436	4240.75

Options & Production	Production	Price
Leather Seats	1601	$79.00
Soft Ray Tinted Glass, all	11,331	15.80
Soft Ray Tinted Glass, windshield	6558	10.55
Power Windows	4036	57.95
Headrests	1762	42.15
Shoulder Belts	1426	26.35
Auxiliary Hardtop	6880	231.75
Vinyl Covering	1966	52.70
Heater and Defroster Delete (credit)	35	97.85
Air Conditioning	3788	412.90
Special Front and Rear Suspension	2198	36.90
Positraction Rear Axle, all ratios	20,308	42.15
Power Brakes	4766	42.15
Special Heavy Duty Brakes	267	342.30
Air Injection Reactor	2573	44.75
Transistor Ignition System	5759	73.75
390 hp Engine	3832	200.15
400 hp Engine	2101	305.50
435 hp Engine	3754	437.10
350 hp Engine	6375	105.35
430 hp Engine	20	947.90
Aluminum Cylinder Heads for L71	16	368.65
4-Speed Manual Transmission	9157	184.35
4-Speed Manual Transmission, close ratio	11,015	184.35
4-Speed Manual Transmission, close ratio, heavy duty	20	237.00
Powerglide Automatic Transmission	2324	194.85
36 Gallon Fuel Tank (coupe)	2	198.05
Off Road Exhaust System	2326	36.90
Side Mount Exhaust System	4209	131.65
Telescopic Steering Column	2415	42.15
Power Steering	5747	94.80
Cast Aluminum Bolt-On Wheels	720	263.30
Whitewall Tires, 7.75×15	13,445	31.35
Redline Tires, 7.75×15	4230	46.65
Speed Warning Indicator	2108	10.55
AM/FM Radio	22,193	172.75

Color Choices & Production

	Production		Production
Tuxedo Black	815	Ermine White	1423
Rally Red	2341	Marina Blue	3840
Lynndale Blue	1381	Elkhart Blue	1096
Goodwood Green	4293	Sunfire Yellow	2325
Silver Pearl	1952	Marlboro Maroon	3464

1968

Vehicle Specifications	convertible	coupe
Wheelbase, in.	98.0	98.0
Length, in.	182.1	182.1
Width, in.	69.2	69.2
Track, in.	front: 58.3	front: 58.3
	rear: 59.0	rear: 59.0
Height, in.	47.8	47.8
Curb weight, lb	3425	3260

Mechanical Specifications	2-door convertible/coupe
Suspension	**front:** Independent; upper and lower A-arms, coil springs, tubular hydraulic shock absorbers, antiroll bar
	rear: Independent, lateral leaf springs, struts, U-joint halfshafts, trailing arms, tubular hydraulic shock absorbers

Wheels/Tires	7×15		
Brakes	front: 11.75-inch disc		
	rear: 11.75-inch disc		
Transmission	3-speed manual (std)		
	4-speed manual (opt)		
	3-speed Hydra-Matic (opt)		
Standard axle ratio	3.70:1		

Engine Specifications

Type	ohv V-8	ohv V-8	ohv V-8 ohv
Displacement, liters/cu in.	5.35/327	5.35/327	7.0/427
Bore × Stroke, in. × in.	4.00 × 3.25	4.00 × 3.25	4.25 × 3.76
Fuel management	1 × 4-bbl.	1 × 4-bbl.	1 × 4-bbl.
Horsepower @ rpm	300 @ 5000	350 @ 5800	390 @ 5400
Torque @ rpm, lb-ft	360 @ 3400	360 @ 3600	460 @ 3600

Type	ohv V-8	ohv V-8	ohv V-8
Displacement, liters/cu in.	7.0/427	7.0/427	7.0/427
Bore × Stroke, in. × in.	4.25 × 3.76	4.25 × 3.76	4.25 × 3.76
Fuel management	3 × 2-bbl.	3 × 2-bbl.	1 × 4-bbl.
Horsepower @ rpm	400 @ 5400	435 @ 5800	430 @ 5200
Torque @ rpm, lb-ft	460 @ 3600	460 @ 4000	450 @ 4400

Published Performance Numbers

	300 hp, 4-speed manual
0-60 mph, sec	6.5
0-100 mph, sec	NA
1/4-mile, sec @ mph	13.41 @ 109.5

Base Prices & Production

	Production	Price
2-door coupe	9936	$4663.00
2-door convertible	18,630	4320.00

Options & Production

	Production	Price
Leather Seats	2429	$79.00
Soft Ray Tinted Glass, all	17,635	15.80
Soft Ray Tinted Glass, windshield	5509	10.55
Power Windows	7065	57.95
Headrests	3197	42.15
Custom Shoulder Belts (std w/coupe)	350	26.35
Auxiliary Hardtop	8735	231.75
Vinyl Covering	3050	52.70
Rear Window Defroster	693	31.60
Air Conditioning	5664	412.90
Special Front and Rear Suspension	1758	36.90
Positraction Rear Axle, all ratios	27,008	46.35
Power Brakes	9559	42.15
Special Heavy Duty Brakes	81	384.45
Transistor Ignition System	5457	73.75
390 hp Engine	7717	200.15
400 hp Engine	1932	305.50
435 hp Engine	2898	437.10
350 hp Engine	9440	105.35
430 hp Engine	80	947.90
Aluminum Cylinder Heads with L71	624	805.75
4-Speed Manual Transmission	10,760	184.35
4-Speed Manual Transmission, close ratio	12,337	184.35
4-Speed Manual Transmission, close ratio, heavy duty	80	263.30
Turbo Hydra-Matic Automatic Transmission	5063	226.45
Off Road Exhaust System	4695	36.90
Telescopic Steering Column	6477	42.15
Power Steering	12,364	94.80
Bright Metal Wheel Cover	8971	57.95
Red Stripe Tires, F70×15 nylon	11,686	31.30
White Stripe Tires, F70×15 nylon	9692	31.30

Alarm System	388	26.35
Speed Warning Indicator	3453	10.55
AM/FM Radio	24,609	172.75
AM/FM Radio, stereo	3311	278.10

Color Choices & Production

	Production		Production
Tuxedo Black	708	Polar White	1868
Rally Red	2918	LeMans Blue	4722
International Blue	2473	British Green	4779
Safari Yellow	3133	Silverstone Silver	3435
Cordovan Maroon	1155	Corvette Bronze	3374

1969

Vehicle Specifications

	convertible	coupe
Wheelbase, in.	98.0	98.0
Length, in.	182.5	182.5
Width, in.	69.0	69.0
Track, in.	front: 58.7	front: 58.7
	rear: 59.4	rear: 59.4
Height, in.	47.9	47.9
Curb weight, lb	3425	3260

Mechanical Specifications — 2-door convertible/coupe

Suspension	**front:** Independent; upper and lower A-arms, coil springs, tubular hydraulic shock absorbers, antiroll bar
	rear: Independent, lateral leaf springs, struts, U-joint halfshafts, trailing arms, tubular hydraulic shock absorbers
Wheels/Tires	8×15
Brakes	front: 11.75-inch disc
	rear: 11.75-inch disc
Transmission	3-speed manual (std)
	4-speed manual (opt)
	3-speed Hydra-Matic (opt)
Standard axle ratio	3.36:1

Engine Specifications

Type	ohv V-8	ohv V-8	ohv V-8
Displacement, liters/cu in.	5.7/350	5.7/350	7.0/427
Bore × Stroke, in. × in.	4.00 × 3.48	4.00 × 3.48	4.25 × 3.76
Fuel management	1 × 4-bbl.	1 × 4-bbl.	3 × 2-bbl.
Horsepower @ rpm	300 @ 4800	350 @ 5600	400 @ 5400
Torque @ rpm, lb-ft	380 @ 3200	380 @ 3600	460 @ 3600

Type	ohv V-8	ohv V-8
Displacement, liters/cu in.	7.0/427	7.0/427
Bore × Stroke, in. × in.	4.25 × 3.76	4.25 × 3.76
Fuel management	3 × 2-bbl.	1 × 4-bbl.
Horsepower @ rpm	435 @ 5800	430 @ 5200
Torque @ rpm, lb-ft	460 @ 4000	450 @ 4400

Published Performance Numbers

	300 hp, 3-sp automatic
0-60 mph, sec	8.4
0-100 mph, sec	21.7
1/4-mile, sec @ mph	NA

Base Prices & Production

	Production	Price
2-door coupe	22,129	$4781.00
2-door convertible	16,633	4438.00

NA= Not Available

(1969 cont.)

Options & Production	Production	Price
Leather Seats	3729	$79.00
Soft Ray Tinted Glass, all	31,270	16.90
Power Windows	9816	63.20
Headrests	38,762	17.95
Custom Shoulder Belts (std w/coupe)	600	42.15
Auxiliary Hardtop	7878	252.80
Vinyl Covering	3266	57.95
Rear Window Defroster	2485	32.65
Air Conditioning	11,859	428.70
Special Front and Rear Suspension	1661	36.90
Positraction Rear Axle, all ratios	36,965	46.35
Power Brakes	16,876	42.15
Special Heavy Duty Brakes	115	384.45
Engine Block Heater	824	10.55
Transistor Ignition System	5702	81.10
390 hp Engine	10,531	221.20
350 hp Engine	12,846	131.65
400 hp Engine	2072	326.55
435 hp Engine	2722	437.10
430 hp Engine	116	1032.15
Aluminum Cylinder Heads with L71	390	832.05
4-Speed Manual Transmission	16,507	184.80
4-Speed Manual Transmission, close ratio	13,741	184.80
4-Speed Manual Transmission, close ratio, heavy duty	101	290.40
Turbo Hydra-Matic Automatic Transmission	8161	221.80
Side Mount Exhaust System	4355	147.45
Tilt-Telescopic Steering Column	10,325	84.30
Power Steering	22,866	105.35
Deluxe Wheel Covers	8073	57.95
Red Stripe Tires, F70×15 nylon	5210	31.30
White Stripe Tires, F70×15 nylon	21,379	31.30
White Letter Tires, F70×15 nylon	2398	33.15
Front Fender Louver Trim	11,962	21.10
Alarm System	12,436	26.35
Speed Warning Indicator	3561	11.60
AM/FM Radio	33,871	172.75
AM/FM Radio, stereo	4114	278.10
Special L88 (aluminum block)	2	4718.35

Color Choices (production numbers not available)

Tuxedo Black	Can-Am White	Monza Red
LeMans Blue	Riverside Gold	Fathom Green
Daytona Yellow	Cortez Silver	Burgundy
Monaco Orange		

1970

Vehicle Specifications	convertible	coupe
Wheelbase, in.	98.0	98.0
Length, in.	182.5	182.5
Width, in.	69.0	69.0
Track, in.	front: 58.7	front: 58.7
	rear: 59.4	rear: 59.4
Height, in.	47.9	47.9
Curb weight, lb	3720	3425

Mechanical Specifications 2-door convertible/coupe

Suspension **front:** Independent; upper and lower A-arms, coil springs, tubular hydraulic shock absorbers, antiroll bar

rear: Independent, lateral leaf springs, struts, U-joint halfshafts, trailing arms, tubular hydraulic shock absorbers

Wheels/Tires	8×15
Brakes	front: 11.75-inch disc
	rear: 11.75-inch disc
Transmission	3-speed Hydra-Matic; 4-speed manual
Standard axle ratio	3.36:1

Engine Specifications

Type	ohv V-8	ohv V-8	ohv V-8 ohv
Displacement, liters/cu in.	5.7/350	5.7/350	5.7/350
Bore × Stroke, in. × in.	4.00 × 3.48	4.00 × 3.48	4.00 × 3.48
Fuel management	1 × 4-bbl.	1 × 4-bbl.	1 × 4-bbl.
Horsepower @ rpm	300 @ 4800	350 @ 5600	370 @ 6000
Torque @ rpm, lb-ft	380 @ 3200	380 @ 3600	380 @ 4000

Type	ohv V-8	ohv V-8
Displacement, liters/cu in.	7.4/454	7.4/454
Bore × Stroke, in. × in.	4.25 × 3.76	4.25 × 3.76
Fuel management	1 × 4-bbl.	1 × 4-bbl.
Horsepower @ rpm	390 @ 4800	460 @ 5600
Torque @ rpm, lb-ft	500 @ 3400	490 @ 3000

Published Performance Numbers

	390 hp 3-sp auto.	460 hp, 4-sp man.
0-60 mph, sec	7.0	NA
0-100 mph, sec	NA	NA
1/4-mile, sec @ mph	15.0 @ 93	13.8 @ 108
source	Road & Track	Sports Car Graphic

Base Prices & Production	Production	Price
2-door coupe	10,668	$5192.00
2-door convertible	6648	4849.00

Options & Production	Production	Price
Custom Interior Trim	3191	$158.00
Power Windows	4813	63.20
Custom Shoulder Belts (std w/coupe)	475	42.15
Auxiliary Hardtop	2556	273.85
Vinyl Covering	832	63.20
Rear Window Defroster	1281	36.90
Air Conditioning	6659	447.65
Optional Rear Axle Ratio	2862	12.65
Power Brakes	8984	47.40
350 hp Engine	4910	158.00
390 hp Engine	4473	289.65
370 hp Engine	1287	447.60
4-Speed Manual Transmission, close ratio	4383	0.00
4-Speed Manual Transmission, close ratio, heavy duty	25	95.00
Turbo Hydra-Matic Automatic Transmission	5102	0.00
California Emissions	1758	36.90
Tilt-Telescopic Steering Column	5803	84.30
Power Steering	11,907	105.35
Deluxe Wheel Covers	3467	57.95
White Stripe Tires, F70×15 nylon	6589	31.30
White Letter Tires, F70×15 nylon	7985	33.15
Heavy Duty Battery (std w/LS5)	165	15.80
Alarm System	6727	31.60
AM/FM Radio	14,529	172.75
AM/FM Radio, stereo	2462	278.10
Special Purpose Engine Package	25	968.95

Color Choices (production numbers not available)

Classic White	Monza Red	Marlboro Maroon
Mulsanne Blue	Bridgehampton Blue	Donnybrooke Green
Daytona Yellow	Cortez Silver	Ontario Orange
Laguna Gray	Corvette Bronze	

1971

Vehicle Specifications

	convertible	coupe
Wheelbase, in.	98.0	98.0
Length, in.	182.5	182.5
Width, in.	69.0	69.0
Track, in.	front: 58.7	front: 58.7
	rear: 59.4	rear: 59.4
Height, in.	47.9	47.9
Curb weight, lb	3593	3593

Mechanical Specifications 2-door convertible/coupe

Suspension	**front:** Independent; upper and lower A-arms, coil springs, tubular hydraulic shock absorbers, antiroll bar **rear:** Independent, lateral leaf springs, struts, U-joint halfshafts, trailing arms, tubular hydraulic shock absorbers
Wheels/Tires	8×15
Brakes	front: 11.75-inch disc rear: 11.75-inch disc
Transmission	3-speed Hydra-Matic; 4-speed manual
Standard axle ratio	3.36:1

Engine Specifications

Type	ohv V-8	ohv V-8
Displacement, liters/cu in.	5.7/350 5.7/350	
Bore × Stroke, in. × in.	4.00 × 3.48	4.00 × 3.48
Fuel management	1 × 4-bbl.	1 × 4-bbl.
Horsepower @ rpm	270 @ 4800	330 @ 5600
Torque @ rpm, lb-ft	360 @ 3200	360 @ 3600

Type	ohv V-8	ohv V-8
Displacement, liters/cu in.	7.4/454	7.4/454
Bore × Stroke, in. × in.	4.25 × 4.00	4.25 × 4.00
Fuel management	1 × 4-bbl.	1 × 4-bbl.
Horsepower @ rpm	365 @ 4800	425 @ 5600
Torque @ rpm, lb-ft	465 @ 3400	475 @ 4000

Published Performance Numbers

	270 hp, 4-sp man.	330 hp, 4-sp man.
0-60 mph, sec	7.1	6.0
0-100 mph, sec	19.8	14.5
1/4-mile, sec @ mph	15.55 @ 90.4	14.57 @ 100.6
source	*Car and Driver*	*Car and Driver*

	365 hp, 4-sp man.	425 hp, 4-sp man.
0-60 mph, sec	5.7	5.3
0-100 mph, sec	14.1	12.7
1/4-mile, sec @ mph	14.2 @ 100.3	13.8 @ 104.7
source	*Car and Driver*	*Car and Driver*

Base Prices & Production

	Production	Price
2-door coupe	14,680	$5496.00
2-door convertible	7121	5259.00

Options & Production

	Production	Price
Custom Interior Trim	2602	$158.00
Power Windows	6192	79.00
Custom Shoulder Belts (std w/coupe)	677	42.00
Auxiliary Hardtop	2619	274.00
Vinyl Covering	832	63.00
Rear Window Defroster	1598	42.00
Air Conditioning	11,481	459.00
Optional Rear Axle Ratio	2395	13.00
Power Brakes	13,558	47.00
365 hp Engine	5097	295.00
425 hp Engine	188	1221.00
330 hp Engine	1949	483.00
4-Speed Manual Transmission, close ratio	2387	0.00
4-Speed Manual Transmission, close ratio, heavy duty	130	100.00
Turbo Hydra-Matic Automatic Transmission	10,060	0.00
Tilt-Telescopic Steering Column	8130	84.30
Power Steering	17,904	115.90
Deluxe Wheel Covers	3007	63.00
White Stripe Tires, F70×15 nylon	6711	28.00
White Letter Tires, F70×15 nylon	12,449	42.00
Heavy Duty Battery (std w/LS5, LS6)	1455	15.80
Alarm System	8501	31.60
AM/FM Radio	18,078	178.00
AM/FM Radio, stereo	3431	283.00
Special Purpose LT1 Engine Package	8	1010.00
Special Purpose LS6 Engine Package	12	1747.00

Color Choices & Production

	Production		Production
Nevada Silver	1177	Sunflower Yellow	1177
Classic White	1875	Mille Miglia Red	2180
Mulsanne Blue	2465	Bridgehampton Blue	1417
Brands Hatch Green	3445	Ontario Orange	2269
Steel Cities Gray	1591	War Bonnet Yellow	3706

1972

Vehicle Specifications

	convertible	coupe
Wheelbase, in.	98.0	98.0
Length, in.	182.5	182.5
Width, in.	69.0	69.0
Track, in.	front: 58.7	front: 58.7
	rear: 59.4	rear: 59.4
Height, in.	47.9	47.9
Curb weight, lb	3593	3593

Mechanical Specifications 2-door convertible/coupe

Suspension	**front:** Independent; upper and lower A-arms, coil springs, tubular hydraulic shock absorbers, antiroll bar **rear:** Independent, lateral leaf springs, struts, U-joint halfshafts, trailing arms, tubular hydraulic shock absorbers
Wheels/Tires	8×15
Brakes	front: 11.75-inch disc rear: 11.75-inch disc
Transmission	3-speed Hydra-Matic; 4-speed manual
Standard axle ratio	3.36:1

Engine Specifications

Type	ohv V-8	ohv V-8	ohv V-8
Displacement, liters/cu in.	5.7/350	5.7/350	7.4/454
Bore × Stroke, in. × in.	4.00 × 3.48	4.00 × 3.48	4.25 × 4.00
Fuel management	1 × 4-bbl.	1 × 4-bbl.	1 × 4-bbl.
Horsepower @ rpm	200 @ 4400	255 @ 5600	270 @ 4000
Torque @ rpm, lb-ft	300 @ 2800	280 @ 4000	390 @ 3200

NA= Not Available

(1972 cont.)
Published Performance Numbers

	200 hp, 4-sp manual	255 hp, 4-sp manual	270 hp, 4-sp manual
0-60 mph, sec	8.5	6.8	6.9
0-100 mph, sec	NA	NA	NA
1/4-mile, sec @ mph	15.2 @ 83	14.1 @ 93	14.3 @ 92
source			*Motor Trend*

Base Prices & Production

	Production	Price
2-door coupe	20,496	$5533.00
2-door convertible	6508	5296.00

Options & Production

	Production	Price
Custom Interior Trim	8709	$158.00
Three Point Seat Belts	17,693	0.00
Power Windows	9495	85.35
Custom Shoulder Belts (std w/coupe)	749	42.15
Auxiliary Hardtop	2646	273.85
Vinyl Covering	811	158.00
Rear Window Defroster	2221	42.15
Air Conditioning	17,011	464.50
Optional Rear Axle Ratio	1986	12.65
Power Brakes	18,770	47.40
Air Injection Reactor	3912	0.00
270 hp Engine (NA California)	3913	294.90
255 hp Engine	1741	483.45
4-Speed Manual Transmission, close ratio	1638	0.00
Turbo Hydra-Matic Automatic Transmission	14,543	0.00
Tilt-Telescopic Steering Column	12,992	84.30
Power Steering	23,794	115.90
Deluxe Wheel Covers	3593	63.20
White Stripe Tires, F70×15 nylon	6666	30.35
White Letter Tires, F70×15 nylon	16,623	43.65
Heavy Duty Battery (std w/LS5)	2969	15.80
AM/FM Radio	19,480	178.00
AM/FM Radio, stereo	7189	283.35
California Emission Test	1967	15.80
Special Purpose LT1 Engine Package	20	1010.05

Color Choices & Production

	Production		Production
Sunflower Yellow	1543	Pewter Silver	1372
Bryar Blue	1617	Elkhart Green	4200
Classic White	2763	Mille Miglia Red	2478
Targa Blue	3198	Ontario Orange	4891
Steel Cities Gray	2346	War Bonnet Yellow	2550

1973

Vehicle Specifications

	convertible	coupe
Wheelbase, in.	98.0	98.0
Length, in.	182.5	182.5
Width, in.	69.0	69.0
Track, in.	front: 58.7	front: 58.7
	rear: 59.4	rear: 59.4
Height, in.	47.9	47.9
Curb weight, lb	3556	3556

Mechanical Specifications 2-door convertible/coupe
Suspension   **front:** Independent; upper and lower A-arms, coil springs, tubular hydraulic shock absorbers, antiroll bar

rear: Independent, lateral leaf springs, struts, U-joint halfshafts, trailing arms, tubular hydraulic shock absorbers

Wheels/Tires	8×15
Brakes	front: 11.75-inch disc
	rear: 11.75-inch disc
Transmission	3-speed Hydra-Matic; 4-speed manual
Standard axle ratio	3.36:1

Engine Specifications

Type	ohv V-8	ohv V-8	ohv V-8
Displacement, liters/cu in.	5.7/350	5.7/350	7.4/454
Bore × Stroke, in. × in.	4.00 × 3.48	4.00 × 3.48	4.25 × 4.00
Fuel management	1 × 4-bbl.	1 × 4-bbl.	1 × 4-bbl.
Horsepower @ rpm	200 @ 4400	255 @ 5600	270 @ 4000
Torque @ rpm, lb-ft	300 @ 2800	280 @ 4000	390 @ 3200

Published Performance Numbers

	270 hp, 4-sp manual
0-60 mph, sec	7.2
0-100 mph, sec	17.9
1/4-mile, sec @ mph	15.5 @ 94
source	*Road & Track*

Base Prices & Production

	Production	Price
2-door coupe	25,521	$5561.50
2-door convertible	4943	5398.50

Options & Production

	Production	Price
Custom Interior Trim	13,434	$154.00
Power Windows	14,024	83.00
Custom Shoulder Belts (std w/coupe)	788	41.00
Auxiliary Hardtop	1328	267.00
Vinyl Covering	323	62.00
Rear Window Defroster	4412	41.00
Air Conditioning	21,578	452.00
Optional Rear Axle Ratio	1791	12.00
Power Brakes	24,168	46.00
275 hp Engine	4412	250.00
250 hp Engine	5710	299.00
4-Speed Manual Transmission, close ratio	3704	0.00
Turbo Hydra-Matic Automatic Transmission	17,972	0.00
Tilt-Telescopic Steering Column	17,949	82.00
Power Steering	27,872	113.00
Deluxe Wheel Covers	1739	62.00
White Stripe Steel Belted Tires, GR70×15	19,903	32.00
White Letter Steel Belted Tires, GR70×15	4541	45.00
Heavy Duty Battery (std w/LS4)	4912	15.00
AM/FM Radio, stereo	12,482	276.00
AM/FM Radio	17,598	173.00
California Emission Test	3008	15.00
Cast Aluminum Wheels	4	175.00
Off Road Suspension and Brake Package	45	369.00

Color Choices (production numbers not available)

Classic White	Silver	Medium Blue
Dark Blue	Blue-Green	Elkhart Green
Yellow	Metallic Yellow	Mille Miglia Red
Orange		

1974

Vehicle Specifications

	convertible	coupe
Wheelbase, in.	98.0	98.0
Length, in.	185.1	185.1
Width, in.	69.0	69.0
Track, in.	front: 58.7	front: 58.7
	rear: 59.4	rear: 59.4
Height, in.	47.9	47.9
Curb weight, lb	3492	3492

Mechanical Specifications — 2-door convertible/coupe

Suspension	**front:** Independent; upper and lower A-arms, coil springs, tubular hydraulic shock absorbers, antiroll bar **rear:** Independent, lateral leaf springs, struts, U-joint halfshafts, trailing arms, tubular hydraulic shock absorbers
Wheels/Tires	8×15
Brakes	front: 11.75-inch disc rear: 11.75-inch disc
Transmission	3-speed Hydra-Matic; 4-speed manual
Standard axle ratio	3.36:1

Engine Specifications

Type	ohv V-8	ohv V-8	ohv V-8
Displacement, liters/cu in.	5.7/350	5.7/350	7.4/454
Bore × Stroke, in. × in.	4.00 × 3.48	4.00 × 3.48	4.25 × 4.00
Fuel management	1 × 4-bbl.	1 × 4-bbl.	1 × 4-bbl.
Horsepower @ rpm	195 @ 4400	250 @ 5200	270 @ 4400
Torque @ rpm, lb-ft	275 @ 2800	285 @ 4000	380 @ 2800

Base Prices & Production

	Production	Price
2-door coupe	32,028	$6001.50
2-door convertible	5474	5765.50

Options & Production

	Production	Price
Custom Interior Trim	19,959	$154.00
Power Windows	23,490	86.00
Custom Shoulder Belts (std w/coupe)	618	41.00
Auxiliary Hardtop	2612	267.00
Vinyl Covering	367	329.00
Rear Window Defroster	9322	43.00
Air Conditioning	29,397	467.00
Gymkhana Suspension	1905	7.00
Optional Rear Axle Ratio	1219	12.00
Power Brakes	33,306	49.00
270 hp Engine	3494	250.00
250 hp Engine	6690	299.00
4-Speed Manual Transmission, close ratio	3494	0.00
Turbo Hydra-Matic Automatic Transmission	25,146	0.00
Tilt-Telescopic Steering Column	27,700	82.00
Power Steering	35,944	117.00
White Stripe Steel Belted Tires, GR70×15	9140	32.00
White Letter Steel Belted Tires, GR70×15	24,102	45.00
Dual Horns	5258	4.00
AM/FM Radio, stereo	19,581	276.00
AM/FM Radio	17,374	173.00
Heavy Duty Battery (std w/LS4)	9169	15.00
Map Light (on rearview mirror)	16,101	5.00
California Emission Test	NA	20.00
Off Road Suspension and Brake Package	47	400.00

Color Choices (production numbers not available)

Classic White	Silver Mist	Corvette Gray
Corvette Medium Blue	Dark Green	Bright Yellow
Dark Brown	Medium Red	Mille Miglia Red
Corvette Orange		

1975

Vehicle Specifications

	convertible	coupe
Wheelbase, in.	98.0	98.0
Length, in.	185.2	185.2
Width, in.	69.0	69.0
Track, in.	front: 58.7	front: 58.7
	rear: 59.4	rear: 59.4
Height, in.	47.9	47.9
Curb weight, lb	3660	3660

Mechanical Specifications — 2-door convertible/coupe

Suspension	**front:** Independent; upper and lower A-arms, coil springs, tubular hydraulic shock absorbers, antiroll bar **rear:** Independent, lateral leaf springs, struts, U-joint halfshafts, trailing arms, tubular hydraulic shock absorbers
Wheels/Tires	8×15
Brakes	front: 11.75-inch disc rear: 11.75-inch disc
Transmission	3-speed Hydra-Matic; 4-speed manual
Standard axle ratio	3.36:1

Engine Specifications

Type	ohv V-8	ohv V-8
Displacement, liters/cu in.	5.7/350	5.7/350
Bore × Stroke, in. × in.	4.00 × 3.48	4.00 × 3.48
Fuel management	1 × 4-bbl.	1 × 4-bbl.
Horsepower @ rpm	165 @ 3800	205 @ 4800
Torque @ rpm, lb-ft	255 @ 2400	255 @ 3600

Published Performance Numbers — 205 hp, 4-sp manual

0-60 mph, sec	7.7
0-100 mph, sec	NA
1/4-mile, sec	16.1
source	*Car and Driver*

Base Prices & Production

	Production	Price
2-door coupe	33,836	$6810.10
2-door convertible	4629	6550.10

Options & Production

	Production	Price
Custom Interior Trim	NA	154.00
Power Windows	28,745	$93.00
Custom Shoulder Belts (std w/coupe)	646	41.00
Auxiliary Hardtop	2407	267.00
Vinyl Covering	279	350.00
Rear Window Defroster	13,760	46.00
Air Conditioning	31,914	490.00
Gymkhana Suspension	3194	7.00
Optional Rear Axle Ratio	1969	12.00
Power Brakes	35,842	50.00
205 hp Engine	2372	336.00
4-Speed Manual Transmission, close ratio	1057	0.00
Turbo Hydra-Matic Automatic Transmission	473	0.00
Tilt-Telescopic Steering Column	31,830	82.00

NA= Not Available

(1975 cont.)

Power Steering	37,591	129.00
White Stripe Steel Belted Tires, GR70×15	5233	35.00
White Letter Steel Belted Tires, GR70×15	30,407	48.00
Dual Horns	22,011	4.00
AM/FM Radio, stereo	24,701	284.00
AM/FM Radio	12,902	178.00
Heavy Duty Battery	16,778	15.00
Map Light (on rearview mirror)	21,676	5.00
California Emission Test	3037	20.00
Off Road Suspension and Brake Package	144	400.00

Color Choices & Production

	Production		Production
Classic White	8007	Silver	4710
Bright Blue	2869	Steel Blue	1268
Bright Green	1664	Bright Yellow	2883
Medium Saddle	3403	Orange Flame	3030
Dark Red	3342	Mille Miglia Red	3355

1976

Vehicle Specifications

	coupe	
Wheelbase, in.	98.0	
Length, in.	185.2	
Width, in.	69.0	
Track, in.	front: 58.7	rear: 59.4
Height, in.	47.9	
Curb weight, lb	3608	

Mechanical Specifications 2-door coupe

Suspension	**front:** Independent; upper and lower A-arms, coil springs, tubular hydraulic shock absorbers, antiroll bar
	rear: Independent, lateral leaf springs, struts, U-joint halfshafts, trailing arms, tubular hydraulic shock absorbers
Wheels/Tires	8×15
Brakes	front: 11.75-inch disc
	rear: 11.75-inch disc
Transmission	3-speed Hydra-Matic 4-speed manual
Standard axle ratio	3.08:1 (auto) 3.36:1 (manual)

Engine Specifications

Type	ohv V-8	ohv V-8
Displacement, liters/cu in.	5.7/350	5.7/350
Bore × Stroke, in. × in.	4.00 × 3.48	4.00 × 3.48
Fuel management	1 × 4-bbl.	1 × 4-bbl.
Horsepower @ rpm	180 @ 4000	210 @ 5200
Torque @ rpm, lb-ft	270 @ 2400	255 @ 3600

Published Performance Numbers

	180 hp, 4-sp man.	210 hp, 4-sp man.
0-60 mph, sec	6.8	6.8
0-100 mph, sec	20.2	19.5
1/4-mile, sec @ mph	15.4 @ 91.5	15.3 @ 92.1

Base Prices & Production

	Production	Price
2-door coupe	46,558	$7604.85

Options & Production

	Production	Price
Custom Interior Trim	36,762	$164.00
Power Windows	38,700	107.00
Rear Window Defogger	24,960	78.00

Air Conditioning	40,787	523.00
Gymkhana Suspension	5368	35.00
Optional Rear Axle Ratio	1371	13.00
Power Brakes	46,558	59.00
210 hp Engine	5720	481.00
4-Speed Manual Transmission, close ratio	2088	0.00
Turbo Hydra-Matic Automatic Transmission	36,625	0.00
Tilt-Telescopic Steering Column	41,797	95.00
Power Steering	46,385	151.00
White Stripe Steel Belted Tires, GR70×15	3992	37.00
White Letter Steel Belted Tires, GR70×15	39,923	51.00
AM/FM Radio, stereo	34,272	281.00
AM/FM Radio	11,083	187.00
Heavy Duty Battery	25,909	16.00
Map Light (on rearview mirror)	35,361	10.00
California Emission Test	3527	50.00
Aluminum Wheels	6253	299.00

Color Choices & Production

	Production		Production
Classic White	10,674	Silver	6934
Bright Blue	3268	Dark Green	2038
Mahogany	4182	Bright Yellow	3389
Buckskin	2954	Dark Brown	4447
Orange Flame	4073	Red	4590

1977

Vehicle Specifications

	coupe	
Wheelbase, in.	98.0	
Length, in.	185.2	
Width, in.	69.0	
Track, in.	front: 58.7	rear: 59.4
Height, in.	47.9	
Curb weight, lb	3595	

Mechanical Specifications 2-door coupe

Suspension	**front:** Independent; upper and lower A-arms, coil springs, tubular hydraulic shock absorbers, antiroll bar
	rear: Independent, lateral leaf springs, struts, U-joint halfshafts, trailing arms, tubular hydraulic shock absorbers
Wheels/Tires	8×15
Brakes	front: 11.75-inch disc
	rear: 11.75-inch disc
Transmission	3-speed Hydra-Matic (std)
	4-speed manual (opt)
Standard axle ratio	3.36:1

Engine Specifications

Type	ohv V-8	ohv V-8
Displacement, liters/cu in.	5.7/350	5.7/350
Bore × Stroke, in. × in.	4.00 × 3.48	4.00 × 3.48
Fuel management	1 × 4-bbl.	1 × 4-bbl.
Horsepower @ rpm	180 @ 4000	210 @ 5200
Torque @ rpm, lb-ft	270 @ 2400	255 @ 3600

Base Prices & Production

	Production	Price
2-door coupe	49,213	$8647.65

Options & Production

Options & Production	Production	Price
Power Windows	44,341	$116.00
Color Keyed Floor Mats	36,763	22.00
Rear Window Defogger	30,411	84.00
Air Conditioning	45,249	553.00
Sport Mirrors	20,206	36.00
Gymkhana Suspension	7269	38.00
Optional Rear Axle Ratio	972	14.00
Speed Control	29,161	88.00
210 hp Engine	6148	495.00
4-Speed Manual Transmission, close ratio	2060	0.00
Turbo Hydra-Matic Automatic Transmission	41,231	0.00
High Altitude Emission Equipment	854	22.00
Tilt-Telescopic Steering Column	46,487	165.00
White Letter Steel Belted Tires, GR70×15	46,227	57.00
AM/FM Radio, stereo	18,483	281.00
AM/FM Radio	4700	187.00
AM/FM Radio, stereo w/8-track tape	24,603	414.00
Luggage and Roof Panel Rack	16,860	73.00
California Emission Certification	4084	70.00
Aluminum Wheels	12,646	321.00
Trailer Package	289	83.00
Convenience Group	40,872	22.00

Color Choices & Production

	Production		Production
Classic White	9408	Silver	5518
Black	6070	Corvette Light Blue	5967
Corvette Dark Blue	4065	Corvette Chartreuse	1
Corvette Yellow	71	Corvette Bright Yellow	1942
Corvette Orange	4012	Corvette Tan	4588
Medium Red	4057	Corvette Dark Red	3434

1978

Vehicle Specifications

	coupe	
Wheelbase, in.	98.0	
Length, in.	185.2	
Width, in.	69.0	
Track, in.	front: 58.7	rear: 59.4
Height, in.	47.9	
Curb weight, lb	3595	

Mechanical Specifications 2-door coupe

Suspension	**front:** Independent; upper and lower A-arms, coil springs, tubular hydraulic shock absorbers, antiroll bar **rear:** Independent, lateral leaf springs, struts, U-joint halfshafts, trailing arms, tubular hydraulic shock absorbers
Wheels/Tires	P277/70R-15
Brakes	front: 11.75-inch disc rear: 11.75-inch disc
Transmission	3-speed Hydra-Matic 4-speed manual
Standard axle ratio	3.08:1 (auto) 3.36:1 (manual)

Engine Specifications

Type	ohv V-8	ohv V-8
Displacement, liters/cu in.	5.7/350	5.7/350
Bore × Stroke, in. × in.	4.00 × 3.48	4.00 × 3.48
Fuel management	1 × 4-bbl.	1 × 4-bbl.
Horsepower @ rpm	185 @ 4000	220 @ 5200
Torque @ rpm, lb-ft	270 @ 2400	260 @ 3600

Published Performance Numbers — 220 hp, 4-sp manual

0-60 mph, sec	6.5
0-100 mph, sec	17.9
1/4-mile, sec @ mph	15.2 @ 95

Base Prices & Production

Base Prices & Production	Production	Price
2-door coupe	40,274	$9351.89
Limited Edition Corvette (pace car)	6502	13653.21

Options & Production

Options & Production	Production	Price
Power Windows	36,931	$130.00
Power Door Locks	12,187	120.00
Silver Anniversary Paint	15,283	399.00
Removable Glass Roof Panels	972	349.00
Rear Window Defogger	30,912	95.00
Air Conditioning	37,638	605.00
Sport Mirrors	38,405	40.00
Gymkhana Suspension	12,590	41.00
Optional Rear Axle Ratio	382	15.00
Cruise Control	31,608	99.00
220 hp Engine	12,739	525.00
4-Speed Manual Transmission, close ratio	3385	0.00
Automatic Transmission	38,614	0.00
High Altitude Emission Equipment	260	33.00
Tilt-Telescopic Steering Column	37,858	175.00
White Letter SBR Tires, P255/60R15	18,296	216.32
White Letter SBR Tires, P255/70R15	26,203	51.00
Heavy Duty Battery	28,243	18.00
AM/FM Radio, stereo w/8-track tape	20,899	419.00
AM/FM Radio, stereo w/CB	7138	638.00
AM/FM Radio, stereo	10,189	286.00
AM/FM Radio	2057	199.00
Power Antenna	23,069	49.00
California Emission Certification	3405	75.00
Aluminum Wheels	28,008	340.00
Trailer Package	972	89.00
Convenience Group	37,222	84.00

Color Choices & Production

	Production		Production
Classic White	4150	Silver	3232
Silver Anniversary	15,283	Black	4573
Black/Silver	6502	Corvette Light Blue	1960
Corvette Yellow	1243	Corvette Light Beige	1686
Corvette Red	2074	Corvette Mahogany	2121
Corvette Dark Blue	2084	Corvette Dark Brown	1991

1979

Vehicle Specifications

	coupe	
Wheelbase, in.	98.0	
Length, in.	185.2	
Width, in.	69.0	
Track, in.	front: 58.7	rear: 59.4
Height, in.	47.9	
Curb weight, lb	3565	

Mechanical Specifications 2-door coupe

Suspension	**front:** Independent; upper and lower A-arms, coil springs, tubular hydraulic shock absorbers, antiroll bar **rear:** Independent, lateral leaf springs, struts, U-joint halfshafts, trailing arms, tubular hydraulic shock absorbers
Wheels/Tires	P225/70R-15

NA= Not Available

(1979 cont.)

Brakes	front: 11.75-inch disc	
	rear: 11.75-inch disc	
Transmission	3-speed Hydra-Matic	4-speed manual
Standard axle ratio	3.55:1 (auto)	3.36:1 (manual)

Engine Specifications

Type	ohv V-8	ohv V-8
Displacement, liters/cu in.	5.7/350	5.7/350
Bore × Stroke, in. × in.	4.00 × 3.48	4.00 × 3.48
Fuel management	1 × 4-bbl.	1 × 4-bbl.
Horsepower @ rpm	185 @ 4000	220 @ 5200
Torque @ rpm, lb-ft	270 @ 2400	260 @ 3600

Published Performance Numbers

	220 hp, 4-sp manual
0-60 mph, sec	6.6
0-100 mph, sec	18.5
1/4-mile, sec @ mph	15.6 @ 91

Base Prices & Production

	Production	Price
2-door coupe	53,807	$10,220.23

Options & Production

	Production	Price
Power Windows	20,631	$141.00
Power Door Locks	9054	131.00
Removable Glass Roof Panels	14,480	365.00
Rear Window Defogger	41,587	102.00
Air Conditioning	47,136	635.00
Sport Mirrors	48,211	45.00
Spoilers, front and rear	6853	265.00
Gymkhana Suspension	12,321	49.00
Heavy Duty Shock Absorbers	2164	33.00
Optional Rear Axle Ratio	428	19.00
Cruise Control	34,445	113.00
225 hp Engine	14,516	565.00
4-Speed Manual Transmission, close ratio	4062	0.00
Automatic Transmission	41,454	0.00
High Altitude Emission Equipment	56	35.00
Tilt-Telescopic Steering Column	47,463	190.00
Aluminum Wheels	33,741	380.00
White Letter SBR Tires, P255/60R15	17,920	226.20
White Letter SBR Tires, P255/70R15	29,603	54.00
AM/FM Radio, stereo w/8-track tape	21,435	228.00
AM/FM Radio, stereo w/CB	4483	439.00
AM/FM Radio, stereo w/cassette	12,110	234.00
AM/FM Radio, stereo	9256	90.00
Power Antenna	35,730	52.00
Dual Rear Speakers	37,754	52.00
Heavy Duty Battery	3405	21.00
California Emission Certification	3798	83.00
Trailer Package	1001	98.00
Power Windows and Door Locks	28,465	272.00
Convenience Group	41,530	94.00

Color Choices & Production

	Production		Production
Classic White	8629	Silver	7331
Black	10,465	Corvette Light Blue	3203
Corvette Yellow	2357	Corvette Dark Green	2426
Corvette Light Beige	2951	Corvette Red	6707
Corvette Dark Blue	5670	Corvette Dark Brown	4053

1980

Vehicle Specifications

	coupe	
Wheelbase, in.	98.0	
Length, in.	185.3	
Width, in.	69.0	
Track, in.	front: 58.7	rear: 59.4
Height, in.	48.0	
Curb weight, lb	3495	

Mechanical Specifications — 2-door coupe

Suspension	**front:** Independent; upper and lower A-arms, coil springs, tubular hydraulic shock absorbers, antiroll bar **rear:** Independent, lateral leaf springs, struts, U-joint halfshafts, trailing arms, tubular hydraulic shock absorbers
Wheels/Tires	P225/70R-15
Brakes	front: 11.75-inch disc
	rear: 11.75-inch disc
Transmission	3-speed Hydra-Matic 4-speed manual
Standard axle ratio	3.55:1 (auto) 3.07:1 (manual)

Engine Specifications

Type	ohv V-8	ohv V-8	ohv V-8
Displacement, liters/cu in.	5.0/305	5.7/350	5.7/350
Bore × Stroke, in. × in.	3.74 × 3.48	4.00 × 3.48	4.00 × 3.48
Fuel management	1 × 4-bbl.	1 × 4-bbl.	1 × 4-bbl.
Horsepower @ rpm	180 @ 4200	185 @ 4000	220 @ 5200
Torque @ rpm, lb-ft	255 @ 2000	270 @ 2400	260 @ 3600

Base Prices & Production

	Production	Price
2-door coupe	40,614	$13,140.24

Options & Production

	Production	Price
Power Door Locks	32,692	$140.00
Removable Glass Roof Panels	19,695	391.00
Rear Window Defogger	36,589	109.00
Gymkhana Suspension	9907	55.00
Heavy Duty Shock Absorbers	1695	35.00
Cruise Control	30,821	123.00
180 hp Engine (required in California)	3221	-50.00
230 hp Engine	5069	595.00
4-Speed Manual Transmission	5726	0.00
Automatic Transmission	34,838	0.00
Aluminum Wheels	34,128	407.00
White Letter SBR Tires, P225/70R15	26,208	62.00
White Letter SBR Tires, P255/60R15	13,140	426.16
Heavy Duty Battery	1337	22.00
AM/FM Radio, stereo w/8-track tape	15,708	155.00
AM/FM Radio, stereo w/CB	2434	391.00
AM/FM Radio, stereo w/cassette	15,148	168.00
AM/FM Radio, stereo	6138	46.00
Power Antenna	32,863	56.00
Radio Delete	201	-126.00
Dual Rear Speakers	36,650	52.00
Roof Panel Carrier	3755	125.00
California Emission Certification	3221	250.00
Trailer Package	796	105.00

Color Choices & Production

	Production		Production
White	7780	Silver	4341
Black	7250	Dark Blue	4135
Dark Brown	2300	Yellow	2077
Dark Green	844	Frost Beige	3070
Dark Claret	3451	Red	5714

1981

Vehicle Specifications — coupe

Wheelbase, in.	98.0
Length, in.	185.3
Width, in.	69.0
Track, in.	front: 58.7 rear: 59.4
Height, in.	48.0
Curb weight, lb	3345

Mechanical Specifications — 2-door coupe

Suspension	**front:** Independent; upper and lower A-arms, coil springs, tubular hydraulic shock absorbers, antiroll bar **rear:** Independent, lateral leaf springs, struts, U-joint halfshafts, trailing arms, tubular hydraulic shock absorbers
Wheels/Tires	P225/70R-15
Brakes	front: 11.75-inch disc rear: 11.75-inch disc
Transmission	4-speed manual 3-speed Hydra-Matic
Standard axle ratio	2.72:1 (manual) 2.87:1 (auto)

Engine Specifications

Type	ohv V-8
Displacement, liters/cu in.	5.7/350
Bore × Stroke, in. × in.	4.00 × 3.48
Fuel management	1 × 4-bbl.
Horsepower @ rpm	190 @ 4200
Torque @ rpm, lb-ft	280 @ 1600

Published Performance Numbers — 190 hp, 4-sp manual

0-60 mph, sec	8.1
0-100 mph, sec	NA
1/4-mile, sec @ mph	NA

Base Prices & Production

	Production	Price
2-door coupe	40,606	$16,258.52

Options & Production

	Production	Price
Power Door Locks	36,322	$145.00
Power Driver Seat	29,200	183.00
Removable Glass Roof Panels	29,095	414.00
Rear Window Defogger	36,893	119.00
Electric Sport Mirrors	13,567	117.00
Two-Tone Paint	5352	399.00
Gymkhana Suspension	7803	57.00
Heavy Duty Shock Absorbers	1128	37.00
Performance Axle Ratio	2400	20.00
Cruise Control	32,522	155.00
4-Speed Manual Transmission	5757	0.00
Aluminum Wheels	36,485	428.00
White Letter SBR Tires, P225/70R15	21,939	72.00
White Letter SBR Tires, P255/60R15	18,004	491.92
Radio Delete	315	-118.00
AM/FM Radio, etr stereo w/8-track	8262	386.00
AM/FM Radio, etr stereo w/8-track & CB	792	712.00
AM/FM Radio, etr stereo w/cassette	22,892	423.00
AM/FM Radio, etr stereo w/cassette & CB	2349	750.00
AM/FM Radio, stereo	5145	95.00
Power Antenna	32,903	55.00
Roof Panel Carrier	3303	135.00
California Emission Certification	4951	46.00
Trailer Package	916	110.00

Color Choices & Production

	Production		Production
Mahogany Metallic	1092	White	6387
Code 13 Silver Metallic	2590	Black	4712
Code 33 Silver Metallic	3369	Code 28 Dark Blue Metallic	2522
Bright Blue Metallic	1		
Code 39 Charcoal Metallic	613	Code 38 Dark Blue Metallic	496
Code 84 Charcoal Metallic	3485	Code 50 Beige	2239
Dark Bronze	432	Code 59 Beige	3842
Maroon Metallic	1618	Autumn Red	1505
Red	4310	Dark Claret Metallic	NA
Yellow	1031	Silver/Charcoal	NA
Silver/Dark Blue	NA	Autumn Red/Dark Claret	NA
Beige/Dark Bronze	NA		

1982

Vehicle Specifications — coupe/hatchback

Wheelbase, in.	98.0
Length, in.	185.3
Width, in.	69.0
Track, in.	front: 58.7 rear: 59.4
Height, in.	48.0
Curb weight, lb	3345

Mechanical Specifications — 2-door coupe/hatchback

Suspension	**front:** Independent; upper and lower A-arms, coil springs, tubular hydraulic shock absorbers, antiroll bar **rear:** Independent, lateral leaf springs, struts, U-joint halfshafts, trailing arms, tubular hydraulic shock absorbers
Wheels/Tires	P225/70R-15 P255/60R-15 (Collector Edition)
Brakes	front: 11.75-inch disc rear: 11.75-inch disc
Transmission	3-speed Hydra-Matic
Standard axle ratio	2.72:1

Engine Specifications

Type	ohv V-8
Displacement, liters/cu in.	5.7/350
Bore × Stroke, in. × in.	4.00 × 3.48
Fuel management	Cross-Fire Throttle Body Fuel Injection
Horsepower @ rpm	200 @ 4200
Torque @ rpm, lb-ft	283 @ 2800

Published Performance Numbers — 200 hp, 3-sp automatic

0-60 mph, sec	7.9
0-100 mph, sec	24.8
1/4-mile, sec @ mph	16.1 @ 85

Base Prices & Production

	Production	Price
2-door coupe	18,648	$18,290.07
Corvette Collector Edition Hatchback	6759	22,537.59

Options & Production

	Production	Price
Power Door Locks	23,936	$155.00
Power Driver Seat	22,585	197.00
Removable Glass Roof Panels	14,763	443.00
Rear Window Defogger	16,886	129.00
Electric Sport Mirrors	20,301	125.00
Two-Tone Paint	4871	428.00
Gymkhana Suspension	5457	61.00
Cruise Control	24,313	165.00
Aluminum Wheels	16,844	458.00
White Letter SBR Tires, P225/70R15	5932	80.00

NA = Not Available

(1982 cont.)

	Production	Price
White Letter SBR Tires, P255/60R15	19,070	542.52
Radio Delete	150	-124.00
AM/FM Radio, etr stereo w/8-track	923	386.00
AM/FM Radio, etr stereo w/cassette	20,355	423.00
AM/FM Radio, etr stereo w/cassette & CB	1987	755.00
AM/FM Radio, stereo	1533	101.00
Power Antenna	15,557	60.00
Heavy Duty Cooling	6006	57.00
Roof Panel Carrier	1992	144.00
California Emission Certification	4951	46.00

Color Choices & Production

	Production		Production
White	2975	Silver	711
Black	2357	Silver Blue	1124
Dark Blue	562	Bright Blue	567
Charcoal	1093	Silver Green	723
Gold	648	Silver Beige	6759
Red	2155	Dark Claret	853
White/Silver	664	Silver/Charcoal	1239
Silver/Dark Claret	1301	Silver Blue/Dark Blue	1667

1984

Vehicle Specifications
hatchback

Wheelbase, in.	96.2
Length, in.	176.5
Width, in.	71.0
Track, in.	front: 59.6 rear: 60.4
Height, in.	46.7
Curb weight, lb	3200

Mechanical Specifications
2-door hatchback

Suspension	**front:** Independent; unequal length upper and lower A-arms, transverse fiberglass leaf spring, tubular hydraulic shock absorbers, antiroll bar
	rear: Independent, upper and lower trailing arms, lateral arms, tie rods, halfshafts, transverse fiberglass leaf springs, tubular hydraulic shock absorbers, antiroll bar
Wheels/Tires	P255/50VR-16
Brakes	front: 11.5-inch disc
	rear: 11.5-inch disc
Transmission	4-speed automatic *4+3-speed manual
Standard axle ratio	2.73:1 (auto) 3.07:1 (manual)

Engine Specifications

Type	ohv V-8
Displacement, liters/cu in.	5.7/350
Bore × Stroke, in. × in.	4.00 × 3.48
Fuel management	Cross-Fire Throttle Body Fuel Injection
Horsepower @ rpm	205 @ 4300
Torque @ rpm, lb-ft	290 @ 2800

Published Performance Numbers
205 hp, 4-sp automatic

0-60 mph, sec	7.0
0-100 mph, sec	NA
1/4-mile, sec @ mph	15.5 @ 88

Base Prices & Production

	Production	Price
2-door coupe	51,547	$21,800.00

*4+3= 4-speed manual with overdrive in 3rd and 4th gears

Options & Production

	Production	Price
Power Driver Seat	48,702	$210.00
Sport Seats, cloth	4003	625.00
Base Seats, leather	40,568	400.00
Power Door Locks	49,545	165.00
Removable Transparent Glass Roof Panel	15,767	595.00
Two-Tone Paint	8755	428.00
Delco-Bilstein Shock Absorbers	3729	189.00
Performance Axle Ratio	410	22.00
Engine Oil Cooler	4295	158.00
Cruise Control	49,832	185.00
4-Speed Manual Transmission	6443	0.00
P255/50VR16 Tires/16 Wheels	51,547	561.20
Radio Delete	104	-331.00
AM/FM Radio Stereo Cassette	6689	153.00
AM/FM Radio Stereo, CB	178	215.00
Stereo System, Delco-Bose	43,607	895.00
Heavy Duty Radiator	12,008	57.00
California Emission Requirements	6833	75.00
Performance Handling Package	25,995	600.20
Rear Window + Side Mirror Defoggers	47,680	160.00

Color Choices & Production

	Production		Production
White	6417	Bright Silver Metallic	3109
Medium Gray Metallic	3147	Black	7906
Light Blue Metallic	1196	Medium Blue Metallic	1822
Gold Metallic	2430	Light Bronze Metallic	2452
Dark Bronze Metallic	1371	Bright Red	12,942
Silver/Medium Gray	3629	Light Blue/Medium Blue	1433
Light Bronze/Dark Bronze	3693		

1985

Vehicle Specifications
hatchback

Wheelbase, in.	96.2
Length, in.	176.5
Width, in.	71.0
Track, in.	front: 59.6 rear: 60.4
Height, in.	46.7
Curb weight, lb	3230

Mechanical Specifications
2-door hatchback

Suspension	**front:** Independent; unequal length upper and lower A-arms, transverse fiberglass leaf spring, tubular hydraulic shock absorbers, antiroll bar
	rear: Independent, upper and lower trailing arms, lateral arms, tie rods, halfshafts, transverse fiberglass leaf springs, tubular hydraulic shock absorbers, antiroll bar
Wheels/Tires	P255/50VR-16
Brakes	front: 11.5-inch disc
	rear: 11.5-inch disc
Transmission	4-speed automatic *4+3-speed manual
Standard axle ratio	2.73:1 (auto) 3.07:1 (manual)

Engine Specifications

Type	ohv V-8
Displacement, liters/cu in.	5.7/350
Bore × Stroke, in. × in.	4.00 × 3.48
Fuel management	Tuned Port Injection
Horsepower @ rpm	230 @ 4000
Torque @ rpm, lb-ft	330 @ 3200

Published Performance Numbers	230 hp, 4-sp manual
0-60 mph, sec	5.7
0-100 mph, sec	NA
1/4-mile, sec @ mph	14.1 @ 97
source	*Car and Driver*

Base Prices & Production	Production	Price
2-door coupe	39,729	$24,403.00

Options & Production	Production	Price
Power Driver Seat	37,856	$215.00
Sport Seats, leather	NA	1025.00
Base Seats, leather	NA	400.00
Sport Seats, cloth	5661	625.00
Power Door Locks	38,294	170.00
Removable Transparent Glass Roof Panel	28,143	595.00
Two-Tone Paint	6033	428.00
Delco-Bilstein Shock Absorbers	9333	189.00
Performance Axle Ratio	5447	22.00
Cruise Control	38,369	185.00
4-Speed Manual Transmission	9576	0.00
California Emission Requirements	6583	99.00
Radio Delete	172	-256.00
AM/FM Radio Stereo Cassette	2958	122.00
AM/FM Radio Stereo, CB	16	215.00
Stereo System, Delco-Bose	35,998	895.00
Heavy Duty Cooling	17,539	225.00
Performance Handling Package	14,802	470.00
Rear Window + Side Mirror Defoggers	37,720	160.00

Color Choices & Production

	Production		Production
Silver Metallic	1752	Medium Gray Metallic	2519
Light Blue Metallic	1021	Medium Blue Metallic	2041
White	4455	Black	7603
Gold Metallic	1411	Light Bronze Metallic	1440
Dark Bronze Metallic	1030	Bright Red	10,424
Silver/Gray	2170	Light Blue/Medium Blue	1470
Light Bronze/Dark Bronze	2393		

1986

Vehicle Specifications	hatchback	convertible
Wheelbase, in.	96.2	96.2
Length, in.	176.5	176.5
Width, in.	71.0	71.0
Track, in.	front: 59.6	front: 59.6
	rear: 60.4	rear: 60.4
Height, in.	46.7	46.4
Curb weight, lb	3101	3279

Mechanical Specifications 2-door hatchback/convertible
Suspension — **front:** Independent; unequal length upper and lower A-arms, transverse fiberglass leaf spring, tubular hydraulic shock absorbers, antiroll bar
rear: Independent, upper and lower trailing arms, lateral arms, tie rods, halfshafts, transverse fiberglass leaf springs, tubular hydraulic shock absorbers, antiroll bar
Wheels/Tires — P255/60VR-16
Brakes — front: antilock 11.5-inch disc
rear: antilock 11.5-inch disc

Transmission	4-speed automatic	*4+3-speed manual
Standard axle ratio	2.59:1 (auto)	3.07:1 (manual)

Engine Specifications

Type	ohv V-8
Displacement, liters/cu in.	5.7/350
Bore × Stroke, in. × in.	4.00 × 3.48
Fuel management	Tuned Port Injection
Horsepower @ rpm	230 @ 4000
Torque @ rpm, lb-ft	330 @ 3200

Base Prices & Production	Production	Price
2-door coupe	27,794	$27,027.00
2-door convertible	7315	32,032.00

Options & Production	Production	Price
Power Driver Seat	33,983	$225.00
Sport Seats, leather	13,372	1025.00
Base Seats, leather	NA	400.00
Power Door Locks	34,215	175.00
Radiator Boost Fan	8216	75.00
Custom Feature Package	4832	195.00
Dual Removable Roof Panels	6242	895.00
Removable Roof Panel, blue tint	12,021	595.00
Removable Roof Panel, bronze tint	7819	595.00
Electronic Air Conditioning Control	16,646	150.00
Two-Tone Paint (coupe)	3897	428.00
Delco-Bilstein Shock Absorbers	5521	189.00
Performance Axle Ratio, 3.07:1	4879	22.00
Engine Oil Cooler	7394	110.00
Cruise Control	34,197	185.00
4-Speed Manual Transmission	6835	0.00
California Emission Requirements	5697	99.00
Radio Delete	166	-256.00
AM/FM Radio Stereo Cassette	2039	122.00
Stereo System, Delco-Bose	32,478	895.00
Heavy Duty Radiator	10,423	40.00
Performance Handling Package (coupe)	12,821	470.00
Rear Window + Side Mirror Defoggers (coupe)	21,837	165.00
Malcolm Konner Special Edition (coupe)	50	500.00

Color Choices & Production

	Production		Production
Silver Metallic	1209	Medium Gray Metallic	1603
Medium Blue Metallic	128	Yellow	1464
White	4176	Black	5464
Gold Metallic	777	Silver Beige Metallic	1383
Copper Metallic	4	Medium Brown Metallic	488
Dark Red Metallic	5002	Bright Red	9466
Silver/Gray	1049	Gray/Black	1138
White/Silver	693	Silver Beige/Medium Brown	1014
Silver Beige/Black	50		

1987

Vehicle Specifications	hatchback	convertible
Wheelbase, in.	96.2	96.2
Length, in.	176.5	176.5
Width, in.	71.0	71.0
Track, in.	front: 59.6	front: 59.6
	rear: 60.4	rear: 60.4
Height, in.	46.7	46.4
Curb weight, lb	3216	3279

NA= Not Available

(1987 cont.)

Mechanical Specifications 2-door hatchback/convertible

Suspension	**front:** Independent; unequal length upper and lower A-arms, transverse fiberglass leaf spring, tubular hydraulic shock absorbers, antiroll bar **rear:** Independent, upper and lower trailing arms, lateral arms, tie rods, halfshafts, transverse fiberglass leaf springs, tubular hydraulic shock absorbers, antiroll bar
Wheels/Tires	P245/60VR-15
Brakes	front: antilock 11.5-inch disc rear: antilock 11.5-inch disc
Transmission	4-speed automatic *4+3-speed manual
Standard axle ratio	2.59:1 (auto) 3.07:1 (manual)

Engine Specifications

Type	ohv V-8
Displacement, liters/cu in.	5.7/350
Bore × Stroke, in. × in.	4.00 × 3.48
Fuel management	Tuned Port Injection
Horsepower @ rpm	240 @ 4000
Torque @ rpm, lb-ft	345 @ 3200

Published Performance Numbers   240 hp, 4-sp manual

0-60 mph, sec	6.3
0-100 mph, sec	NA
1/4-mile, sec @ mph	15.11 @ 93.8
Source	*Motor Trend*

Base Prices & Production

	Production	Price
2-door coupe	20,007	$27,999.00
2-door convertible	10,625	33,172.00

Options & Production

	Production	Price
Power Passenger Seat	17,124	$240.00
Power Driver Seat	29,561	240.00
Sport Seats, leather	14,119	1025.00
Base Seats, leather	14,579	400.00
Power Door Locks	29,748	190.00
Callaway Twin Turbo (not GM installed)	184	19,995.00
Radiator Boost Fan	7291	75.00
Dual Removable Roof Panels	5017	915.00
Removable Roof Panel, blue tint	8883	615.00
Removable Roof Panel, bronze tint	5766	615.00
Electronic Air Conditioning Control	20,875	150.00
Twin Remote Heated Mirrors (convertible)	6840	35.00
Illuminated Driver Vanity Mirror	14,992	58.00
Two-Tone Paint (coupe)	1361	428.00
Delco-Bilstein Shock Absorbers	1957	189.00
Performance Axle Ratio, 3.07:1	7285	22.00
Engine Oil Cooler	6679	110.00
Cruise Control	29,594	185.00
4-Speed Manual Transmission	4229	0.00
California Emission Requirements	5423	99.00
Radio Delete	247	-256.00
AM/FM Radio Stereo Cassette	2182	132.00
Stereo System, Delco-Bose	27,721	905.00
Heavy Duty Radiator	7871	40.00
Performance Handling Package (coupe)	1596	470.00
Rear Window + Side Mirror Defoggers (coupe)	19,043	165.00

Color Choices & Production

	Production		Production
Silver Metallic	767	Medium Gray Metallic	1035
Medium Blue Metallic	2677	Yellow	1051
White	3097	Black	5101
Gold Metallic	397	Silver Beige Metallic	950
Copper Metallic	87	Medium Brown Metallic	245
Dark Red Metallic	5578	Bright Red	8285
Silver/Gray	403	Gray/Black	316
White/Silver	195	Silver Beige/Medium Brown	447

1988

Vehicle Specifications

	hatchback	convertible
Wheelbase, in.	96.2	96.2
Length, in.	176.5	176.5
Width, in.	71.0	71.0
Track, in.	front: 59.6	front: 59.6
	rear: 60.4	rear: 60.4
Height, in.	46.7	46.4
Curb weight, lb	3216	3279

Mechanical Specifications 2-door hatchback/convertible

Suspension	**front:** Independent; unequal length upper and lower A-arms, transverse fiberglass leaf spring, tubular hydraulic shock absorbers, antiroll bar **rear:** Independent, upper and lower trailing arms, lateral arms, tie rods, halfshafts, transverse fiberglass leaf springs, tubular hydraulic shock absorbers, antiroll bar
Wheels/Tires	P255/50ZR-16
Brakes	front: antilock 11.5-inch disc rear: antilock 11.5-inch disc
Transmission	4-speed automatic *4+3-speed manual
Standard axle ratio	2.59:1 (auto) 3.07:1 (manual)

Engine Specifications

Type	ohv V-8	ohv V-8
Displacement, liters/cu in.	5.7/350	5.7/350
Bore × Stroke, in. × in.	4.00 × 3.48	4.00 × 3.48
Fuel management	Tuned Port Injection	Tuned Port Injection
Horsepower @ rpm	240 @ 4300	245 @ 4300
Torque @ rpm, lb-ft	340 @ 3200	340 @ 3200

Published Performance Numbers   240 hp, 4-sp automatic

0-60 mph, sec	5.6
0-100 mph, sec	16.3
1/4-mile, sec @ mph	14.3 @ 95
Source	*Car and Driver*

Base Prices & Production

	Production	Price
2-door coupe	15,382	$29,489.00
2-door convertible	7407	34,820.00

Options & Production

	Production	Price
Power Passenger Seat	18,779	$240.00
Power Driver Seat	22,084	240.00
Sport Seats, leather	12,724	1025.00
Base Seats, leather	9043	400.00
Callaway Twin Turbo (not GM installed)	124	25,895.00
Radiator Boost Fan	19,035	75.00
Dual Removable Roof Panels	5091	915.00
Removable Roof Panel, blue tint	8332	615.00
Removable Roof Panel, bronze tint	3337	615.00

*4+3= 4-speed manual with overdrive in 3rd and 4th gears

Electronic Air Conditioning Control	19,372	150.00
Twin Remote Heated Mirrors (convertible)	6582	35.00
Illuminated Driver Vanity Mirror	14,249	58.00
Delco-Bilstein Shock Absorbers	18,437	189.00
Performance Axle Ratio, 3.07:1	4497	22.00
Engine Oil Cooler	18,877	110.00
4-Speed Manual Transmission	4282	0.00
California Emission Requirements	3882	99.00
Radio Delete	179	-297.00
Stereo System, Delco-Bose	20,304	773.00
Heavy Duty Radiator	19,271	40.00
35th Special Edition Package (coupe)	2050	4795.00
Performance Handling Package (coupe)	1309	1295.00
Rear Window + Side Mirror Defoggers (coupe)	14,648	165.00

Color Choices & Production

	Production		Production
Silver Metallic	385	Medium Blue Metallic	1148
Dark Blue Metallic	1675	Yellow	578
White	3620	Black	3420
Dark Red Metallic	2878	Bright Red	5340
Gray Metallic	644	Charcoal Metallic	1046
White/Black	2050		

1989

Vehicle Specifications	hatchback	convertible
Wheelbase, in.	96.2	96.2
Length, in.	176.5	176.5
Width, in.	71.0	71.0
Track, in.	front: 59.6	front: 59.6
	rear: 60.4	rear: 60.4
Height, in.	46.7	46.4
Curb weight, lb	3229	3269

Mechanical Specifications 2-door hatchback/convertible

Suspension	**front:** Independent; unequal length upper and lower A-arms, transverse fiberglass leaf spring, tubular hydraulic shock absorbers, antiroll bar **rear:** Independent, upper and lower trailing arms, lateral arms, tie rods, halfshafts, transverse fiberglass leaf springs, tubular hydraulic shock absorbers, antiroll bar
Wheels/Tires	P275/40VR-17
Brakes	front: antilock 12.0-inch disc rear: antilock 12.0-inch disc
Transmission	4-speed automatic 6-speed manual
Standard axle ratio	2.59:1 (auto) 3.33:1 (manual)

Engine Specifications

Type	ohv V-8
Displacement, liters/cu in.	5.7/350
Bore × Stroke, in. × in.	4.00 × 3.48
Fuel management	Tuned Port Injection
Horsepower @ rpm	245 @ 4300
Torque @ rpm, lb-ft	340 @ 3200

Published Performance Numbers

245 hp, 6-sp manual

0-60 mph, sec	5.4
0-100 mph, sec	14.42
1/4-mile, sec @ mph	NA

Base Prices & Production

	Production	Price
2-door coupe	16,663	$31,545.00
2-door convertible	9749	36,785.00

Options & Production

	Production	Price
Power Passenger Seat	20,578	$240.00
Power Driver Seat	25,606	240.00
Sport Seats, leather	1777	1025.00
Base Seats, leather	23,364	400.00
Callaway Twin Turbo (not GM installed)	69	25,895.00
Radiator Boost Fan	20,281	75.00
Auxiliary Hardtop	1573	1995.00
Dual Removable Roof Panels	5274	915.00
Removable Roof Panel, blue tint	8748	615.00
Removable Roof Panel, bronze tint	4042	615.00
Electronic Air Conditioning Control	24,675	150.00
Illuminated Driver Vanity Mirror	17,414	58.00
Selective Ride and Handling, electronic	1573	1695.00
Performance Axle Ratio	10,211	22.00
Engine Block Heater	2182	20.00
Engine Oil Cooler	20,162	110.00
6-Speed Manual Transmission	4113	0.00
California Emission Requirements	4501	100.00
Low Tire Pressure Warning Indicator	6976	325.00
Stereo System, Delco-Bose	24,145	773.00
Heavy Duty Radiator	20,888	40.00
Luggage Rack (convertible)	616	140.00
Performance Handling Package (coupe)	2224	575.00

Color Choices & Production

	Production		Production
White	5426	Medium Blue Metallic	1428
Dark Blue Metallic	1931	Black	4855
Dark Red Metallic	3409	Bright Red	7663
Gray Metallic	225	Charcoal Metallic	1440

1990

Vehicle Specifications	hatchback	hatchback (ZR-1)
Wheelbase, in.	96.2	96.2
Length, in.	176.5	177.4
Width, in.	71.0	74.0
Track, in.	front: 59.6	front: 61.9
	rear: 60.4	rear: 61.9
Height, in.	46.7	46.4
Curb weight, lb	3223	3465

Mechanical Specifications 2-door hatchback/convertible

Suspension	**front:** Independent; unequal length upper and lower A-arms, transverse fiberglass leaf spring, tubular hydraulic shock absorbers, antiroll bar **rear:** Independent, upper and lower trailing arms, lateral arms, tie rods, halfshafts, transverse fiberglass leaf springs, tubular hydraulic shock absorbers, antiroll bar
Wheels/Tires	P275/40ZR-17 (P315/35ZR-17 ZR-1, rear)
Brakes	front: antilock 12.0-inch disc rear: antilock 12.0-inch disc
Transmission	4-speed automatic 6-speed manual
Standard axle ratio	2.59:1 (auto) 3.33:1 (manual)

NA= Not Available

(1990 cont.)

Engine Specifications

Type	ohv V-8	dohc V-8
Displacement, liters/cu in.	5.7/350	5.7/350
Bore × Stroke, in. × in.	4.00 × 3.48	3.90 × 3.66
Fuel management	Multi-Port Injection	Multi-Port Injection
Horsepower @ rpm	250 @ 4400	375 @ 5800
Torque @ rpm, lb-ft	350 @ 3200	370 @ 4800

Published Performance Numbers

	250 hp, 6-sp man	375 hp, 6-sp man
0-60 mph, sec	5.7	4.9
0-100 mph, sec	NA	11.5
1/4-mile, sec @ mph	14.3 @ 97.1	13.4 @ 108.5
source	*Motor Trend*	*Road & Track*

Base Prices & Production

	Production	Price
2-door coupe	16,016	$31,979.00
2-door convertible	7630	37,264.00

Options & Production

	Production	Price
Power Passenger Seat	20,419	$270.00
Power Driver Seat	23,109	270.00
Sport Seats, leather	11,457	1050.00
Base Seats, leather	11,649	425.00
Callaway Twin Turbo (not GM installed)	58	26,895.00
Auxiliary Hardtop	2371	1995.00
Dual Removable Roof Panels	6422	915.00
Removable Roof Panel, blue tint	7852	615.00
Removable Roof Panel, bronze tint	4340	615.00
Electronic Air Conditioning Control	22,497	180.00
Selective Ride and Handling, electronic	7576	1695.00
Performance Axle Ratio	9362	22.00
Engine Block Heater	1585	20.00
Engine Oil Cooler	16,220	110.00
6-Speed Manual Transmission	8100	0.00
California Emission Requirements	4035	100.00
Low Tire Pressure Warning Indicator	8432	325.00
Stereo System, Delco-Bose	6401	823.00
Stereo System w/CD, Delco-Bose	15,716	1219.00
Luggage Rack (convertible)	1284	140.00
Performance Handling Package (coupe)	5446	460.00
Special Performance Pkg (ZR-1 coupe)	3049	27,016.00

Color Choices & Production

	Production		Production
White	4872	Steel Blue Metallic	813
Black	4759	Turquoise Metallic	589
Competition Yellow	278	Dark Red Metallic	2353
Quasar Blue Metallic	474	Bright Red	6956
Polo Green Metallic	1674	Charcoal Metallic	878

1991

Vehicle Specifications

	hatchback	hatchback (ZR-1)	convertible
Wheelbase, in.	96.2	96.2	96.2
Length, in.	176.5	177.4	176.5
Width, in.	71.0	74.0	71.0
Track, in.	front: 59.6	front: 61.9	front: 59.6
	rear: 60.4	rear: 61.9	rear: 60.4
Height, in.	46.7	46.4	46.4
Curb weight, lb	3294	3470	3294

Mechanical Specifications 2-door hatchback/convertible

Suspension — **front:** Independent; unequal length upper and lower A-arms, transverse fiberglass leaf spring, tubular hydraulic shock absorbers, antiroll bar
rear: Independent, upper and lower trailing arms, lateral arms, tie rods, halfshafts, transverse fiberglass leaf springs, tubular hydraulic shock absorbers, antiroll bar

Wheels/Tires	P275/40ZR-17 (P315/35ZR-17 ZR-1, rear)
Brakes	front: antilock 12.0-inch disc
	rear: antilock 12.0-inch disc
Transmission	4-speed automatic 6-speed manual
Standard axle ratio	2.59:1 (auto) 3.07:1 (manual)

Engine Specifications

Type	ohv V-8	dohc V-8
Displacement, liters/cu in.	5.7/350	5.7/350
Bore × Stroke, in. × in.	4.00 × 3.48	3.90 × 3.66
Fuel management	Multi-Port Injection	Multi-Port Injection
Horsepower @ rpm	250 @ 4400	375 @ 5800
Torque @ rpm, lb-ft	350 @ 3200	370 @ 4800

Base Prices & Production

	Production	Price
2-door coupe	14,967	$32,455.00
2-door convertible	5672	38,770.00

Options & Production

	Production	Price
Base Seats, leather	NA	$425.00
Sport Seats, leather	10,650	1050.00
Power Passenger Seat	17,267	290.00
Power Driver Seat	19,937	290.00
Callaway Twin Turbo (not GM installed)	62	33,000.00
Auxiliary Hardtop	1230	1995.00
Dual Removable Roof Panels	5031	915.00
Removable Roof Panel, blue tint	6991	615.00
Removable Roof Panel, bronze tint	3036	615.00
Electronic Air Conditioning Control	19,233	180.00
Selective Ride and Handling, electronic	6894	1695.00
Performance Axle Ratio	NA	22.00
Engine Oil Cooler	7525	110.00
6-Speed Manual Transmission	5875	0.00
California Emission Requirements	3050	100.00
Low Tire Pressure Warning Indicator	5175	325.00
Stereo System, Delco-Bose	3786	823.00
Stereo System w/CD, Delco-Bose	15,345	1219.00
Luggage Rack (convertible)	886	140.00
Adjustable Suspension Package (coupe)	733	2155.00
Special Performance Pkg (ZR-1 coupe)	2044	31,683.00

Color Choices & Production

	Production		Production
White	4305	Steel Blue Metallic	835
Yellow	650	Black	3909
Turquoise Metallic	1621	Dark Red Metallic	1311
Quasar Blue Metallic	1038	Bright Red	5318
Polo Green Metallic	1230	Charcoal Metallic	417

1992

Vehicle Specifications

	hatchback	hatchback (ZR-1)	convertible
Wheelbase, in.	96.2	96.2	96.2
Length, in.	178.6	178.6	176.6
Width, in.	71.0	73.2	71.0
Track, in.	front: 57.7	front: 57.7	front: 57.7
	rear: 59.1	rear: 60.6	rear: 59.1
Height, in.	46.7	46.4	46.4
Curb weight, lb	3223	3465	3263

Mechanical Specifications 2-door hatchback

Suspension	**front:** Independent; unequal length upper and lower A-arms, transverse fiberglass leaf spring, tubular hydraulic shock absorbers, antiroll bar **rear:** Independent, upper and lower trailing arms, lateral arms, tie rods, halfshafts, transverse fiberglass leaf springs, tubular hydraulic shock absorbers, antiroll bar
Wheels/Tires	P275/40ZR-17 (P315/35ZR-17 ZR-1, rear)
Brakes	front: antilock 11.9-inch disc rear: antilock 11.9-inch disc
Transmission	4-speed automatic; 6-speed manual
Standard axle ratio	3.45:1

Engine Specifications

Type	ohv V-8	dohc V-8
Displacement, liters/cu in.	5.7/350	5.7/350
Bore × Stroke, in. × in.	4.00 × 3.48	3.90 × 3.66
Fuel management	Multi-Port Injection	Multi-Port Injection
Horsepower @ rpm	300 @ 5000	375 @ 5800
Torque @ rpm, lb-ft	330 @ 4000	370 @ 4800

Published Performance Numbers

	300 hp, 6-speed manual
0-60 mph, sec	5.7
0-100 mph, sec	NA
1/4-mile, sec @ mph	14.1 @ 99.9
source	*Motor Trend*

Base Prices & Production

	Production	Price
2-door coupe	14,604	$33,635.00
2-door convertible	5875	40,145.00

Options & Production

	Production	Price
Base Seats, leather	10,565	$475.00
Base Seats, white leather	752	555.00
Sport Seats, leather	7973	1100.00
Sport Seats, white leather	709	1180.00
Power Passenger Seat	16,179	305.00
Power Driver Seat	19,378	305.00
Auxiliary Hardtop	915	1995.00
Dual Removable Roof Panels	3739	950.00
Removable Roof Panel, blue tint	6424	650.00
Removable Roof Panel, bronze tint	3005	650.00
Electronic Air Conditioning Control	18,460	205.00
Selective Ride and Handling, electronic	5840	1695.00
Performance Axle Ratio	2283	50.00
6-Speed Manual Transmission	5487	0.00
California Emission Requirements	3092	100.00
Low Tire Pressure Warning Indicator	3416	325.00
Stereo System, Delco-Bose	3241	823.00
Stereo System w/CD, Delco-Bose	15,199	1219.00
Luggage Rack (convertible)	845	140.00
Adjustable Suspension Package (coupe)	738	2045.00
Special Performance Package (coupe)	502	31,683.00

Color Choices & Production

	Production		Production
White	4101	Yellow	678
Black	3209	Bright Aqua Metallic	1953
Polo Green II Metallic	1995	Black Rose Metallic	1886
Dark Red Metallic	1148	Quasar Blue Metallic	1043
Bright Red	4466		

1993

Vehicle Specifications

	hatchback	hatchback (ZR-1)	convertible
Wheelbase, in.	96.2	96.2	96.2
Length, in.	178.5	178.6	178.6
Width, in.	70.7	73.1	70.7
Track, in.	front: 57.7 rear: 59.1	front: 57.7 rear: 60.6	front: 57.7 rear: 59.1
Height, in.	46.3	46.4	47.3
Curb weight, lb	3333	3465	3383

Mechanical Specifications 2-door hatchback/convertible

Suspension	**front:** Independent; unequal length upper and lower A-arms, transverse fiberglass leaf spring, tubular hydraulic shock absorbers, antiroll bar **rear:** Independent, upper and lower trailing arms, lateral arms, tie rods, halfshafts, transverse fiberglass leaf springs, tubular hydraulic shock absorbers, antiroll bar
Wheels/Tires	front, P255/45ZR-17 (ZR-1, P275/40ZR-17) rear, P285/40ZR-17 (ZR-1, P315/35ZR-17)
Brakes	front: antilock 11.9-inch disc rear: antilock 11.9-inch disc
Transmission	4-speed automatic; 6-speed manual
Standard axle ratio	3.45:1

Engine Specifications

Type	ohv V-8	dohc V-8
Displacement, liters/cu in.	5.7/350	5.7/350
Bore × Stroke, in. × in.	4.00 × 3.48	3.90 × 3.66
Fuel management	Multi-Port Injection	Multi-Port Injection
Horsepower @ rpm	300 @ 5000	405 @ 5800
Torque @ rpm, lb-ft	340 @ 4000	385 @ 5200

Published Performance Numbers

	300 hp, 6-sp man	405 hp, 6-sp man
0-60 mph, sec	5.6	4.9
0-100 mph, sec	NA	NA
1/4-mile, sec @ mph	14.0 @ 101.7	13.1 @ 109.6
source	*Motor Trend*	*Motor Trend*

Base Prices & Production

	Production	Price
2-door coupe	15,898	$34,595.00
2-door convertible	5692	41,195.00

Options & Production

	Production	Price
Base Seats, leather	8509	$475.00
Base Seats, white leather	766	555.00
Sport Seats, leather	11,267	1100.00
Sport Seats, white leather	622	1180.00
Power Passenger Seat	18,067	305.00
Power Driver Seat	20,626	305.00
Auxiliary Hardtop	976	1995.00
Dual Removable Roof Panels	4204	950.00
Removable Roof Panel, blue tint	6203	650.00
Removable Roof Panel, bronze tint	4288	650.00
Electronic Air Conditioning Control	19,550	205.00
Selective Ride and Handling, electronic	5740	1695.00
Performance Axle Ratio	2630	50.00
6-Speed Manual Transmission	5330	0.00
California Emission Requirements	2401	100.00

NA= Not Available

(1993 cont.)

	Production	Price
Low Tire Pressure Warning Indicator	3353	325.00
Stereo System, Delco-Bose	2685	823.00
Stereo System w/CD, Delco-Bose	16,794	1219.00
Luggage Rack (convertible)	765	140.00
Adjustable Suspension Package (coupe)	824	2045.00
40th Anniversary Package	6749	1455.00
Special Performance Pkg (ZR-1 coupe)	448	31,683.00

Color Choices & Production

	Production		Production
Arctic White	3031	Black	2684
Bright Aqua Metallic	1305	Polo Green II Metallic	2189
Competition Yellow	517	Ruby Red	6749
Torch Red	3172	Black Rose Metallic	935
Dark Red Metallic	325	Quasar Blue Metallic	683

1994

Vehicle Specifications

	hatchback	hatchback (ZR-1)	convertible
Wheelbase, in.	96.2	96.2	96.2
Length, in.	178.5	178.6	178.6
Width, in.	70.7	73.1	70.7
Track, in.	front: 57.7	front: 57.7	front: 57.7
	rear: 59.0	rear: 60.6	rear: 59.0
Height, in.	46.3	46.4	47.3
Curb weight, lb	3309	3465	3361

Mechanical Specifications 2-door hatchback

Suspension	**front:** Independent; unequal length upper and lower A-arms, transverse fiberglass leaf spring, tubular hydraulic shock absorbers, antiroll bar **rear:** Independent, upper and lower trailing arms, lateral arms, tie rods, halfshafts, transverse fiberglass leaf springs, tubular hydraulic shock absorbers, antiroll bar
Wheels/Tires	front, P255/45ZR-17 (ZR-1, P275/40ZR-17) rear, P285/40ZR-17 (ZR-1, P315/35ZR-17)
Brakes	front: antilock 11.9-inch disc rear: antilock 11.9-inch disc
Transmission	4-speed automatic; 6-speed manual
Standard axle ratio	3.45:1

Engine Specifications

Type	ohv V-8	dohc V-8
Displacement, liters/cu in.	5.7/350	5.7/350
Bore $\times$ Stroke, in. $\times$ in.	4.00 $\times$ 3.48	3.90 $\times$ 3.66
Fuel management	Sequential Injection	Sequential Injection
Horsepower @ rpm	300 @ 5000	405 @ 5800
Torque @ rpm, lb-ft	340 @ 3600	385 @ 5200

Published Performance Numbers

	300 hp, 6-sp man	405 hp, 6-sp man
0-60 mph, sec	5.7	5.2
0-100 mph, sec	13.3	12.4
1/4-mile, sec @ mph	14.1 @ 103.0	13.6 @ 106.0
source	*Road & Track*	*Motor Trend*

Base Prices & Production

	Production	Price
2-door coupe	17,984	$36,185.00
2-door convertible	5346	42,960.00

Options & Production

	Production	Price
Sport Seats	9023	$625.00
Power Passenger Seat	17,863	305.00
Power Driver Seat	21,592	305.00
Auxiliary Hardtop	682	1995.00
Dual Removable Roof Panels	3875	950.00
Removable Roof Panel, blue tint	7064	650.00
Removable Roof Panel, bronze tint	3979	650.00
Selective Ride and Handling, electronic	4570	1695.00
Performance Axle Ratio	9019	50.00
6-Speed Manual Transmission	6012	0.00
New York Emission Requirements	1363	100.00
Low Tire Pressure Warning Indicator	5097	325.00
Stereo System w/CD, Delco-Bose	17,579	396.00
Tires, Extended Mobility	2781	70.00
California Emission Requirements	2372	100.00
Adjustable Suspension Package (coupe)	887	2045.00
Special Performance Pkg (ZR-1 coupe)	448	31,258.00

Color Choices & Production

	Production		Production
Arctic White	4066	Admiral Blue	1584
Black	4136	Bright Aqua Metallic	1209
Polo Green Metallic	3534	Competition Yellow	834
Copper Metallic	116	Torch Red	5073
Black Rose Metallic	1267	Dark Red Metallic	1511

1995

Vehicle Specifications

	hatchback	hatchback (ZR-1)	convertible
Wheelbase, in.	96.2	96.2	96.2
Length, in.	178.5	178.6	178.6
Width, in.	70.7	73.1	70.7
Track, in.	front: 57.7	front: 57.7	front: 57.7
	rear: 59.0	rear: 60.6	rear: 59.0
Height, in.	46.3	46.4	47.3
Curb weight, lb	3203	3465	3360

Mechanical Specifications 2-door hatchback/convertible

Suspension	**front:** Independent; unequal length upper and lower A-arms, transverse fiberglass leaf spring, tubular hydraulic shock absorbers, antiroll bar **rear:** Independent, upper and lower trailing arms, lateral arms, tie rods, halfshafts, transverse fiberglass leaf springs, tubular hydraulic shock absorbers, antiroll bar
Wheels/Tires	front, P255/45ZR-17 (ZR-1, P275/40ZR-17) rear, P285/40ZR-17 (ZR-1, P315/35ZR-17)
Brakes	front: antilock 12.9-inch disc rear: antilock 11.9-inch disc
Transmission	4-speed automatic; 6-speed manual
Standard axle ratio	3.45:1

Engine Specifications

Type	ohv V-8	dohc V-8
Displacement, liters/cu in.	5.7/350	5.7/350
Bore $\times$ Stroke, in. $\times$ in.	4.00 $\times$ 3.48	3.90 $\times$ 3.66
Fuel management	Sequential Injection	Sequential Injection
Horsepower @ rpm	300 @ 5000	405 @ 5800
Torque @ rpm, lb-ft	340 @ 4000	385 @ 5200

Base Prices & Production	Production	Price
2-door coupe	15,771	$36,785.00
2-door convertible	4971	43,665.00

Options & Production	Production	Price
Power Driver Seat	19,012	$305.00
Power Passenger Seat	15,323	305.00
Sport Seats	7908	625.00
Auxiliary Hardtop	459	1995.00
Dual Removable Roof Panels	2979	950.00
Removable Roof Panel, blue tint	4688	650.00
Removable Roof Panel, bronze tint	2871	650.00
Selective Ride and Handling, electronic	3421	1695.00
Performance Axle Ratio	10,056	50.00
6-Speed Manual Transmission	4784	0.00
New York Emission Requirements	268	100.00
Spare Tire Delete	418	-100.00
Low Tire Pressure Warning Indicator	5300	325.00
Stereo System w/CD, Delco-Bose	15,528	396.00
Tires, Extended Mobility	3783	70.00
California Emission Requirements	2026	100.00
Adjustable Suspension Package (coupe)	753	2045.00
Indy 500 Pace Car Replica	527	2816.00
Special Performance Pkg (ZR-1 coupe)	448	31,258.00

Color Choices & Production

	Production		Production
Dark Purple Metallic	1049	Dark Purple/White	527
Arctic White	3381	Admiral Blue	1006
Black	3959	Bright Aqua Metallic	909
Polo Green Metallic	2940	Competition Yellow	1003
Torch Red	4531	Dark Red Metallic	1437

1996

Vehicle Specifications	hatchback	convertible
Wheelbase, in.	96.2	96.2
Length, in.	178.5	178.6
Width, in.	70.7	70.7
Track, in.	front: 57.7	front: 57.7
	rear: 59.0	rear: 59.0
Height, in.	46.3	47.3
Curb weight, lb	3298	3360

Mechanical Specifications	2-door hatchback/convertible
Suspension	**front:** Independent; unequal length upper and lower A-arms, transverse fiberglass leaf spring, tubular hydraulic shock absorbers, antiroll bar **rear:** Independent, upper and lower trailing arms, lateral arms, tie rods, halfshafts, transverse fiberglass leaf springs, tubular hydraulic shock absorbers, antiroll bar
Wheels/Tires	front, P255/45ZR-17 rear, P285/40ZR-17
Brakes	front: antilock 12.9-inch disc rear: antilock 11.9-inch disc
Transmission	4-speed automatic; 6-speed manual
Standard axle ratio	3.45:1

Engine Specifications

Type	ohv V-8	ohv V-8
Displacement, liters/cu in.	5.7/350	5.7/350
Bore × Stroke, in. × in.	4.00 × 3.48	4.00 × 3.48
Fuel management	Sequential Injection	Sequential Injection

Horsepower @ rpm	300 @ 5000	330 @ 5800
Torque @ rpm, lb-ft	335 @ 3600	340 @ 4500

Published Performance Numbers	300 hp, 6-sp manual
0-60 mph, sec	5.1
0-100 mph, sec	12.7
1/4-mile, sec @ mph	13.7 @ 104.0
source	*Car and Driver*

Base Prices & Production	Production	Price
2-door coupe	17,167	$37,225.00
2-door convertible	4369	45,060.00

Options & Production	Production	Price
Power Driver Seat	19,798	$305.00
Power Passenger Seat	17,060	305.00
Sport Seats	12,016	625.00
Auxiliary Hardtop	429	1995.00
Dual Removable Roof Panels	3983	950.00
Removable Roof Panel, blue tint	6626	650.00
Removable Roof Panel, bronze tint	2492	650.00
Selective Real Time Damping, electronic	2896	1695.00
Performance Axle Ratio	9801	50.00
330 hp Engine	6359	1450.00
6-Speed Manual Transmission	6359	0.00
Spare Tire Delete	986	-100.00
Low Tire Pressure Warning Indicator	6865	325.00
Compact Disc, Delco-Bose (reqs PEG 1)	17,037	396.00
Tires, Extended Mobility	4945	70.00
Collector Edition	5412	1250.00
Grand Sport Package ($2880 w/convertible)	1000	3250.00
Performance Handling Package	1869	350.00

Color Choices & Production

	Production		Production
Dark Purple Metallic	320	Arctic White	3210
Sebring Silver Metallic	5412	Admiral Blue	1000
Black	3917	Bright Aqua Metallic	357
Polo Green Metallic	2414	Competition Yellow	488
Torch Red	4418		

1997

Vehicle Specifications	hatchback	
Wheelbase, in.	104.5	
Length, in.	179.7	
Width, in.	73.6	
Track, in.	front: 62.0	rear: 62.0
Height, in.	47.7	
Curb weight, lb	3230	

Mechanical Specifications	2-door hatchback
Suspension	**front:** Independent; upper and lower A-arms, transverse composite monoleaf spring, tube shock absorbers, antiroll bar **rear:** Independent, upper and lower A-arms, toe links, transverse composite monoleaf springs, tube shock absorbers, antiroll bar
Wheels/Tires	front, P245/45ZR-17 rear, P275/40ZR-18
Brakes	front: antilock 12.8-inch disc rear: antilock 12.0-inch disc
Transmission	4-speed automatic 6-speed manual
Standard axle ratio	2.73:1 (auto) 3.42:1 (manual)

NA= Not Available

439

(1997 cont.)

Engine Specifications

Type	ohv V-8
Displacement, liters/cu in.	5.7/350
Bore × Stroke, in. × in.	3.90 × 3.62
Fuel management	Sequential Injection
Horsepower @ rpm	345 @ 5600
Torque @ rpm, lb-ft	350 @ 4400

Published Performance Numbers

345 hp, 6-sp manual

0-60 mph, sec	4.8
0-100 mph, sec	11.5
1/4-mile, sec @ mph	13.3 @ 108.0
source	*Road & Track*

Base Prices & Production

	Production	Price
2-door coupe	9752	$37,495.00

Options & Production

	Production	Price
Memory Package	6186	$150.00
Power Passenger Seat	8951	305.00
Sport Seats	6711	625.00
Floor Mats	9371	25.00
Body Side Moldings	4366	75.00
Dual Removable Roof Panels	416	950.00
Removable Roof Panel, blue tint	7213	650.00
Electronic Dual Zone Air Conditioning	7999	365.00
Luggage Shade and Parcel Net	8315	50.00
Selective Real Time Damping, electronic	3094	1695.00
Performance Axle Ratio (Automatic only)	2739	100.00
6-Speed Manual Transmission	2809	815.00
Massachusetts/New York Emissions	677	170.00
Fog Lamps	8829	69.00
Delco Stereo System w/CD	6282	100.00
Remote Compact 12-Disc Changer	4496	600.00
Front License Plate Frame	2258	15.00
California Emissions	885	170.00
Performance Handling Package	1077	350.00

Color Choices & Production

	Production		Production
Arctic White	1341	Sebring Silver Metallic	2164
Nassau Blue Metallic	292	Black	2393
Light Carmine Red Metallic	381	Torch Red	3026
Fairway Green Metallic	155		

1998

Vehicle Specifications

	hatchback	convertible
Wheelbase, in.	104.5	104.5
Length, in.	179.7	179.7
Width, in.	73.6	73.6
Track, in.	front: 62.0	front: 62.0
	rear: 62.0	rear: 62.0
Height, in.	47.7	47.7
Curb weight, lb	3245	3246

Mechanical Specifications 2-door hatchback/convertible

Suspension	**front:** Independent; upper and lower A-arms, transverse composite monoleaf spring, tube shock absorbers, antiroll bar **rear:** Independent, upper and lower A-arms, toe links, transverse composite monoleaf springs, tube shock absorbers, antiroll bar
Wheels/Tires	front, P245/45ZR-17

rear, P275/40ZR-18

Brakes	front: antilock 12.8-inch disc rear: antilock 12.0-inch disc
Transmission	4-speed automatic 6-speed manual
Standard axle ratio	2.73:1 (auto) 3.42:1 (manual)

Engine Specifications

Type	ohv V-8
Displacement, liters/cu in.	5.7/350
Bore × Stroke, in. × in.	3.90 × 3.62
Fuel management	Sequential Injection
Horsepower @ rpm	345 @ 5600
Torque @ rpm, lb-ft	350 @ 4400

Published Performance Numbers

345 hp, 4-sp automatic

0-60 mph, sec	5.1
0-100 mph, sec	12.5
1/4-mile, sec @ mph	13.5 @ 104.7
source	*Motor Trend*

Base Prices & Production

	Production	Price
2-door coupe	19,235	$37,495.00
2-door convertible	11,849	44,425.00

Options & Production

	Production	Price
Memory Package	24,234	$150.00
Power Passenger Seat	28,575	305.00
Sport Seats	22,675	625.00
Floor Mats	30,592	25.00
Body Side Moldings	17,070	75.00
Dual Removable Roof Panels	5640	950.00
Removable Roof Panel, blue tint	6957	650.00
Electronic Dual Zone Air Conditioning	26,572	365.00
Luggage Shade and Parcel Net	16,549	50.00
Selective Real Time Damping, electronic	8374	1695.00
Performance Axle Ratio	13,331	100.00
(3.25 ratio for automatic)		
Active Handling System	5356	500.00
6-Speed Manual Transmission	7106	815.00
Massachusetts/New York Emissions	2701	170.00
Fog Lamps	29,310	69.00
Delco Stereo System w/CD	18,213	100.00
Remote Compact 12-Disc Changer	16,513	600.00
Front License Plate Frame	16,087	15.00
California Emissions	3111	170.00
Indy Pace Car Replica ($5804 w/manual)	1163	5039.00
Performance Handling Package	4249	350.00

Color Choices & Production

	Production		Production
Arctic White	3346	Light Pewter Metallic	3276
Sebring Silver Metallic	4637	Pace Car Purple	1163
Nassau Blue Metallic	1098	Navy Blue Metallic	14
Black	6597	Aztec Gold	15
Light Carmine Red Metallic	1567	Torch Red	8767
Fairway Green Metallic	223	Medium Purple Metallic	381

1999

Vehicle Specifications

	hatchback	convertible	coupe
Wheelbase, in.	104.5	104.5	104.5
Length, in.	179.7	179.7	179.7
Width, in.	73.6	73.6	73.6
Track, in.	front: 62.0	front: 62.0	front: 62.0
	rear: 62.0	rear: 62.0	rear: 62.0
Height, in.	47.8	47.7	47.9
Curb weight, lb	3245	3246	3153

Mechanical Specifications	2-door hatchback/convertible/coupe
Suspension	**front:** Independent; upper and lower A-arms, transverse composite monoleaf spring, tube shock absorbers, antiroll bar **rear:** Independent, upper and lower A-arms, toe links, transverse composite monoleaf springs, tube shock absorbers, antiroll bar
Wheels/Tires	front, P245/45ZR-17 rear, P275/40ZR-18
Brakes	front: antilock 12.6-inch disc rear: antilock 11.8-inch disc
Transmission	4-speed automatic 6-speed manual
Standard axle ratio	2.73:1 (auto) 3.42:1 (manual)

Engine Specifications

Type	ohv V-8
Displacement, liters/cu in.	5.7/350
Bore × Stroke, in. × in.	3.90 × 3.62
Fuel management	Sequential Injection
Horsepower @ rpm	345 @ 5600
Torque @ rpm, lb-ft	350 @ 4400

Published Performance Numbers

345 hp, 6-sp man (hardtop)

0-60 mph, sec	5.3
0-100 mph, sec	11.7
1/4-mile, sec @ mph	13.6 @ 107.3
source	*Road & Track*

Base Prices & Production

	Production	Price
2-door hatchback	18,078	$39,171.00
2-door coupe	4031	38,777.00
2-door convertible	11,161	45,579.00

Options & Production

	Production	Price
Memory Package	23,829	$150.00
Power Driver Seat	3716	305.00
Power Passenger Seat	28,575	305.00
Sport Seats	24,573	625.00
Parcel Net	2738	15.00
Floor Mats	32,706	25.00
Body Side Moldings	19,348	75.00
Dual Removable Roof Panels	6307	950.00
Removable Roof Panel, blue tint	5235	650.00
Dual Zone Air Conditioning	25,672	365.00
Luggage Shade and Parcel Net	18,058	50.00
Selective Real Time Damping	7515	1695.00
Performance Axle Ratio	14,525	100.00
(3.25 ratio for automatic)		
Active Handling System	20,174	500.00
6-Speed Manual Transmission	13,729	825.00
Telescopic Steering, Power	16,847	350.00
Magnesium Wheels	2029	3000.00
Twilight Sentinel	18,895	60.00
Fog Lamps	28,546	69.00
Lighting Package	3037	95.00
Delco Stereo System w/CD	20,442	100.00
Head Up Instrument Display	19,034	375.00
Bose Speaker Package	3348	820.00
Remote Compact 12-Disc Changer	16,997	600.00
Front License Plate Frame	17,742	15.00
California Emissions	3336	170.00
Performance Handling Pkg	10,244	350.00
Magnetic Red Metallic Paint	2733	500.00

Color Choices & Production

	Production		Production
Arctic White	2756	Light Pewter Metallic	6164
Sebring Silver Metallic	3510	Nassau Blue Metallic	1034
Navy Blue Metallic	1439	Black	7235
Torch Red	8361	Magnetic Red Metallic	2733

2000

Vehicle Specifications

	hatchback	convertible	coupe
Wheelbase, in.	104.5	104.5	104.5
Length, in.	179.7	179.7	179.7
Width, in.	73.6	73.6	73.6
Track, in.	front: 62.1 rear: 62.2	front: 62.1 rear: 62.2	front: 62.1 rear: 62.2
Height, in.	47.8	47.7	47.9
Curb weight, lb	3246	3248	3173

Mechanical Specifications	2-door hatchback/convertible/coupe
Suspension	**front:** Independent; upper and lower A-arms, transverse composite monoleaf spring, tube shock absorbers, antiroll bar **rear:** Independent, upper and lower A-arms, toe links, transverse composite monoleaf springs, tube shock absorbers, antiroll bar
Wheels/Tires	front, P245/45ZR-17 rear, P275/40ZR-18
Brakes	front: antilock 12.6-inch disc rear: antilock 11.8-inch disc
Transmission	4-speed automatic 6-speed manual
Standard axle ratio	2.73:1 (auto) 3.42:1 (manual)

Engine Specifications

Type	ohv V-8
Displacement, liters/cu in.	5.7/350
Bore × Stroke, in. × in.	3.90 × 3.62
Fuel management	Sequential Injection
Horsepower @ rpm	345 @ 5600
Torque @ rpm, lb-ft	350 @ 4400

Base Prices & Production

	Production	Price
2-door hatchback	18,113	$39,475.00
2-door coupe	2090	38,900.00
2-door convertible	13,479	45,900.00

Options & Production

	Production	Price
Memory Package	26,595	$150.00
Power Driver Seat	1841	305.00
Power Passenger Seat	29,462	305.00
Sport Seats	27,103	700.00
Parcel Net	938	15.00
Floor Mats	33,188	25.00
Body Side Moldings	18,773	75.00
Dual Removable Roof Panels	6280	1100.00
Removable Roof Panel, blue tint	5605	650.00
Dual Zone Air Conditioning	29,428	365.00
Luggage Shade and Parcel Net	15,689	50.00
Selective Real Time Damping	6724	1695.00
Performance Axle Ratio	14,090	100.00
(3.25 ratio for automatic)		
Active Handling System	22,668	500.00
6-Speed Manual Transmission	13,320	815.00
Telescopic Steering, Power	22,182	350.00

NA= Not Available

(2000 cont.)

Magnesium Wheels	2652	2000.00
Polished Aluminum Wheels	15,204	895.00
Twilight Sentinel	23,508	60.00
Fog Lamps	31,992	69.00
Lighting Package	1527	95.00
Delco Stereo System w/CD	24,696	100.00
Head Up Instrument Display	26,482	375.00
Bose Speaker Package	1766	820.00
Remote Compact 12-Disc Changer	15,809	600.00
Front License Plate Frame	17,280	15.00
California Emissions	3628	0.00
Performance Handling (std w/hardtop)	7775	350.00
Millennium Yellow	3578	500.00
Magnetic Red Metallic Paint	2941	500.00

Color Choices & Production

	Production		Production
Arctic White	1979	Light Pewter Metallic	5125
Sebring Silver Metallic	2783	Nassau Blue Metallic	851
Navy Blue Metallic	2254	Black	5807
Torch Red	6700	Millennium Yellow	3578
Dark Bowling Green Metallic	1663	Magnetic Red Metallic	2941

2001

Vehicle Specifications

	hatchback	convertible	coupe
Wheelbase, in.	104.5	104.5	104.5
Length, in.	179.7	179.7	179.7
Width, in.	73.6	73.6	73.6
Track, in.	front: 62.1	front: 62.1	front: 62.1
	rear: 62.2	rear: 62.2	rear: 62.2
Height, in.	47.8	47.7	47.9
Curb weight, lb	3212	3207	3130

Mechanical Specifications 2-door hatchback/convertible/coupe

Suspension	**front:** Independent; upper and lower A-arms, transverse composite monoleaf spring, tube shock absorbers, antiroll bar **rear:** Independent, upper and lower A-arms, toe links, transverse composite monoleaf springs, tube shock absorbers, antiroll bar
Wheels/Tires	front, P245/45ZR-17 (Z06, P265/40ZR-17) rear, P275/40ZR-18 (Z06, P295, 35ZR-18)
Brakes	front: antilock 12.6-inch disc rear: antilock 11.6-inch disc
Transmission	4-speed automatic 6-speed manual
Standard axle ratio	2.73:1 (auto) 3.42:1 (manual)

Engine Specifications

Type	ohv V-8	ohv V-8
Displacement, liters/cu in.	5.7/350	5.7/350
Bore × Stroke, in. × in.	3.90 × 3.62	3.90 × 3.62
Fuel management	Sequential Injection	Sequential Injection
Horsepower @ rpm	350 @ 5600	385 @ 6000
Torque @ rpm, lb-ft	375 @ 4400	385 @ 4800

Published Performance Numbers

385 hp, 6-sp manual

0-60 mph, sec	4.6
0-100 mph, sec	10.5
1/4-mile, sec @ mph	13.0 @ 110.5
source	*Road & Track*

Base Prices & Production

	Production	Price
2-door hatchback	15,681	$40,475.00
2-door Z06 coupe	5773	47,500.00
2-door convertible	14,173	47,000.00

Options & Production

	Production	Price
Preferred Equipment Group (hatchbk)	2514	$1639.00
Preferred Equipment Group (conv)	1710	1769.00
Preferred Equipment Group (hatchbk)	11,558	2544.00
Preferred Equipment Group (conv)	11,881	2494.00
Memory Package	4780	150.00
Floor Mats	34,907	25.00
Body Side Moldings	20,457	75.00
Dual Removable Roof Panels	5099	1100.00
Removable Roof Panel, blue tint	4769	650.00
Electrochromic Mirrors	4576	120.00
Selective Real Time Damping	5620	1695.00
Performance Axle Ratio (3.25 ratio for automatic)	12,882	300.00
6-Speed Manual Transmission	16,019	815.00
Magnesium Wheels	1022	2000.00
Polished Aluminum Wheels	22,980	895.00
Corvette Museum Delivery	457	490.00
Delco Stereo Cassette (replaces std radio)	6844	-100.00
Delco Stereo System w/CD	28,783	100.00
Remote 12-Disc Changer	14,198	600.00
Front License Plate Frame	18,935	15.00
Performance Handling Pkg	7817	350.00
Millennium Yellow w/tint coat	3887	600.00
Magnetic Red Metallic Paint	3322	600.00

Color Choices & Production

	Production		Production
Light Pewter Metallic	3462	Quicksilver Metallic	4822
Navy Blue Metallic	2587	Speedway White	2465
Black	6971	Torch Red	7192
Millennium Yellow	3887	Magnetic Red Metallic	3322
Dark Bowling Green Metallic	919		

2002

Vehicle Specifications

	hatchback	convertible	coupe
Wheelbase, in.	104.5	104.5	104.5
Length, in.	179.7	179.7	179.7
Width, in.	73.6	73.6	73.6
Track, in.	front: 62.1	front: 62.1	front: 62.1
	rear: 62.2	rear: 62.2	rear: 62.2
Height, in.	47.8	47.7	47.9
Curb weight, lb	3246	3248	3118

Mechanical Specifications 2-door hatchback/convertible/coupe

Suspension	**front:** Independent; upper and lower A-arms, transverse composite monoleaf spring, tube shock absorbers, antiroll bar **rear:** Independent, upper and lower A-arms, toe links, transverse composite monoleaf springs, tube shock absorbers, antiroll bar
Wheels/Tires	front, P245/45ZR-17 (Z06,P265/40ZR-17) rear, P275/40ZR-18 (Z06, P295/35ZR-18)
Brakes	front: antilock 12.6-inch disc rear: antilock 11.6-inch disc

Transmission	4-speed automatic	6-speed manual
Standard axle ratio	2.73:1 (auto)	3.42:1 (manual)

Engine Specifications

Type	ohv V-8	ohv V-8
Displacement, liters/cu in.	5.7/350	5.7/350
Bore × Stroke, in. × in.	3.90 × 3.62	3.90 × 3.62
Fuel management	Sequential Injection	Sequential Injection
Horsepower @ rpm	350 @ 5600	405 @ 6000
Torque @ rpm, lb-ft	375 @ 4400	400 @ 4800

Published Performance Numbers

405 hp, 6-sp manual

0-60 mph, sec	4.37
0-100 mph, sec	9.85
1/4-mile, sec @ mph	12.77 @ 113.65
source	*Car and Driver*

Base Prices & Production

	Production	Price
2-door hatchback	14,760	$41,450.00
2-door Z06 coupe	8297	50,150.00
2-door convertible	12,710	47,975.00

Options & Production

	Production	Price
Preferred Equipment Group-1SB (htchbck)	10,791	$1700.00
		(convertible 1800.00)
Preferred Equipment Group-1SC (htchbck)	2746	2700.00
		(convertible 2600.00)
Memory Package	33,544	150.00
Selective Real Time Damping	4773	1695.00
Z51 Performance Handling Pkg	6106	350.00
6-Speed Manual Transmission	8553	815.00
Performance Axle 3.15 ratio for automatic	9646	300.00
Delco Stereo Cassette	19,948	-100.00
Remote 12-Disc Changer	13,725	600.00
Electrochromic Mirrors	NA	120.00
Corvette Museum Delivery	NA	490.00
Dual Removable Roof Panels	5079	1200.00
Removable Roof Panel, blue tint	4208	750.00
Body Side Moldings	21,422	75.00
Front License Plate Frame	19,948	15.00
Millennium Yellow w/tint coat	4040	600.00
Magnetic Red Metallic Paint	3298	600.00
Polished Aluminum Wheels	22,597	1200.00

Color Choices & Production

	Production		Production
Light Pewter Metallic	2650	Quicksilver Metallic	4618
Electron Blue Metallic	5407	Speedway White	1763
Black	7129	Torch Red	6862
Millennium Yellow	4040	Magnetic Red Metallic	3298

2003

Vehicle Specifications

	hatchback	convertible	coupe
Wheelbase, in.	104.5	104.5	104.5
Length, in.	179.7	179.7	179.7
Width, in.	73.6	73.6	73.6
Track, in.	front: 62.1	front: 62.1	front: 62.1
	rear: 62.2	rear: 62.2	rear: 62.2
Height, in.	47.8	47.7	47.9
Curb weight, lb	3246	3248	3118

Mechanical Specifications 2-door hatchback/convertible/coupe

Suspension **front:** Independent; upper and lower A-arms, transverse composite monoleaf spring, tube shock absorbers, antiroll bar
rear: Independent, upper and lower A-arms, toe links, transverse composite monoleaf springs, tube shock absorbers, antiroll bar

Wheels/Tires	front, P245/45ZR-17 (Z06, P265/40ZR-17) rear, P275/40ZR-18 (Z06, P295/35ZR-18)
Brakes	front: antilock 12.6-inch disc rear: antilock 11.6-inch disc

Transmission	4-speed automatic	6-speed manual
Standard axle ratio	2.73:1 (auto)	3.42:1 (manual)

Engine Specifications

Type	ohv V-8	ohv V-8
Displacement, liters/cu in.	5.7/350	5.7/350
Bore × Stroke, in. × in.	3.90 × 3.62	3.90 × 3.62
Fuel management	Sequential Injection	Sequential Injection
Horsepower @ rpm	350 @ 5600	405 @ 6000
Torque @ rpm, lb-ft	375 @ 4400	400 @ 4800

Published Performance Numbers

350 hp, 6-speed manual

0-60 mph, sec	4.9
0-100 mph, sec	11.5
1/4-mile, sec @ mph	13.4 @ 101.1
source	*Road & Track*

Base Prices & Production

	Production	Price
2-door hatchback	12,812	$43,895.00
2-door Z06 coupe	8635	51,155.00
2-door convertible	14,022	50,370.00

Options & Production

	Production	Price
Preferred Equipment Group (hatchback)	7310	$1200.00
Preferred Equipment Group (convertible)	6643	1200.00
50th Anniversary Edition (hatchback)	4085	5000.00
50th Anniversary Edition (convertible)	7547	5000.00
Commerative Edition (convertible)	2659	3700.00
Memory Package (Z06)	8241	175.00
Body Side Moldings	22,243	150.00
Dual Removable Roof Panels	5184	1200.00
Removable Roof Panel, blue tint	3150	750.00
Electrochromatic Mirrors (Z06)	8227	120.00
Magnetic Selective Ride Control	14,992	1695.00
Performance Axle Ratio (3.15 ratio, automatic only)	9785	395.00
6-Speed Manual Transmission	8590	915.00
Magnesium Wheels	293	1500.00
Polished Alloy Wheels	10,290	1295.00
Corvette Museum Delivery	787	490.00
Stereo with Cassette (replaces std radio)	4664	00.00
Remote 12-Disc Changer	15,979	600.00
Front License Plate Frame	20,605	15.00
Performance Handling Pkg	2592	395.00
Millennium Yellow w/tint coat	3900	750.00

Color Choices

	Production		Production
Quicksilver	2387	Electron Blue	2770
Speedway White	679	Black	5597
Torch Red	5205	Millennium Yellow	3900
Medium Spiral Gray	3299	Anniversary Red	11,632
Torch Red	5023		

NA= Not Available

2004

Vehicle Specifications

	hatchback	convertible	coupe
Wheelbase, in.	104.5	104.5	104.5
Length, in.	179.7	179.7	179.7
Width, in.	73.6	73.6	73.6
Track, in.	front: 62.1	front: 62.1	front: 62.1
	rear: 62.2	rear: 62.2	rear: 62.2
Height, in.	47.8	47.7	47.9
Curb weight, lb	3246	3118	3248

Mechanical Specifications 2-door hatchback/convertible/coupe

Suspension	**front:** Independent; upper and lower A-arms, transverse composite monoleaf spring, tube shock absorbers, antiroll bar **rear:** Independent, upper and lower A-arms, toe links, transverse composite monoleaf springs, tube shock absorbers, antiroll bar
Wheels/Tires	front, P245/45ZR-17 (Z06, P265/40ZR-17) rear, P275/40ZR-18 (Z06, P295, 35ZR-18)
Brakes	front: antilock 12.6-inch disc rear: antilock 11.6-inch disc
Transmission	4-speed automatic 6-speed manual
Standard axle ratio	2.73:1 (auto) 3.42:1 (manual)

Engine Specifications

Type	ohv V-8	ohv V-8
Displacement, liters/cu in.	5.7/350	5.7/350
Bore × Stroke, in. × in.	3.90 × 3.62	3.90 × 3.62
Fuel management	Sequential Injection	Sequential Injection
Horsepower @ rpm	350 @ 5600	405 @ 6000
Torque @ rpm, lb-ft	375 @ 4400	385 @ 4800

Published Performance Numbers   405 hp, 6-sp manual

0-60 mph, sec	4.2
1/4-mile, sec @ mph	12.4 @ 117.0
source	*Motor Trend*

Base Prices & Production

	Production	Price
2-door hatchback	16,165	$44,535.00
2-door Z06 coupe	5683	52,385.00
2-door convertible	12,216	51,535.00

Options & Production

	Production	Price
Preferred Equipment Group (hatchback)	11,446	$1200.00
Preferred Equipment Group (convertible)	9334	1200.00
Commerative Edition (Z06)	2026	4335.00
Commerative Edition (hatchback)	2215	3700.00
Commerative Edition (convertible)	2659	3700.00
Memory Package (Z06)	5446	175.00
Body Side Moldings	20,626	150.00
Dual Removable Roof Panels	5079	1400.00
Removable Roof Panel, blue tint	4356	750.00
Auto-dimming Mirrors (Z06)	5446	160.00
Magnetic Selective Ride Control	5843	1695.00
Performance Axle Ratio (3.15 ratio, automatic only)	10,367	395.00
6-Speed Manual Transmission	6928	915.00
Magnesium Wheels	1022	2000.00
Polished Alloy Wheels	1110	995.00
Corvette Museum Delivery	142	490.00
Stereo with Cassette (replaces std radio)	3860	00.00
Remote 12-Disc Changer	14,668	600.00
Front License Plate Frame	19,520	15.00
Performance Handling Pkg	3672	395.00
Millennium Yellow w/tint coat	2641	750.00
Magnetic Red Metallic Paint	3596	750.00

Color Choices & Production

	Production		Production
Arctic White	1741	LeMans Blue	6899
Black	6212	Millennium Yellow	2641
Medium Spiral Gray	3286	Machine Silver	4666
Magnetic Red II	3596	Torch Red	5023

2005

Vehicle Specifications

	hatchback	convertible
Wheelbase, in.	106.0	106.0
Length, in.	174.6	174.6
Width, in.	72.6	72.6
Track, in.	front: 62.1	front: 62.1
	rear: 60.7	rear: 60.7
Height, in.	49.0	49.0
Curb weight, lb	3179	3199

Mechanical Specifications 2-door hatchback/convertible/coupe

Suspension	**front:** Independent; upper and lower A-arms, transverse composite monoleaf spring, tube shock absorbers, antiroll bar **rear:** Independent, upper and lower A-arms, toe links, transverse composite monoleaf springs, tube shock absorbers, antiroll bar
Wheels/Tires	front, P245/45ZR-18 rear, P285/35ZR-19
Brakes	front: antilock 12.8-inch disc rear: antilock 12.0-inch disc
Transmission	4-speed automatic 6-speed manual
Standard axle ratio	2.73:1 (auto) 3.42:1 (manual)

Engine Specifications

Type	ohv V-8
Displacement, liters/cu in.	6.0/364
Bore × Stroke, in. × in.	4.00 × 3.62
Fuel management	Sequential Injection
Horsepower @ rpm	400 @ 6000
Torque @ rpm, lb-ft	400 @ 4400

Published Performance Numbers   350 hp, 6-speed manual

0-60 mph, sec	4.3
0-100 mph, sec	9.9
1/4-mile, sec @ mph	12.7 @ 113.0
source	*Car and Driver*

Base Prices & Production

	Price
2-door hatchback	$43,710.00
2-door convertible	51,445.00

Options & Production

	Price
Preferred Equipment Group 1SA (hatchback)	$1405.00
Preferred Equipment Group-1SB (hatchback)	4360.00
Preferred Equipment Group-1SB (convertible)	2955.00
Magnetic Selective Ride Control	1695.00
Z51 Performance Handling Pkg	1695.00
4-Speed Automatic Transmission	NC
Navigation System	1600.00
OnStar Assistance System	695.00

NA= Not Available

XM Satellite Radio	325.00
Power Top (convertible)	1995.00
Corvette Museum Delivery	490.00
Transparent Roof Panel	750.00
Dual Roof Panels	1400.00
Polished Alloy Wheels	1295.00

Color Choices (production numbers not available)

Light Pewter Metallic	Victory Red	Precision Red
LeMans Blue	Black	Millennium Yellow
Magnetic Red Metallic	Sunset Orange Metallic	
Machine Silver Metallic	Artic White	

INDEX